Antique
ENAMELED JEWELRY

Dale Reeves Nicholls
with Robin Allison

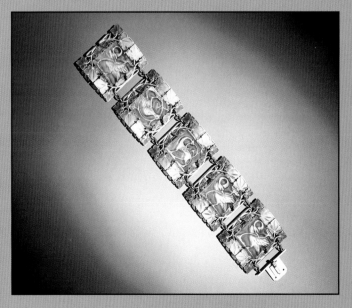

Schiffer Publishing Ltd®

4880 Lower Valley Road, Atglen, PA 19310 USA

Dedication

This book is dedicated to my mother, Elizabeth Bodette Reeves,
who passed on to me her love of jewelry
And to the memory of my father, Robert Grier LeFevre Reeves
And to the memory of my brother, Edward Reeves

From quiet homes and first beginning,
Out to the undiscovered ends,
There's nothing worth the wear of winning,
But laughter and the love of friends.

—Hilaire Belloc, "Dedicatory Ode"

Designed by John P. Cheek
Cover design by Bruce Waters
Type set in BernhardMod BT/Aldine721 Lt BT

ISBN: 0-7643-1991-4
Printed in China

Published by Schiffer Publishing Ltd.
4880 Lower Valley Road
Atglen, PA 19310
Phone: (610) 593-1777; Fax: (610) 593-2002
E-mail: Info@schifferbooks.com

For the largest selection of fine reference books on this and related subjects, please visit our web site at
www.schifferbooks.com
We are always looking for people to write books on new and related subjects. If you have an idea for a book please contact us at the above address.

This book may be purchased from the publisher.
Include $3.95 for shipping.
Please try your bookstore first.
You may write for a free catalog.

In Europe, Schiffer books are distributed by
Bushwood Books
6 Marksbury Ave.
Kew Gardens
Surrey TW9 4JF England
Phone: 44 (0) 20 8392-8585; Fax: 44 (0) 20 8392-9876
E-mail: info@bushwoodbooks.co.uk
Free postage in the U.K., Europe; air mail at cost.

Acknowledgments, Accompanied by an Awareness of Gratitude

A joyful and pleasant thing it is to be thankful...

I am thankful for the help of many friends, some of long acquaintance, and some as yet unmet.

For the kindness of strangers: all of the dealers who sent me pictures, even though they knew me only as a voice on the phone. Among these are Malcolm Logan, of Nelson Rarities, whose kindness was immense, whose help was invaluable, whose wisdom was most welcome. Also Karen Perlmutter, of Acanthus Antiques, unfailingly helpful, who generously photographed items from her collection and for sale in her store; Jonathan Norton and Max Michelson of S. J. Phillips, who so kindly sent pictures of pieces in their large collection of flower pins; Gary Berg, of Kensington House Antiques, who was kind enough to let me use pictures of charming pieces; Mimi Dee of Mimi Dee Artwear, who generously sent photographs; and Judith and Arthur Anderson, of Bijoux Extraordinaire, who very kindly let me have several slides of beautiful pieces, and who first introduced me to suffragette jewelry.

And, most especially to my co-author Robin Allison, who responded to my inquiry about using photos of some terrific enameled pieces from her web site with incredible enthusiasm and generosity, sharing her amazing collection with me and with all readers interested in collecting enameled jewelry, or those merely wishing to browse through a book with pictures of pieces created with care and exquisite craftsmanship. So, thanks Robin! You for the pictures, me for the words!

Friends are flowers of the heart.

The friends who helped are also numerous, and include Theresa Hetrick-Peregoy, manager of Classic Facets, who helped in many ways, and was always willing to furnish facts from her vast store of knowledge, and Jackie Cuyler and Shannon Morgan, also of Classic Facets; my friend Karryl Salit, who took time out of her busy career as a wildlife artist to photograph items at Classic Facets; Sol Varon, of Portland, who lent items to be photographed with a trust for which I am truly grateful; Peter Diehl, of Uncommon Treasures, who also lent pieces that truly were uncommon treasures; and Maureen Flanagan, also of Uncommon Treasures.

To others I am grateful for taking the time to share their knowledge: Ralph Esmarion, the collector and dealer, who graciously gave of his time and showed me the many beautiful pieces of Newark enameled jewelry in his collection; Janet Bliss, who was so very kind and helpful; Ulysses G. Dietz, of the Newark Museum, who generously shared both time and information; Emily Wheat, at the Newark Museum, who cheerfully answered questions and found rare pieces in the vaults; Scott Hankins, assistant registrar at the Newark Museum, who sent pictures; and last but by no means least, Shelly Foote, of the Smithsonian Museum–thank you, Shelly, not only for help with this project, but for all the years of friendship as well.

Also to be thanked is my instructor, Kristin Mitsu Shiga, wonderful teacher, incredibly talented jeweler, and enthusiastic enamelist, who patiently put up with me even when I: forgot to use a trowel and set my leather mitt on fire; put the trivet too close to the kiln's cord, and burned a small hole in it; sprayed a fellow student with Klyr-fire; melted cloisonné wire to a trivet; brought the wrong materials to class; and was oblivious to the difference between opaque and translucent enamels. You only *thought* I wasn't listening; you taught me a lot more than you will ever guess.

And to my editors Nancy Schiffer and Ginny Parfitt, and all of the terrific people at Schiffer Publishing: Thank you for agreeing to take on this project. Thanks as well for your help and guidance.

Now what is love? I pray thee, tell.

Love is one of the ingredients that went into this book. And this book would never have become reality if not for the unwavering love and support of my mother, Bodette Reeves. Thank you. Your support was love in action, and I can never repay you. And thank you, Robert and Jonathan, for putting up with your flower pin–obsessed mother and listening to disquisitions on jewelry and enamel which must have bored you to tears–tears you politely never let fall. And deepest gratitude to my late brother Ward, who patiently supplied support and encouragement over the years, without ever once complaining. On our last trip together, Ward, though by then terminally ill and bravely concealing it, took me to New York and Newark to further research for this book. (Love and miss you always, baby brother.) Also, thank you, Stephanie, for giving me the added nudge I needed, and for believing that this project might succeed.

And finally, thank you to Mark Scattergood, for putting up with my (of course extremely rare) periods of ill humor, for providing encouragement and shelter, for giving me great support –and for learning to use a digital camera just so you could take all those photographs. And then later, when those pictures weren't quite high resolution enough, for taking the time to devise a set-up that actually worked, and teaching this photographobic neophyte to take acceptable pictures. Many, many thanks.

And now, the usual disclaimer: The characters in this book are... Oops, wrong disclaimer. While I did a good deal of research, and drew upon the knowledge of many generous persons, much of the material in this book is based on my own experiences as a collector and a beginning enamelist; any mistakes are purely of my doing. Unfortunately, this is really true.

Contents

Preface
Confessions of an Enameled Jewelry Junkie

When I was young, I used to gaze covetously at the cover of *National Geographic*. The *back* cover. Not for me ballooning over the Alps or sailing solo across the Atlantic. No, the back cover had everything I wanted. Enthralling, I found it; much more interesting than the jungles and jaguars, deserts and dromedaries depicted inside. For on the back cover of *National Geographic* was Jewelry.

And not just any jewelry. *Enameled* jewelry. What I particularly yearned for were the earrings and matching pin with tiny blue enameled forget-me-nots. At that time, I had no idea what a forget-me-not was, much less what it symbolized. I probably could have identified a rose or an iris–although of course I was equally unaware of their symbolism–but the forget-me-not was just a cute little blue enameled flower. I desperately wanted one.

But my parents were obliviously old-fashioned, and in their view, little girls did not wear costume jewelry. Not even cute costume jewelry. We lived in Brazil, and they generously gave me amethysts and aquamarines, gold and pearls. My yearning for little enameled flowers seemed to them a bizarre and probably passing fancy.

It wasn't.

Although I went without the little blue forget-me-nots, I stayed true to their name, and never forgot them.

However, times changed. I reached adulthood. I went to college, graduate school, and yet more graduate school. I still liked jewelry, but it played a marginal role in my life. Then one day an acquaintance who owns an antique jewelry store in Boulder, Colorado, where I lived, showed me a Victorian flower pin. I had never seen anything quite so beautiful. It was set in a ring of five pearls interspersed with ten small leaves set with seed pearls. The petals were in matte enamel shading from a creamy white at the center to a delicate pink at the edges. The small stamens surrounding the diamond-like crown were enchanting. The diamond in the center glistened like a dewdrop.

It was love at first sight.

The pin had a bail that folded so that it could be worn as a pendant as well as a brooch. It also had a watch or chatelaine hook in back, which I later learned was a not uncommon feature in pins of that era. It was, in short, very versatile. As my acquaintance said, it did everything: "It chops, it slices, it dices."

Unfortunately my wonderful flower pin was lost or stolen when I wore it on a jacket lapel. I was devastated. Periodi-cally I would wander into the jewelry store and mourn my flower pin. Finally, a bit exasperated by my lamentations, my acquaintance advised, "Get over it."

I tried, but no other piece of jewelry had ever had that effect on me. Then, one day, my acquaintance called. Someone had just sent her a collection of flower pins. Would I like to come down and look at them? My then-husband and I went. I gazed down on nine, yes, *nine* flower pins. Each was different: They ranged from a small pin with two tiny violets inside two small linked hearts to a large iridescent cherry blossom. Which ones, my husband asked, did I want. I stared at them, each one like a fugitive from a jeweled garden. Which ones? I asked myself. The little violets were so cute. The orchid was so realistically rendered, down to the speckling on its petals. The small forget-me-not was so *Victorian*. The cherry blossom was simply gorgeous. *Which one?* All of them, I finally said. And so started my collection–a collection that might not have happened if I'd still had my first flower pin.

Several years later, I first read about the Victorian language of flowers. In this language, each flower conveyed a different and specific meaning. As someone with a background in linguistics, I was fascinated. I read more. And the more I read, the more I was convinced that at least some flower pins also conveyed a message. Looking at a little pansy would make me think of some young woman, perhaps dressed primly in a high-collared dress, who had a century before received the pin as a token of affection from her fiancé. Think of me, perhaps he said as he handed her a small blue velvet box with tied with a gold ribbon bow. Or the pale peach orchid, shimmering with iridescent enamel–had that been presented to a debutante on the occasion of her coming out? Of course I would never know, but it was fun to create scenarios of days gone by, when courtship rituals were more formal, and at the same time more imbued with hidden meanings.

Today, almost twenty years later, I am still a flower pin junkie. The sight of an enameled orchid, lotus, iris, violet, to me is more beautiful than the most wonderful of diamonds or pearls. However, I have shifted my focus slightly, trying to find examples of more unusual flowers, or pins with unusual themes, or pins that are exquisitely enameled.

And, with a course in enameling having further fueled my passion for glass fused onto metal, I now think that enamel is perhaps the most perfect jewel of all.

Because I loved enamel, and had amassed a fairly sizable collection–especially of flower pins–I decided to write this book. In a sense, though, this book has already had two lives. The first version, in which some of the photographs needed to be retaken, was sent back to me for revisions the same week I learned that my younger brother had gone to the hospital for the final time. After his death, I was depressed and discouraged, and had almost decided to give up the project. Then, after the depression had lifted somewhat, I realized that it would be foolish to give up on something I enjoyed so much. I contacted dealers who had so generously shared photographs of their inventory or collections, and asked for new photographs. All responded with the same enthusiasm for the project they had expressed before, and with the same level of generosity. Malcolm Logan of Nelson Rarities sent higher resolution digital photographs of the fabulous pieces acquired over the years by his firm. Karen Perlmutter of Acanthus Antiques sent more pictures of her charming collection of enameled pansies. Gary Begin of Kensington House Antiques sent high-resolution pictures of some wonderful pieces in their inventory.

One collector especially, however, changed the nature and scope of this book. I wrote to Robin Allison, a prodigious collector who also runs Red Robin Antiques. I had purchased a couple of pieces from her before, and wanted to buy an orchid brooch from her web site. And, by the way, I added, would she mind if I used a few pictures of some of the terrific pieces on her web site in a book I was writing on enameled jewelry?

Robin's response was overwhelming. As she later put it in one of our wonderful marathon phone conversations, she was hooked from the word "Hello." Yes, she would be more than happy to share pictures from her web site, but would I also be interested in pictures of her collection? She had been thinking about writing a book about her collection, but... Her forte was really photography, yet she wanted to share the many pieces she had acquired during the course of nearly twenty years of collecting.

Robin's collection left me breathless. I was totally in awe not only of the depth of her collection, but its breadth as well. It spans decades and continents, ranging from Victorian to contemporary, from American and Mexican to European and Asian. In many areas our tastes overlap, but she had acquired pieces I could only dream about. We occasionally found ourselves bidding for the same piece in online auctions. Usually I hate losing an auction; when Robin won, I could only be happy: She would end up with a lovely piece of jewelry, and I would have a picture for the book!

In the end, we decided to make the book a collaborative effort, as approximately half of the photographs in the book would come from her collection. Not only would her collection form a significant part of the book, and add areas, such as Mexican jewelry, which in the first version were small or nonexistent, but her own knowledge, experience, and expertise gained over years of serious collecting would help inform the book. Without her generous help, this book would have been merely a shadow of what it has grown to be with her participation.

With Robin, I almost feel as if I have met my complementary half. While I adore writing, photography had always been difficult for me; for Robin, it was the opposite–she loves photography, but finds writing a chore.

So... Thanks, Robin! Here's to a fun and fruitful collaboration–and to many more years of exciting and eclectic collecting!

Guide to Pricing

The prices given throughout may cover a fairly wide range, as prices today seem to vary more than ever. In large part, we believe, this is due to the internet, which has influenced buying in several ways: through online auctions that allow a buyer to purchase a piece at less–often significantly less–than what was traditionally asked by dealers and/or shops; through dealers who sell exclusively through their web sites–virtual stores rather than real stores–thus cutting their overhead to almost nothing, and letting them in turn reduce their prices; and by allowing buyers to comparison shop more easily and conveniently than ever before. However, there are still a number of dealers who sell higher-end merchandise to an upscale clientele. Their asking prices for both pieces by famous designers and those from lesser-known makers are generally higher; on the other hand, the pieces they sell are almost always in perfect condition. In addition, they often carry one-of-a-kind items by to-die-for makers.

The prices in this book also reflect the authors' shopping experiences. Robin in particular has not only inherited the collecting gene, but also has a real feel for bargains–along with the knowledge, mobility, and determination that drives her to find them. Dale's experience is different, as she paid higher-end retail prices for years before realizing that comparison shopping pays off; that customer loyalty is all well and good, but should never lead to being taken advantage of; and that

in most cases, if a piece is not in great condition, or the asking price is too high, another like it will come along sooner or later. That being said, both Robin and Dale would agree that, if it's a once-in-a-lifetime find and you've wanted it forever, buy it! Even if it means paying a bit more than you'd like. Of course, if it's totally prohibitive… then there's really nothing to do but grit your teeth and walk away.

For the most part, prices in this guide–especially for pieces in Robin's collection–are in the low-to-medium range; some dealers will charge more for similar pieces. For Dale's collection, the prices are more in the mid-to-high range. Her prices often also have a wider range than Robin's.

Also, please note that while Robin and Dale have shared prices for almost all pieces in their respective collections, a number of the photographs in this book were contributed by dealers who did not agree to have prices for their jewelry included. Therefore, there will be some items for which no price is given. The captions for those pieces will have a *Courtesy of…* line at the end of the caption. (However, to distinguish Robin's collection from Dale's, captions for her pieces will also have a *Courtesy of…* line.)

Please refer to the following list of abbreviations when using the pricing guides. Unless otherwise specified (usually in karats for gold items but occasionally for costume or gold-filled items too) the item is in silver.

Abbreviations Used for Makers or Manufacturers of Jewelry

# indicates costume manufacturer, + indicates a New York or Newark maker, ★ indicates a Norwegian maker, ★★ indicates a British maker, ★★★ a German manufacturer; unless otherwise noted, makers were based in the United States.

A.C.	Alice Caviness (mostly did costume pieces, but the pieces shown in this book are in sterling silver, of German manufacture)	Crd.	Creed	M.B.★★	Murrle Bennett (actually, this firm is usually referred to as Anglo-German, as their jewelry was made in Pforzheim, but marketed in Britain)
		C.T.+	Crane-Theurer		
		D.A.★	David Anderson		
		D.deW.B.+	D. de W. Brokaw		
		Eis.#	Eisenberg		
		F.&B.	Foster & Brothers (var. Foster & Brooks)		
A.Hn.★	Aksel Holmsen	H.L.★★★	Heinrich Levinger		
A.J.H.+	A.J. Hedges.	H.P.★	Hroar Prydz	M.H.★	Marius Hammer
All.+	Alling Co.	J.A.&S.★★	John Atkins and Sons	Mm.Hsk.#	Miriam Haskell
B.G.&O.+	Bippart, Griscom & Osborn	Kr.+	Krementz Co. (although their later pieces are mostly costume)	M.M.★★★	Meyle and Mayer
				R.Bro.+	Riker Brothers
C.&C.★★	Child & Child			T.F.★★★	Theodor Fahrner
C.H.★★	Charles Horner			Tiff.+	Tiffany & Co.
C.Her	Carl Herman	Mar.+	Marcus & Co.	Trf.#	Trifari
C.H.&G.+	Carter, Howe & Gough (var. Carter & Howe)	M. de T.	Margot de Taxco (Mex)	W.	Watson Co.
				W.&B.+	Whiteside & Blank
		Mat.#	Matisse (var. Matisse Renoir)	Wls.#	Wells Co.
C.Rob.	Charles Robinson Co.			Wss.#	Weiss

List of Abbreviations Used in Pricing Guides

A&C	Arts and Crafts	exp	export	pail	paillons
AD	Art Deco	fest	festoon	p-d-v	pate de verre
A-H	Austro-Hungarian	fich-p	fichu pin	pend	pendant
amlt	amulet	fil	filigree	perf	perfume
amth	amethyst	flr	flower	phrh	pharaoh
AN	Art Nouveau	f-m-n	forget-me-not	plq	plique-à-jour
ant	antique	Fr	French	pnk	pink
art	articulated	fthr	feather	porc	porcelain
BA	beaux arts	fx	faux	ppl	purple
bclt	bracelet	garn	garnet	pr	pair
bkgd	background	Ger	German	prof	profile
bkl	buckle	gf	gold-filled	pre-R	pre-Raphaelite
bl	blue	gls	glass	prl	pearl
blk	black	glss	glossy	pst	paste(s)
bot	bottom	gp	group	p-wtch	pendant or pocket
bq-prl	baroque pearl	gr	gray		watch
br	brooch	grn	green	qtrfl	quatrefoil
br/pend	brooch/pendant	Gth rev	Gothic revival	qtz	quartz
brd	border	guil	guilloche	r.	right
Brit	British	hon-p	honeymoon pin	rect	rectangular
brn	brown	hrt	heart	Ren rev	Renaissance revival
bt	basse taille	ht-p	hatpin	rep	reproduction
btrfl	butterfly	irid	iridescent	rh-st	rhinestone
Byz	Byzantine	It	Italian	saph	sapphire
cam	cameo	Jap	Japanese	scrb	scarab
carn	carnelian	jgstl	Jugendstil	sl-lckt	slide locket
cflnk	cufflinks	K	karat	sl-mrr	slide mirror
chmp	champlevé	l.	left	sm	small
chmp f-m-n	champlevé forget-me-	lav	lavender	Sp	Spanish
	nots	lckt	locket	s-prl	seed pearl
chat	chatelaine	lf	leaf	st-p	stickpin
chrb	cherub	lg	large	styl	stylized
Chin	Chinese	Lim	Limoges	styl-lot	stylized lotus
chry	chrysoprase	l/l	lapis lazuli	suff	suffragette
cir	circle	lt	light	t-d'ep	taille d'épargne
cit	cit	lvs	leaves	trnsl	translucent
clsn	cloisonné?	m.	middle	trsfr	transfer
co bl	cobalt blue	med	medium	turq	turquoise
cost	costume	Mex	Mexican	v	very
cpt	compact	mod	modern	Vict	Victorian
crl	coral	Mog	mogul	vint	vintage
dam	damascene	m-o-p	mother-of-pearl	w/	with
Dan	Danish	mrng	mourning	wg	winged
drgfl	dragonfly	mtt	matte	wg-scrb	winged scarab
dk	dark	neck	necklace	wh	white
dmd	diamond	nie	niello	w/o	without
dngl	dangle	Nk	Newark-New York	wtch-p	watchpin
ea	each	Nor	Norwegian	w-w	wristwatch
Edw	Edwardian	n-pad	notepad	xifrm	cruciform
Eg rev	Egyptian revival	opq	opaque	yell	yellow
e/r	earrings	orig	original		

Introduction
The Golden Age of Enamel

Once in three years came the navy of Tharshish, bringing gold, and silver, ivory, and apes, and peacocks.

—I Kings 10:22

At some time in the distant past, one of our ancestors found a nugget of gold and examined it to discover gold's properties. These turned out to be wonderful: Gold was malleable, and could be formed into beautiful things–beads, talismans, coiled bracelets, weighty rings, thin foil masks. Whoever that long-ago person was, whether Egyptian or Chinese, of the Andes or the Indus Valley, he or she created a trend. Ever since that discovery veiled by the mists of time, gold has been among the most prized and precious of materials.

My beloved is white and ruddy, the chiefest among ten thousand. …His hands are as gold rings set with the beryl; his belly is as bright ivory overlaid with sapphires.

—Song of Solomon 5:10-11

Later, polished stones were added to gold to create even more beautiful jewels. Amethyst, carnelian, turquoise, lapis lazuli, jade…Ivory, coral, pearls…Rubies, sapphires, emeralds… And still later, diamonds. All of these took their place among the rare and beautiful gems used to fashion jewelry for the wealthy and powerful who walked the earth.

For millennia, fine jewelry, finely wrought out of the finest materials, has been a coveted symbol of wealth and power. And not just for this world, but in the next: Kings the world over filled their tombs with treasures. Tutankhamon took with him a legendary treasure of gold and lapis and turquoise and carnelian; the so-called Agamemnon found by Heinrich Schliemann at Mycenae was buried with a royal ransom's worth of gold; Inca chieftains were sent into the afterlife with gold and jade. Jewelry was about ornamentation, true, but it was also about status and privilege.

A rooster was once strutting up and down the farmyard among the hens when suddenly he spied something shining among the straw. "Ho! Ho!" said he, "that's for me," and soon rooted it out from beneath the straw. What did it turn out to be but a pearl that by some chance had been lost in the yard? "You may be a treasure," said the rooster, "to men that prize you, but for me, I would rather have a single barleycorn than a peck of pearls."

—Aesop, Fables

However, for a period at the end of the nineteenth century, when the Arts and Crafts and Art Nouveau movements rebelled against the heaviness and gaucheness of nineteenth century design, the fashion for precious gems waned. Like the rooster in Aesop's fable, not everyone was impressed by the largest of

pearls–or the most glittering of diamonds. Such jewels, some felt, did not create jewelry that was beautiful enough to be considered art. Instead, the "important" gems were replaced by lesser substances, among them horn, mother-of-pearl…

And enamel. Powdered glass that could be fused onto metal to create color and detail, and that could even replicate gemstones.

Enameling was actually not a new technique. Among the most beautiful of early jewelry was that of the ancient Egyptians, who fashioned gold into *cloisons*, or cells, empty and ready to be filled with pieces of turquoise or carnelian or lapis lazuli cut to fit each cell's outline precisely. It was a laborious process, but it produced objects of great beauty.

And then, at some point, the Egyptians discovered that a combination of sand covered with a glaze could be substituted for the stones. Instead of sawing a piece of carnelian, shaving a nugget of turquoise, or sanding a chunk of lapis lazuli to fit exactly a small space, a bit of sand could be packed into the cell, covered with glaze–which, it should be noted, could be almost any color–and fired to create the same effect.

Although the technique was not quite enameling, it was close. This frit of sand and glaze, often called faience, was the first approximation to what later became a technique to substitute an easier, less costly material: enamel made of glass.

Enameling was used extensively during the Renaissance by, among others, the great Italian goldsmith and jeweler, Benvenuto Cellini. Although it seems to have fallen in and out of fashion, it continued to be used, to add color and interest to items fashioned of metal; but it was not given the status of a precious gem.

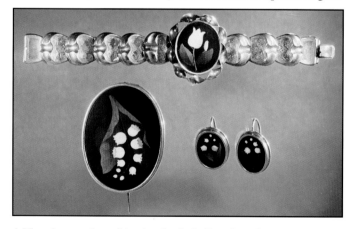

A Victorian set of matching jewelry, in Italian *pietra dura* depicting lilies-of-the-valley, from 1856. This type of work was painstaking and difficult, fashioning designs with tiny pieces of stone cut to fit the pattern. As the ancient Egyptians discovered, enameling was one way of creating floral and other patterns, often with greater detail, in a less time-consuming way. *Courtesy of the Department of Costume and Social History, Smithsonian Institution, Washington, D.C.*

During the nineteenth century, trends and new techniques added to the repertoire of enameling used by jewelers and other metalsmiths. Cloisonné enamel, introduced from the Orient, came into vogue. Metal artists in Limoges, France had centuries earlier learned how to paint with enamel; some Arts and Crafts jewelers used this technique to create pictures of handsome young men and beautiful young women in old-fashioned dress. Machines were used to create *guilloche* work, geometric patterns over which translucent enamel produced a shimmering effect. Still, for most of the nineteenth century, jewelry was viewed as a source of wealth; and diamonds, sapphires, rubies, emeralds, pearls were preferred to their poor relations, the enamels made of powdered glass.

And then, almost as if by some alchemical transformation, as if glass had suddenly been transmuted into sapphire or emerald, the status of enamel changed. It became *important*. Great designers such as Alexis and Lucien Falize, Parisian jewelers who worked with enamel, created pieces of unparalleled beauty. In Russia, the legendary Carl Peter Fabergé fabricated a treasure of enameled and gem-encrusted jewels for Tsar Nicholas II and his family. The genius designer René Lalique made enamel a signature of the beautiful Art Nouveau jewelry, which was produced for such a short time, but which made such a lasting impression. Enamelists in the Arts and Crafts movement developed an iridescent blue-green enamel the color of a peacock's feathers. The great designers and jewelers of that era used enamel so translucent that details sculpted on their pieces stood out: ridges on a flower's petal, the feathers on a bird's wing, the molding of a woman's eyebrow. They perfected new techniques such as plique-à-jour enamel, transparent enamel pierced by light like stained glass. They invented enamel *sur paillons*, translucent enamel applied over tiny pieces of gold foil that glistened like gothic gems.

Above left:
An Art Nouveau pendant in 10K gold, Limoges enameling, and seed pearls, with the head in profile of a young woman with a distinctly Renaissance or even medieval style. Her long, flowing hair, dreaming expression, and simple dress are typical both of Art Nouveau and pre-Raphaelite women. Her only adornment is a fillet around her head from which are draped pearl festoons. Typical of Limoges enameling are the painterly detail, and the use of foil to highlight clothing and to add interest to the background. The frame is fairly elaborate, more Victorian than Art Nouveau in design, and like many Victorian pieces is set with seed pearls. The Limoges enamel may have been added to an extant Victorian frame. Measures 1.5" x .875". *Courtesy of Robin Allison.*

Above right:
A lovely Art Nouveau slide locket in 900 silver and enamel, by Meyle & Mayer, with a beautifully enameled woman against a wavy green guilloche background, which admirably simulates draperies or wallpaper. The silver borders of the locket have characteristic curving lines as well as floral decoration. Measures 1.75" x 1.375" and is marked depose, sterling, and Meyle & Mayer. *Courtesy of Robin Allison.*

An elaborate pendant in sterling silver, enamel, paste, and pearls, from the German jewelry manufacturing center of Pforzheim. The pendant has a woman playing a violin, her undulating hair floating as she dances to the strains of her music. Plique leaves emerge from the silver frame, which has a rather Arts and Crafts–like angularity and ends in a baroque pearl drop. What might be a lily pad with a stylized blossom forms a design on the woman's dress. The piece came with its original box, which is marked Ehreugabe zum Festsehiessen von Wilh Lichterberger, Pforzheim; measures 3.75" x 2.125". *Courtesy of Robin Allison*

A marvelous bracelet in 14K gold, enamel, rubies, pearls, and diamonds, by Alling Co. This lovely bracelet, with an enameled "Byzantine" lady in profile, is typical of the pieces for which this company was known. Their Byzantine lady can be found in pieces small and large: stickpins, brooches, lockets, and bracelets. While this lady is larger than most, she nonetheless contains the same elements found in her smaller counterparts: the waving hair, which here as in other pieces hangs just below the circle comprising the bracelet's central element; the beautifully enameled face, with its wonderful detail extending to eyebrows, lids, and lashes; and the fantastic headdress ending in a circular dangle. However, she is also somewhat more elaborate than most such ladies, with rubies and diamonds forming the fillet of her headdress, which also has an enameled circular dangle set with a diamond. The central circle, measuring 1.25", is also set with pearls at intervals, adding to the Byzantine appearance of the bracelet. *Courtesy of Robin Allison.*

An interesting Arts and Crafts pendant displaying beautiful iridescent enamel in shades of blues and greens, almost a signature of Arts and Crafts jewelry, as well as the angularity typical of British Arts and Crafts pieces. Also typical of such pieces are the hand-fashioned look, the use of chains joined by a loop at the top, and a small drop in this case enameled, although in some cases a baroque pearl was used. Unmarked sterling; measures 1.875" x 1.375". *Courtesy of Robin Allison.*

Art Nouveau stickpin of a woman's head, a much smaller version of the Byzantine woman in the bracelet pictured above, in 14K gold, enamel, and with a single small pearl, probably made in Newark or New York c. 1900, possibly by Alling Co. The woman's head measures only .50" x .75", but on this small area the maker managed to include a wealth of detail. A diadem with waves and dangles, topped with a single pearl, encircles the flowing hair, which forms a frame for the lower edge of the pin. The woman's face, painted in iridescent enamel, is so finely drawn that it shows even an eyebrow, eyelashes, and a nostril. Darker enamel defines the cheek.

A 14K gold and enamel bird brooch, with two small diamonds, 1.5" x 1", probably of American manufacture. The enamel is a deep translucent red that reveals an underlying basse taille design engraved to create the look of feathers. The enameling is beautifully done and very even, except where it has been applied more heavily at the edges of the wings and tail to create a darker effect. Stylistically, the piece seems more Victorian than Art Nouveau, with a rather formal rather than flowing design; yet the translucent enamel work and the feathered effect seem more in keeping with Art Nouveau. The pin's plain c-clasp and lack of a maker's mark—the pin rather than the clasp is stamped 14K—point to an earlier rather than later date, perhaps c. 1885-1890. Like many brooches from the late Victorian period, this one has a hinged folding bail that allows the piece to be worn as a pendant.

Two beautifully enameled watches by famous maker Phillipe Patek, each in a different style, and a lorgnette. The red Patek, with its sentimental scene with cherubs and clouds edged by pearls, is typically Victorian. The green one, with its twisted leaves and pearl fruit or flowers, borders on Art Nouveau. The lorgnette, with its green champlevé enamel, incorporates classical motifs such as the laurel wreath and acanthus leaves–both of which are very symbolic. *Courtesy of Nelson Rarities, Portland, ME.*

The techniques they introduced were not just impressive, but dazzling; and, in a way, enamel became a jewel in its own right.

Symbolism

O day and night, but this is wondrous strange! …There are more things in heaven and earth, Horatio, than are dreamt of in your philosophy.

—William Shakespeare, *Hamlet*

Symbolism was an important part of nineteenth century jewelry, whether Victorian, Arts and Crafts, or Art Nouveau. Dragons and dragonflies, fauns and fairies, lotuses and lilies, gorgons and griffons, peacocks and pigeons, swans and swallows, primroses and pansies–each of these usually meant *something*, whether in the language of flowers beloved of the Victorians or the elaborate symbolic lexicon embraced by Art Nouveau.

Symbolism was in many cases inspired and informed by Classical mythology; Christian iconography also played a role. And, with the archaeological revival movements of the mid-to-late nineteenth century and the Asian influence created by the opening of Japan's ports to Western trade, other traditions also introduced new motifs as well as new meanings. The crane of China and the chrysanthemum of Japan were added to the motifs used by nineteenth century jewelers. Egyptian revival jewelry created a host of new symbols: the ankh and the scarab, the eye of Horus and the girdle of Isis.

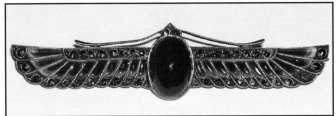

A marvelous winged scarab brooch in 935 silver, carnelian, marcasites, and enamel. The carnelian scarab is a plain cabochon stone, not carved with the usual scarab markings that replicate ancient Egyptian scarabs. This simplicity extends to the monochromatic wings, in plique-à-jour enamel that echoes the color of the carnelian scarab, and the overall design, which has only two graceful feelers rather than the customary fore- and hindlegs pushing circles representing the solar orb. In Art Deco fashion, marcasites decorate the wings' edges. Measures 2.75" x .625". *Courtesy of Robin Allison.*

A necklace in 14K gold, enamel, and pearls, comprising seven pansies done in a beautiful iridescent enamel. Undoubtedly of New York or Newark manufacture, the pansies are realistically painted, with their markings those of real flowers, and their petals nicely dimensional, as is typical of the best of American floral jewelry of the era. While such pansies are relatively common in pins or brooches, they are much less often found in necklaces or dog collars. Interestingly, the necklace takes a much-loved Victorian motif, the pansy, and places it in a piece with Art Nouveau overtones, such as the iridescent enamel and the use of baroque pearls to accent the chains between the flowers. Undeciphered maker's mark, 14K; measures 15.5" x 1.125". *Courtesy of Robin Allison.*

A pendant in sterling silver, enamel, marcasites, and paste in the form of a stylized winged scarab. Egyptian revival jewelry was popular in Victorian times, and retained– or possibly regained–popularity into the 1950s, with costume jewelry designers such as Hattie Carnegie creating elaborate pieces in the Egyptian style. In Art Deco Egyptian revival jewelry, the winged scarab seemed to hold pride of place, and examples of the genre abound. This pendant, of German origins, has the plique-à-jour wings so often found in Art Deco pieces, combined with unusually clean, geometric lines and an elegant symmetry. Undeciphered maker's mark; measures 2.75" x 1.25". *Courtesy of Robin Allison.*

A fascinating Art Nouveau piece, in carved gold, enamel, diamonds, and a pearl. The woman's head, with the typical flowing Art Nouveau hair, is set against a circle of deep blue guilloche enamel, the night sky. A diamond crescent frames the left edge of the piece, while diamond-set stars surround the woman's head. Plique-à-jour wings frame the lower half of the piece. *Courtesy of Nelson Rarities, Portland, ME.*

However, when we seek to interpret the meaning of the plethora of Arts and Crafts peacocks or the myriad Art Nouveau dragonflies, we should also pause to consider that jewelers in many cases used these motifs simply because they were beautiful, or because they lent themselves to enameling. But whether they intended to create symbols or to fashion expressions of beauty, the designers and makers of late nineteenth and early twentieth century jewelry were significantly aided in their efforts to achieve the impressions they sought by the brilliant enameling techniques of the age. How much more beautiful the Art Nouveau dragonfly with plique-à-jour wings than his poor Victorian ancestor, whose wings were embellished merely with the dull gleam of garnets! How bland the flower that blooms without color, fashioned from glittering diamonds that do little to convey the warmth and beauty of a living blossom!

A late Victorian circle pin in 14K gold, enamel, and pearls, approximately 1.5" in diameter, c. 1895. The matte enameling on the three diminutive flowers is shaded from lighter at the center to darker at the edge of the petals. The small stamens are characteristic of many Newark pieces produced at this time.

A wonderful transitional Art Nouveau/Edwardian brooch in silver-topped gold, diamonds, pearls, sapphires, and enamel, in that archetypical Art Nouveau figure, a dragonfly. The dragonfly's gracefully curving body is set with diamonds, which also decorate the upper edges of the insect's wings, and the stems of the plique-à-jour leaves on which it alights. The plant's flowers are, in very Art Nouveau fashion, suggested by pearls. A diamond and pearl drop finishes this exquisite piece. Unmarked; measures 2.75" x 2.125". *Courtesy of Robin Allison.*

A brooch/pendant in 18K silver-topped gold, enamel, diamonds, and a pearl dangle, c. 1885, of French origins. This beautifully enameled brooch falls somewhere between Renaissance revival and Art Nouveau. The flowers are enameled in a shimmery coral, while the enamel on the leaves has an almost patina-like quality. Measures approximately 2.75" x 2".

The innovations created by the Falizes, by Lalique, by Fabergé and others were picked up by American firms such as Tiffany & Co. and Marcus & Co. Smaller companies, for the most part located in Newark, New Jersey, created their own small enameled gems, flowers and birds, and women, emulating Art Nouveau design in shimmering iridescent enamels.

It was the Golden Age of enamel, and nothing like the enameling of the late nineteenth and early twentieth centuries had ever been achieved before–or, some might say, since– that time.

A large cherry blossom in 14K gold, iridescent enamel, and a diamond, c. 1900. This flower, with the folded edges to its petals and other naturalistic details, very strongly resembles a similar brooch/pendant made by the American firm Marcus & Co., at one time rival to the great jewelry house Tiffany & Co. However, there is no maker's mark, and it is marked only 14K on the back. Measures approximately 1.5" in diameter.

The jewelry created around 1900 in New York and Newark ranged from the exquisite and sublime, as in the pansy choker shown above, the moderately large, as the cherry blossom above, to the dainty and diminutive. This child's ring has a small four-petaled flower that measures about .360" in diameter, yet even so, shows several details for which Newark enamels are noted: It has slightly wavy edges to the petals; the enamel shades from lighter at the center to darker at the edges; and there are small spots of dark enamel intended to represent markings on the petals.

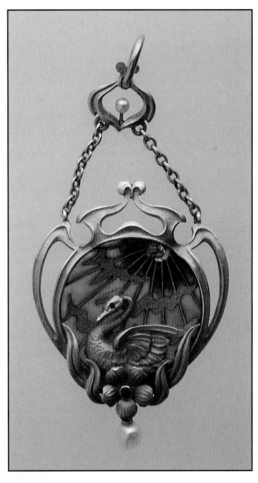

A wonderful Russian Art Nouveau gold, ruby, diamond, and plique-à-jour swan pendant. The swan swims against the plique-à-jour background with colors suggesting sunrise, a diamond at the top corner perhaps representing the sun. *Courtesy of Nelson Rarities, Portland, ME.*

A 19th century Swiss bracelet in 18K gold and enamel. The women portrayed on the bracelet, which is painted using the Limoges enameling technique, each represent a different canton, or province, of Switzerland. *Courtesy of Nelson Rarities, Portland, ME.*

A lovely Art Nouveau/Jugendstil bracelet in 900 silver and plique-à-jour enamel, c. 1900, by Carl Hermann of Germany. Silver chains link four plaques with stylized, geometric flowers incorporating a series of circular elements, perhaps meant to represent leaves, hanging from the flowers. Interestingly, the second plaque from the right is larger than the other three, identical, plaques and contains two flowers rather than one. Measures 7.25" x 2". *Courtesy of Robin Allison.*

Two late 19th century necklaces, probably of Newark, New Jersey manufacture, showing characteristics of both Victorian and Art Nouveau jewelry. The small flowers are more realistically rendered than most Art Nouveau flowers, with small stamens surrounding the central pearls. However, the curving frames, pearl dangles, iridescent enamel, and–in the upper necklace –chain festoons point to Art Nouveau intentions, or pretensions.

An Art Nouveau brooch in 14K (or possibly 10K sold as 14K) gold, enamel, and pearls, featuring a woman's head in profile against a crescent of pearls, of American origin. Typically, the Art Nouveau woman is depicted with long, swirling hair, which in this piece both creates the background texture against which the face is set, and forms part of the frame. The beautiful iridescent enameling of the face is nicely shaded, and very detailed, down to the eyelids and eyelashes. Measures 1.25" x 1.25". *Courtesy of Robin Allison.*

A Continuing Tradition

Be not the first by whom the new are tried,
Nor yet the last to lay the old aside.
—Alexander Pope, *An Essay on Criticism*

However, because enamel is a wonderful means of adding great beauty to a piece of jewelry for much less time and expense than setting stones to create a similar look, it has never gone completely out of style. Art Deco jewelry made use of enamel, either as an integral part of a design, or as an accent. Later jewelers, such as the Scandinavian and Mexican jewelers working in the Arts and Crafts tradition, continued to use enamel as a basic element of their designs. Recently, enameling has made a major comeback, as artisan/artist jewelers create stunning jewelry by reviving techniques from the past, or even devising new techniques, such as the use of wet-packed enamel without cloisonné cells.

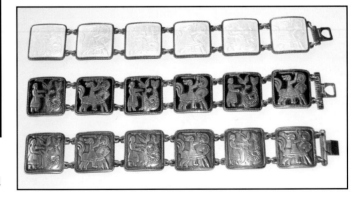

A wonderful contrasting group of bracelets by noted Norwegian designer David Andersen, in silver. The three bracelets, all with the same Scandinavian designs–alternating plaques with a woman feeding a mythical beast and a stylized knight on horseback–show perfectly the difference that enamel can make, as the bottom bracelet is unenameled, while the middle bracelet has the designs set against red enamel, and the top has the design completely covered by enamel. Each marked for David Andersen, Norway, with silver content marks ranging from 830S to 925S; each measures 7.25" x 1". *Courtesy of Robin Allison.*

Enamel, especially guilloche enamel, remained popular for such "useful" decorative objects as perfume bottles and compacts. The set above, by the American company Foster and Brothers, shows a masterful use of guilloche to form light radiating from the moon. The seagull compact at top right uses guilloche only as a border for the marvelously drawn seascape. Both marked F & B and sterling; green compact measures 2.125" x 2.125", seagull compact measures 2.375" in diameter. *Courtesy of Robin Allison.*

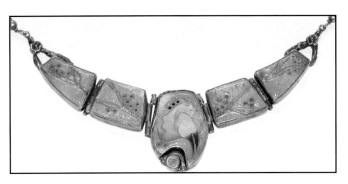

A contemporary necklace in sterling silver, enamel, and a moonstone, featuring unusually shaped, graduated plaques with stylized branches, blossoms, and, in the central piece, a peacock in cloisonné enamel. The art of enameling has, in recent years, made a comeback in artisan jewelry, such as this fascinating piece. The light blue enamel that forms the background has a wonderful textured look to it; marked BW and measures 4" x 1.25". *Courtesy of Robin Allison.*

Possibly the most unusual enameled piece Robin has ever seen, this pendant from Hungary is done in platinum and diamonds, with a very three-dimensional woman's face in enamel. The face is so ghostlike that it almost re-sembles a death mask, and rises about .5" from the base of the pendant. Measures 2.75" x 1" . Unmarked. Most likely 1911-1919, transitional between Victorian/Edwardian and Art Deco. *Courtesy of Robin Allison.*

Price Guide for Introduction

p. 11: AN Lim 14K w/ s-prls lady pend $750-$900; M.M. guil sl-mrr $1000-$1200; Ger AN plq lady w/ violin pend $3500-$4500; **p. 12:** All. 14K w/ dmds, prls & rub Byz. lady bclt $6000-$9000; Nk AN Byz. 14K w/ sm prl lady st-p $550-$650; Vict 14K w/ sm dmds trnsl enam red bird br-pend $750-$1250; **p. 13:** A&C bl & gr pend $200-$250; Nk AN 14K w/ prls pansy neck $7500-$10,000; Eg rev plq wg-scrb br w/ carn $350-$400; Eg rev grn plq wg-scrb pend $400-$500; M.M. AN plq styl-lot neck w/ grn pst $2000-$2500; **p. 14:** Fr AN 18K w/ dmd, prls, rub & saph drgnf br $5000-$7000; Nk Vict 14K cir br w/ 3 flrs $750-$1250; Fr AN 18K w/ dmds & prl irid crl bellflower br-pend $6000-$8500; **p. 15:** M. lg 14K w/ dmd irid pnk flr br-pend $2500-$3000; Nk 14K v sm chld rng $150-$250; Nk AN 14K w/ prl cres irid lady br $1000- $2000; AN grn plq bclt $2500-$3000; AN 14K w/ prl neck $750-$1500; 3 D.A. bclts: w/o enam $150-$175, w/ enam $400-$450; **p. 16:** F.&B. cpt in orig box $500-$600; vint seagull cpt $400-$500; AD plat w/ dmds lady pend $2500-$3000; mod bl peacock neck $200-$300.

Chapter One
Oh, What a Time It Was!

Now has come the last age according to the oracle at Cumae;
the great series of lifetimes starts anew. Now too the virgin god-
dess returns, the golden days of Saturn's reign return, now a
new race descends from heaven.

—Virgil, *Ecologue*

Praise they that will times past, I joy to see
My self now live: this age best pleaseth me.
—Robert Herrick, "The Present Time Best Pleaseth"

The end of the nineteenth century was, arguably, the last great age of enameled jewelry. It was a time when the prophesied "golden days of Saturn's reign" were fulfilled by some of the most talented jewelers and enamelists ever to work their magic in gold and gems and glass. It was, in short, one of the most exciting times in the history of decorative arts.

As Queen Victoria's long reign drew to a close, two influential movements arose to challenge the traditional concept of jewelry: the Arts and Crafts movement in Great Britain, and Art Nouveau in France and Belgium. Both viewed jewelry as art rather than wealth, and introduced a new lexicon of enameling techniques, as well as a wealth of symbolism. At the same time, more traditional makers also turned to enamel, and produced charming miniature works of art in their delicate flower and other figural pins.

For a collector of period jewelry, though, the end of the nineteenth century can be not only exciting, interesting, but, well... confusing. Awash with so many movements, so many names. Victorian, Edwardian, Arts and Crafts, Aesthetic, Art Nouveau, Art Deco, *fin-de-siècle, beaux arts, belle époque*, Romantic Period, Grand Period. And so many of them overlap, like waves on a shore, that it is sometimes hard not to feel inundated. And–to extend the metaphor–hard not to feel swept away in confusion and, as a result, left completely at sea.

A brief description of periods and movements might help clarify some of the terms mentioned above. The following list is intended to serve as an introduction to a more detailed discussion of trends in late nineteenth and early twentieth century jewelry, especially the enameled jewelry of the period.

What Time *Was* It?

Victorian–This term sometimes evokes a certain atmosphere, one of rigid social conventions, heavy dark furniture, and florid brick buildings inhabited by prim young women and proper young men. A certain type of jewelry fit in with the era: heavy, elaborate, often set with dark garnets.

In reality, the term *Victorian* is the name of the era covered by Queen Victoria's reign in Great Britain, which lasted for almost two-thirds of the nineteenth century. It is really a historical term rather than the name of a style or trend, although like other such terms it covers art, architecture, and literature produced during her reign, as well as the manners and customs of the period. It also is often applied to jewelry made in the United States (and elsewhere) as well as in Great Britain. For the purpose of convenience, it will sometimes be used to refer not only to British jewelry but to American and even European jewelry as well, in place of the more cumbersome (but more accurate) phrase *late nineteenth century*.

Because Victoria's reign lasted so long, it is frequently divided into three distinct periods: *early Victorian*, also known as the *Romantic Period* (1837-1860); *mid-Victorian*, also called the *Grand Period* (1860-1885); and *late Victorian*, also sometimes called the *Aesthetic Period* (not to be confused with the Aesthetic Movement) (1885-1901).

Edwardian–Like the term Victorian, *Edwardian* is also a historical term, and refers to the reign of Victoria's son Edward VII, who reigned from 1901 to 1910. And, again like the term Victorian, Edwardian is used to refer to manners, literature, art, costume, and jewelry of the time. It also conjures up a certain spirit. It was a graceful age, its gracefulness that of the swan-necked Gibson girl or the equally swan-necked Queen Alexandra, Edward VII's wife. It also had a certain innocence, or lightness; it was a time when young women and men dressed in white linen and straw hats played croquet or tennis on pleasant lawns shaded by broad elms. They wore jewelry that was as airy as Victorian was dark: It sparkled with diamonds and white metals in clean geometric lines, with long festoons of pearls, and close-fitting dog collars. The clothing and jewelry fit them and the more casual, carefree life they led–a way of life which was largely to end with the onset of World War I in 1914.

fin-de-siècle–Like Victorian and Edwardian, *fin-de-siècle* is a historical term that simply refers to the "end of the century," the transition between the nineteenth and twentieth centuries (or, in a sense, the transition between Victoria's reign and that of her son). Perhaps even more than the preceding terms, it implies a certain spirit of the times, a sort of decadence, but exuberance as well: half-clad dancers at the *Moulin Rouge*, the designs of Mucha, jewelry draped with swags as glittering as crystal chandeliers.

belle époque–This is a rather tricky term; meaning "beautiful age," it is most often used to refer to the Edwardian era. However, it has also been applied to French jewelry of the mid- to late nineteenth and early twentieth centuries when great makers such as Boucheron, Fouquet, Lalique, and Vever made their names at world fairs and expositions.

Aesthetic Movement–This phrase refers to a movement that spread through western Europe in the 1850s and 1860s, lasting roughly for most of the rest of the century. It embraced an aesthetic sense that spurned usefulness and embraced the exotic, including the art of Japan, newly opened to Western trade in 1853 by the American, Commodore Matthew Perry. One of its adherents, the French author Théodore Gautier, wrote in the preface to his novel *Mademoiselle de Maupin*: "Nothing is really beautiful unless it is useless; everything useful is ugly, for it expresses a need and the needs of man are ignoble and disgusting..." (Gauthier then went on to opine that the most useful room in the house was the lavatory.) Art for art's sake became a credo of the movement. Among its followers were the American-born painter James McNeill Whistler; the poet, playwright, and novelist Oscar Wilde; the British artists Aubrey Beardsley and Sir Lawrence Alma-Tadema; and the French poet Charles Baudelaire. One of the signature motifs of the Aesthetic Movement, the peacock, was picked up by makers of Arts and Crafts jewelry and metalwork.

Aesthetic Period–A term sometimes given to the late Victorian period, not to be confused with the earlier Aesthetic Movement.

Arts and Crafts–A seminal movement, one of the two most important in late Victorian jewelry, it largely embraced the philosophy of artist-designer William Morris and critic John Ruskin. Enamel, along with other non-traditional materials such as opals, mother-of-pearl, and semi-precious rather than precious stones, was one of the materials favored by artists and artisans who made Arts and Crafts jewelry (and other metal objects). In a number of ways, it was influenced by the Aesthetic Movement as well as the Pre-Raphaelite Brotherhood formed by poet-painter Dante Gabriel Rossetti and artist John Everett Millais.

Art Nouveau–The second movement that influenced the jewelry of the late nineteenth century, Art Nouveau emerged in Belgium around 1880-1885, but is most identified with France. Like the Arts and Crafts movement (which to some extent influenced it; Karlin, in her book on Arts and Crafts jewelry and metalwork, sees the two movements as intertwined), its goals were to create jewelry that broke away from the poor design of conventional jewelry. It also disdained the notion of jewelry as wealth, concentrating instead on jewelry as Art. It too made great use of enamel.

beaux arts–Like Arts and Crafts, Art Nouveau, and Art Deco, this term describes a genre–or, more accurately, a somewhat limited sub-genre–rather than a particular period. From the French meaning "fine (or beautiful) arts," this phrase has recently come to refer to pieces that do not fall distinctly into any historical or aesthetic category. Pieces in this sub-genre might have been created during the late Victorian or early Edwardian period, and might overlap with Arts and Crafts and/or Art Nouveau, but they have their own particular style and (fairly limited) subject matter. Perhaps the most obvious examples of enameled *beaux arts* pieces produced in the United States c. 1900 are the lions and tigers that manage to appear both realistic and stylized at the same time. Tigers especially were produced in some quantity by Newark and New York makers. Usually these are shown with the mouth open, in a somewhat menacing snarl, holding a diamond in their enameled red mouths.

Art Deco–Perhaps because of the similarity of the terms, Art Deco jewelry is sometimes confused with Art Nouveau. However, the two styles could not be more different. Where Art Nouveau embraced the curve and the complex, Art Deco embodied the simple, bold, and angular. It grew out of the prevailing styles and tastes that largely distinguished Edwardian jewelry from late Victorian. Late Victorian jewelry, especially for the middle classes, was heavy, ornate, and favored gold and garnets. Edwardian jewelry was lighter, geometric, favored filigree work, diamonds, and white metal–platinum for the costlier jewelry, white gold and silver for less expensive pieces. Art Deco design characteristic of the 1920s and early 1930s was also geometric, and like Edwardian jewelry, favored white metal and diamonds. It also used bold, contrasting colors, especially sapphires and emeralds and rubies set alongside diamonds, as well as the contrast of black (often onyx) and white (often diamonds, but sometimes pearls or mother-of-pearl). Unlike Art Nouveau jewelry, many Art Deco pieces used enamel sparingly, often as an accent rather than as an integral feature of the design. The exceptions are plique-à-jour enamel, found especially in the Egyptian revival jewelry popular at the time; and guilloche enamel, which remained popular for objects such as compacts, cigarette cases, and cufflinks, as well as some jewelry. Enamel was also used by some innovative designers; however, most pieces of important Art Deco jewelry are not enameled.

vintage–Technically, this term can be used to describe any piece of jewelry that is not actually antique–that is, over one hundred years old–and is also not new or modern. However, while Art Deco falls within this range, it has its own unique style and can be considered a separate category; therefore, in this book vintage will be used to describe non-Art Deco jewelry from about 1930 up to modern jewelry. Often vintage is used to refer to jewelry from the 1940s, 1950s, and 1960s; but, as it is often difficult to date a vintage piece with certainty, there is probably a fair amount of latitude.

Traipsing Through Time: Aesthetic Awareness

The nineteenth century was rich in movements, many of which influenced–however indirectly–late nineteenth-century jewelers and their customers, and through them more general taste. The most influential movements were:

Mid-Victorian (1860–1885)

♦ *The Pre-Raphaelite Brotherhood*–This was formed in 1848 by the artist and poet Dante Gabriel Rossetti and artist John Everett Millais after a chance encounter. Its emphasis on an older artistic aesthetic–one that influenced art before the works of late Renaissance Italian painter Raphael–can be seen in Arts and Crafts works and jewelry, as well as in some Limoges enamels created in France.

♦ *The Aesthetic Movement*–This movement began in the 1850s, and included among its followers the famous poet, playwright, and novelist Oscar Wilde; the American-born painter James McNeill Whistler; and the artists Sir Lawrence Alma-Tadema and Aubrey Beardsley. Its direct influence can be found in the multitude of Arts and Crafts peacocks.

♦ *The Symbolist Movement*–This is said to have begun in 1857 with the publication of French poet Charles Baudelaire's *Les fleurs du mal* (*The Flowers of Evil*). Baudelaire was also an adherent of the Aesthetic Movement. The Symbolists heavily influenced Art Nouveau designers, whose jewelry was replete with hidden meaning.

♦ *Japonisme*–Precipitated by Commodore Perry's trip to Japan, this movement in some ways seems to be a subset of the Aesthetic Movement, as it inspired some of the same artists. For example, Whistler's 1864 painting *Rose and Silver: The Princess from the Land of Porcelain*, shows his model clothed in a kimono in front of a Japanese screen. It also inspired some of French jeweler Lucien Falize's most beautiful pieces, which employ cloisonné enamel in Asian designs.

♦ *Style Cathédrale*–This French Gothic-inspired trend to some extent seems to correspond to the English pre-Raphaelite movement in its aims and sympathies, as well as to archaeological revivals in jewelry, of which it might be considered a part. It led to Gothic-style jewelry designed by some famous French makers, including Falize father and son, who created jewelry with Gothic letters using enamel *sur paillons*.

♦ *Arts and Crafts*–One of the two most important artistic and philosophical movements in decorative arts at the end of the nineteenth century, this revolt against the mediocrity of machine-age design and fabrication was largely inspired by the writings of William Morris and John Ruskin; its spiritual ancestors are the Pre-Raphaelite Brotherhood and the Aesthetic Movement. It began in Great Britain in the 1870s (thus straddling the mid- and late Victorian periods), but its influence soon spread, not least of all to Art Nouveau.

Late Victorian (1885-1901)

♦ *Art Nouveau*–The other important artistic movement for decorative arts at the end of the nineteenth century, this was a jewelry-driven movement fueled in large part by the artistic genius of René Lalique; its spiritual and aesthetic antecedents are the Arts and Crafts, the Symbolist, and the Aesthetic movements.

Edwardian (1901-1910)

♦ *Art Deco*–This design movement, popular during the 1920s, can be said to have its beginnings in the more geometric designs popular during the Edwardian period. As did jewelry in the Edwardian era, Art Deco jewelry favored diamonds and platinum and a certain cleanness of line. Other prominent features of Art Deco design are bold geometric designs, the use of black and white, and splashes of brightly colored stones such as emeralds, rubies, and sapphires, as well as opaque or translucent semi-precious gems such as coral, onyx, and jade. Enamel is not usually a major feature of Art Deco jewelry, with the exception of guilloche enamel, which remained popular for objects such as powder compacts, cigarette cases, and cufflinks; and plique-à-jour enamel, often found in Egyptian revival jewelry.

A cigarette case in silver and enamel, with Dante Gabriel Rossetti's painting *Proserpina* (Persephone). Rossetti and his sister Christina were among the leading members of the Pre-Raphaelite Brotherhood. The Pre-Raphaelites' philosophy as well as their art influenced the Aesthetic and the Arts and Crafts movements in Great Britain. Measures 5.5" x 3.75"; hallmarks for British sterling, Birmingham, and signed J. Cl. Co. Ltd. *Courtesy of Robin Allison.*

Victorian Jewelry

The Early Victorian–or Romantic–Period

'Beauty is truth, truth beauty,'–That is all
Ye know on earth, and all ye need to know.
—John Keats, *Ode on a Grecian Urn*

Early Victorian jewelry continued many trends of the immediately preceding Georgian period. Common to both was what Luthi, in her book *Sentimental Jewellery*, calls "the language of stones."

This "language of stones" used the first letters of the names of stones to spell out words, most often REGARD (**R**-uby, **E**-merald, **G**-arnet, **A**-methyst, **R**-uby, **D**-iamond) or DEAREST (**D**-iamond, **E**-merald, **A**-methyst, **R**-uby, **E**-merald, **T**-opaz, or **T**-urquoise).

A late Georgian REGARD locket, in 18K gold and colored stones, c. 1830, from England. In this type of piece, the first letters of the names of the stones used–ruby, emerald, garnet, amethyst, ruby, diamond–spell out the word. This locket, intended to hold a lock of hair, was fashioned to look like a book. Unmarked 18K gold and stones, measures approximately 1.125" x .825".

Two early to mid-Victorian rings, in 14K gold, with **d**iamond, **e**merald, **a**methyst, **r**uby, **e**merald, **s**apphire, and **t**opaz, spelling out the word "dearest" in what has been called "the language of stones." The larger ring, c. 1855, measures approximately .50" in diameter, the smaller approximately .367". Although many such rings have the stones arranged side-by-side in a row, these two rings display the stones set in a flower-like circle, with the diamond in the center.

Mourning jewelry, popular during the late Georgian period, continued to be worn in Queen Victoria's time. Often this took the form of a locket intended to hold a lock of a loved one's hair, or of jewelry actually fashioned with hair as a main component. It sometimes included a miniature portrait of the person being mourned. Occasionally mourning jewelry incorporated black enamel, sometimes with pearls, less frequently with diamonds; other gems seem to have been considered too colorful or gaudy for something as serious as a mourning piece.

A small collection of Victorian mourning jewelry. The early to mid-Victorian bracelet is of 14K gold and glossy black enamel, with diamonds arranged to form floral sprays. The pansy, which bears the maker's mark for A. J. Hedges & Co. of Newark, is in 14K gold and black enamel, c. 1895, approximately 1" in diameter. Pansies were a favorite theme for mourning and other Victorian flower jewelry. The flower, despite its monochrome enamel, is otherwise much like other pieces from Newark and New York, with five separate petals linked by a rivet and arched wire supports in back. Its appearance is also characteristic, naturalistic in form. The enamel on both pieces is very glossy, lacking the matte or iridescent finish of later enamel. The earrings are of 10K gold, jet, and seed pearls. *Bracelet courtesy of Sol Varon, Portland, OR.*

While not enameled in black, this lovely brooch is a memorial piece, engraved with a woman's name and the date of her death. The center, in the vivid cobalt blue popular during the 18th and 19th centuries, contains a diamond butterfly, which appears to emerge from its chrysalis–quite possibly a symbol of the soul leaving the body. The surrounding enamel is done in the lovely shade of turquoise blue that became popular around 1845, with lovely gold scrollwork. In 14K gold, enamel, and diamonds. An inscription reads "In memory of Elizabeth Guest, Sept. 10, 1845 at 47." Unmarked, measures 1.625" x 1.375". *Courtesy of Robin Allison.*

When not used for mourning jewelry, Victorian enamel-work was often flowery and ornate, as in the brightly hued enameled watch shown on this page.

An early to mid-Victorian watch in gold, enamel, and pearls. The flowers, beautifully enameled against a blue ground, are set off nicely by the scalloped pearl edging. Elaborate design, sometimes executed in enamel, is typical of some Victorian jewelry. In many cases these designs were created by the use of transfer enameling. *Courtesy of Judith Anderson, Bijoux Extraordinaire, Manchester, NH.*

Also popular were pieces enameled in the cobalt blue enamel of the previous century. When Prince Albert became engaged to the young Queen Victoria, he gave her a snake bracelet; snake bracelets with cobalt blue enamel set with diamonds became the rage.

French slide bracelet, with the cobalt blue enamel so prevalent in the late 18th and 19th centuries. The bracelet, in 18K woven gold with diamonds and half pearls, has the fleur-de-lis motif sometimes associated with the Napoleonic period. Cobalt enamel remained popular during the early and mid-Victorian periods. Unmarked; slide portion measures approximately 1.625" in diameter.

French snake bangle bracelet in 18K gold, enamel, diamonds, and pearls. While this French bracelet is earlier than the one given by Albert to Victoria, it is very similar to bracelets that remained popular during the Victorian era. Good luck charms–a horseshoe in pearls, and a star–hang from the snake's mouth. Later, such charms were sometimes replaced by a diamond or ruby dangle.

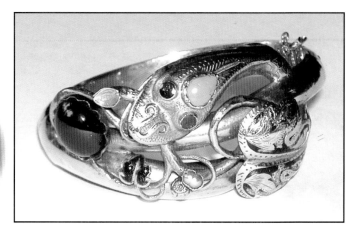

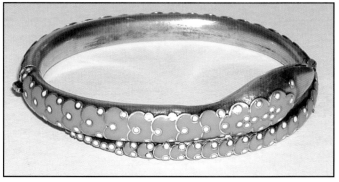

Another of the snake bracelets of which Victorians were so fond, and which they produced in some quantity, especially with cobalt blue enamel. This bracelet, in 18K gold, enamel, turquoise, pearl, and garnets is–like the bracelet below left–most likely of French origin. In this case, the cobalt blue enamel is applied to leaves that garland the snake, a somewhat different design for this type of bracelet. While many snakes have heads enameled in cobalt blue and set with diamonds, some are also found with an opal on the head; the turquoise in this piece is much more unusual. Undecipherable gold hallmark. This large bracelet measures 1.5" across. *Courtesy of Robin Allison.*

This snake bracelet, unlike like the other two, is in silver; its enameling, however, is in many ways superior to its more expensive counterparts in 18K gold. Like many pieces from the mid-Victorian era, it is enameled in a light turquoise blue that simulated the Persian turquoise so fashionable at the time. Unlike the other two snake bracelets, this one is fully enameled, with a scalloped edge punctuated by the white dots that also decorate the middle of each enameled cell. In some ways, the enameling is reminiscent of later Scandinavian enamel work, which occasionally makes use of dots to enhance monochrome enameling, possibly to simulate pearls. European origin, 800 silver. *Courtesy of Robin Allison.*

Snake jewelry other than bracelets was also made during this period. This necklace, with a cobalt blue enameled oval studded with diamond leaves and a pearl perhaps meant to represent an apple, has a frame formed by two snakes entwined at heads and tails. The necklace itself is formed of enameled links interspersed with pearls. In 18K gold, enamel, diamonds, rubies, and pearls. Pendant portion of necklace measures approximately 1.5" x 1.875".

For nature then… to me was all in all.

—William Wordsworth, "Lines composed
a few miles above Tinturn Abbey"

The very beginning of Victoria's reign was also influenced by the waning Romantic movement. Although the foremost of England's Romantic poets, Lord Byron, John Keats, and Percy Bysshe Shelley had breathed their last a decade earlier, the Romantic Period exemplified by their poetry carried over into the early years of Victoria's reign. The Romantics exalted nature and the past, and described them both in detail. In jewelry, Romantic influence can be seen in pieces decorated with leaves, flowers, birds, insects; these themes, however, are not confined to early Victorian jewelry, but persisted throughout her reign. The *execution* of such motifs, however, did change; they are often heavier and darker in late Victorian jewelry. The lily-of-the-valley became a motif set into black onyx or jet, the ivy leaves–and other leaves and flowers–often appeared in black enamel.

A charming early Victorian locket with an enameled fly surrounded by green enameled ivy leaves and lilies-of-the-valley in white enamel with green leaves. The fly, with white enamel wings and a darker enameled body, is realistically rendered, befitting an era that glorified nature. *Courtesy of Nelson Rarities, Portland, ME.*

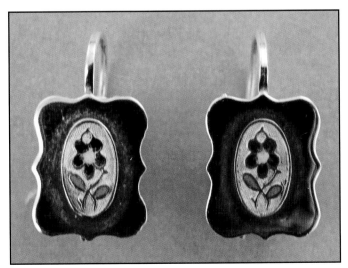

A pair of small late Georgian or early Victorian earrings, in gold and enamel. The flowers, with stems and leaves, seem to be in a combination of a rather simple cloisonné and champlevé enamel. Unmarked gold, probably 14K; measure approximately .625" x .75".

The Mid-Victorian, or Grand, Period

Her tears fell with the dew at even;
Her tears fell ere the dews were dried.

—Alfred, Lord Tennyson, *Marianna*

The mid-Victorian period may have been the Grand Period, but it was also the Grand Age of Mourning. In 1861, Victoria's beloved husband, Prince Albert, died; and the queen went into perpetual mourning. Memorial pieces, not uncommon before this time, suddenly became ubiquitous. Miniature portraits, hair jewelry, black jet earrings, brooches, and lockets–all these became standard in the jewel boxes of the day. Because black enamel was suitable for mourning, it was frequently used in mourning pieces. Even flower pins, more often found naturalistically painted with colored enamels, were enameled in black for mourning.

Two mourning brooches, one in unmarked 14K gold, matte black enamel, and a pearl, in the form of a violet–or, perhaps, a johnny-jump-up–the other a wreath of flowers carved in black jet. Floral jewelry was extremely popular during this period, and a number of flower brooches were enameled in black for mourning pieces. The violet, probably c. 1900 and measuring 1" x .625", converts to a pendant; the jet brooch measures 1" in diameter. *Courtesy of Red Robin Antiques.*

Three floral mourning pieces, including a locket in rose gold and onyx, with a basket of flowers overlying the onyx; a violet in 14K gold and a pearl, measuring about .75", quite possibly by the New York firm Black, Starr & Frost; and a gold-filled handkerchief pin with a movable head, measuring .50" x .75", in the form of a pansy (today this would be called a johnny-jump-up, but up until c. 1850, when the modern pansy was first developed at London's Kew Gardens, this was the flower people referred to as a pansy). Like many flowers of New York and Newark origin, the violet has tiny stamens surrounding the pearl; however, these can scarcely be seen, as they too are enameled in black.

A demi-parure of Victorian mourning jewelry, comprising a locket and earrings in sterling silver, enamel, and pearls. Black enamel and pearls were a hallmark of Victorian mourning jewelry, in which diamonds are occasionally–but much less frequently–found. In typical Victorian style, the pearls are set into a floral design. The locket, which converts to a brooch, measures 2.25" x 1.375"; the earrings measure 2" x .5". Unmarked silver. *Courtesy of Robin Allison.*

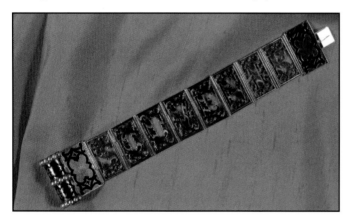

A gold and enamel S-O-U-V-E-N-I-R ("to remember") bracelet, with each letter spelled out in one link, which folds up to look like a book. Bracelets with lettering, especially Gothic lettering, were popular c. 1880, and were made by some noted makers, including Falize. *Courtesy of Nelson Rarities, Portland, ME.*

Another type of enamel popular for mourning jewelry was *taille d'épargne* (sometimes also spelled *taille d'épergne*) enamel. Taille d'épargne literally means "figure (or size) of economy," and consists of shallow, usually machine-made designs filled with opaque enamel, most often black. This black enamel set against an engraved gold background was stately and subdued, eminently suitable for mourning, and became very common in Victorian pieces.

A mourning locket in 18K gold and black taille d'épargne enamel with the words IN MEMORIAM on the front, British or American, c. 1880. The beautifully engraved back of this mourning locket most likely bears the deceased person's initials. *Locket courtesy of Classic Facets, Boulder, CO; photograph by Karryl Salit.*

A watch in 18K gold and taille d'épargne enamel, c. 1885. This type of enameling was popular in late Victorian British and American jewelry, possibly in part because the restrained black enamel made a piece in taille d'épargne suitable for mourning.

Not all jewelry in taille d'épargne enamel was intended for mourning, as this set of wedding bracelets in gold and taille d'épargne enamel attests. The bracelets, c. 1870, in unmarked gold, and inscribed with the bride's name (Maggie M. Wiley), have a floral motif that is very typical of Victorian taille d'épargne enameling. Unmarked gold; measure .375" in width. *Courtesy of Robin Allison.*

An unusual Victorian watch holder brooch in gold, coral, and taille d'épargne enamel in the shape of a coral hand with a fan or wide cuff. Another piece that might have been suitable in or out of mourning. *Courtesy of Nelson Rarities, Portland, ME.*

A pair of earrings c. 1845, in unmarked gold (as is common for the period), pearls, and enamel, measuring 1.75" x .625". The earrings, typically mid-Victorian, are in the turquoise blue enamel that became popular as a means of creating the effect of the Persian turquoise gemstones very much in demand at the period. The earrings have delicate gold swirls, as well as a circle in twisted gold, with a pearl, at the center. *Courtesy of Robin Allison.*

Not all enamel of the period was black. When Persian turquoise became fashionable around 1850-1860, a light turquoise blue enamel also became popular, emulating or simulating the beautiful blue stone. French jewelry, as well as British and American, used this attractive enamel. When mourning jewelry was not involved, mid-Victorian jewelry was often flowery and sentimental, as it had been in the first part of Victoria's reign.

A brooch of agate, gold, and Persian turquoise, c. 1880, approximately 1.5" x 1.125". When Persian turquoise became readily available to the Western market from the Ottoman Empire, a light turquoise blue enamel was developed to simulate its color. Persian turquoise remained popular throughout most of the mid- and late Victorian periods, as did the turquoise enamel.

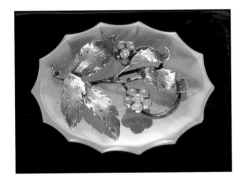

A bangle in gold, enamel, and pearls, c. 1880. This lovely bracelet has three raised roundels in basket-weave light blue champlevé enamel, with pearls set in the spaces formed by the woven enamel. This light blue enamel became fashionable in the 1860s, when Persian turquoise was also popular. *Courtesy of Nelson Rarities, Portland, ME.*

French day-night earrings and locket in 18K gold and the turquoise blue color fashionable c. 1860. The rich color shows how 19th century jewelers used enamel that emulated or replaced gemstones. *Earrings and locket courtesy of Classic Facets, Boulder, CO; photograph by Karryl Salit.*

A small bow in 14K gold, enamel, seed pearls, and a diamond, c. 1880. Bows were popular motifs in Victorian jewelry, and can be found not just alone, but as decoration on other, more elaborate, pieces. Marked 14K; measures approximately 1.125" in width. *Pin courtesy of Bodette Reeves, Odessa, TX.*

The mid-Victorian period also marked the beginning of the age of archaeological revivals. This trend was due primarily to the Italian Fortunato Piu Castellani and his son Alessandro who, inspired by finds of Classical and Etruscan jewelry by the Duke of Sermonta and others, managed to recreate the granulé and filigree work so commonly found in Greek and Etruscan jewelry.

A pair of Etruscan revival earrings in 18K gold and coral, c. 1880, approximately 1" diameter, probably French. Etruscan revival pieces are easily identified by their extensive use of granulé work (or granulation), supposedly rediscovered by Castellani in the middle of the 19th century. They also feature filigree and other twisted wire work.

For political reasons, Alessandro moved to Paris. There his premises formed the nucleus of the French Archaeological School of Jewelry. While he professed to disdain Renaissance jewelry and scultpure[1] he nevertheless added a line of Renaissance jewelry to his Classical revival jewelry. In 1860 a fellow archaeological revival jeweler, Carlo Giuliano, accompanied Alessandro to London. Giuliano was largely responsible for bringing archaeological revival jewelry to England, where he stayed and registered his own mark in 1863. Snowman (1990) notes that Giuliano was considered a kindred spirit by the Pre-Raphaelite Brotherhood, and lent pieces of jewelry to artists such as Sir Lawrence Alma-Tadema to use in their paintings. Although many of Giuliano's designs incorporate enamel accents, most Classical revival jewelry is primarily in gold, sometimes embellished with cabochon stones. Revival jewelry, whether Etruscan, Greek, Gothic, Renaissance, or Egyptian, was to remain in vogue for much of the rest of the century.

Earrings in perhaps the Etruscan revival style (but with some appearance of Renaissance revival in the enameled flowers), of 18K gold, enamel, and seed pearls, c. 1880, possibly French or English, .50" x 1.5" (excluding wires). These earrings were manufactured with delicate filigree work surrounding teardrop-shaped enameled plaques painted with small pink and blue flowers. Cobalt blue enamel frames the earrings, which end in a fringe of tiny seed pearl dangles.

A ring in 14K gold, diamonds, and Limoges enameling, showing a young woman wearing a Renaissance or medieval cap sparked with small diamonds, which also form the border of her square-cut bodice. Her distant gaze and abstracted expression, as well as her long straight hair and antique raiment, show definite pre-Raphaelite tendencies. Top measures .75" x .5". *Courtesy of Robin Allison*

An Egyptian revival bracelet in 18K gold, enamel, and diamonds, possibly c. 1880, the center portion approximately 1.75" x 1". The central scarab is realistically rendered, and set off by 24 small diamonds. Two lotus blossoms and four buds, in champlevé enamel, flank the scarab. The links are topped with champlevé lotus buds. It may have been inspired by the discovery of Queen Aahotep's Eighteenth Dynasty tomb in 1859, or by the later discovery of Twelfth Dynasty royal jewelry at Lisht and Dashur. Scarabs and lotuses were both very symbolic to the ancient Egyptians.

A striking bracelet in the Gothic revival style, featuring plaques with gargoyles or demons and dragons or griffons in base metal, interspersed with plaques of young men and women in Renaissance dress. Measures 7" x 1". *Courtesy of Robin Allison.*

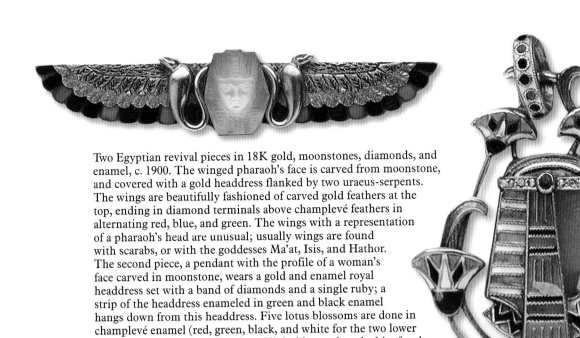

Two Egyptian revival pieces in 18K gold, moonstones, diamonds, and enamel, c. 1900. The winged pharaoh's face is carved from moonstone, and covered with a gold headdress flanked by two uraeus-serpents. The wings are beautifully fashioned of carved gold feathers at the top, ending in diamond terminals above champlevé feathers in alternating red, blue, and green. The wings with a representation of a pharaoh's head are unusual; usually wings are found with scarabs, or with the goddesses Ma'at, Isis, and Hathor. The second piece, a pendant with the profile of a woman's face carved in moonstone, wears a gold and enamel royal headdress set with a band of diamonds and a single ruby; a strip of the headdress enameled in green and black enamel hangs down from this headdress. Five lotus blossoms are done in champlevé enamel (red, green, black, and white for the two lower blossoms and the dangle; dark and light blue, red, and white for the upper two). The use of vivid colors, often imitating the dark blue lapis, red carnelian, and light blue turquoise favored by Egyptian jewelers, is common in Egyptian revival jewelry.

Egyptian revival jewelry especially, in part because of the discovery of King Tutankhamon's treasure in 1922, was to go in and out of fashion during the twentieth century as well.

The archaeological revival style was apparently popular not just for jewelry, but for a complete line of silver serving dishes, all embellished with archaeological motifs. (From an 1868 edition of *Frank Leslie's Illustrated News*.)

Traipsing Through Time: The Age of Archaeological Adventure

Archaeological revival jewelry enjoyed great popularity in the mid- and late Victorian periods. Revival jewelry was everywhere: Greek revival, Etruscan revival, Egyptian revival, Gothic revival. Women wore items of jewelry that had been out of fashion for centuries, even in some cases millennia: Their jewel boxes contained fibulae and bullae and scarabs. One of the reasons archaeological revival jewelry became popular in mid- and late Victorian times was that there were so many prototypes upon which to draw, as adventurers and archaeologists turned up find after find:

♦ 1763–Systematic excavation of the ancient Roman city of Pompeii begins; excavation continues under Napoleon's domination of Italy (1806-1814); the Bourbon rulers actively support the excavation; and in 1861 the government takes over the excavation using a more scientific approach developed by G. Fiorelli.
♦ 1799–The Rosetta Stone, which eventually unlocks secrets of Egyptian hieroglyphic writing, is found by Napoleon's army in the Nile Delta.
♦ 1802–Dominique Vivant Denon, a member of the team of scholars and scientists sent by Napoleon to Egypt after the French conquest of the country, publishes his *Voyage dans la basse et la haute Égypte (Voyage in Lower and Upper Egypt)*, published in English in 1803 as *Egypt*.
♦ 1822–Jean François Champollion (using Englishman Thomas Young's insight that cartouches in the Rosetta Stone's text held royal names) deciphers ancient Egyptian hieroglyphs.
♦ 1848–Henry Layard, after excavating Ninevah (1845-1847), returns to England and publishes *Ninevah and Its Remains*.
♦ 1855–Layard's further explorations in Mesopotamia result in his publishing *Discoveries in the Ruins of Ninevah and Babylon*.
♦ 1859–The Egyptian Antiquities Service, in its first year of operation under French archaeologist Auguste Mariette, discovers the tomb of Queen Aahhotep at Dra Abu Naga, on the west bank of Thebes; her mummy is found to contain her personal jewelry, which Mariette secures for the Cairo Museum.
♦ 1861–Cavaliere Campana, a noted Italian collector of antiquities, helps fuel the archaeological revival trend in jewelry by having his collection of over a thousand pieces of ancient Greek, Roman, and Etruscan jewelry installed in Paris's Louvre Museum.
♦ 1876–Heinrich Schliemann, having found what he and the world hail as the remains of Troy, discovers the "Gold of Agamemnon" at Mycenae, and in 1877 publishes his *Mycenae* to great acclaim.
♦ 1894-1895–Excavations at the city of Dashur by Egyptian Antiquities Service director J. de Morgan reveal jewelry belonging to Egyptian princesses of the Twelfth Dynasty.
♦ 1901-1903–Egyptian jewelry dating back to Dynasty I is found by British Archaeologist Flinders Petrie at Abydos, and by American excavator George Reisner at Nag ed-Der, north of Abydos.

Late Victorian Jewelry

Rules and models destroy genius and art.
—William Hazlitt, noted critic, "On Taste"

Some jay of Italy,
Whose mother was her painting, hath betrayed him:
Poor I am stale, a garment out of fashion.
—William Shakespeare, *Cymbeline*

The late Victorian period might be stigmatized by some as an era in which tasteless design ruled. Revival pieces, which had raised the idea of jewelry as art, continued to be popular during the this period, with jewelers such as London's Giuliano and the Paris- and Rome-based Castellanis largely filling the void in innovative design with designs from the past.

In general, later nineteenth century jewelry was not particularly noted for freshness or spontaneity. The excesses and questionable taste exhibited by some of the jewelry of this period (and the years preceding it, as for example when French jewelers copied flowers to the smallest detail in diamond sprays, without the least moderating effect of interpretation or insight) might be said to contain the roots of dissent and discontent that led to Arts and Crafts and Art Nouveau jewelry.

A decorative pendant in gold, diamonds, and white champlevé enamel by French designer Lucien Gautrait, c. 1880. Gautrait later designed pieces in the Art Nouveau tradition. With its profusion of ribbons and floral motifs, this design shows the nineteenth century emphasis on wealth and elaborate design in jewelry. Nonetheless, it is very attractive, and the fine quality of the workmanship is obvious. *Courtesy of Nelson Rarities, Portland, ME.*

In some cases, it appears that designers and manufacturers of jewelry were more interested in technical innovations than in artistic merit. The design of the sash brooch pictured here was apparently subordinate to its new type of clasp, the patent for which is proudly touted on the back.

Some of the jewelry, such as the patented sash pin, was too large, too gaudy, or too dark for modern tastes to admire. However, this period was also one of miniaturization, including miniature scenes carved as cameos, that most archetypal Victorian form of jewelry. While these carved gems are not usually associated with enamel, a number were set in enameled frames.

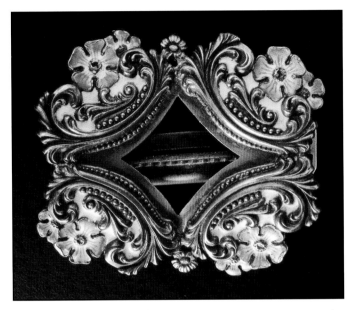

Three Victorian cameos, one showing a Classical theme, the other two possibly portraits, set in enameled frames that range from the flowery and colorful, to the somber and subdued. The Classical-themed cameo with the blue enameled flowers is in 18K gold with French hallmarks and measures 2.625" x 2.5"; the cameo with the austere black-and-white enamel is in 14K gold and measures 1.5 x 1.25"; the cameo with the pearls is in 18K gold with undecipherable French hallmarks, and measures 2" x 1.25". *Courtesy of Robin Allison.*

This American-made sterling silver and enamel sash pin, patented on April 23, 1895, shows the oppressive over-ornamented ugliness of Victorian design against which Arts and Crafts and Art Nouveau jewelers rebelled. The pin, 2.5" x 2", has curlicues, dots, flowers–both enameled and plain–and other embellishments to spare. The blue champlevé flowers, set against white champlevé enamel, might be forget-me-nots. While the enameling on the flowers is not incompetent, and some attempt has been made to provide detail in the form of painted veins on the petals, it in no way compares with the much finer enameling done by the best makers in the United States. It almost appears at this point that clever new–and patentable–devices such as the pin's clip, took priority over any real attempt at attractive design. Marked sterling, Pat. Pending Apr. 23.95, with unidentified maker's mark

A marvelous Victorian locket in (unmarked) 18K gold, diamonds, pearls, and enamel, with that most Victorian of subjects, a cherub, in that most Victorian of jewelry genres, a cameo. The cherub is shown with typical Victorian charm, swathed in swirling draperies and about to clap two cymbals together. Measures 2.75" with the bail. *Courtesy of Robin Allison.*

A Victorian demi-parure in 18K gold, enamel, and pearls, with French hallmarks. While the winged children depicted in the pendant and earrings may not be cherubs–they look more like fairy children than *putti*–they do show the mid- to late Victorian sentimentality so often found in jewelry from this period. This beautifully enameled set has the two children from the pendant each reprised in an earring, though in a different pose. Pendant measures 3" x 1.5"; earrings 2.5" x .875". *Courtesy of Robin Allison.*

As the cherub cameo, and the myriad other cherubs found in Victorian jewelry show, the age was also unabashedly sentimental. Besides cherubs, scenes of angels, often with children, can be found in late Victorian jewelry, whether American, English, or Continental.

A Jugendstil-style slide locket in 900 silver and enamel, with an attractive sentimental scene composed of an angel embracing a child at bedtime. While cherubs are often represented in Victorian jewelry, adult angels are less common. An interesting feature of this piece is its graceful plique-à-jour frame. Measures 3.125" x 1.375". *Courtesy of Robin Allison.*

Lockets, popular in Georgian and earlier Victorian jewelry, remained fashionable, often as memorial jewelry–such as the "IN MEMORIUM" locket on p. 24. Originally, as their name implies, they were intended to hold a lock of hair belonging to a dear one, whether living or dead. Later, with the advent of photography, their function changed to that of a wearable picture frame. Lockets could be plain, engraved, have designs in bas relief, or be decorated with enamel. They were most commonly worn around the neck as a pendant, but less often could be found as bracelets or brooches.

A locket adorned with a Sigma Chi fraternity pin in unmarked gold, enamel, and diamonds. Enamel was often used on fraternity pins and jewelry for organizations such as the Masons, as well as in tourist jewelry.

Another type of jewelry in miniature, the stickpin, also abounded in Victorian times, and was worn by both men and women. Many were somewhat plain, set with a single stone, or worked into a design in gold (in France, for some reason, mistletoe and griffins were especially popular themes for stickpins); but sometimes they were also enameled. The rather elusive term *beaux arts* can be applied to the lion and tiger shown in the group of four figural stickpins.

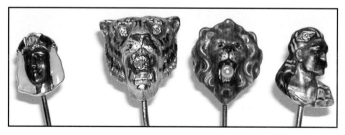

A group of four figural stickpins in 14K gold and enamel, including motifs common in jewelry of the period: a pharaoh, a tiger, a lion, and a Barbary pirate. The lion and tiger pieces might be said to fall under the *beaux arts* rubric. Tigers were produced in some quantity by Newark makers, often holding a diamond in the mouth. The lion, looking as adorably whimsical as the cowardly lion in *The Wizard of Oz*, is a bit more unusual. Despite their small size (from about .5" for the pirate to .625" for the tiger), these miniature jewels manage to incorporate a wealth of detail. *Courtesy of Robin Allison.*

A locket bracelet in unmarked silver and enamel with Cyrillic lettering on the back. While lockets are more commonly found as pendants to be worn as necklaces, they are also occasionally found in bracelets and pins. The bracelet is beautifully enameled in bright turquoise and orange, bordered by a Greek key design in black; and is 1.25" wide. *Courtesy of Robin Allison.*

A locket pin in unmarked 10K gold and enamel, with a design of pansies done through a transfer. The back of the pin opens, allowing its owner to insert a photograph or a lock of hair. Probably c. 1890; measures approximatey 1.125" x .875".

My strength is as the strength of ten,
Because my heart is pure.
    —Alfred, Lord Tennyson, "Sir Galahad"

Often, lockets were in the shape of a heart. Hearts were a favorite motif in Victorian jewelry. From ancient times, the heart had variously been considered the seat of intelligence (by the Egyptians); of intention (in literature, virtue and evil, purity and dishonor were often ascribed to the heart); or of emotion. The Victorians, with all their sentimentality, with their language of flowers, their language of stones, and their other covert methods of communication, were in love with Love. Especially associated in the Victorian mind with love, hearts abounded in jewelry of that period—and beyond.

A large Victorian heart-shaped locket in sterling silver and enamel. Hearts, with all of the sentimentality they implied, were a theme often used in Victorian jewelry. Here the enamel is in the turquoise blue originally created to resemble Persian turquoise. Marked sterling, and measures 2.5" x 2". *Courtesy of Red Robin Antiques.*

A Happiness of Hearts: Hearts Through Time

Kind hearts are more than coronets…
    —Alfred, Lord Tennyson, "Lady Vere de Vere"

As tokens of love, hearts have been popular in jewelry for well over a hundred years. They seem to be found especially often as lockets and as charms. Even in the less sentimental Art Nouveau movement, hearts were fashioned into jewelry–sometimes with a special unsentimental little twist. During the 1940s and 1950s, hearts were collected and made into charm bracelets. Today these charms, whether vintage or Victorian, enameled or not enameled, are considered especially collectible.

A Victorian heart-shaped locket in silver, enameled in a beautiful red guilloche and painted with a cherub modeled after one by the Italian Renaissance painter Raphael. This unabashedly sentimental locket practically whispers "Be mine, Valentine" down through time. Unmarked silver, measuring 1.25" x 1". *Courtesy of Robin Allison.*

A beautiful German or Austrian Art Nouveau locket in 935 silver and enamel. The enamel, in iridescent yellow, peach, and lavender over swirling guilloche, is painted with lovely stylized irises, a flower often found in Art Nouveau jewelry. Undecipherable maker's mark. *Courtesy of Robin Allison.*

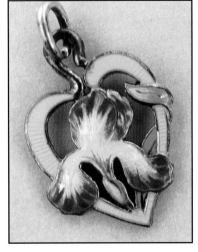

Another Art Nouveau heart with an iris, this one a pendant in silver and enamel, French c. 1900. The detailed iris, which curls out of the heart-shaped frame, was quite likely created in transfer enamel. Measures approximately 1" across.

A heart-shaped locket in 900 silver and enamel, by the prolific and versatile German firm Meyle & Mayer, with a beautifully painted Art Nouveau woman against a spider web, possibly indicating the provocative woman's ability to ensnare the unwary. A wonderful Art Nouveau piece, measuring 1.75" x 1.5". *Courtesy of Robin Allison.*

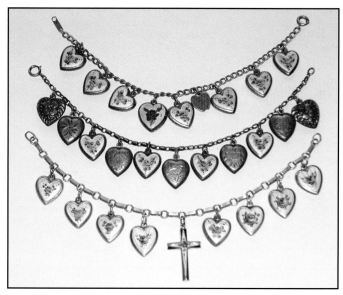

A heart of a somewhat different sort, this one in an Arts and Crafts pendant in unmarked silver and enamel, with a pearl dangle. The hand-fashioned look and the geometry of the design–the heart is framed by what almost look like two single quote marks–as well as the wonderful blue-green enamel, are all hallmarks of Arts and Crafts design. Measures 2.75" x 1.25". *Courtesy of Robin Allison.*

Three charm bracelets, the charms of which are almost all enameled with guilloche and roses, all in sterling silver c. 1940. Roses against a guilloche background have been a favorite motif since Victorian days, and have graced everything from charms, bracelets, and brooches, to compacts and perfumes. The charms measure from .625" to .75". *Courtesy of Robin Allison.*

Three charm bracelets with sterling silver hearts, some enameled and some not. The charms are from various eras, but mostly Victorian c. 1900. Some include such Victorian favorites as tiny enameled blue forget-me-nots, while others are enameled in guilloche, with or without tiny roses. Such hearts have become increasingly collectible. The charms measure from .625" to 1.25". *Courtesy of Robin Allison.*

Eight sterling silver guilloche with roses charms by mid-20th century designer Walter Lampl, whose jewelry is quite collectible, c. 1940. Although all are similar, closer examination shows that each heart is slightly different: larger or smaller, with a keyhole or without, on a white background or one of a different color. In addition, the guilloche patterns differ: Some are wavy, some have a striped effect, others radiate out from the center like rays of sunshine. As with most guilloche and roses pieces, the roses are not fully realized, suggesting a rose rather than rendering it in complete detail. Marked WL for Walter Lampl, measure from .625" to .75". *Courtesy of Robin Allison.*

In late Victorian jewelry, hearts were also fashionable as frames for small enameled flowers, especially in those flower pins sometimes called Newark enamels, after the New Jersey city where many of them were made.

A violet, probably manufactured in Newark c. 1900, in a simple heart-shaped frame. The pin, in 14K gold and enamel, measures approximately 1" x 1". While many of the larger New York or Newark floral pieces stand alone, it is usual for smaller flowers to be enclosed in a frame. Hearts were only one of a number of different types of frames found in such pieces; others include wishbones, navette-shaped frames, and, of course, crescents.

A small unmarked gold heart with two tiny forget-me-nots enameled in blue. These little forget-me-nots were very popular in Victorian jewelry.

Right:
Another bluebird in sterling silver and enamel, this one by the well-known British maker Charles Horner. Perhaps dating to a slightly later period than the bluebird above, this brooch is enameled in a slightly darker blue; Horner often used the iridescent blue-green enamel associated with the British Arts and Crafts jewelers. The brooch is marked with the CH for Charles Horner, along with marks identifying sterling silver, the city of Chester, and the year, and measures approximately 2" x .5".

Natural Instincts

The richness I achieve comes from nature, the source of my inspiration...
—French impressionist Claude Monet

The late Victorians also continued their predecessors' love affair with nature. Flora and fauna, pansies and primroses, birds and bugs abounded in their jewelry. Much of this jewelry was symbolic–bluebirds, for example, were harbingers of happiness–but it was also very decorative.

A lovely Victorian bracelet in unmarked silver and enamel, depicting a bluebird flying over a nest with eggs, most likely of American manufacture. The bluebird, an emblem of happiness, is for some reason often depicted in Victorian jewelry with a swallow tail. Small blue flowers are painted on either side of the central oval containing the picture of the bluebird. Everything about this piece–the carefully realized nest with its tiny eggs, the swoop of the bird in flight, the delightful sprays of flowers–shows the Victorians' love of nature, and their desire to depict it as faithfully as possible. Measures 1.5" in width. *Courtesy of Robin Allison.*

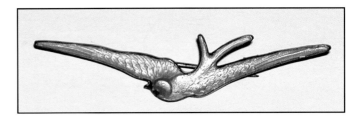

A brooch in sterling silver and enamel, in the form of a swallow-tailed bluebird. The bird is shown in flight, its head slightly averted to one side to reveal the hint of a red breast. This bird is slightly more abstract than the painterly bird depicted on the bracelet above. Marked CMC and sterling; measures 2.5 x .5". *Courtesy of Robin Allison.*

Mourning pieces were also still in vogue, but not all late Victorian jewelry was dark and heavy. Knot pins, usually with four loops overlapping to form a quatrefoil design, were popular. A variation on the knot pin, the "target" pin is shown enameled in matte pink and white enamel.

An interesting brooch/watch pin in 14K gold, enamel, and a small diamond, c. 1900, probably of Newark or New York manufacture. While the brooch has the underlying quatrefoil shape (sometimes referred to as a "target" broach) found in many Victorian pins, the pink and white enameling and the interesting curlicues around the edge of the brooch have an almost Renaissance revival look. Marked 14K, 1" in diameter.

A Victorian lover's knot brooch in sterling silver, guilloche enamel, seed pearls, and opal, approximately 1.125" in diameter. While this brooch embodies a common late Victorian motif, more often this design is found in gold (or gold-filled) pieces, sometimes with small champlevé forget-me-nots. However, in spite of being done in silver, this pin is very well made, with a seed pearl set in the middle of each loop. Marked sterling; old c-clasp.

In American-made jewelry, the preoccupation with natural themes, possibly coupled with the tendency toward miniaturization, marked the beginnings of beautiful nuanced enameling that carried over into Art Nouveau pieces.

One fashion innovation had dainty blue champlevé forget-me-nots against a usually gold (or gold-filled) background. This design probably originated with the Newark manufacturing firm Krementz & Co.; or, if not with them, with a more obscure company whose design Krementz and others soon picked up. It was the enamel trend *du jour*, and lasted until about the end of the nineteenth century.

Victorian gold-filled pin with champlevé enamel forget-me-nots, c. 1890, approximately 1.25" x .75". This pin contains elements of both Victorian design, notably the champlevé enameled forget-me-nots (like taille d'épargne enamel, another somewhat commonly used Victorian enamel motif/technique), and Art Nouveau, with a flowing stylized iris and a curving frame.

This type of champlevé enamel was included in various types of jewelry, including pins with tiny enameled flowers such as honeymoon pins and flowers in heart-shaped frames, as well as knot pins.

Three small pieces decorated with the blue champlevé forget-me-nots so popular for decorating, among other things, lovers' knots (like the one in the stickpin) and crescents in honeymoon pins; the double heart frame with the two small violets is less commonly found. The double heart–shaped pin with the violets measures approximately 1" x .625".

Enameled Flower Pins

It was also during this period, a period in which delight in gardening and the popularity of the language of flowers blossomed, that enameled flower pins and other floral jewelry first came into their own.

These pins were still recognizably of the age. Some are set in wishbones, hearts, and knots, popular motifs of the era. Others are set in frames set with the seed pearls that seem so ubiquitous in Victorian jewelry.

While knots are often associated with Celtic jewelry, they were also fairly commonly used in Victorian jewelry–usually, however, as lovers' knots. Here, a knot in twisted and braided gold holds three small flowers, possibly forget-me-nots (although the color of two of the flowers might suggest another flower). This pin is in 10K gold, c. 1885, and measures approximately 1.75" x .5".

A small pin in 14K gold, enamel, and a diamond, in the shape of a wishbone holding a pansy. Wishbones, as symbols of good luck, are occasionally found in Victorian jewelry, and as pansies were among the favorite floral motifs in Victorian jewelry, it is not surprising to find one in a pin of this type–even one with Art Nouveau pretensions, as evinced by the iridescent enameling and the stylized rather than naturalistic flower, with four petals instead of five. Measures approximately 1.375" x .75".

Just as the settings show late Victorian taste, so do the flowers depicted in flower pins. The most popular flower by far was the pansy, of innocent appearance and blameless significance–in the Victorian language of flowers, the pansy stood for "thoughts."

Two floral pins in seed pearl frames, in 14K gold, enamel, pearls, and–in the larger of the two–a small diamond. The smaller pin has a generic flower with petals that have basse taille markings under iridescent enamel shading from gold to pink at the petal's edges. The enamel is rather harsh and metallic, and bears little resemblance to the best of Newark–or New York or European–enameling. The larger brooch, which also serves as a watch pin, has a fleur-de-lis enameled in hues shading from gold to deep purple at the edges. Seed pearl–set frames are fairly common in smaller Victorian floral pieces; the fleur-de-lis pin measures 1.375" x 1.375", the smaller pin 1.125" x .875".

Three pansy necklaces and a pansy brooch, in 14K gold, enamel, diamonds, or pearls. The pansies, as is typical of flowers at the end of the 19th century, have realistic markings, and are nicely dimensional, with (except in the case of the smallest pendant) each petal formed separately and attached to the others by arches on the underside of the piece. The largest of the necklaces is in iridescent enamel, while the second largest is in matte enamel; the smallest pansy and the brooch are done in glossy enamel. The brooch measures approximately .875" in diameter.

A pair of pansy earrings in 14K (unmarked) gold, enamel, and pearls. Like the other pansies, these are realistically marked (against matte enamel) and have each petal formed separately, and attached to the others with arches underneath. Probably American-made, c. 1885, measuring approximately .875" x .875".

An unusual late Victorian flower pin in 14K gold, enamel, pearls, and a small diamond, composed of a sickle set with seed pearls holding a central violet flanked by daisies and forget-me-nots. Although the flowers are typically Victorian, the sickle adds an interesting touch. Despite its small size, the violet shows all the hallmarks of fine Newark or New York enameled flowers: It has small stamens surrounding the central diamond, the petals curl up, and are painted with extremely fine lines to indicate the petals' veining. Unusually, the center diamond is in a buttercup setting. Marked 14K, and measures approximately 1.75" x .875".

Four pansy stickpins. Stickpins and pansies both were popular during this period, and often are found in conjunction. Two of the stickpins show naturalistic detail, while the third enameled one is much less realistic. The fourth pansy, dark red and white, is made of carved garnet and quartz.

Also frequently found in pins of this time are forget-me-nots.

A Victorian flower pin in 14K gold, enamel, diamond, and seed pearls in the form of a forget-me-not, perhaps c. 1890, approximately 1.75" x .75". While the flower and its leaves are somewhat stylized, pointing to a transition toward Art Nouveau, the leaves set with seed pearls are typically Victorian. The pin, with its enamel shaded from lighter blue in the middle to darker at the edges, was most likely made in Newark or New York.

A navette-shaped frame with three small forget-me-nots, in 14K gold, enamel, and seed pearls, c. 1895, 1.5" x .625". As small as the petals on the flowers are, some attempt was made to give them a naturalistic look by painting a dark stripe down the center of each petal.

Honeymoon Pins

One of the more charming innovations in late Victorian jewelry, at least in the United States, was the honeymoon pin. While crescents–enameled black, or set with diamonds or pearls–were fashionable during the latter part of Victoria's reign, the honeymoon pin added enameled flowers to crescent pins. True to the Victorian delight in veiled meanings, the honeymoon pin was something of a rebus–the crescent represented the moon, and the flower represented the nectar, or the "honey" part of the puzzle. And, true to the prevailing taste in flowers, most of these pins contain enameled forget-me-nots, violets, pansies, or shamrocks.

A crescent pin in 14K gold, black matte enamel, and pearls, by the Newark maker Crane Theurer. While crescent pins, especially those set with diamonds and/or pearls, were popular among Victorians, they would have been considered inappropriate for mourning attire–for which this pin was almost certainly made. Marked with CT for the maker, and 14K; approximately 1.75" long.

Four honeymoon pins, each with three forget-me-nots inside the crescent moon, of gold, enamel, and seed pearls, c. 1890, each about .75" in diameter except for the elongated one on the left, which is almost 1.25" long. The longer one bears a maker's mark for the Newark jewelry firm of Krementz, and is in 14K gold. The largest of the other pins may also have been made by Krementz; the c-clasp with identifying marks has been replaced with a newer safety clasp, but the petals are the same shape and have the exact same brownish lines painted in the center. The other two pins have no maker's marks, are of 10K gold, and may have been less expensive pins inspired by the Krementz piece. While these pins are similar, small differences can be seen, indicating either different makers or possibly different manufacturing dates. Honeymoon pins were popular in late Victorian jewelry, but as these four similar-looking pins might seem to indicate, those with forget-me-nots appear to have been especially common.

A selection of five honeymoon pins, ranging from Victorian in style–the elongated crescent on the left with the small matte pink flower and the crescent with the small violet–to Art Nouveau–the poppy, the iridescent violet in the crescent so rounded it almost forms a circle, and the iridescent flower in the crescent set with pearls. Honeymoon pins were especially popular during the late Victorian period, and retained their popularity after the emergence of Art Nouveau; jewelers merely modified their designs to adapt to the new look, adding iridescent enamel and flowers that are a bit more stylized. All except the longer pin measure approximately 1" in length; the longer one measures approximately 1.25".

As can be seen, the Victorian taste for pearls and enameled forget-me-nots showed up in honeymoon pins; some of the crescents are set with pearls, while others have the champlevé forget-me-nots.

"Circa 1900"

C. 1900 is the date given for any number of pieces of enameled floral jewelry produced in the United States. And indeed, it is difficult to distinguish pieces that were often created by the same firm using the same molds over a period of years. However, sometimes distinctions can be made between earlier pieces and later pieces, especially if one can identify a flower or leaf as being late Victorian, Art Nouveau, or–less frequently–Arts and Crafts.

Certain signals point to a piece's being Victorian (and thus perhaps older). Late Victorian jewelry often

♦ Has a flower or leaf standing alone, rather than in a frame.
♦ If there is a frame, it tends to be less fluid and more formal; it may be decorated with seed pearls or, sometimes, small champlevé forget-me-nots.
♦ Is realistically rendered, with painted veins and other markings over petals or leaves that show folds, curled edges, or other features.
♦ If the flower has a stem or leaves, these also may be set with seed pearls.
♦ The enamel tends to be occasionally glossy but often is matte (matte to some extent having replaced the glossy enamel found in earlier Victorian jewelry; it is easier to paint details on matte enamel than glossy) rather than iridescent.

Other markers indicate an Art Nouveau–possibly later–piece. American Art Nouveau jewelry often, though not always

♦ Has a curved frame, rather than a navette-shaped or other stiff type of frame.
♦ Has a frame in which striated markings on the gold, under enamel as basse taille work or not, suggest a ribbon or the veins in an elongated leaf.
♦ Has a flower or bud suggested by a pearl or other gem, rather than one that is realistically rendered.
♦ If the piece of jewelry is a necklace, an Art Nouveau one often will have a pearl dangle, a curvy frame, and chain festoons.
♦ May "suggest" a flower, rather than realistically depicting it in painstaking detail.
♦ Is enameled in iridescent enamel, rather than matte or glossy enamel.

However, this being said, it should be noted that late Victorian and Art Nouveau jewelry in America often overlapped, with manufacturers such as Krementz producing jewelry in both styles to please different tastes during the same period. Still, there are trends, and a discerning eye can make use of enameling and other hints to distinguish the different styles.

Two pins with about the same dimensions and each containing a violet–and the resemblance ends there. The top one, with its tiny Newark-style violet and small pearls, its rigid frame, is typically Victorian. The lower one, set with milky quartz instead of a pearl or a diamond, and done in iridescent enamel in a frame that curves and winds, its striations suggesting the marks on leaves or (less likely) a ribbon, clearly intends to suggest Art Nouveau. The iridescent enamel shows some wear, unfortunately not uncommon with this type of enamel; it is, however, somewhat less noticeable in person. Each is approximately 1" wide.

An Art Nouveau pansy necklace in 14K gold, enamel, pearls, and a central diamond, c. 1900, approximately 1" x 1" (excluding largest baroque pearl drop). The curving frame, the pearl dangles, the iridescent enamel, and the chain festoons are all indicative of Art Nouveau style.

Otherwise the pansy, which though unmarked appears to be of Newark or New York manufacture, looks much like earlier Victorian pansy pendants and necklaces; the major difference being that earlier pansies appear alone, lacking the Art Nouveau trappings. The flower is delicately enameled, with a central pale green shading to a peach at the edges, and with dark lines suggesting a pansy's markings. Underlying the enamel, basse taille lines–curved to match the petals' shape–suggest the flower's veining.

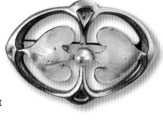

Three Art Nouveau brooches, in 14K gold, iridescent enamel, and pearls, c. 1900. The first has lily pads enameled, oddly enough, in pink. Its winding frame that suggests leaves, as well as tiny pearls instead of actual lily blossoms, are very representative of Art Nouveau design. This pin has an unidentified maker's mark and measures 1" x 1". The middle pin, by the Newark firm Whiteside & Blank, suggests stylized lotus blossoms, and also has a more geometric look leaning toward Edwardian design. The last pin, with three stylized blossoms, shows the lack of concern with portraying flowers naturalistically so common in Art Nouveau jewelry, and so different from the Victorian objective of rendering recognizable flowers. The latter two pins show varying degrees of enamel loss. Each marked 14K, and measure approximately 1.125" in width.

A Clutch of Cloverleaves: Cloverleaves Through Time

May good luck be your friend in whatever you do, and may trouble always be a stranger to you.

—Irish Blessing

You are in clover.

—Charles Lamb, in a letter to a friend

Just as hearts are tokens of love, the four-leaf clover–or, as used by Charles Lamb, clover in general–has stood for luck. In Victorian days, four-leaf clovers were popular tokens in honeymoon pins and other jewelry. And, over the years, cloverleaves have remained in fashion, as charms and pendants, in pins and brooches, as earrings, and even on bracelets.

A Victorian watch in gold, enamel, and rose-cut diamonds (on the back), of Swiss origin. While Victorian honeymoon pins were popular as bridal presents in the United States, with many featuring enameled cloverleaves, here the bridal present is a watch, and the cloverleaves occupy a less prominent position in the border around the guilloche enamel center on the front of the watch. Like many guilloche pieces of the period, this watch is decorated with painted roses, although in this case the painting is more detailed than most, a full bouquet rather than the usual sketchily rendered roses, and also includes sentimental forget-me-nots. The back of the watch is nicely enameled in opaque white, with a stylized flower rendered in rose-cut diamonds. Engraved: Bridal Present from J. R. Russell to Mary Wilkinson. Measures 1" in diameter and is 14-18K gold (unmarked). Also marked Geneve and Elffroth. *Courtesy of Robin Allison.*

A brooch/pendant and earrings in 14K gold, enamel, seed pearls, and (in the brooch) a small diamond. While the brooch is marked with Krementz's maker's mark, the earrings are unmarked, except for the screw backs, which are gold-filled and marked Van Del (the name of a company that produced gold-filled costume jewelry). However, given the resemblance of the earrings to the brooch, it is fairly certain that they too were made by Krementz; Krementz produced a number of floral pieces with seed pearls either as a border around the petals, or at the tips of the petals. Brooch measures approximately 1.25" in diameter, earrings approximately .875" in diameter.

A Victorian/Edwardian bracelet in silver and enamel, showing a series of good luck symbols, including a four-leaf clover, and cloverleaves with a horseshoe and the unlucky number thirteen. Other tokens of good fortune are a ladybug, the number seven, and a black cat–symbols still found on charm bracelets today. European in origin and marked 835; measures 7" x .5". *Courtesy of Robin Allison.*

Two Victorian honeymoon pins set with cloverleaves, both probably by Krementz (although only the one with the champlevé forget-me-nots and chased edges to the leaves bears their maker's mark). Both 14K gold, approximately 1.125" in length.

A selection of small pieces with enameled cloverleaves, including a small Arts and Crafts pendant, a small cloverleaf brooch, and a wishbone with a four-leaf clover. All are c. 1900 and in 14K gold, except for the pendant on the right, which is in silver gilt by Norwegian David Andersen and measures .75" in diameter.

A brooch in silver and enamel, by Charles Horner, c. 1912. The three-leaf clovers are in champlevé enamel, while the background and the border are guilloche. Horner, who mass-produced jewelry both in the Arts and Crafts style and in more traditional themes, made a number of these pins; often, however, they are found with moderate to severe enamel damage. Has maker's mark CH, mark for British sterling, mark for Chester, and marked M for the year; measures approximately 1.125" x .875".

A pair of costume earrings, c. 1940 which, despite being in base metal and set with paste or rhinestones, are nicely enameled, with basse taille striations to the leaves.

A vintage pin in silver and enamel, reprising the Victorian cloverleaf in wishbone motif.

A darling brooch in sterling silver, enamel, and marcasites, by designer Alice Caviness, in the form of a four-leaf clover with a ladybug perched on it, of German manufacture. As with so many cloverleaves, from so many different periods, this one has painted stripes to suggest the leaves' striations. While Victorian/Art Nouveau cloverleaves tended to have darker lines in tight bands, this cloverleaf has lighter and freer lines. Like so many of the finer vintage German pieces, this one is decorated with marcasites. The ladybug adds a cute, colorful touch. Measures 1.25" in diameter and is marked sterling silver, maker, Germany. *Courtesy of Robin Allison.*

Austro-Hungarian Jewelry

A Bavarian is halfway between an Austrian and a human-being.

—Otto von Bismark,
nineteenth-century chancellor of Germany

When it comes to late nineteenth and early twentieth century jewelry, Otto von Bismark's somewhat biased words might well apply to Austro-Hungarian jewelry, rather than the Austrians themselves. The jewelry of this Eastern European empire was not quite like other European jewelry of the era, but was also not so totally different that it forms a completely separate category. Because it is often misidentified, a separate section has been devoted to it.

As some have described it, Austro-Hungarian jewelry tended toward a rather ornate, almost Renaissance revival look. It was also at times a bit heavy. One characteristic seems to be an unusual combination of materials: precious stones set in silver, rather than gold (which was much more rarely used in fine jewelry there than it was elsewhere); large pearls and paste stones appearing in the same piece.

Robin's collection includes enameled Austro-Hungarian jewelry, pictured below.

A pair of earrings in 935 silver, enamel, and lapis lazuli. While these earrings show the intricate metal-work characteristic of Austro-Hungarian jewelry, oddly enough the small enameled forget-me-nots are rather similar to those fashionable in some American jewelry c. 1885-1900. However, these earrings are probably a bit later; Robin believes they date perhaps to the 1920s. Austro-Hungarian jewelry frequently did use flower motifs. Measure 2.5" x .625" and marked 935 with an undecipherable hallmark. *Courtesy of Robin Allison.*

A brooch by the well-known costume jewelry maker Trifari, in enamel and rhinestones. The blue is a bit unusual for clover-leaves, but makes a nice change. Marked TRIFARI. Measures approximately 1.5" in diameter.

A fascinating pendant in vermeil, enamel, paste, and a large baroque pearl, of Austro-Hungarian origin. This piece contains several elements characteristic of Austro-Hungarian jewelry, including the juxtaposition of the patrician–in this case the wonderful baroque pearl–with the pedestrian–here the use of vermeil rather than a more precious metal, and paste rather than the rubies and sapphires one might expect to find set together with such a fine pearl. Also typical of Austro-Hungarian jewelry, but hardly limited to it, is the use of medieval and Renaissance motifs or styles; here, the use of the mythological griffon. The pearl "person" has eyes, and wears a necklace with a heart pendant set with a paste stone, making this piece truly unique. Measures 3.5" x 2", and is marked Hungary, with the Hungarian hallmark for 800 silver and the letter B. *Courtesy of Robin Allison.*

An Austro-Hungarian pendant in vermeil, citrine, pearls, and enamel, with a beautiful ornate setting that seems to harken back to an earlier age. Perhaps in part because it is not as often seen as jewelry of French, British, Italian, German, or even Russian origins, and in part because it embodies rather elusive design characteristics, Austro-Hungarian jewelry can be difficult to identify. Robin feels that it is perhaps one of the most often misidentified genres of the period. Measures 2.75" (including bail) x 1.75" and is unmarked. *Courtesy of Robin Allison*

An Austro-Hungarian locket with a miniature on ivory, set in unmarked silver with enamel and paste and measuring 3" x 2" (the bail adds another inch). Again, the juxtaposition of the valuable–the miniature on ivory is of fine quality–with the ordinary, in this case faux jewels rather than gemstones. *Courtesy of Robin Allison.*

The front and back of a lovely Renaissance-inspired Austro-Hungarian necklace in silver, amethysts, pearls, and enamel, with matching earrings. Interestingly, the back of the necklace, with its ornate curlicues enlivened by enamel, is to a true enamel enthusiast possibly even more attractive than the sumptuous front. While counter-enameling is stressed for beginning enamelists, as it helps avoid distortion of the metal by the weight of the enamel, there is no real reason to counter-enamel a piece such as this, other than to create a fully finished piece. Marked AA, HB and an undeciphered mark; necklace measures 16" with pendant 3.75" x 1.875", earrings 1.625" x .5". *Courtesy of Robin Allison.*

Left:
An ornate Austro-Hungarian necklace in unmarked silver, (probably faux) emeralds, and pearls. An interesting feature of Austro-Hungarian pieces–in addition to their often medieval or Renaissance revival tendencies–is their tendency to set fine precious gems in silver, rather than in gold or platinum, metals usually used elsewhere for such stones. Chain measures 18", with pendant measuring 3.5" x 2.5". *Courtesy of Red Robin Antiques.*

"Art for Art's Sake"–The Two Seminal *Fin-de-Siècle* Movements

Mediocrity knows nothing higher than itself, but talent instinctively recognizes genius.
—Sir Arthur Conan Doyle, *The Valley of Fear*

If it can be said that the end of the nineteenth century marked the high point of enameling, it can also be said that it was quite possibly the most exciting period in the history of jewelry. Two important movements that changed decorative arts and design and challenged the conventional idea of jewelry arose: the Arts and Crafts movement in Great Britain, and Art Nouveau in France and Belgium. Although they diverged, at the onset the goals of both movements seemed similar.

Revival jewelry had brought back from the past the idea of the jewel as a work of art. However, the great jeweler and chronicler of jewelry, Henri Vever, noted in 1898 that the public was "saturated with *déjà vu*." (Becker, 1985, 8). Revivals, no less than jewelry in the prevailing fashion, were stale. The need for a new theory of design, for new standards of taste, was apparent. And the two great movements, Arts and Crafts and Art Nouveau, stepped in to fill that need.

Both wished to break away from the conventions that had prevailed over much of the nineteenth century, and both were interested in creating jewelry that was art, rather than a symbol of wealth. As such, both movements made use of new and different materials, and in many cases the list of materials used by the two movements overlaps: Both showed a preference for opals, for example, and used mother-of-pearl, ivory, and baroque pearls.

And both placed a good deal of emphasis on enamel. Enamel was already an important factor in jewelry design; the great French jeweler Frédéric Boucheron, for example, inspired by the writings of the Renaissance jeweler and goldsmith Benvenuto Cellini, was already using translucent and other enamels in his jewelry (Snowman, 1990, 78). However, with both Arts and Crafts and Art Nouveau jewelry, enamel became not merely an accessory, but a central feature, almost a hallmark.

And, perhaps most of all, both were driven in large part by the genius and vision of two great names in design: William Morris for Arts and Crafts, and René Lalique for Art Nouveau.

Arts and Crafts, or Art Nouveau?

As Karlin (1993) notes, the line between Arts and Crafts and Art Nouveau is not always a clear, fixed boundary. This is not really surprising, given that to some extent Art Nouveau was influenced by the Arts and Crafts movement; in fact, the guiding force behind Art Nouveau jewelry, René Lalique, studied in England, and one cannot help but assume that he was influenced by the British movement. In some cases, the two genres seem to overlap, or even become indistinguishable. Both had their favored themes, materials, and even enamels: Arts and Crafts jewelers favored a brilliant blue-green iridescent enamel, while Art Nouveau is most often identified with plique-à-jour enameling, but both used Limoges enameling to some extent. Arts and Crafts artists favored leaves, peacocks, and galleons, Art Nouveau flowers, Woman, and insects, especially the dragonfly. Arts and Crafts jewelers worked primarily with silver; Arts and Crafts pieces in gold are far rarer. On the other hand, Art Nouveau jewelers worked primarily in gold, although some Art Nouveau jewelry, such as that produced by Meyle & Mayer, is found in silver. Arts and Crafts pieces tend to be more angular, Art Nouveau pieces more flowing. But, occasionally we find the Arts and Crafts dragonfly, or the plique-à-jour piece that seems to have more of an Arts and Crafts angularity about it, or a hand-made look.

A wonderful Art Nouveau plaque au cou, in 900 silver, plique-à-jour enamel, and opals. The piece, meant to be worn on a ribbon or held by several strands of pearls as a dog collar, is in a rather formal, geometric design that suggests leaves and a central flower–set with a large opal–rather than formally depicting them. The fine, fiery opals, which add a great deal of beauty to the piece, were favored by designers in both the Arts and Crafts and the Art Nouveau movements. Marked 900, depose, undeciphered mark; measures 3.125" x 2". *Courtesy of Robin Allison.*

An unusual Arts and Crafts brooch in silver, enamel, shell, and a pearl. Interestingly, this piece combines a shell cameo, so quintessentially Victorian, in an Arts and Crafts setting. The symmetry of the setting, its champlevé enamel, its small dangling stylized flower ending with a pearl drop, its so obviously hammered silver, are all as representative of Arts and Crafts design as the cameo is of Victoriana. Measures 2" x 1.5" and is unmarked. *Courtesy of Robin Allison.*

A dragonfly brooch in silver and enamel, combining aspects of both Arts and Crafts and Art Nouveau style. The dragonfly was in some ways emblematic of Art Nouveau, with myriad examples created by designers such as René Lalique and Louis Comfort Tiffany, who were captivated by its beauty and evanescence, as well as its aspects of the grotesque. However, this brooch is more Arts and Crafts in style, the blue-and-green enameling being especially typical of Arts and Crafts workmanship, as is the symmetry and angularity of the piece. Measures 2.5" x 1.75", and marked s silv. *Courtesy of Robin Allison.*

A rather unusual necklace that contains some elements of both Arts and Crafts and Art Nouveau design. The geometric nature of the piece points to Arts and Crafts, as do the silver wire–wrapped pearl at the center of the crescent and the (seemingly) handmade chains. The plique-à-jour enameling, however, is more often associated with Art Nouveau, while the pearl dangles could belong to either genre. In fact, this necklace is probably a German Jugendstil piece. Sterling, and measures 2" x 1.75". *Courtesy of Robin Allison.*

And, just as Arts and Crafts is sometimes hard to distinguish from Art Nouveau, there are a few instances in which Victorian design blends with Arts and Crafts.

A Victorian festoon necklace in 900 silver, turquoise, enamel, and pearls. This piece has something of an Arts and Crafts feel to it, with its chains, baroque pearl drops, and turquoise dangles, but also looks rather Middle Eastern, in keeping with the Victorian love of things new and different–and exotic. Robin has seen a similar piece with the same enameling listed as Arts and Crafts; this piece, however, is far more elaborate, with its drops and quarter moon sections, and has elements of both periods. European origin. Festoon section measures 8" x 3.25". *Courtesy of Robin Allison.*

A necklace in silver, enamel, green pastes, and moonstones very much in the Arts and Crafts style of the Gaskins. Festoons of chains were popular with some Arts and Crafts designers, as were the use of less expensive materials such as moonstones instead of pearls or diamonds and silver rather than gold or platinum. While Victorian and Art Nouveau jewelry made much use of floral elements, some Arts and Crafts jewelers seem to have preferred the simplicity of leaves rather than more flamboyant flowers. The festoon section measures 4.25" x 1.5". Unmarked. *Courtesy of Robin Allison.*

The Arts and Crafts Movement

Dreamer of dreams, born out of my due time,
Why should I strive to set the crooked straight?
Let it suffice that my murmuring rhyme
Beats with light wing against the ivory gate.
—William Morris, *The Earthly Paradise*

I believe the right question to ask, regarding all adornment,
is simply this: Was it done with enjoyment—was the carver happy
while he was about it?
—John Ruskin, *The Seven Lamps of Architecture*

One of the most influential design movements of the nineteenth century, if not of the modern age, was the Arts and Crafts movement. It arose primarily in reaction to the industrial age, whose shoddy designs and mediocre workmanship it abhorred. It also disliked the conditions under which most artisans and crafters toiled. Although it had its roots partly in the Aesthetic Movement, it was largely the product of William Morris's philosophy and views on design. In 1861, Morris started the firm later known as Morris and Company, which was noted for, among other things, its stained glass designs.

Although in his poem *The Earthly Paradise*, Morris asked why he should strive to set the crooked straight, in many ways "setting the crooked straight" was his life's work. Others before him had tried; the Aesthetic Movement's Owen Jones, for example, set forth his vision of design in the influential *Grammar of Ornament*. None, however, seems to have had the influence Morris ultimately wielded.

William Morris was born to a wealthy British industrial family in 1834. He studied architecture, but decided that his true vocation lay in decorative arts. To some extent Morris was influenced by other nineteenth century ideas, besides those of the Aesthetic Movement; he also knew and sympathized with members of the Pre-Raphaelite Brotherhood. His one surviving painting, *La Belle Iseult*, shows the influence of his pre-Raphaelite friend Dante Gabriel Rossetti.

In a speech given in 1877 before the Trades' Guild of Learning, Morris articulated his philosophy of design. He felt strongly that the decorative arts should not be considered less worthy than the "great arts" of painting, sculpture, and architecture. Good design was, he asserted, necessary, and worthy of attention; it must also be in accordance with nature:

> …there is scarce anything that they [builders and craftsmen] use, and that we fashion, but it has always been thought to be unfinished till it has had some touch or other of decoration about it. True it is, that in many or most cases we have got so used to this ornament, that we look upon it as if it had grown of itself, and note it no more than the mosses on the dry sticks with which we light our fires. So much the worse! for there is the decoration, or some pretence of it, and it has, or ought to have, a use and a meaning. For, and this is at the root of the whole matter, everything made by man's hands has a form, which must be either beautiful or ugly; beautiful if it is in accord with Nature, and helps her; ugly if it is discordant with Nature, and thwarts her… Now it is one of the chief uses of decoration, the chief part of its alliance with Nature, that it has to sharpen our dulled senses in this matter: for this end are those wonders of intricate patterns interwoven, those strange forms invented, that men have so long delighted in: forms and intricacies that do not necessarily imitate Nature, but in which the hand of the craftsman is guided to work in the way that she does, till the web, the cup, or the knife, look as natural, nay, as lovely, as the green field, the river bank, or the mountain flint.

> To give people pleasure in the things they must perforce use, that is one great office of decoration; to give people pleasure in the things they must perforce make, that is the other use of it.

Morris was not only a designer–his stained glass designs, for example, were noted for their beautiful foliage, and he drew from nature as well in his textile designs–but he was also a poet. His dislike of industrialized England echoes in his poetry; one can almost hear the nostalgia for a simpler time in the prologue to his poem "The Wanderer": "Forget six counties overhung with smoke,/ Forget the snorting steam and piston stroke,/ Forget the spreading of the hideous town;/ Think rather of the pack-horse on the down,/ And dream of London, small and white and clean,/ The clear Thames bordered by its gardens green." Morris's last venture was the founding of Kelmscott Press, for which he designed three different type faces based on fifteenth century typography.

Morris's politics–he was a leading Socialist–also influenced his ideas on the status of craftspersons. He firmly believed, as he stated in his 1877 address, that the crafter should take as much pleasure in creating an item as its owner did in using it.

Words to Work By

Goals for Those Working in the Arts and Crafts Tradition

The Arts and Crafts movement's goals for jewelers and metalworkers were, like those for other designers and creators, basically straightforward.

In theory, followers of the Arts and Crafts movement subscribed to several basic tenets, among them:

♦ The artist/craftsperson should undertake every step of creating a piece her- or himself, from design to finished product.
♦ The finished product should not only be made by hand, it should *look* as if it were made by hand.
♦ Design should be attractive, and in keeping with an aesthetic found in and derived from Nature.
♦ The status of the craft should be raised to that of an art; a craftsperson should be able to take pride in her or his work, and find satisfaction in the process as well as the finished product.
♦ Good design should be made affordable not just for the wealthy few, but for the masses.
♦ Artists/craftspersons should be organized into guilds, much as medieval tradesmen had been.

In practice, these goals translated into some fairly interesting results. Among them was a preference for working in silver and copper (as these metals showed hammer-marks better than gold, and thus revealed the hand-made nature of a piece). Semi-precious materials were also preferred over the traditional precious gems such as diamonds and rubies. Enamel, especially the iridescent blue-green enamel characteristic of much of Arts and Crafts jewelry, but also the painted Limoges enameling technique mastered by one of the movement's foremost jewelers, Charles Ashbee, was also a favored material.

Another interesting aspect of the Arts and Crafts movement was the relatively egalitarian status accorded women. Of the English Arts and Crafts jewelers and metalworkers listed by Karlin (1993), seventy-four out of one hundred and seventy-six were women. Only nine of these were wives or daughters of others in the Arts and Crafts movement; and the wives, such as Georgina Cave Gaskin, were as productive, if not more productive, than their husbands.

Like the women portrayed in pre-Raphaelite paintings, women in the Arts and Crafts movement wore simple, flowing gowns with jewelry to match, rather than the constricting clothing of the fashionable Victorian woman. And some of the crafts embraced by the movement were those traditionally considered "women's work," most notably hand embroidery and weaving.

A lovely pendant in the Arts and Crafts style, in unmarked silver, enamel, and mabe pearls. This pendant, with the beautiful blue-green enamel often used by Arts and Crafts jewelers, shows its Arts and Crafts origins in the symmetrical simplicity of the design, the small pendant drop, and its use of nontraditional materials, in this case mabe pearls. Measures 2.5" x 1.5" and is unmarked. *Courtesy of Robin Allison.*

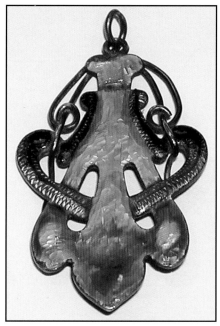

Two fine examples of Arts and Crafts jewelry, in the form of two pendants in silver, enamel, mabe pearl, and–in the pendant on the right–opals. The pendants, both having the wonderful handcrafted appearance of Arts and Crafts pieces, look like they may have been created by the same artist. Both seem to have the same dotted basse taille work, and the same green enameling, as well as the central mabe pearl. In addition, both make use of champlevé work to set off different elements in the design. While the pendant on the right has a more figural appearance, with its stylized butterfly and bird, the pendant on the left also seems to draw on nature for inspiration, with stylized leaves at the top from which depends a circular, almost fruit-like, element. The bird measures 3.25" x 1.5", the pendant, 2.75" x 1.75". Both are unmarked. *Courtesy of Robin Allison.*

An interesting Arts and Crafts-style pendant in blues and greens, with what appear to be hammer marks under some of the enameling, and basse taille markings under other portions. With its obviously handmade look, including bent wire, this piece is very much in the Arts and Crafts spirit. Unmarked; measures 1.625" x 1". *Courtesy of Robin Allison.*

An Arts and Crafts pendant that, unusually, is in 15K gold (thus pointing to a British origin) rather than silver, with the iridescent blue-green enamel so commonly found in Arts and Crafts pieces. Also somewhat unusual is the very figural nature of the piece, as Arts and Crafts designers often seemed to prefer working in the geometrical abstract. The most unusual thing about this pendant, however, is the inscription on the back, which reads: Om mane padme AUM. This is a Buddhist chant meaning "hail to the jewel in the lotus"–which is exactly what this pendant embodies: a jewel (the mother-of-pearl) set in a lotus. Measures approximately 1.375" in width.

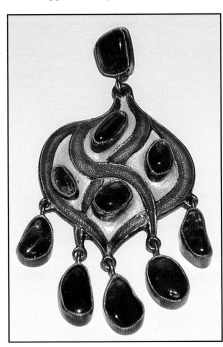

A European (most likely Austrian or German) Arts and Crafts pendant in silver, enamel, and pink tourmaline. This piece shows the influence of British insistence on simplicity, elegance, and the use of nontraditional gemstones such as the tourmaline, here in cabochon form and bezel-set. One particularly nice element of this design is the use of snaking lines enameled in blue against white enamel, with the lines ending in tourmaline drops giving something of the appearance of a peacock's tail. Measures 2.75" x 1.25"; the silver hallmark is undecipherable, but the piece is also marked H and BE. *Courtesy of Robin Allison.*

Not all Arts and Crafts pieces were large: This small hand-made Arts and Crafts pendant in 10K gold, enamel, green tourmaline, a small diamond, and a pearl dangle, c. 1900, measures only .5" x 1.0" (excluding bail). Enamel and non-precious gems such as tourmaline were popular with Arts & Crafts jewelers, as they were relatively inexpensive and helped keep the jewelry more affordable. The champlevé enamel in this pendant is of a light opalescent green that resembles serpentine.

Central to the Arts and Crafts philosophy was the idea of simplicity, whether in dress or design. The influential writer and critic John Ruskin, whose philosophy helped inspire the Arts and Crafts movement, designed a brooch named for him. Typically, this brooch consists of a "Ruskin stone"–an enameled, usually round, ceramic piece with an often monochromatic glaze–in a very simple round silver or lesser metal (such as pewter) setting, as shown in the picture above. *Courtesy of Robin Allison.*

One interesting type of jewelry, sometimes enameled but more often not, was the "Ruskin stone." The influential nineteenth century critic John Ruskin propounded the virtue of simplicity, in both design and in life. The brooch named after him usually has a round ceramic "stone," sometimes glazed to look like a semi-precious stone, set in a very plain silver or pewter frame. Other designers took this idea, and expanded upon it, making a somewhat more interesting Ruskin-style brooch.

An unmarked and undated Arts and Crafts necklace in sterling silver and enamel, probably from Great Britain. The hammermarks on the silver squares are a signature of Arts and Crafts work, as is the simplicity of design. The classic appearance of this piece, however, with its alternating hammered silver squares and red enameled rings, gives it a timeless air and makes it difficult to date. *Necklace courtesy of Classic Facets, Boulder, CO; photograph by Karryl Salit.*

Two pendants in sterling silver and Limoges enamel, 1.5" in diameter, c. 1880, having both a Renaissance revival and an Arts & Crafts look. Each pendant has a miniature portrait of a young woman in period dress, painted with great detail and expressiveness, and set in an enameled frame. Silver foil, often used in Limoges enamels, provides metallic highlights for the jewelry worn by one of models, and a hat worn by the other. *Courtesy of Uncommon Treasures, Portland, OR.*

Unfortunately, some of the movement's goals conflicted. For example, it was almost impossible for an artisan to make goods that were affordable not just for the middle and upper classes but for the average worker, and still earn a living wage her- or himself. It was this conflict that ultimately led to the dissolution of the Guild of Handicraft–for which Charles Ashbee primarily blamed the London department store Liberty.

Give Me Liberty's...

Liberty, the London department store noted for its textile designs–some of which were inspired by the Aesthetic Movement–commissioned a line of Arts and Crafts–style jewelry that it marketed under the name Cymric. This jewelry was simple, attractive, wearable, and affordable. It was also very often enameled.

One of the foremost designers for Liberty's Cymric line was Charles Horner. His pieces were eclectic–some, for example, were in the Egyptian revival style, while still others took *fin-de-siècle* styles and simplified them. One of his Egyptian revival pieces can be seen in the grouping of pieces below. Horner's winged scarab is noticeably different from the other, more conventional, one: Its stylized wings, for example, set it apart.

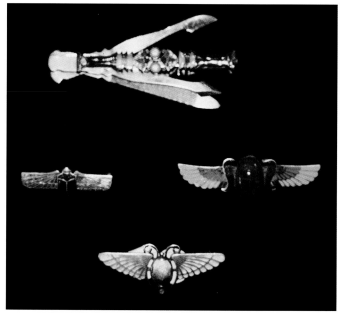

Four Arts and Crafts pieces in silver and enamel, all of which are in the Egyptian revival fashion. The manicure set (top) is British, from the 1920s, and shows its Egyptian revival nature both in its use of color–the traditional dark blue for lapis lazuli, the turquoise, and the red for carnelian, which were the stones most often found in ancient Egyptian jewelry–and its design, including *djed*-pillars (for more on which please see chapter four, p. 136) representing the backbone of the god Osiris, at either end of the piece. The rightmost of the two winged scarabs, a common theme in Egyptian revival jewelry, also used Egyptian colors (with the addition of green) and a carnelian scarab; it is unsigned and dates to about 1920. The bottom-most piece is by the noted designer Charles Horner, and is marked for the year 1912. It looks much less Egyptian than the other three pieces, in part because its wings are more stylized, and have a less colorful–and less Egyptian-like enameling–than would be found in an ancient Egyptian piece or a more conventional revival piece. Also, note the large, curlicue antennae. *Jewelry courtesy of Classic Facets, Boulder, CO; photograph by Karryl Salit.*

Jewelry of the Arts and Crafts–and its sister Art Nouveau–movement was so identified with Liberty that in Italy Arts and Crafts and Art Nouveau styles were sometimes referred to as Stile Liberty.

Arts and Crafts Elsewhere

Then I felt like some watcher of the skies
When a new planet swims into his ken;
Or like stout Cortez when with eagle eyes
He star'd at the Pacific–and all his men
Look'd at each other with a wild surmise—
Silent, upon a peak in Darien.

—John Keats, "On First
Looking into Chapman's Homer"

The Arts and Crafts movement had a transformative effect in countries other than England. Designers elsewhere were equally ready to discard the old and unworkable in favor of the new and fresh. The movement spread to a number of countries in Europe, including Germany (where it was known as Jugendstil, or "youth style") and Scandinavia.

Today probably the most famous name associated with German Arts and Crafts–or Jugendstil–jewelry is that of Theodor Fahrner, whose firm bought from a number of designers and makers, and sold its work in Great Britain. He worked from the German city of Pforzheim which, thanks to Fahrner and other manufacturers, became an important jewelry manufacturing center, much like Birmingham in England and Newark in the United States. (For more information on Fahrner, please see chapter three.)

A pendant in sterling silver, paste, marcasites, and plique-à-jour enamel. This piece shows the difficulty of classifying jewelry as "fine" or "costume"–silver Arts and Crafts jewelry is often classified as "fine" jewelry by dealers and auction houses, while lower karat gold or gold-filled jewelry (especially the latter) is often considered costume jewelry. Here a paste stone, usually associated with costume jewelry, is found in a piece with fine plique-à-jour enameling and good design. *Courtesy of Red Robin Antiques.*

A Scandinavian brooch in 925 silver and enamel, possibly c. 1910. This painterly piece, with its theme "After the Storm," has elements typical of Scandinavian design, including a shimmery guilloche background against which the detailed scene is painted. Also typical of the best Scandinavian design is the masterful use of the guilloche turning to create an effect of sunlight breaking through clouds, and the watery reflections of the rocks. The guilloche turning is not merely an interesting and attractive effect, as it is in most jewelry and toilet articles, but here forms an integral part of the scene. However, while the enamel elements are typical of Scandinavian pieces, the subject matter is very unusual: Most pieces like this have flowers or Scandinavian scenes. Robin notes that she has not seen another Scandinavian piece like this one, which is also sometimes titled "The Storm." Measures 2.125" in diameter and is marked G.B.925N.M. *Courtesy of Robin Allison.*

In Scandinavia, Georg Jensen produced jewelry and silver objects in the Arts and Crafts tradition, little of it enameled. Norway's Marius Hammer also produced Art jewelry, as did a number of other Norwegian designers, probably the best-known of whom is David Andersen. Enameled goods formed a large part of his company's output; he and other Scandinavian jewelers are for some reason noted especially for their enameled leaves and butterflies.(For more on Scandinavian and German designers, please see chapter three, and for more examples of Scandinavian butterflies, please refer to the section in chapter four on Butterflies Through Time.) Andersen's firm is still in existence, and still known for quality enameled pieces.

German and Scandinavian designers followed many of the precepts of the Arts and Crafts movement. Like their British counterparts, they worked primarily in the more affordable (for both crafter and buyer) silver and semi-precious stones. They too rebelled against the soullessness of machine-made, mass-produced goods. However, by the 1920s, most Art jewelers in Germany and Scandinavia had turned to the "functional" jewelry then in vogue, and their jewelry became less decorated and more machine-made. (Karlin, 1993, 222)

Scandinavian Jewelry

While Scandinavian designers often produced jewelry almost indistinguishable from that made in other countries–Aksel Holmsen, for example, produced a number of guilloche brooches with roses that closely resemble those by England's Charles Horner and America's Thomae Co.–many Scandinavian pieces have their own special flair. Some incorporate figural Scandinavian themes, such as reindeer and Viking ships, while others use traditional Scandinavian designs. Such designs appear in both older and more modern pieces. Scandinavian designers are noted for their use of enamel, especially guilloche and basse taille work, which they employ to very fine effect.

Another older Scandinavian brooch, this one depicting a typical Scandinavian theme: a Viking ship sailing past snow-covered mountains. This piece also makes good use of guilloche enameling to represent what some consider a depiction of the midnight sun. Marked 925S, measures 1.125".

A cuff bracelet in silver and enamel by the Norwegian firm Andersen & Scheinpflug. The bracelet has a stylized, possibly Scandinavian, wavelike design in black enameled cartouches, with stylized floral elements flanking the cartouches. The bracelet, while essentially modern in effect, also has a rather timeless quality about it, and could possibly even be described as Art Deco. Marked 925S, and measures 1.125" in width. *Courtesy of Robin Allison.*

A Scandinavian bracelet in silver and enamel by Tone Vigeland, with the guilloche panels each hand-painted with a different flower. While guilloche with roses is a common theme, and can be found in enamels from many countries, it is more unusual to see a variety like this. Marked Norway, sterling, and measures 7" x .75". *Courtesy of Robin Allison.*

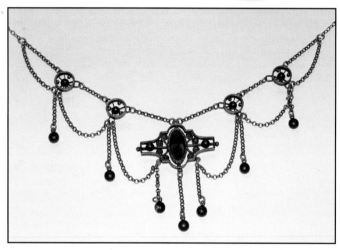

A wonderful festoon necklace by Danish designer Bernard Hertz, in silver and enamel. This piece, with its guilloche enamel in vivid cobalt blue, its chains and dangles, its severe symmetry could fall into a number of genres: Arts and Crafts, Art Deco, or Jugendstil. Marked BH, 925S; festoon section measures 6" x 1.25". *Courtesy of Robin Allison.*

Below:
Another Scandinavian piece, this one a bracelet in silver and enamel, with five panels, each of which shows a different scene relating to Scandinavia: a polar bear, a moose pulling a sleigh or perched on a ledge, a Viking ship, and a fjord. These scenes too use guilloche to create an effect. The scenes are linked by squares enameled in black, with a traditional design in turquoise. Marked with an undeciphered mark, 925S, and measures 7" x .5". *Courtesy of Robin Allison.*

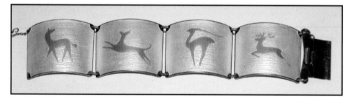

A wonderful wide bracelet in 925 silver and enamel, from Norway, consisting of four links each painted with a different stylized impression of a deer. The shimmery white guilloche background gives the impression of sunlit snow against which the deer gambol and leap, showing yet another masterful use of guilloche to create an effect that is so typical of Scandinavian enameled pieces. By Tone Vigeland, marked Norway, sterling, and 925; measures 6.75" x 1.25". *Courtesy of Robin Allison*

The Arts and Crafts movement in Europe largely ended with the onset of World War I; after the war, Functionalism and Art Deco became the prevailing styles. However, unlike Art Nouveau, which lasted for a very short time, the Arts and Crafts tradition lingered. In Great Britain, jewelers returned to their studios after the war and continued to produce handmade jewelry or to design jewelry that contains elements of Arts and Crafts style.

Mexican Jewelry

Oddly enough, half a world away, the Arts and Crafts tradition took hold in Taxco, Mexico. Taxco had long been–and still is–a city noted for its silver production. But during the 1930s it was transformed by an American, William Spratling, who envisioned it becoming a city noted for its jewelry production, much as Birmingham, Newark, and Pforzheim were leading producers of jewelry for their countries. A good deal of the jewelry produced in Taxco, just as jewelry produced in Birmingham, Newark, and other major centers, was derivative and not especially interesting. However, a few designers, notably Margot de Taxco, produced enameled silver jewelry of the highest quality. Margot used both the basse taille and champlevé techniques to create jewelry that is highly collectible, and left a legacy of fine enameling that still exists in Taxco today.

A necklace and matching earrings in sterling silver and enamel, by Margot de Taxco. The lovely clean lines of the necklace, geometric swirls ending in a stylized flower, and the simple colors, blue and white champlevé enameling with basse taille markings, show her work at its best. Brooch/pendant measures 2.75" x 1.25" and the detachable chain measures 14.25". Earrings measure 1.375" x .875". All are marked Margot de Taxco, sterling, and #5685. *Courtesy of Robin Allison.*

A necklace, bracelet and matching earrings in silver and enamel by famed Mexican designer Margot de Taxco. Taxco, which to this day remains famous for its silver jewelry, produced a number of designers/artisans, of whom Margot is by far the best known. Her work, like that of modern Scandinavian designers such as David Andersen and Aksel Holmsen, covers a wide range of subjects and styles. Here both the colors, the yellow and black with accents of red and green, and the intricate stylized geometric design, seem perhaps inspired by Mayan or Aztec carvings. *Courtesy of Robin Allison.*

Two fun Taxco pieces, a brooch in the form of a fish and a brooch/pendant in silver and enamel, in the form of a mermaid playing a guitar. The fish, which measures approximately 1.375" in diameter, is marked silver, Taxco, Mexico, and signed by Maya de Taxco; the mermaid is marked Taxco, but is unsigned.

Art Nouveau

Beauty is Nature's brag, and must be shown
In courts, at feasts, and high solemnities,
Where most may wonder at the workmanship
        —John Milton, *Comus*

I went hunting wild
After the wildest beauty in the world.
        —Wilfred Owen, "Strange Meeting"

In many ways, Art Nouveau is the changeling sister of the Arts and Crafts movement, the sister that grew up to become a swan. While there is no doubt that a number of the same fundamental goals underlay both movements, Art Nouveau fast outgrew its roots and became something almost ethereally different.

49

Art Nouveau emerged first in Belgium, around 1885, and spread quickly to France, inspiring, among others, René Lalique. It did not receive its "new art" name until the 1900 International Exposition in Paris at which Belgian innovator Samuel Bing displayed his designs in a pavilion called "Art Nouveau Bing." Sinuous and graceful in its beauty, its reign was brief, lasting about fifteen years; most accounts give 1910 as the date for its "swan song."

Conditions in France that led to Art Nouveau were similar to those in Britain leading to Arts and Crafts. In France as well as in Britain, archaeological revival jewelry had filled a void left by the need for innovative design. Becker (1985, 8) notes that

> By the late nineteenth century, jewelry design was ripe for drastic transformation: stagnating, robbed of artistic merit by the industrial age, it was long overdue for an injection of fresh talent. With no new artistic impetus of its own, the mid nineteenth century forced its jewelers to turn to the past for inspiration. A spiritual longing for the Middle Ages, an idealized 'age of chivalry', ushered in a revamped Gothic style... while the neo-Renaissance look occupied the last part of the nineteenth century.

Jewelry had become stiff, innovation replaced with reproductions of pieces from antiquity, or detailed renditions of nature's flowers, leaves, birds encrusted in diamonds. Perhaps worst of all, jewelry had become Wealth. It was a status symbol, judged by the richness of its settings and the size and brilliance of its stones rather than any artistic merit.

It may accurately be said that both artistic movements arose from the same ideals and constraints. Both were influenced by the Aesthetic Movement, and both reacted to the same heaviness and over-ornamentation common in late nineteenth century jewelry. It should also be noted that the great genius jeweler of the Art Nouveau movement, René Lalique, studied in England for two years during the early 1880s. Karlin (1993, 157) makes clear the connection between the two artistic trends: "The Arts and Crafts tradition was certainly a factor in the origins of the Art Nouveau movement. The desire to create a fresh new style handcrafted by individual artisans was an ethic primary to both movements."

Similar aesthetic concerns led designers in both countries to rely heavily on nature for inspiration, and similar views led Art Nouveau designers to use materials previously not thought appropriate for fine jewelry. Art Nouveau jewelers, like their counterparts in Great Britain, "focused on the artistic value of materials rather than the intrinsic value" (Karlin, 1993, 157). The French, like the British, used opals, ivory, and other semi-precious stones.[2]

And both made great use of enamel; as Karlin (1993, 157) notes, "Enamel, which was so important to the Arts and Crafts designers, was equally important in Art Nouveau jewelry, although here the two movements took divergent paths." For the Arts and Crafts jewelers, Limoges, champlevé, and cloisonné were the favored techniques; for Art Nouveau, it was plique-à-jour enamel.

Two Paths Diverge

Different preferences in enamel was hardly the only area in which Art Nouveau differed from Arts and Crafts. For one thing, it eschewed the handmade look so prevalent in Arts and Crafts pieces. Not for Art Nouveau the hammer marks on copper and silver, or the fine hand-twisted wire found in Arts and Crafts jewelry. Most of the better-known designers created jewelry in 18K gold, and many designs, even those in non-precious materials like horn and enamel, are set with diamonds. And most of the pieces they produced, often with the help of experts in one particular area (such as the noted enamelist Antoine Tard, who worked with the Falizes and other designers) are beautifully finished works.

Stylistically, Arts and Crafts and Art Nouveau also diverged considerably. Probably the signature stylistic element of Art Nouveau is the curvy or wavy line. "Sinuous" is one of the words that perhaps best describes much of Art Nouveau design. The wavy line is seen in the flowing hair of women, in the drape of their dresses, in the leaves framing flowers, in feathers, in water.

Art Nouveau Woman

Themes, too, differed dramatically. While both Art Nouveau and Arts and Crafts drew heavily on the peacock motif, Art Nouveau glorified Woman and Nature. The heads of women appeared on pins and lockets; the full female form is occasionally found in pendants and necklaces.

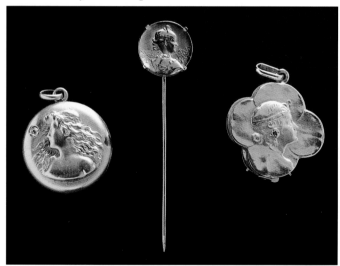

Not all Art Nouveau women were in enamel, although there did seem to be a preference, especially among some American firms, for creating beautifully enameled women. These three depictions of women's heads in Art Nouveau jewelry are, from left, a U. S.-made locket in 14K gold and a diamond, .875" in diameter, c. 1900; center, a French stickpin with a woman's head in 18K gold and small diamonds, .50" in diameter, c. 1895, signed A. Vaudet; right, a French locket in 18K gold and a small diamond, approximately 1" in diameter, c. 1900. Note the flowing hair of the woman on the American locket, typical of Art Nouveau and, earlier, pre-Raphaelite women. The woman on the French locket, however, has her hair worn in a mock-classical "nymph" style. The quatrefoil shape of the French locket is fairly often found in pins and lockets of the period.

Beguiling Beauties: Women Through Time

She walks in beauty, like the night
Of cloudless climes and starry skies;
And all that's best of dark and bright
Meets in her aspect and her eyes....
—George Gordon, Lord Byron, "She Walks in Beauty"

Since ancient Egypt, when Nefertiti's bust was sculpted to immortalize beauty that has beguiled the ages, women have been a favorite subject of sculptors, painters–and jewelers. During the period when Art Nouveau flowered, women were an especially strong source of inspiration. However, women as a subject were hardly neglected by designers both before and after the Art Nouveau period.

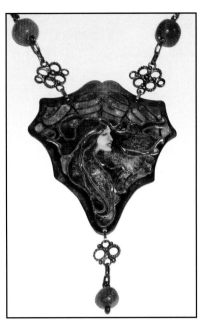

A necklace in silver, enamel, and carnelian, showing the Art Nouveau–Arts and Crafts crossover. Idealized Woman, with long, flowing hair, was a common theme in both Art Nouveau and Arts and Crafts jewelry; in the latter, it seems to have been influenced especially by pre-Raphaelite ideals such as those embodied in the paintings of Dante Gabriel Rossetti. Additionally, the use of plique-à-jour enamel is associated primarily with Art Nouveau jewelry, rather than Arts and Crafts. However, the use of silver and carnelian, and the symmetrical, rather geometric–even weblike–centerpiece, are very much in the spirit of Arts and Crafts jewelry. Unmarked; pendant measures 3.625" x 2.125". *Courtesy of Robin Allison.*

A Victorian watch in 800 silver vermeil and enamel, showing a fashionable lady of the era painted on a cobalt blue guilloche enamel. The woman, with her vivacious smile and her rigidly coiffed hair (which is accented with two rose cut diamonds), her earrings, and her elaborate gown, forms a nice contrast with the archetypal Art Nouveau and Arts and Crafts lady, with her dreamy expression, simple–if any– garb, and long flowing hair. This woman's personality comes through very strongly, making her anything but an archetype or stereotype. The back is enameled in cobalt blue and black enamel. Marked Jules Mathey and L'OCLE. Measures 1.5" in diameter. *Courtesy of Robin Allison.*

A lovely Limoges necklace in sterling silver, enamel, garnet pastes, pearls, and turquoise, with the beautifully detailed bust of a woman. Her hair, embellished with a flower, and her unstructured, draped clothing show her to be an Art Nouveau woman, although to Robin she also has elements of Arts and Crafts. As in many Limoges enamels, this one uses foil underneath the draped cloth to add interest and richness to the piece, which is done in the fine painterly tradition long established at Limoges. Matching chain is set with garnet pastes and pearls and is quite ornate. Pendant measures 2.5" x 1.625", and the chain is 20" long. This is most likely an American piece and is marked sterling. *Courtesy of Robin Allison.*

A slide locket in sterling silver and enamel, with the head and torso of a woman. As in many Art Nouveau portrayals of Woman, here the subject is semi-nude. Her flowing tresses are also typical of Art Nouveau Woman, and show some pre-Raphaelite influence, as in the rose tucked into her locks. The realism with which she is rendered also seems to have pre-Raphaelite roots, and is rather reminiscent of paintings by Sir Lawrence Alma-Tadema, who was noted for his appropriation of Classical themes and settings. As in many Limoges enamels, the woman's necklace is created by the use of foil, or paillons, as is the gold star in her hair. Measures 1.625" in diameter and is marked sterling silver. *Courtesy of Robin Allison.*

An Arts and Crafts woman in silver and enamel, painted in profile without a great deal of detail, rather in the fashion of Phoebe Traquair. The woman's hair seems long and blowing rather than long and flowing, wrapping partway around her face like a frame. She is set in a leaf-shaped frame enameled in traditional Arts and Crafts blues and greens. The difficult Limoges style of painting was adopted by some–especially British–Arts and Crafts jewelers. The rather sophisticated profile of the woman contrasts nicely with the handcrafted nature of the somewhat asymmetrical setting. Measures 2" x 1.75" and is unmarked. *Courtesy of Robin Allison.*

A brooch in unmarked 14K gold and enamel, with a Limoges-style painting of the head and shoulders of a woman. The woman, her long hair garlanded with ribbon and flowers, her expression dreaming, her features ethereal, and her dress distinctly un-Victorian, harking back possibly to the Renaissance, shows pre-Raphaelite influence.

The gold star-shaped paillons and the foil used to accent clothing and hair adornments are typical of Limoges enameling, which made very effective use of metal foil under enamel to highlight jewelry and raiment, and to add interest to backgrounds. Measures 1.125" in diameter. *Courtesy of Robin Allison.*

A slide locket in 935 silver and enamel, this one with a Byzantine lady against a guilloche background. Rather than the usual profile, the lady here is depicted in three-quarter view. Different also is her hair, which instead of curling–as it usually does in depictions of Byzantine women–is straight in the manner of pre-Raphaelite maidens. Yet she is recognizably the Byzantine woman, with the same beautifully detailed features, the same expression, wearing the typical headdress, which here adds flowers to the usual geometric elements. Measures 2" x 1.375" and is marked 935 and sterling. *Courtesy of Robin Allison.*

Two pieces in 900 silver and enamel, each with an Art Nouveau woman surrounded by a plique-à-jour frame. The pendant on the left, with a the woman ethereally playing a harp and wearing a dress emblazoned with stars, is set in a frame with geometric, stylized flowers. The slide locket on the right is set in a frame that resembles the daisies its subject holds her in hand and wears in her hair. In some ways this woman is reminiscent of Levinger's lady with roses, but she is a bit more restrained, and also has something of an Edwardian Gibson girl look about her hair and clothing. The pendant measures 3" x 2"; the slide locket measures 2.75" x 1.75". *Courtesy of Robin Allison.*

A notepad by German Heinrich Levinger in 900 silver, enamel, and pastes, measuring 2.5" x 1.625", with a detailed depiction of a woman much in the spirit of those created by the Czech artist Alphonse Mucha, who was noted for his Art Nouveau women. This one sniffs a rose, twin to the ones she wears in her cascading hair, while her eyes are closed as if to allow her more fully to breathe in the sensuous heavy scent of the rose. Marked HL, with British hallmarks. *Courtesy of Robin Allison.*

Woman *with* Nature

In a number of Art Nouveau pieces, Woman was depicted with nature, especially with flowers. The woman may be holding a flower, wearing it, or simply juxtaposed with it.

An Art Nouveau woman in a pendant in 14K gold, plique-à-jour enamel, and diamonds, shown with a stylized flower that forms part of the frame, as does in part her flowing hair. Her hair also is adorned with a stylized flower, held in place by a fillet of diamonds. The plique in this piece is in lovely shades of pink and green, colors often favored by Art Nouveau enamelists. Measures 1" x .875". *Courtesy of Robin Allison.*

A lovely Art Nouveau woman in silver and enamel, with a pearl dangle. The woman, shown in profile against green plique-à-jour enamel, wears green flowers in her upswept blue hair. Brooch measures 1.75" x 1.125". *Courtesy of Robin Allison.*

A charming and unusual Art Nouveau brooch in 935 sterling silver, enamel, and plique-à-jour enamel, showing a woman with a very expressive face, next to a stylized flower with a baroque pearl bud. Measures 1.125" in diameter. *Courtesy of Robin Allison.*

A beautiful brooch by the German firm Meyle & Mayer, in 900 silver and enamel, showing a woman against a pale plique background with which a vibrantly enameled iris forms a contrast. The flowing striated leaves of the iris form the greater part of the frame of this wonderful piece, which measures 1.125" x 1.125". *Courtesy of Robin Allison.*

A brooch in unmarked silver and enamel, 1" in diameter, with the head, neck, and shoulders of a woman. Unlike many such pieces, this one has enamel in a light lavender forming the background, while the woman's face, ever so slightly averted, is in silver. A flower, leaf, and bud also add splashes of color to the piece. *Courtesy of Robin Allison.*

Woman *as* Nature

In other pieces, women were given wings; they were angels or fairies. Other pieces depicted butterfly women and dragonfly women, as in the famous piece by Lalique, now in Lisbon's Calouste Gulbenkian Museum, of a woman's body carved in chrysoprase given dragonfly wings. Women were also depicted *as* flowers, not merely *with* flowers.

A beautiful brooch in silver, enamel, and chrysoprase, by Meyle & Mayer, showing a butterfly-woman. The woman's face is beautifully carved, almost ethereal, surrounded by a swirl of hair adorned with a chrysoprase cabochon matching one in the nearer wing, and melding her even further with the butterfly. This merging of woman with nature was a popular theme for Art Nouveau designers; Lalique's dragonfly woman is famous, and even Newark makers created such pieces (as the one by Whiteside & Blank). Marks for Meyle & Mayer; measures 2" x 1.5". *Courtesy of Robin Allison.*

Woman as Iris, in a brooch in 900 silver and enamel, by the Italian firm Brevetatto, noted also for its silver products. The woman's face, very much in the Mucha style popular with afficionados of Art Nouveau, grows out of an iris beautifully enameled in deep purple and gold over basse taille striations. Measures 1.125" x 1". *Courtesy of Robin Allison.*

A wonderful adaptation of a French Art Nouveau concept, by the Newark company of Whiteside & Blank. The brooch, in 14K gold, enamel, and diamonds, depicts a butterfly-woman with plique-à-jour wings and an iridescent enamel dress. The enameling is first-rate, and the overall appearance of this piece is stunning. *Courtesy of the Newark Museum, Newark, NJ.*

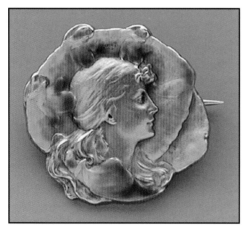

A fascinating Art Nouveau brooch that shows the tendency to blur the lines between Woman (or Man) and nature. Here a woman's head in typical Art Nouveau profile, flowing hair and all, is set against–almost emerges from–green enameled lily pads, the violet flowers of which surround her face. *Courtesy of Nelson Rarities, Portland, ME.*

The matching locket, brooch, and stickpin to the lorgnette pictured above (and to the Alling Co. bracelet shown in the introduction). All have the beautifully enameled Byzantine woman, complete with elaborate headdress–each feature rendered in detail, no matter how large or small the piece. According to one expert, the stickpins especially were produced in some quantity, and it is easy to see why they were so popular. Unmarked locket measures 1.625" in diameter; brooch, also unmarked, measures 1.125" x 1"; stickpin measures .75" in diameter. *Courtesy of Robin Allison.*

Byzantine Woman

Another sub-genre of Art Nouveau Woman, especially popular with American makers such as Alling Co., was the Byzantine woman. Stylistically, however, the Byzantine woman really had less in common with Art Nouveau Woman than at first glance might appear. The Byzantine woman almost seems to form a bridge between revival pieces of the Victorian era, and Art Nouveau depictions of woman. The Byzantine woman might have long, curling hair–though this in fact is usually rather static–but she is much more stylized and formal than the true Art Nouveau Woman, with her flowing tresses and expressive face. Many Byzantine women, though beautiful to look at, reveal little, if any, emotion. One feature especially common to Byzantine women is an exotic, carefully detailed headdress, often studded with diamonds or other precious stones, from which depend circles and hoops.

A lorgnette in 14K gold and enamel, with diamond accents, with the head in profile of a "Byzantine" lady. In typical Art Nouveau fashion, the hair is flowing, although here adorned with an elaborate headdress enlivened by diamonds. Also typical of American Art Nouveau jewelry, her face is enameled in translucent, or iridescent, enamel. The enameling is beautiful and detailed, so that her features are very much alive. Measures 4.5" x .25". *Courtesy of Robin Allison.*

Another Byzantine lady stickpin in 14K gold, diamonds, and a pearl. Much like the other Byzantine women in Newark jewelry, she wears a diadem–this one set with diamonds and ending in a pearl–on her long, curling hair. Otherwise, she is almost identical to the Byzantine lady stickpin in the introduction–though given her diamonds, she was probably the more expensive version. Producing much the same piece in different sizes, or with diamonds instead of pearls, was a fairly common practice among Newark manufacturers.

A lovely slide locket in 800 silver and enamel, showing a dragonfly, whose wings–in a beautiful iridescent enamel shading from blue to green to gold–somewhat resemble a stylized lotus blossom. The daisies among which the dragonfly has alit are also nicely enameled, with pink-tipped petals that curve up ever so slightly. Measures 2" x 1.375". *Courtesy of Robin Allison.*

A different version of the Art Nouveau Byzantine lady, this time in a 935 sterling silver and enamel slide locket. The enameling–possibly done using the transfer process–has created a great deal of detail and shading in hair, face, headdress, and costume, but otherwise this Byzantine lady looks very much like her counterparts in gold and iridescent enamel, with the same features and expression, and the same detail to the eyes, nose, and lips. As in some Limoges enamels, gold accents–here created by enamel rather than metal foils–add life and sparkle to the extremely elaborate headdress and the necklace she wears. Measures 2" x 1.375". *Courtesy of Robin Allison.*

Art Nouveau Nature

Nature will bear the closest inspection. She invites us to lay our eye level with her smallest leaf, and take an insect view if its plan.
—Henry David Thoreau, *On Walden Pond*

Nature, along with Woman, is abundantly represented in Art Nouveau jewelry. The Art Nouveau dragonfly, found not only in jewelry but in the stained glass of Louis Comfort Tiffany, is almost a cliché. However, Art Nouveau also created bats and birds, butterflies and bees.

In some instances, Art Nouveau design may present a more realistic depiction of nature than Arts and Crafts. Both used flowers, leaves, butterflies, insects, and snakes as inspiration, but "[i]n the British movement these motifs tend to be quite stylized and static whereas the French designers made them startlingly real, almost grotesque, by depicting all states of nature including decay and death." (Karlin, 1993, 157) Art Nouveau design was thus a mixture of intense realism coupled with grotesque imaginings.

A marvelous necklace by Meyle & Mayer, of a bird in silver, enamel, and pearls. While the wings are beautifully enameled in plique-à-jour enamel shading from pale yellow to a deep pink, almost red, at the tips, in cells that suggest feathers, the bird's head and neck are wonderfully dimensional, and done in iridescent enamel that, like the wings, shades from gold through deep pink. The head, cocked to one side, extends away from the wings, and holds a pearl in its beak, which is enameled black. The tips of the wings curve down to meet, forming a frame from which is suspended a pearl drop. Measures 2" x 1.75". *Courtesy of Robin Allison.*

A dragonfly in silver, enamel, and pastes, its wings vibrant with blue enamel that shows the basse taille veining below. The body and wings are accented with paste stones, the red eyes further adding to this extremely colorful piece, created by the German firm of Meyle & Mayer. Measures 2" x 1.75". *Courtesy of Robin Allison.*

A brooch in sterling silver and plique-à-jour enamel, in the form of a bat. The bat, whose wings are enameled in green, flits against a blue plique sky enlivened by stars affixed to beams radiating up from the moon at the very bottom edge of the piece. It measures 1.125" in diameter. *Courtesy of Robin Allison.*

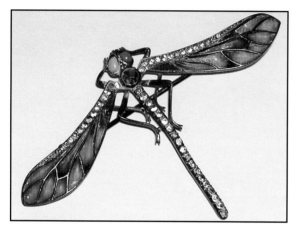

Another dragonfly, possibly (other than Woman) the motif most associated with Art Nouveau jewelry. This dragonfly, in silver, enamel, and pastes, has large turquoise eyes that make it appear very realistically an insect. Its wings, in plique-à-jour enamel, are in a wealth of colors that range from greens and blues through red. Marked 925 silver, undeciphered mark; measures 3" x 2". *Courtesy of Robin Allison.*

As the observant reader has probably noticed, Meyle & Mayer is among Robin's favorite makers of Art Nouveau and other jewelry. And for good reason, as this charming bee in silver, enamel, and a pearl shows. The wings are beautifully enameled in plique-à-jour that shades from green through violet. The body, curving down around legs that clutch a pearl, is also done in iridescent violet enamel, with black stripes. Marked for Meyle & Mayer, 900 silver depose, and measures 1.75" x 1.75". *Courtesy of Robin Allison.*

Religious Medals

A subset of Art Nouveau jewelry was religious medals, which were especially popular in France. Many of them were done with plique-à-jour backgrounds, in blue primarily but sometimes with other colors as well. This type of jewelry remained popular into the 1930s.

A religious medallion in 18K gold and plique-à-jour enamel, c. 1910-1920, depicting Mary with angels. Probably French or Belgian; measures .875" in diameter.

A small Madonna pendant in 18K gold and plique-à-jour enamel, the frame surrounded by small seed pearls. *Courtesy of Bodette Reeves, Odessa, TX.*

Two madonna pendants. The one on the left is late 19th century, probably French, of 18K gold, plique-à-jour enamel, and diamonds set in a carved ivory frame. The one on the right is also French, in 18K gold, platinum, enamel, and mother-of-pearl. Dating from the 1930s, it shows its Art Deco style in its angular geometric forms and its use of pink, green, and black enamel. *Jewelry courtesy of Classic Facets, Boulder, CO; photograph by Karryl Salit.*

It may be that, on the whole, the well-articulated philosophy underlying the Arts and Crafts movement did not translate well into the French Art Nouveau. While Arts and Crafts was a definite philosophy not merely of design, but also of working conditions, of execution, of an entire way of life, it appears that for Art Nouveau, aesthetics alone mattered. Could it be that this lack of a serious underpinning was to prove the downfall of such a stellar movement? Was Art Nouveau ultimately built upon quicksand, rather than a more solid philosophical foundation? While Arts and Crafts had the brilliant William Morris to delineate its goals and desires, no such spokesperson emerged to define Art Nouveau. At best, the Symbolist poet Stéphane Mallarmé was quoted; his ideal of "suggesting" nature, rather than replicating it, was the aim: "To suggest it, that's the dream."

Whatever the cause of the evanescence of Art Nouveau design, the movement lasted only ten years into the new century. Design became stale, trite, in danger of becoming the very thing it had rebelled against: stagnant. The great jewelers who fueled the movement, Lalique, Fouquet, Gaillard, Aucoc, began to abandon it. Lalique turned his genius to glass design, and became famous for the perfume bottles, vases, and bowls he created.

A Panoply of Peacocks: Peacocks Through Time

The pride of the peacock is the glory of God.
—William Blake, *Proverbs of Hell*

The peacock, long a symbol of beauty as well as ostentatious display, was a favorite subject of both Arts and Crafts and Art Nouveau designers. Peacocks, with their iridescent feathers and bright coloring, lent themselves perfectly to enameled jewelry. Like other beautiful or sentimental motifs, they have remained popular in jewelry over the years.

Another wonderful peacock piece, this one in unmarked silver, enamel, opals, and a pearl, attributed to the great British Arts and Crafts jeweler George Hunt. Here the peacock is almost abstract, but the enameling, especially of the dappled feathering on its body, is exquisite. The opals pick up the colors of the peacock, setting it off nicely. Peacocks were among the favored subjects of Arts and Crafts designers, and this is a striking example. Measures 4.25" x 2.75". *Courtesy of Robin Allison.*

A beautiful quatrefoil brooch depicting a peacock perched in a tree. The basse taille detail to the feathers and the iridescent enamel make this a very lovely portrait of a peacock; the white pearlescent drops forming the eyes of the tail feathers are an especially nice touch. Marked sterling; measures 2.25" x 1.875". *Courtesy of Robin Allison.*

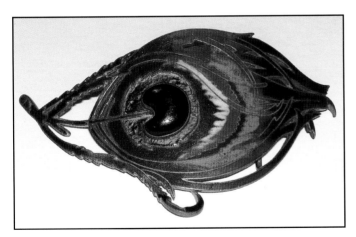

A marvelous belt buckle in the form of a peacock feather, by the noted French Art Nouveau jewelers, Piels Frères. The buckle is richly enameled in blues and green to simulate a peacock's tail feather, its eye set with a cobalt blue glass cabochon. A wonderful example of the best of Art Nouveau design, the feather is just stylized enough "to suggest the dream" rather than fully replicating it. Marked depose PF; measures 4.5" x 2.5". *Courtesy of Robin Allison.*

A brooch in 935 silver by Norwegian designer Marius Hammer, with a peacock surrounded by red and green flora. As with many of the more effective Scandinavian pieces, this one uses the underlying guilloche to achieve a wonderful, shimmery effect which, because the rest of the brooch is done in opaque enamel, shows through to create iridescence only for the peacock and the vegetation. Marked 935S, with Marius Hammer's maker's mark. Measures approximately 2.25" x 1.5".

Three bird brooches–two peacocks and a grouse–in silver and paste, c. 1910. The peacocks are quite dissimilar, one having its tail fanned open, its rather dimensional head turned to one side, while the other shows the peacock in profile, running with its tail streaming behind it. Both birds have, in addition to the usual blues and greens, topaz-colored paste stones, giving them a superficial resemblance that fades at a second, closer, look. The grouse too looks as if he belongs, having roughly the same colored pastes. The heads of the grouse and the fan-tailed peacock are enameled. The grouse measures 1.5" x 1", the peacock in profile 2.875" x .75", and the fan-tailed peacock 2" x 1.75". *Courtesy of Robin Allison.*

A gorgeous Art Deco peacock pendant in sterling silver, enamel, and glass. The peacock's tail, enameled in the traditional blues and greens, with red accents that make it rather unusual in the lexicon of peacocks, curves sinuously around the oval of frosted glass on which the peacock is perched. Measures 3.25" x 1". *Courtesy of Robin Allison.*

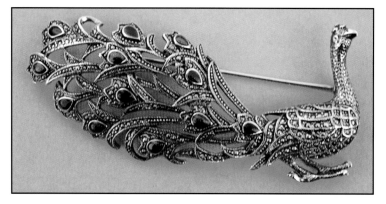

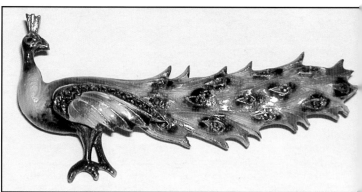

A large Art Deco brooch in silver, enamel, and marcasites, in the form of a peacock in profile. The only accents of color to this piece are teardrops in different colors of iridescent enamel. Interestingly, there is one teardrop in black enamel on the reverse side of the brooch. Unmarked; measures approximately 3.25" x 1.25".

A beautiful later peacock brooch in sterling silver, enamel, and marcasites, by designer Alice Caviness, probably of German manufacture. The tail feathers trail behind the peacock, enameled in bright blues and greens, with a marcasite forming the center of each eye. Marcasites also add interest to the curve of the wing. Measures 2.5" x 1.5". *Courtesy of Robin Allison.*

A smaller peacock brooch in silver filigree, with only its body and the eyes on its tail feathers enameled, in champlevé. While this piece is unmarked, it resembles the many peacocks produced in Portugal by the firm Topazio. Measures 1.5" x 1.5".

A pair of peacock earrings in silver and enamel, from Taxco, Mexico. The earrings, enameled in the traditional peacock hues of blue and green, strike a balance between a representational and a stylized portrayal of the peacock.

A vintage peacock brooch, gold-filled and enameled, by Trifari, c. 1960. Unlike most peacocks, this one is done in rather drab colors, browns and greens; however, it is nicely dimensional, with a sculptural body riveted to the tail section. Marked for Crown Trifari; measures 1" x 1.25".

Art Nouveau in America

While the Arts and Crafts movement appears not to have had a major impact on jewelry manufactured in the United States (aside from the output of independent jewelers working from their studios, little jewelry in the Arts and Crafts style was produced in this country), Art Nouveau made a major impression. One of the greatest of all American designers, Louis Comfort Tiffany, created decidedly Art Nouveau pieces, not only jewelry, but his famous stained glass lamps as well, with their dragonflies and lilies and poppies. Marcus & Co., in New York, also made Art Nouveau jewelry, and–along with Tiffany & Co., Riker Brothers, and Whiteside & Blank– was one of the few American firms to make jewelry with plique-à-jour enamel.

Newark, New Jersey, was already a major manufacturing center for jewelry by 1890, home to firms such as Krementz, Whiteside & Blank, and Bippart, Griscom, & Osborn. These companies mass-produced jewelry that was affordable for the middle class, but which was also fashionable, attractive, and well made. When Art Nouveau became the rage, Newark companies followed the fashion, and began to create Art Nouveau pieces. Many of them produced pieces with women, such as the Byzantine woman previously discussed.

And many of these pieces took the form of flower pins, pendants, and earrings. Such jewelry was not a novelty. During late Victorian times, Newark had produced its share of Victorian flower pins. Firms in other parts of the country, such as the Massachusetts-based Watson Co., already noted for its fine silver work, also began to manufacture Art Nouveau flower brooches.

There was one major difference between Victorian floral jewelry and Art Nouveau pieces: preferences in flowers. If pansies, forget-me-nots, and cloverleaves were the favored floral motifs for late Victorian jewelry, irises and poppies and water lilies (or lotuses) were no less emblematic for Art Nouveau. (For more on Newark and other American makers, please refer to chapter three; for more on floral jewelry, please see chapter five.)

Three brooches in sterling silver and enamel, with irises against a guilloche background. All three are alike, save for the color of the irises, which are a silvery white, purple, and yellow (and also some variation in the color of the element separating the two flowers in each brooch). The craftsmanship in these brooches is very fine, with basse taille markings indicating the striations of the leaves– which in sinuous Art Nouveau fashion curve around to form part of the frame–and adding a feeling of dimensionality to the flowers' petals. Each measures 2.75" x 1.5"; while all three were likely made by the same manufacturer, the yellow and purple ones have the maker's mark for the Shepard Co. (a Massachusetts-based company). *Courtesy of Robin Allison.*

Another iris, a flower much represented in Art Nouveau design, in sterling silver and enamel, set in a quatrefoil frame. While the design is perhaps not quite as obviously Nouveau as that of the three irises shown above–the quatrefoil setting is a bit less flowing, more traditional–the lovely shimmering enamel does give it that special Art Nouveau glow. Also marked for Shepard Co.; measures 2.25" x 1.875". *Courtesy of Robin Allison.*

A lovely Art Nouveau water lily in silver and enamel, with some nice champlevé work giving it almost a look of cloisonné, and basse taille markings for the leaves, the petals, and the center of the flower visible through the bright, translucent enamel. The piece has an almost hand-fashioned look reminiscent of Arts and Crafts pieces, and its artful lack of symmetry is rather refreshing. Maker's mark for the Watson Co.; measures 2.25" x .75". *Courtesy of Robin Allison.*

Traipsing through Time: Trends in Enamel

Tastes in enameled jewelry changed dramatically over the course of the nineteenth and early twentieth centuries. The beginning of the nineteenth century saw the continued popularity of cobalt blue enamel, which had been prevalent during the eighteenth century. However, over the course of Victoria's long reign, fashion changed considerably, and these changes are reflected in tastes in enameled jewelry as well as in other jewelry and decorative arts. The following is a list of some of the more distinctive trends:

♦ 1800 on–Cobalt blue enamel is popular, and is often seen on the fashionable snake bracelets of the period.
♦ c. 1860–Persian turquoise jewelry becomes fashionable, and a light turquoise blue enamel is produced to emulate or simulate this newly fashionable gemstone.
♦ 1861–Prince Albert dies, and Queen Victoria goes into mourning; black enamel and taille d'épargne enamel are much in vogue for use in mourning jewelry.
♦ 1860s on–the opening of China (in 1848) and Japan (1853) to Western trade makes the use of cloisonné enamel popular, especially by master jewelers such as Lucien Falize, with the help of the talented enamelist Antoine Tard.
♦ c. 1880–in the United States, the popularity of glossy enamel, especially in 14K gold floral jewelry, gives way to a taste for matte enamel realistically painted with veins and markings on leaves and petals.
♦ 1880s–The Arts and Crafts movement in Great Britain makes use of non-traditional materials such as semi-precious gems, mother-of-pearl, and enamel in jewelry; especially popular are Limoges enamels, and a vivid iridescent blue-green enamel.
♦ 1880–The use of guilloche enamel, machine turned engravings on metal overlain with transparent or translucent enamel, becomes popular; the talented Falizes develop a technique using guilloche enamel and cloisonné together. Guilloche enamel remains popular during the Art Deco period.
♦ c. 1885–In the U. S. especially, a motif of champlevé enamel filled with a light blue enamel in a forget-me-not pattern, sometimes with green leaves and contrasting white enamel, becomes popular; such enameling is found on the crescents in honeymoon pins, and against a gold or gold-filled background.
♦ c. 1895–The Art Nouveau movement in Europe and the United States finds plique-à-jour enamel especially suited for creating delicate wings on fairies and butterflies, angels and dragonflies, dragons and grotesques, as well as sky and water in its nuanced jeweled landscapes.
♦ 1897–Bright iridescent enamels, known sometimes as Jubilee enamels, are developed in honor of Queen Victoria's diamond jubilee celebrating her sixty years on the throne.
♦ c. 1900–U.S. manufacturers of mass-produced Art Nouveau jewelry begin to use iridescent enamels on women and flowers, birds and leaves, and other creations.

East Was East and West Was West–Until They Met: Asian Jewelry

East my pleasure lies…
—William Shakespeare, *Antony and Cleopatra*

Because Asian decorative arts inspired a number of gifted nineteenth century designers and artists, and because Asia not only gave Western jewelers the cloisonné enameling technique but lent certain motifs as well, it seems appropriate to mention Asian jewelry briefly.

An Art Nouveau notepad in silver and enamel, with what appears to be a stylized lotus design. Such notepads were often attached to chatelaines. Here a functional object is elevated beyond the merely useful through its lovely design and fine enameling. The top is pierced to allow the next layer of aqua foil to show through. Measures 3.25" (with loop) x 2.125" and is unmarked. *Courtesy of Red Robin Antiques.*

A good deal of the Asian jewelry seen in this country is Chinese jewelry made for export to the west and is, in fact, sometimes called "Chinese export jewelry." Chinese export jewelry is characterized by cloisonné enameling, often in cells laid over a mesh background.

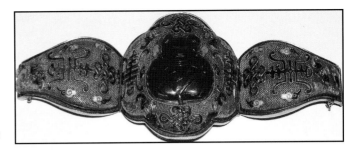

A Chinese bracelet in silver gilt and cloisonné enamel, with a carved carnelian panda. The Chinese made a large number of pieces for export to the west, often in silver or vermeil filigree, and often with cloisonné enameling, at which they excelled. Sometimes the pieces contain gemstones such as jade, lapis lazuli, or, in this case, carnelian. Measures 2.5" x 6.75". This is an older piece, from 1920 or before. *Courtesy of Robin Allison.*

A lovely Chinese bracelet in silver, turquoise, and enamel. Like many Chinese export pieces, this one has a light gold wash. The cloisonné enamel beautifully sets off the turquoise cabochons, which have the robust deep greenish blue of Chinese turquoise, rather than the lighter, bluer hues of Persian and some southwest American turquoise. Approximately 1920 or earlier. Measures 1.625" x 6.75"; marked silver and MG. *Courtesy of Robin Allison.*

Other Asian pieces can, of course, be found. India created some beautiful enameled jewelry, some of which is classified as "Mogul" jewelry, after the Mogul empire founded by Babur in the mid-fifteenth century. Mogul jewelry, as other aspects of Mogul culture, has a very rich look–a look that is perhaps best exemplified by the Taj Mahal. Not all Mogul jewelry is extremely old; even relatively modern pieces, created while India was under British rule, are sometimes labeled Mogul.

A pair of handmade earrings from India, in silver, enamel, coral, and pearls, in the so-called mogul style (named after the Islamic Mogul empire in India founded by Babur). These earrings, like other mogul pieces, are ornate, enameled in an elaborate pattern, and incorporate fine quality gems. Measure 2" x 1" and are unmarked. *Courtesy of Robin Allison.*

A pair of egg-shaped Chinese earrings, in silver gilt and enamel. Like many pieces exported from China early in the 20th century, these are formed of mesh, over which cloisons with enamel have been applied. *Courtesy of Robin Allison.*

Japan also created some lovely enameled pieces. However, some Japanese "enameled" jewelry is really painted porcelain, known as Toshikane after the primary manufacturer of such jewelry.

Interestingly, Thailand is also a fairly major exporter of enameled jewelry. A number of Thai pieces, usually in silver, are in the shape of fans, with or without stylized Thai dancers. The other item of Thai jewelry often encountered is a peacock brooch with a tail that is hinged to fold up or down.

A Toshikane bracelet in silver and enameled porcelain, from Japan. The links in this attractive bracelet alternate a charming bluebird with a stylized yellow flower. Marked silver; measures 7.5" x .75". *Courtesy of Robin Allison.*

A peacock brooch in silver and enamel, from Thailand. This is a fairly standard piece from a country noted for its export of enameled jewelry, many pieces of which are decorated with stylized Thai dancers. The brooch is hinged so that the peacock's body may be worn closer to or farther away from its tail.

Two beautiful Japanese floral items in silver and enamel: The first is a belt, each link of which contains a different flower or group of flowers; the second is a belt buckle with two brightly enameled peonies, the one in the forefront being done in pinks and reds shading to white, the one behind it in white shading to a deep plum color. The belt measures 26", with the buckle measuring 1.875" and the other links 1.25", and is marked TOKIO with Japanese hallmarks. The belt buckle, which measures 2.5" x 2.25" and is unmarked, has an exotic oriental flair. *Courtesy of Robin Allison.*

The Edwardian Age

Beautiful as sweet!
And young as beautiful! and soft as young!
And gay as soft! and innocent as gay.

—Thomas Young, *Night*

When Queen Victoria died in 1901, the Victorian age and its ethos died with her. The century was new, and new fashions quickly sprang up to greet it. Whereas Victoria and her subjects had worn heavy jewelry set with dark colored stones, Edward VII's subjects preferred platinum in airy filigree settings that were perfect for the diamonds then in fashion. When platinum was too expensive for a smaller or less important piece of jewelry, white gold was often used. Pearls too were popular, worn either in long strands, or in multiple strands in dog collars. Accents of color were provided by the occasional sapphire or emerald–and, of course, enamel. The jewelry was much less sentimental. In part it was less figural, too; geometric design largely replaced the taste for natural motifs found in nineteenth century jewelry.

Bar pin by Newark maker Bippart, Griscom, & Osborn, c. 1910, .125" x 2.25". This pin displays a number of elements characteristic of Edwardian jewelry: It is made of white metal, in this case white gold overlying gold; its single stone is a diamond; it contains delicate filigree work that is geometric in nature, with circles enclosing diamond shapes; and the entire piece has a geometric look, with an elongated ellipse forming the body of the pin, diamond-shaped tips at either end of the pin, and a central circle holding the diamond.

A lovely locket in silver, enamel, and marcasite, by Meyle & Mayer, demonstrating the versatility of that particular manufacturer, which also produced outstanding Art Nouveau pieces. The lovely, formal guilloche and the pale blue enamel are characteristic of the age, and found in other Edwardian pieces, including some made by American firms. Measures 1.125" in diameter. *Courtesy of Robin Allison.*

A beautiful Edwardian pendant in silver, enamel, and an amethyst (or, possibly, a paste stone), 1.75" in diameter. The design, with its stylized flowers and proportionate design, is very clean and attractive. The white enameled band surrounding the central stone is an interesting touch, and seems to embody Edwardian tastes: the geometric and orderly, the clean and bright. The plique-à-jour enameling, however, is in the shades often found in Art Nouveau pieces: pinks shading into green. *Courtesy of Robin Allison.*

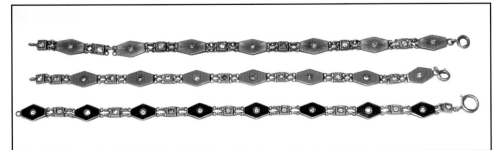

Three very similar Edwardian bracelets in silver, enamel, and paste, showing the angularity of the new aesthetic in design as it made the transition into Art Deco. The underlying guilloche work is especially visible under the translucent lavender enamel of the topmost bracelet. Marked sterling; 7" x .25". *Courtesy of Robin Allison.*

Festoon necklaces, found in both late Victorian and Arts and Crafts jewelry, remained popular. However, there was a geometric feel even to these, with some of the central elements having an overlying grid.

Another type of pin that was popular at this time was the so-called "beauty pin." This pin is an elongated oval, often decorated with enamel, such as guilloche.

Two pins, in 14K gold, enamel, and pearls, both by Newark makers. The smaller pin, white with three small seed pearls, is described as a baby's bib pin, and dates probably c. 1915; it was made by the Newark company Link & Angell. The larger pin, by Whiteside & Blank, was popular c. 1900, and is of the type known as a beauty pin. The design of the beauty pin fit the era's emphasis on clean lines and muted colors. Larger pin is approximately 1.5" wide; smaller approximately 1.125". Both fully marked for maker and karat content.

Flower jewelry retained some popularity, but even it has a more angular look. For example, a pin with the traditional tiny forget-me-nots found in Victorian hearts or honeymoon pins, might now appear in a geometric grid.

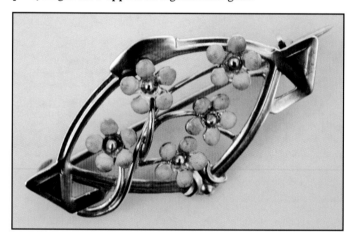

A small pin in 10K gold and enamel, c. 1905, 1.25" wide. While this pin contains the tiny enameled forget-me-nots so often found in smaller Victorian pins, the frame is angular and geometric, and totally Edwardian.

Top left & left:
Two Edwardian festoon necklaces, the first in vermeil, enamel, marcasites, pearls, and paste, the second in unmarked silver, enamel, pearls, and paste. The festoon necklace, while also found in Victorian jewelry, was especially popular with the Edwardians. Both necklaces have guilloche enamel in soft colors overlain by a geometric design in silver. The geometrical nature of this jewelry is a precursor of the clean, geometric lines favored in Art Deco design. Festoon sections measure 2.125" x 1.75". *Courtesy of Robin Allison and Red Robin Antiques.*

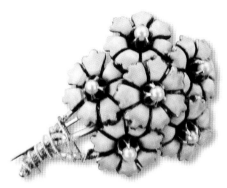

An Edwardian flower pin, possibly forget-me-nots, 1.75" (including stem) by 1". The pin, in 14K gold, enamel, and pearls has no maker's mark but was probably manufactured in Newark or New York c. 1905. Enameled flower pins were much less popular during the Edwardian years than they had been previously. This one, unlike its earlier counterparts, is rather stylized–the petal edges appear more serrated than folded–and the overall effect seems more geometric. The enameling, too, lacks the detail found in earlier pins; it simply shades from cream to light blue at the edges. Some details, however, are reminiscent of Victorian jewelry: The carved and textured stems and the wire tying the flowers together add a rather Victorian touch.

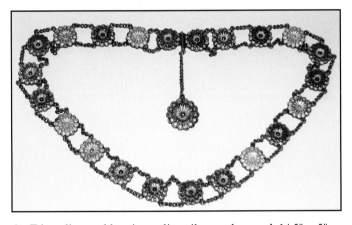

An Edwardian necklace in sterling silver and enamel, 14.5" x .5". While the stylized flowers and the dangle are typical of Edwardian jewelry, the multi-hued flowers are less typical of a period in which white metal, diamonds, and pearls predominated, and in which color, when used, was usually fairly subdued. *Courtesy of Robin Allison.*

Suffragette Jewelry

"My lige lady, generally," quod he, "wommen desiren to have soverynetee as wel over hir housband as hir love."
—Chaucer, "The Wife of Bath's Tale"

March, march–many as one, sister to sister, friend to friend.
—British Suffragette Anthem

In a century filled with brutality–two world wars, murderous totalitarian tyrants, genocide, horrible disasters, and civil strife–it is easy to forget that one of the great struggles in Great Britain and America at the end of the nineteenth and beginning of the twentieth centuries was the fight for women's rights. Women, as Chaucer had remarked over five hundred years before, generally desired to have sovereignty–and not just over their hearts and husbands, as Chaucer wrote, but over their lives and circumstances.

They wanted the vote.

The fight was not new. At the turn of the century, it had already marked its one-hundredth birthday. However, as the new century arrived, the suffrage movement gained momentum. It veered into violence, as British suffragettes shattered windows, set fire to empty houses, slashed paintings, and rioted. Women were arrested, jailed, force-fed.

Public sentiment and politicians' opinions were not favorable. When British suffragette Emily Davidson threw herself under the King's horse at a race and was killed, cartoonists were cruel–as they had been all along. Not surprisingly, suffragettes developed their own secret sign of belonging: suffragette jewelry.

A suffragette pin, in 14K gold, enamel, plique-à-jour enamel, with a small pearl, 1" x 1.25", probably made in Newark or New York between 1900 and 1905. The suffragette colors are found in the violet and white flower (possibly a poppy or an anemone) and its buds, while the green is found in the plique-à-jour enamel background, as well as a touch of iridescent green enamel in the buds' capsules. The torch at the top of this heart-shaped pin is undoubtedly symbolic, perhaps of liberty.

Early suffragette jewelry, dating from about 1885 until 1919, used colored stones to spell out the initials of the suffragette motto: **G**reen, **W**hite, and **V**iolet, for **G**ive **W**omen **V**otes, was "written" with peridot, pearl, and amethyst, reminiscent of the earlier "language of stones" in which the first letter of stones' names spelled out DEAREST or REGARD. Although later suffragette jewelry continued to use this combination of stones, some pieces made in both the United States and in Great Britain were enameled. In addition to the suffragette colors, the jewelry could incorporate other emblems: the torch of liberty, for example, or the head of Liberty personified. As one expert on suffragette jewelry–right now a fairly intense area for collectors–noted, when a woman wore a piece of jewelry with the suffragette colors into a garden party, other women knew she was "a sister."

WOMEN AT THE POLLS.

Women at the Polls,

Previous to a late municipal election at Sturgis, Michigan, an appeal was made to the ladies to aid the cause of prohibition by their influence at the polls. The fair ones agreed to the proposition, on condition that they should be allowed to cast votes for their favorite candidates. A committee of twelve ladies was appointed, who set themselves to work canvassing the village and urging upon all females the necessity and propriety of their coming out on election day, and showing that they were not afraid to demand those rights to which by nature they were entitled, but which the male population were unwilling to accord them. On election day they marched to the balloting-place, and one hundred and twenty females exercised the high prerogative of the elective franchise. Their conduct was orderly and dignified; and by their presence at the ballot-box they exerted a healthful influence over the men there congregated, so that the election was characterized as the most quiet one that had ever been held.

A snippet of news from *Frank Leslie's Illustrated News*, in 1868. In spite of the favorable review given of women at the polls, it would be over fifty more years before women were given the vote.

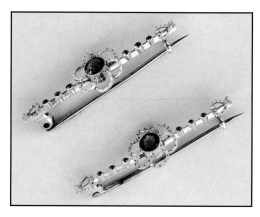

An Arts and Crafts suffragette pin in sterling silver, plique-à-jour (or, possibly, glass that was inset into the pin) and champlevé enamel c. 1905, approximately 1.25" x .875". The suffragette colors of green, white, and violet, for Give Women the Vote, are found in the plique-à-jour enamel (or glass), shading from one to the next without intervening metalwork. Violet champlevé enamel is also found on either side of the plique-à-jour enamel. The woman's head in profile may represent a symbolic idea, such as Liberty personified. The garlands, which cross at the top and bisect the champlevé enamel, are undoubtedly significant–although it's not clear of what (they are possibly laurel leaves, but this is merely a guess).

A rather morbid political cartoon depicting the bones of suffragette Emily Davison, who was killed when she threw herself under the King of England's horse at a race meet.

A pair of suffragette pins, in gold, enamel, amethysts, and demantoid garnets, c. 1900-1905, approximately 1.5" x .50". "Hearts and flowers" seems to underlie the suffragette message here, with stylized enameled flowers in the center, and small stylized hearts (or possibly leaves) at the tips of the pins. The suffragette colors are displayed in the white enamel, the violet amethysts, and the green demantoid garnets. These pins, in their original box, were sold by the London jeweler Percy Edwards Ltd., of Piccadilly.

An unusual pin in unmarked gold (but probably lower karat or even gold-filled), enamel, pearl, and pink sapphire, c. 1900. This pin, with basse taille markings on its leaves, the leaf motif itself, and the rather hand-formed look point to an Arts and Crafts designation, but it also has elements of Art Nouveau. This pin might conceivably have both a pearl and a pink sapphire because it is a suffragette piece, as stones other than the amethyst were sometimes used to represent the violet in "Give Women Votes": One dealer listed a suffragette piece set with a pink tourmaline rather than an amethyst, while another catalogued a suffragette pendant set with an almandine garnet.

Three pins that might have been–or equally well might not have been–worn by suffragettes. The bar pins were both sold as suffragette pins, although it might be that the colors are merely a design element, rather than a political statement. The pin on top is sterling, and enameled in the restrained colors fashionable during the Edwardian period. The flower pin, in enameled base metal but possibly set with real amethysts, is more likely a suffragette pin, as there is no compelling reason to embellish the white flowers with purple stones. The pin on the bottom is possibly of more interest to an enamelist than a historian: It is in brass, but the enamel was applied over a thin layer of gold.

Traipsing Through Time: Suffering for Suffrage

The woman suffrage (using the suffragettes' term) movement is considered to have begun with English writer Mary Wollstonecraft's publication of *A Vindication of the Rights of Woman*, in 1792. Other notable events that led to the eventual enfranchisement of women in both England and America are…

♦ 1832–Unmarried woman of property Mary Smith petitions the British Parliament urging the inclusion of women of property among those allowed to vote for members of Parliament. Parliament laughs.

♦ 1848–Elizabeth Cady Stanton and Lucretia Mott organize the Seneca Falls Convention, at Seneca Falls, New York; Stanton drafts a "Declaration of Sentiments" calling for suffrage and other rights based on the Declaration of Independence; all but suffrage pass.

♦ 1869–Wyoming, still a territory, becomes the first to give women the vote; later, achieving statehood in 1890, refuses to "come in without the women."

♦ 1872–Susan B. Anthony leads a delegation of women to the polls in Rochester, New York, with the intention of voting, and is arrested.

♦ 1875–The U. S. Supreme Court, hearing a case that began with Anthony's arrest in 1872, concurs that citizenship does not automatically confer the right to vote, and that woman suffrage must be decided within the individual states.

♦ 1889–Emmeline Pankhurst and her husband Richard form the Women's Franchise League in Manchester, England.

♦ 1888–Susan B. Anthony organizes the International Council of Women.

♦ 1903–Emmeline Pankhurst and daughter Christabel form the Women's Social and Political Union in Manchester, England.

♦ 1904–Susan B. Anthony organizes the International Woman Suffrage Alliance

♦ 1908–Violent protests begin in England, with middle- and upper-class women breaking windows, burning empty buildings, chaining themselves to railings, slashing paintings, and rioting in battles with police.

♦ 1913–A Franchise Reform Bill fails to pass in Britain's Parliament, and suffragette violence escalates as a result (although many suffragettes do not agree with such tactics). Emily Davidson, throwing herself under the King's horse at a race, becomes the movement's first–and only–martyr.

♦ 1914–With the outbreak of World War I, British suffragettes call a truce to violent tactics and support the nation's war effort, filling jobs vacated by men fighting at the front.

♦ 1918–British Parliament passes the Reform Bill granting women the vote and, though he bitterly opposes it, Prime Minister Asquith signs it into law.

♦ 1920–American women join their British sisters as enfranchised voters.

Art Deco–A Bold New Look for a Weary World

Novelty has charms which the human mind can scarcely withstand.

—William Makepeace Thackery

I am ashamed thro' all my nature to have loved so slight a thing.

—Alfred Lord Tennyson, *Lockesley Hall*

At the end of World War I, a world weary of strife and bloodshed was ready for a new aesthetic. It wanted vibrant colors, bold lines, clean design. In Art Deco, it found all of those.

Just as the Arts and Crafts and Art Nouveau movements arose in revolt against the prevailing heavy, stale, to some extent tasteless, decorative arts of the late Victorian era, Art Deco might be called a backlash against the excesses of trite Art Nouveau design.

A brooch in 18K gold and pearls, in the Art Nouveau style. This piece, with its clichéd curving frame, its generic flower with leaves shaped like lily pads, its small pearl dangle, its lack of any real saving interest or grace, shows to what level Art Nouveau design had sunk–and why Art Deco seemed like such a wonderfully refreshing change.

Sylvie Raulet (1985, 15), writes that by the end of the Edwardian period, Art Nouveau had become passé:

> By 1910, Art Nouveau was discredited, victim of a certain mannered academism. The floral image lost ground, the bindweed became untangled, good sense replaced impetuosity. A desire for severity and simplicity emerged, the representational image and the soft focus disappeared gradually, giving way to stylization and geometric shapes.

Worse yet, Art Nouveau had become trite, almost laughable, a cliché. Raulet (1985, 16) quotes the French magazine *La Mode*'s words addressed to a notable critic: "'The song is becoming monotonous. When shall we be done with the peacock feathers, swans, irises, orchids and that sort of thing?'"

Unlike the Arts and Crafts movement, so strongly guided by William Morris, or Art Nouveau, so closely associated with René Lalique, Art Deco was not linked with any one name. Raulet notes that the seeds of Art Deco design were launched early in the first decade of the twentieth century; she cites two designers, Maurice DuFrêsne and Paul Follot, who both published designs for modern jewelry showing a distinct trend toward the use of geometrical forms in design. However, it also appears that this tendency toward "geometricization of forms" was already to be found in some Edwardian jewelry. Raulet herself notes that the idea of austerity in design was not new: Both the Vienna Secessionists and the Glasgow School under the leadership of Charles Rennie Mackintosh favored design based on straight lines and cubes.

Not that there were no stars to be found in the Deco firmament. The fauvist painter Raoul Dufy designed fabric and furniture in a geometric style echoed in the cubist paintings of artists such as Pablo Picasso and Georges Braque. The painter Leon Bakst used a palette of bright colors to evoke the richness of Egypt, Byzantium, Rome. And designer Gabrielle (Coco) Chanel made costume jewelry not merely respectable, but fashionable and desirable.

A number of advances in stone-setting and -cutting aided jewelers in the creation of the new look. Raulet cites platinum as one innovation, although it had been in use for a number of decades. Discovered by Spanish explorers in South America, platinum was first used for setting stones around the mid-nineteenth century. Its properties–strong, durable, not springy–allowed settings that were finer and less noticeable than those in gold or silver. However, platinum remained relatively rare until new deposits were found in South Africa in 1924.

Gem-cutters helped create the new look by adding a number of different cuts to the prevailing rose and brilliant: baguettes, for example, and trapeziums. Calibré cuts allowed stones to be placed together so closely that gaps were almost invisible. Also, pearls were now much more abundant; jewelers were no longer dependent on haphazard harvesting of natural pearls from the sea. The Japanese businessman Kokichi Mikimoto, granted a patent to culture hemispherical mabe pearls in 1896, in 1908 was given a patent to create spherical pearls.

Art Deco was geometric and bold. It used bright colors, or it used black and white. It used hard, opaque or semi-translucent gems such as coral, turquoise, malachite, chrysoprase, onyx, jade. For added sparkle in less expensive pieces, it very commonly added marcasites. When it also used enamel, the colors were for the most part bright, and fused onto geometric forms. Often, enamel was limited to accents, a hint of black against diamonds or paste.

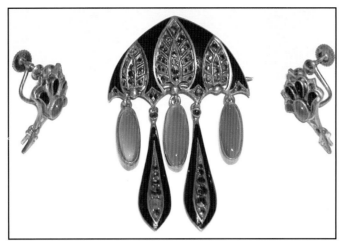

An interesting geometric Art Deco necklace in sterling silver, enamel, and glass, with the central element a piece of green glass with a textured design set into a "diamond" formed by four triangles in silver and plique-à-jour enamel. The design is echoed in the necklace, which also has six-sided oblongs in silver and plique enamel. A very bold and different piece, measuring 24" in length, with the pendant 3" x 1.375". *Courtesy of Robin Allison.*

An interesting Art Deco brooch in 935 silver, enamel, chrysoprase, and marcasites, with matching earrings. The brooch has over-tones, such as the dangles and the spear-shaped elements, that point to Arts and Crafts or Jugendstil design, but the use of chrysoprase cabochons and marcasites seems very Art Deco. Measures 2.125" x 1.875" and is marked 935; probably of German manufacture. *Courtesy of Robin Allison.*

A stunning bracelet in sterling silver, enamel, chrysoprase, and marcasites. Art Deco jewelry, noted for its elegance and geometri-cal designs, also made great use of colored stones, both translucent and opaque. The lovely green chrysoprase is here nicely offset by the black enamel over a geometric swirled pattern. Measures .75" x 6.75"; marked sterling and Germany. *Courtesy of Robin Allison.*

A pair of Art Deco earrings in silver and paste, with enamel accents, showing the very geometrical design characteristic of the period as well as a preference for the look of diamonds and platinum–or, if these didn't quite fit the budget, of silver and paste. Marked 935, HW; 2" x 1". *Courtesy of Robin Allison.*

A selection of three Art Deco bracelets, showing the emphasis on clean lines and color. The top two bracelets are especially similar, with rectangular links. The lower bracelet, with its slightly irregular links alternating with squares, is enameled a bit less vibrantly, in one color. *Courtesy of Robin Allison.*

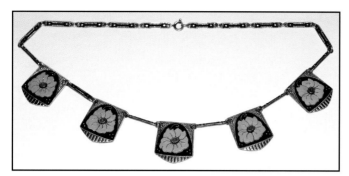

A beautiful Art Deco necklace in silver, enamel, and chrysoprase, with a floral design in green enamel centered with chrysoprase stones of a hue only slightly darker than that of the enameled petals. Opaque or semi-translucent gemstones such as onyx, jade, coral, and chrysoprase are often found in Art Deco pieces. Each section measures .875" x .875", with the necklace measuring 16" in length. *Courtesy of Robin Allison.*

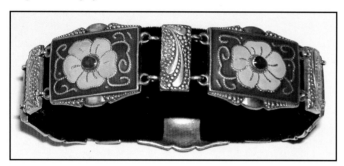

A bracelet that shows a few similarities with the necklace above, especially in the look of the stylized flowers–these enameled in turquoise rather than green, and set with chrysoprase and carnelian cabochons, but still showing the same rather "ropy" wire used to outline the flowers, as well as provide details in the petals. A nice example of the blend of Art Deco style with good champlevé enameling. Undeciphered mark; 7.25" x .75". *Courtesy of Robin Allison.*

Some Art Deco jewelry was whimsical, or fun. A few pieces were enameled with circles in champlevé that resemble balloons.

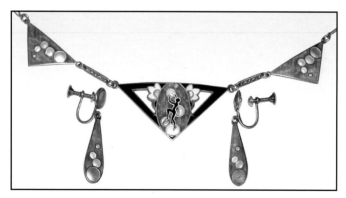

A whimsical Art Deco necklace and matching earrings in sterling silver and enamel. The necklace has a central element showing a sprite-like being, perhaps a clown, balanced on two circles in champlevé enamel, and reaching for a third. Two stylized daisies with basse taille enameling flank the oval cartouche with the clown. The oval itself rests against a triangle in black enamel. The triangular plaques that compose the rest of the necklace, as well as the earrings, are enameled in green with circles that match those in the central part of the necklace. The enamel in the circles has a slightly dimensional look, possibly achieved through a slight rounding in the underlying silver. The enameled section of the necklace measures 3.125" x .75". The earrings measure 1.5" x .25". All are marked sterling, and with the letter E in a square. *Courtesy of Robin Allison.*

A wonderful Art Deco necklace, composed entirely of circles in champlevé enamel, arranged to create triangular elements that form the necklace. A very interesting variation on Art Deco design, in which color and geometry are integral, but which is less angular than many Art Deco pieces. Marked sterling; enameled sections measure 12.5" x .5". *Courtesy of Robin Allison.*

One major addition to the jewelry wardrobe during the Art Deco period was the wristwatch. There are several conflicting stories about the origins of the wristwatch, but the one most often told is that Louis Cartier developed the wristwatch for his friend, the Brazilian aviator Alberto Santos-Dumont. Santos-Dumont had complained about the impossibility of timing his flights while at the controls of an airplane, and asked his friend Cartier to come up with a more practical timekeeper. The result was the wristwatch. Reportedly, Santos-Dumont wore the wristwatch made for him by Cartier in every subsequent flight he made.

The wristwatch fit in perfectly with the new streamlined look in jewelry. Women no longer wore flowery watch pins from which dangled heavy watches. The new watches were almost more a form of jewelry than a means of keeping time. They were worn on thin bands, of leather, or gold, or even bands blazing with diamonds and sapphires; and they often looked more like bracelets than watches. Occasionally, they were decorated with enamel.

A wristwatch in silver and enamel, in a bright green over guilloche. The wristwatch, while not a new invention, became newly popular as a fashion accessory during the 1920s, worn by both men and women. 800 silver; 1" x 1". *Courtesy of Robin Allison.*

Another facet of Art Deco jewelry was the burgeoning popularity of costume jewelry. Although costume jewelry was not a new phenomenon–examples of nineteenth century costume jewelry abound–it gained respectability during the 1920s and 1930s, largely through the influence of designer Gabrielle (Coco) Chanel. Chanel believed that jewelry should not be confined merely to formal occasions; it should fit into everyday life as well. It should also fit one's wardrobe, or costume. Therefore it should be affordable, wearable, and of appropriate size and color. The costume jewelry developed at this time often used base metals instead of gold or platinum, rhinestones instead of diamonds, paste stones instead of rubies or emeralds, and faux pearls rather than cultured ones. Not infrequently, this jewelry was also made with enamel, a fairly inexpensive way of adding color and interest to a brooch or bracelet. (For more about costume jewelry, please see the section on this topic at the end of this chapter.)

Enamel was often used for so-called "useful" objects such as cigarette cases and compacts, for which the enameling tended to be guilloche–with its underlying wavy, geometric patterns, it was the perfect complement to the geometric pieces it adorned. Men's cufflinks too tended occasionally to be enameled, usually in guilloche enamel or geometric champlevé patterns.

A compact in silver and enamel, with a certain Art Deco flair. While the circular center section, with its green guilloche enamel decorated with a garland of flowers, is a timeless design and could have come from many other eras, the corners of this compact not only give it a squared Art Deco look, but they are also enameled in bold colors in a geometric design. Marked 14X (possibly indicating gold rather than silver); 2" x 2". *Courtesy of Robin Allison.*

Egyptian Revival Jewelry

Age cannot wither her, not custom stale
Her infinite variety.
— William Shakespeare, *Antony and Cleopatra*

One subset of Art Deco jewelry often found enameled, sometimes with plique-à-jour enamel, sometimes with cloisonné, basse taille, or champlevé enamel, was Egyptian revival jewelry. Popular during the nineteenth century, Egyptian revival jewelry made a spectacular comeback with the equally spectacular discovery of Tutankhamon's tomb in 1922. While Vivant Denon's description of his travels in Egypt with Napoleon's expeditionary force, published in 1802, provided an entire lexicon for Egyptian design, Tutankamon's tomb provided examples of jewelry quickly emulated by designers. Winged scarabs, perhaps the most common motif found in Egyptian revival jewelry of this period, were fashioned into stickpins, brooches, necklaces, and bracelets. Some necklaces included lotus blossoms, or "amulets" in the form of ankhs and the Egyptian hieroglyph for protection, the *sa* sign, while bracelets show scenes of life in Egypt both past and present.

A marvelous Egyptian revival festoon necklace in sterling silver and enamel, with three stylized lotuses from which depends a scarab. Interestingly, the dangles from both the lotuses and the scarab are in plique-à-jour enamel. The bright blue and the red are often found in such pieces; the yellow is a bit more unusual. Scarabs and lotuses were both important symbols to the ancient Egyptians. Festoon section measures 5.75" x 4". *Courtesy of Robin Allison.*

An unusual Egyptian revival necklace in silver, enamel, turquoise, and amazonite, featuring a very stylized scarab–here little more than an oval cabochon–flanked by creatures with vultures' heads combined with serpent-like bodies which meet in a stylized tail that somewhat resembles a flower, finishing with a pendant amazonite drop. This piece lacks the plique-à-jour wings often associated with such scarab pieces, and also is unusually enameled in blues and greens, rather than the red, lapis blue, and turquoise most often associated with Egyptian revival pieces. Measures 2.75 x 1.5". *Courtesy of Robin Allison.*

An attractive Egyptian revival piece, in silver, enamel, a pearl, and paste stones, in the form of stylized lotus blossoms. Aside from the small lotus dangle at the top of the pendant, this looks as much inspired by Art Deco as ancient Egypt. 800 silver; measures 4" x 1.125". *Courtesy of Robin Allison.*

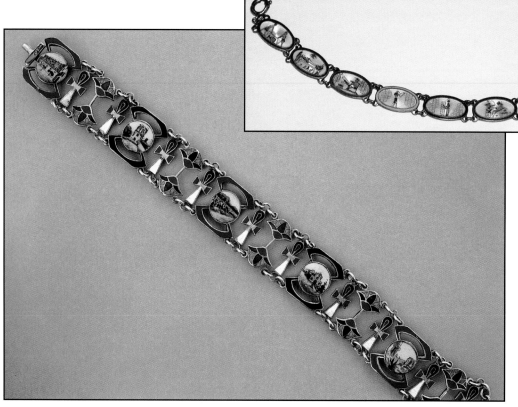

Courtesy of Robin Allison.

Two revival bracelets, both with scenes of life in Egypt. The first bracelet, unusually, shows scenes that might well have come from ancient Egyptian tomb paintings: Bakers bake, scribes write, pharaoh hunts in his chariot. The lower bracelets, with scenes connected by ankhs and lotuses, shows scenes of modern Egypt. Top bracelet measures 7.5" x .375"; lower one measures 7.5" x .5".

A wonderful pair of revival earrings, in silver, enamel, and pastes, in the form of the broad collar worn by Egyptians for special occasions. Interestingly, while the terminals on such collars in ancient Egypt were often in the form of falcons or falcon heads, the broad collars in these earrings end in owls. Falcons were extremely important in ancient Egyptian beliefs, identified with both Horus–and through him with the reigning pharaoh–and with the sun god Ra-Harakhty. Owls, on the other hand, were of little importance, other than serving as the hieroglyph for "m." Stylized scarabs dangle from each of the collars, which measure 2.25" x 1". *Courtesy of Robin Allison.*

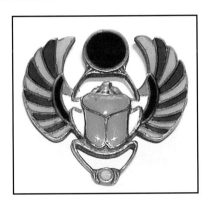

A more usual type of Egyptian revival piece, this one a brooch in silver and enamel, showing a winged scarab pushing the red solar disk before it: In Egyptian mythology, the sun was pushed through the sky on its daily journey, much as the beetle pushed its egg sac before it in daily life. The colors in this piece are also more traditional for revival jewelry of the period. 800 silver; .9375" x .9375". *Courtesy of Robin Allison.*

Vintage and Costume Jewelry

Not all that tempts your wandr'ing eyes
And heedless hearts, is lawful prize;
Nor all, that glisters, gold.

—Thomas Gray, *Ode on … Eton College*

Vintage Jewelry

Jewelry that was made after the Edwardian period, and which does not fall neatly into another category such as Art Deco, is often referred to as vintage. While vintage jewelry is largely beyond the scope of this book, some pieces have been added because they are either fun or fascinating.

Many pieces of vintage jewelry in silver and enamel were manufactured in Germany. Just as Pforzheim had supplied jewelry for Liberty of London (such as that purveyed by the Anglo-British firm of Murrle-Bennett), it later supplied jewelry for designers such as Alice Caviness. A number of these German pieces are extremely well made, and beautifully enameled, and it seemed a shame not to include them. A number of examples of vintage jewelry, besides those few presented in this section, can be found in chapters four and five.

A fun vintage brooch showing a cowboy astride a bucking bronco, in sterling silver, enamel, and marcasites, from Germany. For some reason, Germany was fascinated by the wild west, their imaginations fueled by westerns written by authors such as Karl May. Marked for Alice Caviness, sterling, Germany; 1.5" x 1.5". *Courtesy of Robin Allison.*

A whimsical cat brooch in sterling silver, enamel, and marcasites, also of German origin. A number of the nicer pieces in sterling, enamel, and marcasites were created in Germany, especially in Pforzheim, traditionally a center of jewelry manufacturing. Measures 1.5" x 1.25". *Courtesy of Robin Allison.*

An attractive floral set of brooch and earrings, in silver, enamel, and marcasites. Marked KV for maker, 800 silver; brooch 1.875" x 1.5", earrings, 1.25" x .75". *Courtesy of Robin Allison.*

Just looking at this brooch always makes Dale want to head for the nearest tropical paradise, although this brooch in silver, enamel, and marcasites was actually manufactured not in Tahiti or even Haiti, but in the United States. This wonderful tropical scene has it all–stylized tropical flowers, palm trees, and a colorfully dressed woman carrying a basket on her head. Measures 1.875" in diameter. *Courtesy of Robin Allison.*

A lovely bracelet in sterling silver, enamel, and marcasites, with dimensional-looking stylized daffodils or other flower in different colors. Measures 7" x .875". *Courtesy of Robin Allison.*

Costume Jewelry

Costume jewelry is also not really covered in any depth in this book. In part this is because costume jewelry collectors already have access to a wealth of books on the subject, whether books that cover costume jewelry generally, or books that focus on a specific designer or manufacturer. Also, the topic is so vast that to do it justice would require much more space than that allotted to this book. However, the line between so-called "fine" jewelry and costume jewelry is one that, on close inspection, can be called blurry at best.

In some cases, the line is blurred by the combination of paste or other faux stones in pieces that either also contain gemstones, or are made of silver. A number of pieces included in this book are fine examples of Victorian, Art Nouveau, Arts and Crafts, or Art Deco pieces in silver and enamel, which also happen to be set with paste rather than diamonds, emeralds, rubies, or other precious stones.

In other cases, the line is blurred by a particular designer, who may have chosen to produce both enameled silver jewelry and costume pieces. Alice Caviness is one such designer. The manufacturing firm of Coro, which produced costume pieces in base metal as well as the highly collectible Corocraft pieces in sterling silver, is another example of the cross-over between costume and non-costume jewelry.

In yet other cases, the line seems more like a cultural boundary rather than a general demarcation. In some parts of Europe, for example, jewelry not in 18K gold or platinum is often considered to be costume jewelry. A friend from Ethiopia noted once that a gift of jewelry in anything other than 24K gold is taken almost as an insult. But what about all those wonderful Arts and Crafts pieces that were made primarily in silver, as a philosophical statement against the prevailing view of jewelry as wealth rather than art? What about the Victorian pinchbeck jewelry–gold over lead, the alchemical wonder of the age–set with pearls, amethysts, garnets, or miniatures on ivory?

And in the United States, what did we consider jewelry in 10K gold? In some cases it seems that lower karat gold jewelry was not highly prized–or priced–in this country. Most of the better jewelry from New York and Newark makers was in 14K or 18K gold; 10K gold jewelry seems to have been a mid-range item falling between higher karat gold and gold-filled jewelry.

Therefore a few pieces of costume jewelry have been included in several places in this book, especially in the "Through Time" sections.

The decision to include only a few examples of costume jewelry has nothing to do with relative prices. Or with collectibility: There are collectors who search for a Hattie Carnegie brooch or an Eisenberg ice bracelet with the same dedication we bring to collecting enameled jewelry. Some costume pieces fetch higher prices than many of the pieces of jewelry in this book. In fact, some pieces of costume jewelry fetch sums in the four figures–not including the zeroes to the right of the decimal point!

A gold-filled and enameled costume piece, c. 1900, in the form of a violet set in a partially chased circle. While the attention given to more expensive pieces of the period, such as enameled flower pins in 14K gold, is lacking here–the flower has been stamped out of one piece of metal, rather than being formed of separate petals linked on the underside–some care has been given to its enameling. It, like its gold counterparts, has been enameled in white, over which shaded color and thin lines indicating the petals' veins or markings, has been added. Unmarked; measures approximately 1.125" in diameter.

What Puts the "Cost" in Costume Jewelry?

Some costume jewelry is as expensive as–and in some cases even *more* expensive than–so-called "fine" jewelry. For example, a set of Coro silver, enamel, and rhinestone owls recently sold for more in an online auction than did a pair of 14K gold, enamel, and seed pearl earrings, c. 1900, by Krementz. Recently a Corocraft salamander sold at auction for $1200. A fun Egyptian revival piece by designer Hattie Carnegie in base metal, enamel, and glass beads may sell for several hundred dollars, about the same price asked for a silver and enamel Egyptian revival piece from around 1920. A "rare" Miriam Haskell parure of a necklace, bracelet, and earrings in turquoise-colored glass beads had the asking price of $800, more than was paid for a rare gold and enamel owl brooch by the Newark firm Riker Brothers. Retailers often set even higher prices for costume jewelry–an Alice Caviness parure, comprised of a necklace, earrings, and bracelet, in lavender rhinestones was offered at $900, and a Boucher ivy leaves parure, of a necklace, bracelet, earrings, and brooch, in rhinestones and lucite, had an asking price of $1600.

A striking salamander or lizard brooch by noted maker of costume jewelry, Coro, in silver, rhinestones, and a faux pearl. This piece, especially sought-after by Coro collectors, has sold more than once at online auction for over twelve hundred dollars. Measures 3.25" x 2". *Courtesy of Robin Allison.*

What makes some costume jewelry so, well, costly? Some of the factors are the same for any other collectible item, be it an Art Nouveau bracelet by René Lalique, a Tiffany orchid, or a Newark enameled flower pin:

♦ Famous name brands bring more–Just as a necklace by Louis Comfort Tiffany will sell for more than a similar unsigned necklace, so will a necklace by Miriam Haskell or Hattie Carnegie go for more than one by a lesser known or unknown designer.

♦ Good design is good design–Even if the materials used to manufacture a piece are not particularly costly, the design may influence market value.

♦ Rarity–A scarcer piece can be much more expensive than a more easily found piece. For example, a Charles Horner brooch in silver and enamel, painted to resemble a Russian icon, recently sold for far more than other, larger, pieces made by his company. It was extremely unusual, and quite possibly another piece like it may not be offered for sale in a collector's lifetime. However, with costume jewelry, this truism may be less true. While rare pieces of costume jewelry by a noted designer may cost more, it may also be the case that unusual pieces are ignored–in part because they are not as easily recognized as coming from a certain designer, but possibly also in part because collectors enjoy archetypal pieces by designers or manufacturers.

♦ Desirability–In some ways, rarity factors into this, but other criteria also make a piece desirable. Maker, size, age, and color can all influence how collectible–or desirable–a piece is. An older piece, such as an older Hattie Carnegie piece with the coveted maker's mark of the initials HC enclosed in a diamond, is usually more highly sought after than a newer piece. In part this may be because with age, jewelry can become damaged, destroyed, or lost, thus making earlier pieces scarce. It may also be that fewer pieces were produced in the early stages of a designer's career, before her or his jewelry became fashionable and therefore sold in larger quantities.

♦ More is more (1)–Bigger *is* better–some costume pieces, such as the Egyptian revival pieces by Hattie Carnegie, are quite large; and, as with so-called "fine" jewelry, large pieces are often, though not always, more expensive than smaller pieces. Even though the materials used to manufacture such pieces may not be intrinsically as valuable as the gold and gemstones used in fine jewelry, it is still more expensive to produce large pieces than small ones.

♦ More is more (2)–The more the merrier–a parure, or matched set of jewelry, often costs significantly more than the individual pieces would bring if sold separately. There are exceptions, of course; some people buy sets at auction and then break them up to sell individually. This happened recently with a water lily brooch and earrings by David Andersen; because the design is relatively rare, the buyer was able to sell earrings and brooch separately for a profit. However, a pair of earrings in a desirable color and pattern by the costume jewelry maker Matisse Renoir might sell for approximately $20 at auction, while a matching brooch might sell for $45. Sold together as a set, the matched brooch and earrings might sell for $85 or more.

♦ Putting on the glitz–Rhinestone pieces are often more expensive than those without rhinestones; pieces with more and/or larger rhinestones will in general cost more than pieces without, with fewer, or with smaller, rhinestones.

However, one of the main reasons for focusing less on enameled costume jewelry than we might otherwise have done, both in our collecting and in writing this book, is that most later costume jewelry does not use true hard or vitreous enamel–that is, enamel fused to metal at high temperatures. Most later enameled costume jewelry uses "soft" enamel, which is often an acrylic or other polymer. (For more on hard vs. soft enamel, please see chapter two.)

One costume jewelry firm producing jewelry with true enamel is Matisse Renoir. Their jewelry has an interesting flair, which often includes overlying copper designs over the enamel. Also, some of their jewelry displays unusual enameling techniques, including the use of foil.

A set of leaf brooch and earrings by the maker Matisse (also sometimes known as Matisse Renoir). In hard enamel, often with foil or other accents, theirs is some of the more interesting costume jewelry in true vitreous enamel.

Endnotes Chapter One

[1]Snowman (1990, 14) quotes A. Castellani as saying:
[I]n the decline of painting, sculpture and architecture in the days of Michelangelo, jewellery underwent the same fate. In the seventeenth century it was already in an advanced stage of decay and lost every merit, and every reminiscence of good taste, under the fatal domination of the Spaniards and Austrians over Italy.
[2]There has been some suggestion that not only was the artistic value of materials a factor for Art Nouveau designers, especially Lalique, but so was cost. To some extent Lalique may have wished to evade prohibitive government tariffs on the so-called "precious materials" in France, and thus turned to materials not incurring a heavy tax. (Museu Calouste Gulbenkian, *Sala Lalique*, 1997, 4)

Price Guide for Chapter One

p. 21: Geo 14K REGARD lckt $3000-$6000; 2 Vict DEAREST rngs: lg $2500-$3500, sm $1000-$1500; sm coll Vict mrng jewl: 18K pansy br $600-$800, 14K w/ dmds bclt $1250-$1500, jet e/r $100-$150; Vict 14K w/ sm dmds co & turq enam br $800-$1200; **p. 22 :** Fr Geo 18K w/ dmds & prls co bl sl-bclt $7000-$8500; Fr Geo 18K w/ dmds snake bclt $6500-$9500*; Vict 18K w/ turq, garn & prls snake bclt $2500+; Vict snake turq enam snake bclt $750-$1000; Fr Geo 18K w/ dmds, rub & prl neck $3000-$5500; **p. 23 :** sm Geo/Vict 18K e/r $250-$450; **Mourning:** 2 Vic br: Nk 14K w/ prl mtt blk enam violet $500-$750; 2 Nk Vic flr pins: 14K w/ prl

flr $500-$750, gf st-p $100-$150; **p. 24:** Vict demi w/ s-prls $500-$600; Vict 18K t-d'ep p-wtch $300-$600; pr Vict 14K t-d'ep brclts $400-$500 both; **p. 25 :** Vict 14K w/ sm prls turq enam e/r $350-$500; sm Nk Vict 14K w/ dmd & s-prls bow pin $250-$300; **p. 26 : Revivals:** Etr rev 18K w/ crl e/r $600-$1000; Vict 14K w/ s-prls Etr/Ren rev e/r $1000-$1800; Vict Gth rev Lim bclt $750-$900; Vict 18K w/ sm dmds rng $700-$750; Vict 18K w/ sm dmds scrb bclt $1500-$2200; **p. 29:** Vict bl & wh chmp enam sash-p $125-$175; **Cameos:** Vict 18K w/ sm prls & enam flrs cam br $2000; Vict 18K w/ prls blk enam cam pend $1500-$2000; Vict 14K blk & wh enam cam br $600-$750; Vict 18K w/ prls cherub cam pend $2500-$2750; **p. 30:** Vict/AN plq angel pend $1500-$2000; 4 Vict 14K st-p: phrh $300-$350, tiger $500-$550, lion $500-$550, pirate $450-$475; Vict sigma chi lckt Vict $300-$500; lckt bclt $500-$500; **p. 31:** 10K lckt br $75-$250; **Hearts:** Vict hrt lckt w/ turq enam $200-$250; Vict red guil hrt lckt w/ chrb $400-$450; AN guil enam hrt lckt w/ iris $500-$550; Fr hrt w/ iris $75-$195; **p. 32:** AN sl-lckt w/ lady, web $1000-$1250; A&C hrt pend $250-$300; coll 3 hrt chm bclts $1500-$2000 ea; coll 3 guil hrt chm bclts $750-$1000 ea; W.L. hrt chms $75-$150 ea; **p. 33:** Vict 14K hrt w/ violet $400-$750; sm 10K vict hrt w/ f-m-n $100-$125; Vict bl bird bclt $1250-$1500; Vict bl bird br $75-$125; C.H. bl bird br $275-$550; **p. 34:** Nk Vict 14K w/ sm dmd Ren rev wtch-p $250-$600; Vict wtch-p w/ sm opal $125-$250; Vict gf iris br w/ chmp f-m-n $85-$120; 3 Nk Vict pins w/ chmp f-m-n: 14K st-p w/ sm dmd $200-$225, 10K hon-p w/ enam fl $75-$225, 14K 2hrts w/ violets $225-$550; Nk 14K br w/ 3 sm flrs $300-$600; Nk Vict 14K pansy in w/bn $300-$400; **p. 35: Vict Flowers:** 2 Vict 14K w/ s-prls flr br $375-$650 ea; Nk Vict 14K w/ s-prls & sm dmd flrs in sickle br $450-$800; gp 4 Nk pansies: sm 10K pend $125-$150, med 14K pend $450-$800, lg 14K pend $500-$875, 14K br w/ prl $450-$800; Nk Vict 14K w/ sm prl pansy e/r $800-$1250; 4 14K st-p $225-$450 ea; **p. 36 :** Nk Vict 14K w/ sm dmd & s-prls f-m-n br $600-$750; Nk Vict 14K br w/ 3 sm f-m-n $350-$400; **Honeymoon:** C.T. 14K w/ sm prls blk mtt cres br $200-$425; 4 hon-p w/ f-m-n: 10K $100-$250, 14K $200-$350 ea; 5 hon-p in 14K $250-$450 ea; **p. 37:** 2 Nk 14K br w/ enam flrs: Vict $250-$500; AN $350-$600; Nk AN 14K w/ sm dmd & prls irid pnk pansy fest neck $950-$1500; 3 Nk AN 14K flr br $500-$1200 ea; **p. 38: Cloverleaves:** Vict 14K guil w/ flrs p-wtch $500-$750; Krem Vict 14K demi: br $700-1500, e/r $600-$1200; 2 Krem Vict hon-p $250-$450 ea, sm Nk 14k br $150-$350; coll sm br & pend: Vict 14K in w/b $150-$400, A&C 14K w/ prl pend $250-$450, D.A. pend $40-$75; C.H. br $400-$700; vint br w/ marc $75-$100; Trf bl cost br $35-$60; **Austro-Hungarian:** e/r w/ bl flrs $350-$400, pend w/ lg bq-prl & pst $1200-$1500, **p. 40:** cit pend w/ prls $500-$500, br w/ min & enam flrs & pst $750-$800, demi w/ ame $1750-$2000, qtrfl neck w/ grn pst & prls $1000-$1250; **p. 41 :** Fr AN grn plq w/ opals pl-au-cou $2500-$3000; A&C plq enam w/ cam $500-$700; **p. 42:** A&C drgfly br $300-$400; A&C plq neck w/ bq-prls $750-$1000; Vict/A&C fest neck w/ turq & prls $800-$1000; A&C fest neck w/ mnstn $800-$1000; **p. 44: Arts & Crafts:** 2 pend w/ mabe prl $500-$750 ea; lt bl pend w/ m-o-p $250-$300; bl & gr enam pend $250-$300; **p. 45:** Brit 15K w/ m-o-p lotus pend $600-$1200; Eu A&C pend w/ pnk tour $1500-$1750; U.S. 14K A&C pend w/ tour $450-$600;; Brit A&C wh Ruskin br $30-$60; **p. 47:** Germ jgstl pnk plq pend $700-$800; **Scandinavian**: Vict guil "storm" br $350-$400; **p. 48**: Vict guil ship br $150-$350; B.H. dk bl guil fest neck $500-$600; vint blk & wh cuff bclt $250-$275; vint guil flrs bclt $200-$300; mod reindeer bclt $250-$275; vint reindeer brcl $250-$300; **p. 49: Mexican**: M.deT. blk & yell set $1000-$1500, M.deT. bl & wh demi $1000-$1250, vint mermaid br $75-$150; vint fish br $75-150; **p. 50** : AN lckt w/sm dmd $150-$325; 18K stck-p w/ sm dmds $125-$300; 18K lckt $650-$1200; **p. 51: Women**: Vict -p-wtch w/ bl guil $350-$400; A&C pend $750-$1000; A&C plq neck w/ carn $1500-$2000; A&C/AN Lim neck w/ pst & prls $1000-$1200; AN sl lckt w/ lt bl bkgd $1000-$1200; **p. 52**: AN/pre-R 14K w/ sm dmds, stars in bkgd br $1500-$1750; AN Byz ldy w/ yell guil bkgd sl-lckt $1000-$1250; H.L. red guil bkgd n-pd $1000-$1200; 2 Edw plq: l. pend w/ harp $2000+, r. sl-lckt w/ daisies $1250-$1500; **Woman & nature**: 14K w/ dmds plq pend $1000-$1500; plq w/ bq-prl grn flws bl hair br $750-$800; **p. 53**: bl quil bkgd w/ plq flr & bq-prl br $1200-$1500; M.M. plq w/ ppl iris br $750-$1000; ppl bkgd & bl flrs br $300-$400; plq drgfl ldy w/ grn pst $3500-$4000; It iris ldy $300-$400; **p. 54: AN Byzantine woman**: All. 14K w/ dmds & prls irid enam lrgnt $4000-$7000; coll. 14K All.: lckt w/ dmds & emr $2000-$2500, br $1250-$1500, st-p $500-$650; **p. 55**: All st-p w/dmds & sm prl $450-$750; lckt w/ lt bl bkgd $800-$1000; **AN Nature**: M.M. dk bl w/ pst drgnf br $300-$350; AN drgnfl w/ flrs sl/lckt $500-$500; M.M. plq bird neck $2000-$2500; **p. 56**: U.S. plq bat w/ stars $1500-$1750; AN plq drgnf w/ turq & pst br $1000-$1200; M.M. plq bee w/ bq-prl & pst $1500-$1700; Fr AN 18K w/ s-prls plq Mary pend $250-$300; **p. 57 : Peacocks**: P.Fr. AN brass fthr bkl $1500-$1600; G.H. A&C pend w/ opals & prls $3000-$4500; U.S. qtrfl chmp enam br $375-$460; M.H. AN guil br $275-$400; **p. 58**: 3 Edw br w/ pst: top l. $150-$200, r. $350-$400, bottom $350-$400; AD w/ frst-gl cost pend $300-$325; A.C. br w/ marc br $200-$250; lg. U.S. vint cost br $50-$75; **p. 59**: vint fil br $35-$60; Mex. e/r $35-60; vint Trf. gf br: $25-$60; **U.S. Art Nouveau**: 3 iris br $300-$350 ea; **p. 60**: qtrfl iris br $250-$300; lily br $250-$275; **p. 61: Asian**: chat n-pd $250-$275; vint Chin clsn "egg" e/r $250-$300; vint Chin clsn carn bclt $500-$600; vint Chin turq br $250-$300; vint Ind.Mog w/ crl & prls e/r $350-$400; **p. 62**: Tosh.vint bclt $400-$500; Jap vint flrs: belt $1000-$1250, bkl $500-$500; Siam peacock br: $65-$145; **p. 63: Edwardian**: 3 bclts $100-$150 ea; plq w/ pst pend $1000-$1250; M.M. med bl guil lckt w/ marc $450-$500; **p. 64**: 2 guil enam fest neck w/ bq-prls & pst $500-$600 ea; W.&B. 14K w/ sm prl lav guil pin $200-$450, Nk 14K w/ sm prls bib pin $45-$125; Nk 10K Edw f-m-n br $100-$300; **p. 65**: Nk 14K w/ prls lt bl f-m-n br $800-$2000; styl flrs neck $350-$400; **Suffragette**: Nk AN 14K & prl plq br w/torch & flr $1200-$2400; **p. 66**: U.S. A&C plq br w/ head $250-$750; Brit A&C 15K w/ ame & grn garn pr br in orig box $1500-$2750; **p. 67**: A&C 10K w/ prl & pnk saph lvs br $250-$500; Vict cost br w/ ame $35-$100; 2 Vict bar pins: t. cost $60-$80, b. $75-$150; **p. 69: Art Deco**: plq & gls neck $500-$600; e/r w/ blk enam & pst $350-$400; blk enam w/ chrys & marc demi $350-$450; blk enam w/ grn pst or chrys & mar bclt $400-$500; 3 rect link bclts $150-$200 ea; **p. 70**: blk & turq enam w/ chrys neck $400-$500; turq & brn enam w/ chrys and carn bclt $450-$500; bl enam w/ cir neck $250-$300; "sprite" demi $275-$350; grn guil w/w $250-275; **p. 71**: grn guil cpt **p. AD Egyptian revival**: scrb fest neck $1500-$2000; **p. 72**: plq scrb w/ turq dngl neck $1800-$2000; plq styl-lot neck w/ turq & prls $1800-$2000; "tomb scenes" bclt $275-$425; mod scene bclt $300-$600; **p. 73**: scrb dngl e/r w/ pst $400-$425; wg-scrb br $200-$225; **Vintage**: bronco br w/ marc $125-$150; cat br w/ marc $100-$150; **p. 74**: rose demi w/ marc $400-$450; woman br w/ marc $125-$150; flr bclt w/ marc $150-$200; Vict gf pend $35-$85; **p. 75**: Cc. lizard br w/ fx prl & rh-st $1200-$1500.

⋆These bracelets sometimes have asking prices of $20,000 or more, especially in major metropolitan areas, such as London.

Chapter Two

An Excursus on Enamel

Enameling is a precious art which, owing to its prominence in the works of bygone days, has occupied a privileged place in public and private collections. It is the duty of contemporary artists to create, for our own use and for our museums, works of art that lend themselves to enamel.

—Lucien Falize, 1893 (cited in Snowman, 1990, 62)

A matching pin and bracelet in sterling silver and enamel, by David Andersen of Norway, c. 1950. The bracelet, similar to one shown in chapter one, measures .50" x 8", the pin 1.25" x .875". The enameling, which makes great use of basse taille or guilloche, champlevé, and painted or, more likely, transfer enameling to create scenes, is characteristic of Andersen's jewelry. This set shows the use of several different enameling techniques to create a complex work with pictorial elements. *Courtesy of Uncommon Treasures, Portland, OR.*

A precious art–yes, enameling is that, especially in the hands of the most talented designers and enamelists. But what exactly is enamel?

The easy answer is: Enamel is powdered glass on a metal background, fused to it by extremely high heat. The real answer is a lot more complicated, because enamel, as Falize implied, has a long history. And over its long history, many types and techniques of enameling have been developed.

Although new technologies are blurring the category somewhat, traditional enamel is *vitreous*–that is, it is basically a fusion of silica, soda, and lime–it is glass, finely ground into a powdered form. In most cases it is combined with various substances, such as metallic oxides, that act as coloring agents. Other agents, notably calx, can also be added to create various degrees of opacity, as enamel, like other forms of glass, is inherently transparent or translucent.

Enamel is placed on metal and then baked in a kiln, usually at temperatures above 1400 degrees Fahrenheit.[1] The glass fuses to the metal, forming a smooth, glossy surface. Depending on what technique is being used by the enamelist, the enamel can be sifted onto metal prepared with a binding agent, it can be wet-packed (mixed with a small amount of binding agent and distilled water until it forms a paste and then packed into a cell or a hollow in the metal), or it can be painted onto a metal surface or a previously enameled surface.

A Swiss gold and enamel brooch nicely painted in a scene reminiscent of pre-Raphaelite artists such as Sir Lawrence Alma-Tadema, noted for his scenes of life in antiquity. *Courtesy of Nelson Rarities, Portland, ME.*

Enameling on Metal

While enamel had a long tradition going back almost four millennia, had been used by great jewelers in the past, and figured in some Victorian jewelry, its use became widespread among some Arts and Crafts metalworkers. According the Karlin, Alexander Fisher, one of the finest Arts and Crafts enamelists (Karlin calls him "the undisputed master of enameling at this time"), had studied in France and later taught others. Karlin notes that a variety of enamel techniques were used, including cloisonné, champlevé, and Limoges. (Karlin, 1993, 30) In part, enamel may have been prized by Arts and Crafts jewelers because of their backward-looking world view: Enameling had been an important element in medieval and Renaissance metalworking.

Alexander Fisher was noted not only for his fine enamel work, but also for his writings on enamel. In his writing, he articulated many precepts still used today. Among these were the idea that enamel fused best to pure metals. Copper, fine silver, and 24K gold were considered ideal media for enameling–despite the fact that New York and New Jersey makers used primarily 14K gold, and great French jewelers worked primarily in 18K gold. Surfaces were also to be exceedingly clean before enamel was applied; Fisher recommended dipping them in a warm solution of acid diluted with water before beginning the enameling process. This acid bath, sometimes referred to as "pickle," is still used to clean surfaces that have become tainted while being fired. Fisher also recommended the use of pure, clean enamels. (Although he was a leading enamelist, Fisher worked primarily in copper, with only a few pieces of silver jewelry attributed to him.)

To this day, many enamelists continue to prefer pure metals, claiming that enamel will behave capriciously on less pure metals, and that the desired outcome of the firing process will be less certain.

While it is clear that Fisher's comments on clean surfaces are correct, it is less obvious that only pure metals can be used for enameling. As the many successfully enameled 18K, 14K, 12K, and even 10K gold pieces of antique jewelry show, less pure metals are also suitable for enameling. Sterling silver, as well, is not a pure metal, and there are many pieces of enameled sterling silver jewelry.

However, in one internet enamelists' forum, it was noted that enameling on metals such as bronze or brass does create some difficulties, perhaps because the high tin content of these alloys makes them unsuitable for traditional "hot" enamel; oxidation does not occur satisfactorily. And indeed, the enameled suffragette pin shown in chapter one was enameled on gold *over* brass rather than directly on brass.

Because of the invention of various polymer enamels that can either be applied cold, or that are to be baked at low temperatures in a conventional oven, sometimes a distinction between "hot" and "cold" enamel is made. "Hot" enamel is the traditional vitreous enamel that is fired at high temperatures in a kiln. "Cold" enamel, on the other hand, is usually some type of polymer that is either applied without heat and left to dry, or baked at a low temperature (around 200 degrees Fahrenheit) in a conventional oven. Cold enamel is also sometimes referred to craft enamel, or soft enamel. While cold enamel in no way takes the place of glass enamel that when fired hardens to form a gem-like surface, it does have its uses. It is especially helpful in repairing slight damage to an enameled piece; this topic is addressed in chapter six.

A Short History of Enameling

The first enameling was *cloisonné* although, ironically, the first cloisonné was not enameled. According to most sources, the first cloisonné jewelry was created in ancient Egypt. At first the cloisons, or cells, of Egyptian cloisonné were filled with semi-precious stones–most frequently carnelian, lapis lazuli, and turquoise. However, at some point early on[2] the Egyptians discovered that it was possible to substitute a frit, or non-clay ceramic material[3] covered with soda-lime silica glaze and fired, for the laboriously cut stones. This frit, which could be tinted in a number of different colors, is sometimes called *faience*. Frit, or faience,

was frequently used as a substitute for lapis lazuli and turquoise. While the finest work still used stone, in many cases, either for color or convenience, faience was also used, often alongside semi-precious stones. The frit frequently did not last, as the many empty cloisons in ancient Egyptian jewelry attest.

One enamelist places the earliest surviving true (vitreous) enamels in Minoan and Mycenaean Crete, about 1424-1400 B.C., with repoussé (what we would probably call *champlevé*) enameling and cloisonné enameling on the bezel and band of a ring.[4]

Whatever the merits of this claim, it is known that enameling was used by the Greeks as early as the fifth century B.C. Enameling was also known to the early inhabitants of the British islands, and evidence has been found for enameling on East Anglian Anglo-Saxon metalwork.[5] During late Roman and Byzantine periods (the fourth through the twelfth centuries A.D.), enameling was used to create religious works on metal.

Enameling played an important part in Renaissance jewelry, used by among others the great goldsmith and jeweler Benvenuto Cellini, whose writings on metalworking and jewelry-making are still cited today. Although cloisonné enameling is sometimes said to have been reintroduced to the Western jewelry-making tradition from Asia, an enameled cloisonné cross from seventeenth-century Italy was recently offered for sale. The cross had ornate arms with inlays encircling the letters IC (for Jesus) on the left arm, and XC (for Christ) on the right arm. In the center was a bust of Christ. The enamel, which was thick and much of which had been lost, was in turquoise and dark blue. The use of champlevé enameling also continued during this period.

Perhaps the most interesting innovation in enameling during the late medieval and early Renaissance periods was the introduction of painting with enamels, sometimes referred to as *Limoges* enameling after the French city where it was first developed in the fifteenth century. It remained much in use through the nineteenth century, especially for the enameling of pendants and watches, and lent itself to the flowery jewelry in vogue during the early and mid-Victorian periods. Limoges enameling was also popular with British jewelers and metalworkers in the Arts and Crafts tradition.

Probably the next major innovation in enameling occurred after the industrial revolution. Machine-turning–the creation of repeated exact (usually geometric) patterns created by machines–was used under translucent enamels to create *guilloche* enameling.

During the nineteenth century, a number of innovations in enameling occurred. Among these was the use of enamel *sur paillons* purportedly invented by Alexis and Lucien Falize, the introduction of *iridescent* enamels, and *plique-à-jour* enameling.

Traipsing Through Time: Advances in Enameling

The fine art of enameling has a long and rich history. Before it became one of the major tools of Arts and Crafts and Art Nouveau jewelers, enameling had incorporated a number of innovations and improvements. Among them are:

♦ Around 3000 B.C.–Egyptians develop the technique of creating cells, or cloisons, which they fill with semi-precious stones cut to fit, or a frit composed of a glazed mixture of quartz and other materials.

♦ Around 1400 B.C.–Minoans either discover cloisonné enamel or borrow the concept from Egypt; and also create the first known champlevé enamel, filling depressions in metal with enamel.

♦ Around 500 B.C.–The Greeks use true vitreous enamel on gold.

♦ Around 50 B.C.–Caesar finds inhabitants of the British Isles using enamel.

♦ From around 400-1300 A.D.–Byzantine and medieval artists and craftsmen create religious works using enamel.

♦ Around 1400–Artisans in Limoges, France develop the technique of painting with enamels.

♦ In 1540, Benvenuto Cellini begins work on his famous gold-and-enamel salt cellar; twenty years later, he writes his treatise on goldsmithing and jewelry.

♦ Around 1800–The industrial revolution leads to machine-turned metal used under translucent enamel to create guilloche enamel.

♦ Around 1870– Cloisonné enamel reaches its height with the enamels of Lucien Falize, many of which incorporate Japanese-inspired designs.

♦ Around 1890–Iridescent enamel is introduced and widely used in American-made Art Nouveau jewelry.

♦ Around 1890–Art Nouveau jewelers such as René Lalique perfect plique-à-jour enameling.

♦ 1897–Jubilee enamel–brightly colored iridescent enamel–is introduced as Britain celebrates Queen Victoria's sixty years on the throne.

Types of Enamel and Enameling Techniques

basse taille (pronounced boss tie')–Literally meaning "low figure" in French, basse taille enamel makes used of designs stamped, engraved, or otherwise impressed on metal. Translucent enamel, fired over these designs, allows them to be easily visible.

While this technique in some ways resembles guilloche enamel, there is a noticeable difference. Guilloche enamel creates an even, regular pattern, often of zig-zags or other geometric forms. Basse taille designs, on the other hand, tend not to cover the entire surface of the underlying metal, and are also more irregular, as can be seen in the work of some of the American and Norwegian jewelers, who were masters of basse taille enameling.

An Art Nouveau buckle, 3.5" x 2.875", in silver and enamel that uses both basse taille markings and champlevé enameling (see below) to show dragonflies and pansies. Basse taille lines create stripes that give a feeling of dimensionality to the pansies' petals: The stripes create the illusion that the petals fold down and curve slightly. Basse taille circles add texture to the dragonflies' wings, while lines in bands across the body give it a shimmery effect. Marked STG SIL. *Courtesy of Robin Allison.*

A butterfly by the Danish maker Meka, in silver and enamel. Here basse taille markings are put to a different use: While the basse taille markings above added almost illusory effects to the piece, here the markings–such as the sunburst design and wavy lines–in the wings are purely decorative, and in no way mimic real markings on a butterfly's wing. In fact, they more resemble stylized flowers, stems, and leaves, than anything to do with the butterfly's true appearance. Measures approximately 1.375" across.

champlevé (pronounced shahmp-luh-vey')–This technique literally means "raised field" in French, and refers to enamel placed in indentations in metal. These indentations can be created by hammering; casting; or pressing. This technique is easier than cloisonné, with its shaped wire, but lends itself to less intricate designs. It is also useful when the enamelist wants enameled accents, rather than wishing to cover the entire surface of a piece.

A spherical Victorian watch fob in 14K gold and enamel, approximately .875" in diameter. Here the enamel was used to create the small blue champlevé flowers (here also in light pink with green leaves) commonly found in some jewelry c. 1890. The missing enamel shows how small depressions, formed when the piece was cast, create an effect close to that of cells formed by wire in cloisonné enameling. However, cloisonné is a more complicated technique, and one generally not used by American manufacturers; the Massachusetts-based Thomae & Sons and the Watson Co. are two exceptions.

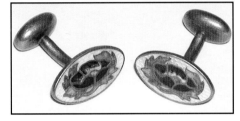

Cufflinks in silver and enamel, c. 1900, .625" x .375", with a design of poppies created through the use of cloisonné enameling. It is somewhat difficult to differentiate this cloisonné enamel from champlevé enamel, but the cufflinks are marked GEN. CLOISONNE, and were manufactured by the Massachusetts-based firm Chas. Thomae & Sons, a rather upscale New England maker that created pieces for Tiffany & Co. This firm also made the brooch with the gold bee paillon shown below, under *paillon*. *Courtesy of Robin Allison.*

Right:
A pair of Chinese earrings in unmarked silver gilt and enamel, with jade dangles, in the form of baskets, 2.625" x 1.125". Here, as on the upper edge of the bracelet above, the cloisonné design is raised above the surface of the earrings, so that the cloisons formed by wire and filled with enamel can be seen clearly. *Courtesy of Robin Allison.*

Far right:
A thimble in cloisonné enamel, again showing the wire that forms divisions or cells into which enamel is wet-packed and then fired. Again, the difference between champlevé and cloisonné enamel can be seen; the wire is much thinner than the walls formed by depressions in the metal in champlevé enameling.

cloisonné (pronounced klwah-zone-nay')–Probably the oldest enameling technique, cloisonné is said to have originated in ancient Egypt, although Minoan Crete has also been suggested as a candidate for the first enameled pieces. In this process, wire is used to create cells, or cloisons, which are then filled with enamel. A number of different colors can thus be used side-by-side to create a crisp design without the enamel running and blurring during firing. This technique is said to have been imported from Japan and China, but a seventeenth century cloisonné cross from Italy indicates that is was used during the Renaissance in Europe. The quality of the cloisonné work displayed in the cross, however, is quite mediocre compared to later cloisonné work by the best nineteenth century enamelists, most notably Lucien Falize. Falize's Japanese-inspired cloisonné pieces are some of the most beautiful ever created.

A Chinese bracelet in silver gilt and cloisonné enamel, .75" wide. Here the cloisons, or cells, form a design of bamboo stalks and leaves in one panel, and of flowers, a butterfly, and a frog in another. While there are some similarities in appearance between the cloisonné shown here and the champlevé shown above, the wire separating the cloisons is much finer than the silver or gold between the depressions in the champlevé. The difference can especially be seen on the top of the bracelet, which interestingly has a cloisonné design without enamel in between the cloisons, so that the way the cells are formed can easily be seen in the raised quatrefoil flowers and the leaves outlined by wire. *Courtesy of Robin Allison.*

grisaille (pronounced greez-eye'-yuh)–One of the most difficult enameling techniques, grisaille requires layering painted enamel in black and white to create a picture that in some ways resembles a black-and-white photograph. There are few examples of this type of enameling (although there are one or two modern enamelists who have chosen to work in this demanding genre), but the locket below shows an attempt to mimic grisaille work through the use of a transfer in black and white.

A Victorian locket in silver and enamel, which is in black and white, similar to the enamel created by the difficult grisaille technique. While here the design was almost certainly created by transfer enameling, true grisaille uses layer upon layer of black and white enamels to create the impression of an etching or an old-fashioned black-and-white photograph (one where the edges are not especially crisp and clear). For an example of monochromatic enameling in the grisaille technique, please see under Boucheron in chapter three. *Courtesy of Robin Allison.*

guilloche (sometimes spelled *guilloché*; pronounced gee-yosh', with a hard g, or gee-yo-shay')–This technique, which uses machine-engraved metal under translucent enamel to create a beautiful geometric effect, is perhaps most widely associated with the great jeweler Carl Fabergé. Many of the pieces designed by him and created by the large number of artists and artisans who worked for him use guilloche enamel as a base for lavishly decorated pieces. Among Fabergé's best-known pieces are the guilloche-enameled Easter eggs created for Tsar Nicholas II and his family at the end of the nineteenth and beginning of the twentieth centuries.

Guilloche enamel was also used in France. Lucien Falize developed a technique that combined cloisonné and guilloche: Cloisons were filled with enamel over machine-turned metal. Guilloche enamel, however, is perhaps more associated with the twentieth century. It was popular for some Edwardian jewelry, including suffragette pins, and in the 1920s and 1930s Art Deco guilloche compacts, cigarette cases, and other objects, as well as some jewelry, were widely manufactured.

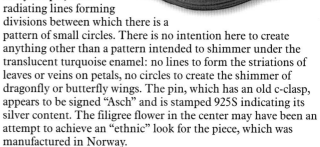

A pin in sterling silver and translucent turquoise blue guilloche enamel, 1.25" x .75", date unknown but probably early 20th century. Here the guilloche design is fairly simple, with radiating lines forming divisions between which there is a pattern of small circles. There is no intention here to create anything other than a pattern intended to shimmer under the translucent turquoise enamel: no lines to form the striations of leaves or veins on petals, no circles to create the shimmer of dragonfly or butterfly wings. The pin, which has an old c-clasp, appears to be signed "Asch" and is stamped 925S indicating its silver content. The filigree flower in the center may have been an attempt to achieve an "ethnic" look for the piece, which was manufactured in Norway.

A rather strange brooch in copper and enamel, which appears to employ cloisonné enameling in conjunction with guilloche–or basse taille–markings. Here the markings both create an effect, such as of leaves in the palm fronds and ripples in the ocean, and also a guilloche-like pattern in the sky. The truly interesting thing about this piece is that a fair amount of time and effort have gone into creating a piece of very little value. And while one might suspect that this piece is in champlevé rather than cloisonné, a close inspection of the brooch allows one to see and feel the wire separations. Approximately 1" in diameter, unmarked. (For another example of guilloche or basse taille and cloisonné enamel please see under pansies in chapter five p. 158; the Watson pansy brooch employs both techniques.)

A Riot of Rosebuds: Guilloche and Roses Through Time

Gather ye rosebuds while ye may,
Old time is still a-flying;
And this same flower that smiles to-day
To-morrow will be dying.

—Robert Herrick, "To the Virgins,
to Make Much of Time"

From the Victorian era through Edwardian and Art Deco, passing on to more modern times, guilloche enameling decorated with roses (and, less often, other flowers) has been an overwhelmingly popular motif. Produced in pins and pendants by Charles Horner, by Scandinavian masters such as Marius Hammer and Aksel Holmsen, by American manufacturers of compacts and perfumes, guilloche and roses have remained an enduring favorite. Most often the roses are rather stylized, even sketchy, but they also appear in naturalistic guise, often   through the use of transfers.

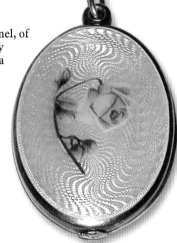

A locket in silver and enamel, c. 1900, probably of British origin. Here the roses painted over the wavy guilloche design are part of a garland strung from two gold foil ribbons, from which also hang blue enameled ribbons ending in a trefoil gold pattern in paillons. Unmarked; measures approximately 1.125" in diameter.

Two brooches in silver and guilloche enameling, both from Norway. The brooch on the top, by well-known Norwegian designer Aksel Holmsen, has two rather sketchily rendered roses and leaves, possibly done with transfer enameling, surrounded by stars. At first glance these stars appear to be created by paillons; a closer examination shows that they are a raised design in the silver, and enameled in gilt. The pin has a simple c-clasp, and probably dates from the early part of the 20th century. The brooch on the bottom, by Ivar T. Holt, was actually sold as having been manufactured by British designer Charles Horner, who produced a number of such guilloche with roses pieces. The somewhat simplified rosebud is surrounded by an oval of black enamel, giving the piece an Art Deco look furthered by the raised, almost fleur-de-lis shaped ends.

A locket in 900 silver and enamel, of French manufacture. The wavy guilloche pattern is topped by a single yellow rose, realistically depicted, possibly through a transfer or transfer enameling. Undeciphered maker's mark; 2.25" x 1.375". *Courtesy of Robin Allison.*

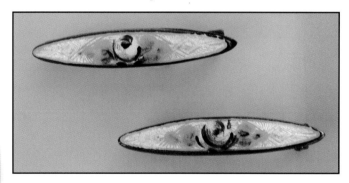

Two tiny "collar" pins in sterling and enamel, by Coro, c. 1910. These small pieces, despite their diminutive size, are done in guilloche enamel with roses. Marked Coro, sterling; measure approximately .75" across.

A bracelet in silver and enamel, Edwardian or possibly transitional between Edwardian and Art Deco, c. 1915. Each square link of the bracelet has a stylized four-pointed design inside another four-pointed design, somewhat like a compass rose and very geometrical, as is typical of both Edwardian and Art Deco pieces. Every fourth link has a small rosebud painted in the center. In addition, each link is bordered on top and bottom by bands of black in champlevé enamel, adding to the spare Art Deco look. Marked sterling; measures 7" x .625". *Courtesy of Robin Allison.*

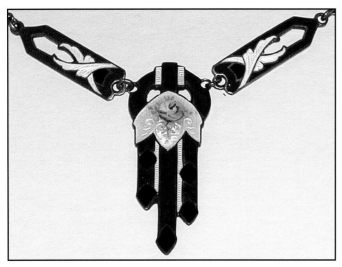

An unusual variation on the guilloche with roses theme, in the form of an Art Deco necklace in silver and enamel. The central element in the necklace, as well as the side panels, are enameled primarily in a deep red, with black and white accents–colors that are very much in the spirit of Art Deco. The shapes, too, are very much Art Deco in nature: the rounded form in the center with three "ribbons" hanging down, each ribbon decorated with diamonds in black enamel; the geometric panels with their stylized leaf pattern; the three-pointed design somewhat reminiscent of the Art Deco brooch in silver and chrysoprase in chapter one. In fact, the only element that seems remotely out of place is the guilloche and rose on this three-point design, which looks very traditional for such a bold Deco design. Undeciphered maker's mark; enameled section measures 2.5" x 1.375". *Courtesy of Robin Allison.*

An Art Deco/vintage perfume bottle and its top–in the form of a bow–in silver and enamel. The perfume and its top are decorated in guilloche with the usual somewhat sketchily rendered rosebuds, and bordered by black. While the use of guilloche with roses (or less often, other flowers) is common for objects such as perfumes and compacts, the black border gives this piece a rather Art Deco look. *Courtesy of Robin Allison.*

A costume pendant by Sarah Coventry, with a guilloche pattern under turquoise enamel, and the usual minimalist rose. Although in a base metal (possibly copper or another metal that has been copper-plated), the enamel is vitreous. The earrings, by Coro, also appear to be in guilloche enamel with the traditional painted rose, but the guilloche work under the enamel consists of choppy, broken lines, failing to create a true shimmery effect.

A more traditional look for a perfume, this lovely flask in silver and enamel is decorated with blue ribbons and bows from which hang swags of leaves centered with rosebuds. Marked Blackington Sterling; measures 1.75" x .75". *Courtesy of Robin Allison.*

A compact in silver and enamel, with two different guilloche patterns. The white guilloche enamel in the center, with its very traditional painted rosebuds, radiates out in wavy, shimmery lines, while the polygonal green border has a geometric design that, from a distance, seems like an optical illusion that one way looks like squares, and the opposite way resembles stairs. *Courtesy of Robin Allison.*

As perhaps might be expected, guilloche and basse taille enameling are often confused. It is not unusual to find, say, a Scandinavian butterfly with basse taille markings described as guilloche. The confusion is easy to understand. After all, both basse taille and guilloche make use of designs on the metal below (usually) translucent enamel to create a visual effect. And in fact, the distinction may in many cases be somewhat arbitrary. For example, throughout this book, basse taille has been used to refer to markings, either made by hand or by machine, intended to create the effect of striation in leaves or markings on butterfly wings, while guilloche is used to refer to machine turning that creates a repetitive pattern that often–though not always–gives a shimmery effect. However, that said, guilloche turning can also be used to create an effect in a piece where a scene in opaque enamel is painted over the guilloche background, so that the guilloche work appears in only small a portion of the enameled piece, where it serves a definite purpose in the design.

iridescent enamel–This appears to be an innovation in enameling that is most associated with Art Nouveau jewelry, particularly in the United States but also in Great Britain, France, and elsewhere in Europe. Iridescent enamel has a subtle shimmer; as one person described it, this shimmer gives it the appearance of having minute particles of gold suspended in it.

In England, a beautiful bright teal blue iridescent enamel, the color of peacock feathers, was developed, and used not only for enameling peacocks but other pieces as well. For the most part, though, iridescent enamel was rather subdued in color: Pale peaches and faint yellows, pearly pinks and whispery lavenders, misty greens and watery blues formed the primary palette of iridescent enamels. However, in some later Victorian and Art Nouveau jewelry, a brighter green iridescent enamel is occasionally used for leaves.

Two brooches in 14K gold with iridescent enamel, both probably of Newark or New York manufacture c. 1900. This shimmery iridescent enamel is characteristic of Art Nouveau pieces made in those two cities. The leaves surrounding the citrine in the first brooch, in translucent enamel over basse taille markings, have a sharp iridescence that has very little of the softer opalescent enamels in it, while the enamel in the other flower brooch appears somewhat softer, perhaps due to the effect of lighting. Citrine brooch measures approximately 1.125" across; the flower brooch 1.5" x 1.375". *Flower brooch courtesy of Robin Allison.*

A wonderful locket in silver and enamel, with a guilloche pattern covered in part by a picture in opaque enamel of a cat staring at its reflection in a mirror. Here the guilloche is used to create a wonderful effect of shimmering in the mirror and, to a lesser extent, in the draperies on either side of the mirror. Swedish hallmarks, 925S; measures 1.5" in diameter. *Courtesy of Robin Allison.*

An Art Nouveau brooch in 14K gold, iridescent enamel, and pearls by the Newark maker Krementz c. 1900. Typical of American Art Nouveau floral jewelry, this brooch has two very stylized blossoms, displays iridescent enamel, and has a pearl dangle. Aside from the dangle, it is very similar to the brooch on p. 113, also by Krementz. Measures 1.25" x 1.25". *Courtesy of Robin Allison.*

In the floral piece below, it is obvious that the background is guilloche–there is a regular, machine-made pattern used to create a visual effect rather than to form an integral part of a design. But what about the striations in the leaves, the markings on the petals? Should those be labeled basse taille, or guilloche?

A large Art Nouveau brooch in silver and enamel, depicting two iris blossoms and their leaves, in what might be termed basse taille enamel by some, guilloche by others. While there is little doubt that the background, with its wavy lines under white enamel simply there to provide a background for the floral design, could and probably should be considered guilloche enamel, what do we call the underlying patterns in petals and leaves? There the patterns serve a purpose: They show the striations of the leaves, and give the petals the shimmery bloom found in the real flower. With their curves, they also create a deceptive illusion of folds and dimensionality in the petals. It seems that a case could be made for calling the underlying machine engraving in the flowers and leaves either guilloche or basse taille, and that neither one would strictly speaking be incorrect. However, throughout this book, engraving that has been created to indicate structures of wings, leaves, petals, etc. is referred to as basse taille. Manufactured by the Shepard Co.; measures 2.375" in diameter. *Courtesy of Robin Allison.*

Jubilee enamel–This bright iridescent enamel was developed at the end of the nineteenth century by enamelists in Great Britain to celebrate, in 1897, Queen Victoria's sixty-year reign. It appears not to have been widely used, possibly because of the difficulties of combining iridescence with vivid colors.

Limoges (pronounced lee-mohzh')–Limoges enameling developed in fifteenth-century France in the city noted for its fine china, still produced there today. Often done over foil, or *paillons*, to create a shiny metallic appearance, Limoges enameling involves using very finely sifted glazes mixed with essential oils–clove oil for the detailed areas, and lavender oil for background and larger areas. In many cases, it appears that the term Limoges enamel is used for any painted enamel; however, Limoges enamel has a distinctly bolder and often glossier look than most other painted enamel.

This technique was popular among some jewelers in the British Arts and Crafts movement, which widely used enamel instead of more expensive jewels to produce a vivid effect. The famed Arts and Crafts designer Charles Ashbee (according to Karlin, 1993, 38, probably the first of the Arts and Crafts designers to make jewelry, and also founder of the influential Guild of Handicraft) was a master of Limoges enameling and this probably encouraged its adoption by others in the movement.

A pair of earrings in gold and enamel, painted in the Limoges style and matching the brooch at the lower left in the group above. Like the masked portrait brooch, the earrings are cleverly made with tiny diamonds sparking the corners of the eyes behind the mask. *Courtesy of Nelson Rarities, Portland, ME.*

matte enamel–Enamel, being made of glass, is inherently both translucent and glossy. As mentioned above, agents added to enamel can create opacity. However, to obtain matte, or flat, non-shiny enamel, enamelists most often treat the surface of the enamel after it has been fired. The two most frequently used methods of creating matte enamel are to etch it with a weak acid solution, or to sand it with a fine grade of sandpaper or emery. This process is sometimes referred to as giving the enamel some "tooth."

Unlike glossy enamel, a matte enamel surface holds paint well; many painted Victorian enamel pieces are done in matte enamel.

Two flower brooches in 14K gold, matte black enamel, and pearls, probably intended as mourning pieces. The first brooch is in the form of a somewhat Arts and Crafts–looking pansy (in its old-fashioned guise, today known as a johnny-jump-up), while the second appears to be a violet, or perhaps an African violet, 1.375" in diameter. Both violets and pansies were extremely popular in late 19th century jewelry, usually painted in more naturalistic colors. However, in this age of mourning, black flowers were also frequently manufactured, often with the same molds used to create their more cheerful counterparts. A flower similar to the black violet also was made in blue (shown below). Like the best Newark flower enamels, this one has tiny stamens surrounding the pearl at its center, their tips also in black. *Violet courtesy of Robin Allison.*

A group of five gold and enamel brooches painted in the Limoges style, showing the detail achieved by the best enamelists working with this technique. Several of them are painted against guilloche or another elaborate background. Some of the pieces are executed in the Renaissance revival style popular in the 1880s; note the headdresses and style of clothing. According to one source, many of the women portrayed in such portraits were famous actresses. *Courtesy of Nelson Rarities, Portland, ME.*

A beautiful necklace in 930 silver and enamel, by the Norwegian master jeweler Marius Hammer, c. 1900. The necklace is enameled in an opalescent enamel that almost resembles melted apple green pearls. This same enamel can also be found in another piece by Hammer shown in chapter five. While opalescent enamel is readily available to modern enamelists, it appears to have been less available–or, at any rate, less commonly used–in the 19th and early 20th centuries. The difference between opalescent and iridescent enamels seems to be almost one of degree, with opalescent enamels being softer, more lustrous than glittering. The festoon section measures 8.5" x 2". *Courtesy of Robin Allison.*

opalescent enamel–This type of enamel, created like opaque enamel by the addition of certain minerals, has a shimmering look that is more subtle than that of the more sparkling iridescent enamel. However, in photographs the two may look rather similar. In real life, opalescent enamel has a luster more like that of a pearl.

A Newark brooch/pendant in 14K gold, enamel, and a diamond in the form of a violet or an African violet, approximately 1" in diameter. The matte enamel is lightly chipped at the edges, revealing upon close scrutiny the matte white underlayer of enamel commonly found in pieces enameled in this fashion. Although similar to the black violet above, this one is in matte blue, with naturalistic shading and painted veins on the petals. Because matte enamel, given "tooth" by sanding or a light acid, takes paint better than glossy enamel, it was popular for enamelists who wished to give their pieces some detail. Typical of many Newark pieces, this one has a folding bail that allows it to be worn as a pendant, and small gold stamens surrounding the center diamond.

opaque enamel–This is enamel to which agents have been added, turning the normally translucent glassy enamel opaque–that is, enamel through which light does not pass.

Opaque enamels were often used in Victorian enameling. The black enamel used for mourning pieces was opaque, as was the usually black enamel found in taille d'épargne enameling. Earlier Victorian floral pins were enameled in colored opaque enamel.

A coat of opaque white under-enamel was used in many of the later Victorian flower pins, which were then painted with shading colors, veins, and other realistic features of plants. A close look at the edges of the pin in the photograph above will show where tiny chips around the edges reveal the white undercoat upon which the naturalistic details of the flower were enameled and painted.

paillon (pronounced pie-yone)–literally meaning foil (the French Larousse dictionary cites for paillon: "A very thin leaf of colored copper, which *bijoutiers en faux*–or costume jewelers–use to make a reflecting background"). Although the French definition cites copper foil specifically, more often jewelers working in enamel use gold or silver foil. Paillons are very often found in Limoges enamels, adding interest to caps and other clothing.

A Limoges pendant in 18K gold and enamel signed L. Clement. The pendant has an irregular six-sided shape with a rope of twisted gold at the edge. Like many other Limoges enamels, this one shows a young woman in medieval or Renaissance dress accented with gold or silver foil accents, also known as *paillons*.

However, as used by British and American jewelers, *paillon* in the singular has another, quite distinct meaning: It refers to a small piece in gold, often in a figural shape–paillons are found as fleur-de-lis, as stars, as ribbons (as in the Victorian locket shown in Guilloche Through Time), and, in the Thomae brooch as a bee.

A brooch in sterling silver and enamel, by the New England maker Thomae. While the brooch has the common guilloche and roses motif, it also has a small paillon in the form of a bee placed in the center of the piece as if hovering between the roses. This type of paillon, one formed into an object or shape, is much less frequently found than the gold or other metal foil in, for example, Limoges pieces. Marked sterling, with maker's marks for Thomae; measures approximately 1.25" in width.

plique-à-jour (pronounced pleek ah zhure')–This type of enameling is usually described as being like cloisonné without the metal backing, and in one sense this is a reasonable description: In plique-à-jour enameling, the enamel is wet-packed, as it is in cloisonné enameling, into cells or empty spaces. However, unlike in cloisonné, in which cloisons or cells are created by shaping wire into the desired pattern and fusing it to a metal back, the empty spaces in plique-à-jour enameling can be created in a number of ways, not only by shaping wire but also by sawing, stamping out, casting, or otherwise piercing spaces in the metal frame.

A small pin in base metal, faience, and plique-à-jour enamel, in the form of a winged scarab. The interesting feature of this piece, which is otherwise unremarkable and similar to many other winged scarabs in terms of design and color, is that the plique enamel somehow did not fire properly, and so left small holes in two of the cloisons–evidence of how difficult and demanding a technique plique-à-jour enameling truly is.

In some major Art Nouveau pieces where the fragility of plique-à-jour enamel presented a challenge, the plique-à-jour enamel was fired on one metal piece which was then attached to another piece in front on which the pattern had been cast; the enamel was thus not fired directly onto the visible part of the piece.

Two halves of a piece that once held plique-à-jour enamel; this fragile enamel was ruined over time, and will undergo re-enameling by an expert enamelist. The piece, made in Newark, shows a crane in a marsh at sunrise. The two parts of this piece show how it was originally constructed, with the difficult plique enamel in the lower half, and the more detailed design placed over the enameled part. *Courtesy of Nelson Rarities, Portland, ME.*

An Art Nouveau necklace in 14K gold, pearl, diamond, and plique-à-jour enamel, possibly of American manufacture c. 1900. Plique-à-jour enamel, similar to cloisonné, uses cloisons or cells formed of metal into which enamel is wet-packed. Unlike cloisonné, however, plique-à-jour enamel has no metal backing, and thus allows light to pass through the enamel, creating a stained glass effect. However, in the best Art Nouveau plique-à-jour enameling, gradations and transitions in color are found, often within a cell, giving a more interesting effect than that created by the monochrome enamel in this piece–which here is more of a background for the gold floral design than an integral part of the design. Pendant measures approximately 1.25" x 1.5".

Left:
A necklace in silver, enamel, citrine or paste, and a pearl, c. 1900. Here the plique shades beautifully from a light blue-gray to a deeper gray. In this piece, too, the plique-à-jour enamel is not simply background for a design, but is itself the design, forming upswept wing-like extensions from the central stone. Marked sterling; measures 1.5" x 1". *Courtesy of Robin Allison.*

The top and bottom halves placed together, though still without enamel, give a better idea of what the finished piece once looked like. *Courtesy of Nelson Rarities, Portland, ME.*

The history of plique-à-jour enameling is as obscure as the meaning of its name. No etymology is given for the word "plique"; however, it is Dale's personal feeling that it is short for "appliqué," as the phrase "applied to [let pass through] the light" truly describes the technique. Perfected by Art Nouveau jewelers, plique-à-jour enamel is a thin membrane of transparent glass that lets light shine through like a piece of stained glass. Perhaps more than anything else, plique-à-jour is *the* hallmark of great Art Nouveau jewelry, but it almost undoubtedly did not originate with Art Nouveau jewelers.

Its origins are as mysterious as it itself is clear. It is claimed by some that the Italian Renaissance goldsmith and jeweler Cellini created plique-à-jour enamel and wrote about the process in his treatise on working with gold. However, one historian who specializes in Renaissance jewelry has said that there is nothing in Cellini's writings to indicate that he created, or even knew about, plique-à-jour enameling.[6] Other accounts have plique-à-jour originating in Russia, perhaps during the seventeenth or eighteenth centuries. Another account, almost certainly wrong, has it that plique-à-jour was developed by the Spanish jewelry firm Masriera, which created some noteworthy Art Nouveau jewelry but was not a pioneer in the movement.

While European Art Nouveau jewelers such as Lalique, Fouquet, and Wolfers created many notable pieces incorporating plique-à-jour enamel, it was less commonly used by American makers of Art Nouveau jewelry other than Tiffany, Marcus, Whiteside & Blank, and Riker Brothers.

soft enamel–Any of a number of types of enamel that can be applied to metal either without heat, or baked at very low temperatures. These enamels tend to be polymers, such as acrylic. The difference between hard and soft enamel is sometimes a bit difficult to distinguish, but generally soft enamel has a softer, less glassy look; it also *feels* softer, and when tapped, can *sound* softer than vitreous enamel. (For the most part, the enamel pieces in this book are not enameled with soft enamel; the focus is on vitreous enamel.)

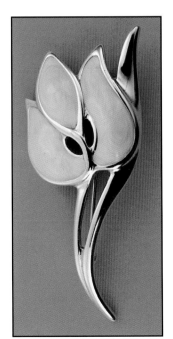

A costume flower brooch by Monet, in the form of a stylized tulip in gold-tone base metal and soft enamel. The enamel in this piece looks soft, in part perhaps because of its pastel color, but it also has a soft feel and sound; and if prodded by a pin, will give way before the pin's point.

sur paillons (pronounced sir pie-yone')–This type of enameling, which literally means "over little pieces of foil," is sometimes said to have been developed by either Alexis Falize or his son Lucien (both claimed credit) or the two of them working together. While gold or silver foil was often used as an accent in Limoges enameling, this innovation used tiny flecks or chips of foil over which translucent enamel was fired. The result was an incredibly rich, shimmering effect. The Falizes used this technique especially when creating their Gothic gems. In fact, Lucien Falize likened his Gothic jewels to illuminated manuscripts, saying that his creations would be passed down to future generations much as illuminated manuscripts had been in the past. (Snowman, 1990, 73)[7]

A pansy stickpin in 14K gold, enamel, and a small diamond, .5" x .625", c. 1900. The enamel is an unusual opalescent pale green, with the gold around the edges of the petals creating a champlevé background. It also appears to have underlying gold foil giving a quasi *sur paillons* effect at the center; gold foil or gold strips also create markings on the petals. The pin is stamped 14K on the back, but otherwise has no maker's information.

taille d'épargne (also sometimes spelled *taille d'épergne*, pronounced d'eh-pahrnh)–This type of enameling, which basically means "size (or figure) of economy," or economical enameling, fills shallow engraved designs (usually created by machine against a machine-patterned background) with opaque enamel, most often black. Because the opaque black enamel designs made taille d'épargne enamel suitable for mourning jewelry, it was relatively common in Victorian jewelry. Designs in taille d'épargne enamel often incorporated leaves and flowers.

A watch slide in 18K gold with taille d'épargne enamel, created using opaque, usually black, enamel in shallow depressions. This type of enamel is commonly found in Victorian jewelry, as it was eminently suitable for mourning. Measures approximately 1.5" x 1".

transfer–A transfer is not really a form of enameling, but rather a device used in enameling. It can be made in several ways, out of several different materials, but in Victorian and later jewelry is most often a design printed on paper and applied to an enameled or unenameled piece, which is then often coated with lacquer or some other preserving agent. A good analogy might be the decals applied to dyed Easter eggs. Because they are glossy and *look* like enamel, pieces with transfers *not* applied to enamel are often unknowingly sold, and unwittingly bought, as enameled pieces.

Transfers are fairly easily recognized by their sharp, crisp edges; unlike true enameled pieces, a transfer does not shade or blend into the background. They should not be confused with *transfer enameling*, which is a form of enameling that uses true enamel with designs transferred by paper from engraved copper plates.

A pair of cufflinks in 10K (unmarked) gold, enamel, and moonstones, and a pendant in black stone, 14K gold, and enamel, both with cherubs created by transfers. The sharp edges of the design against the background material are one way to recognize that a motif or scene has been done with a transfer, rather than with true enameling, either by painting or using the transfer enameling technique. Cufflinks measure .5" in diameter; pendant measures 2.5" (including bail) x 1". *Courtesy of Red Robin Antiques and Robin Allison.*

transfer enameling–This process began, most experts agree, with the Battersea enamels made by York House, London, beginning around 1750. It used paper impressions taken from engraved copper plates, with the still-wet ink of the impression being carefully pressed onto the enamel (or porcelain, or earthenware) surface of the piece being treated in this fashion. Battersea enamels, now very rare and collectible, largely included useful objects or *objets d'art* such as candlesticks, decanter labels, bonbon dishes, and snuffboxes.

A watch in 18K gold and enamel, with an elaborate floral design made up of many types of flowers, all beautifully shaded and detailed. While in an earlier piece it would be logical to assume that the design was hand-painted, in a later piece such as this it is more likely that the design was created through transfer enameling. Transfer enameling allows for a great deal of detail by using printed material pressed onto enamel, thus saving time and also avoiding the mistakes that can occur in hand-crafted pieces. Marked Longines Grand Prix Paris 18K; measures 1.25" in diameter. *Courtesy of Robin Allison.*

A late Victorian or Edwardian watch, in silver and transfer, showing an equestrienne jumping a fence. Unlike the watch above, this one has no enameled background for the transfer to be applied to, and thus should be considered a transfer, rather than transfer enameling. Again, the design applied to the watch has crisp edges, a discontinuity between the enamel and the silver of the background. Marked 935 Rose Watches Swiss; measures 1.75" in diameter. *Courtesy of Robin Allison.*

translucent enamel–Enamel, as already mentioned, is inherently translucent, meaning that it lets light pass though. It is, however, usually not completely transparent, as say clear window glass is, possibly because of the addition of metallic oxides as coloring agents.

Traipsing Through Time: Events and Enameling

Some events resonate much more than others. A major archaeological find, the death of a much-loved spouse, a single naval delegation can change the course of history. This is as true for the history of jewelry as it is for any other human endeavor. In some cases, the aftereffect is almost immediate; in others, it may take almost half a century for the event to produce its reaction. A short list of events that led to trends in enameled jewelry in the nineteenth and early twentieth centuries:

◆ 1750–Innovators at the York factory at Battersea create a new technique for producing detailed scenes, which at the time were painted by master enamelists and took a great deal of time and skill, by using transfer enamels; jewelers learn to incorporate such enameling into sentimental scenes on lockets and watches.

◆ 1839–Prince Albert gives Queen Victoria a snake bracelet as an engagement gift; the public embraces the style, and any number of snake bracelets with the popular cobalt blue enamel are made and sold.

◆ 1840–Lucretia Mott and Elizabeth Cady Stanton, both active abolitionists, meet at the World Anti-Slavery Convention in London; eight years later they stage the Seneca Falls convention and raise a cry for women's rights; some forty years later, Suffragette jewelry makes its appearance with its trademark Green, White, and Violet colors, expressed in enamel as well as gemstones.

◆ 1842–The Treaty of Nanking opens China to Western trade, with the result that new motifs and plants introduced from the East inspire some pieces of Art Nouveau and Arts and Crafts jewelry, such as a beautifully enameled bleeding heart necklace by Gaillard.

◆ 1848–Dante Gabriel Rossetti meets the painter John Everett Millais, and the Pre-Raphaelite Brotherhood is formed, indirectly leading to the Arts and Crafts movement in England and the increased use of different types of enameling, including Limoges.

◆ 1853–Commodore Perry leads a naval delegation to Japan, opening the reclusive island nation to trade with the West; the result is *Japonisme* with an accompanying increase in the use of Japanese motifs and cloisonné enamel in jewelry.

◆ 1861–Prince Albert, beloved husband of Queen Victoria, dies; Victoria raises mourning to a high art form, with the result that the use of black and taille d' épargne enamel, along with jet, ebony, and other dark materials, increases.

◆ 1895–Excavation of the tombs of royal princesses at Dashur leads to finds of beautiful Twelfth Dynasty Egyptian jewelry; Egyptian revival jewelry becomes the rage, often enameled in bright blues, turquoise, greens, and reds; in Art Nouveau jewelry, plique-à-jour enameling is not infrequently used in revival pieces. Famous designers such as René Lalique and Charles Horner create jewelry based on Egyptian themes.

If It Walks Like a Duck but Clucks Like a Chicken: Techniques Sometimes Mistaken for Enameling

Do you think that the things people makes fools of themselves about are any less real and true than the things they behave sensibly about?

—George Bernard Shaw, *Candida*

Certain techniques, such as the transfers previously discussed, are sometimes mistaken for enameling, largely because they resemble enameled work. These techniques may be more difficult to manufacture, rarer, or even–depending on the eye of the beholder–more beautiful than true enamel. Nonetheless, they are *not* enamel; and it seemed appropriate to include a brief section on techniques sometimes misidentified as enameling.

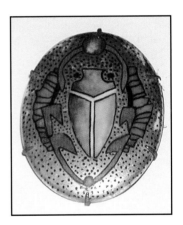

While it is sometimes difficult to distinguish–especially when looking at a photograph–between true enamel, glass fused to metal, and other media, here a piece that is obviously porcelain has been very unconvincingly painted to look as if it were done on brass or another metal. This adorable brooch shows a winged scarab painted against a brass-colored background pocked with dark spots, as if to indicate hammer marks or some other metallic structure. Rust spots? *Courtesy of Robin Allison.*

An item that, in a photograph, looked like enamel–and was sold over the internet as enameled. However, while the backing is metal, the surface with the floral design is in reality some other sort of material, possibly bakelite or another type of plastic.

Another item sold over the internet as being enameled, this antique costume brooch in gold-plated brass and paste stones is in fact painted rather than enameled.

Several of the techniques sometimes confused with–or sold as–enameling are:

damascene work–Sometimes called *damascene enameling*, this technique involved hammering or otherwise incorporating metal(s) into a darker metal background to create a design, sometimes a scene, sometimes a pattern. For some reason, this technique is especially associated with Japan and Spain; frequently it is found in so-called "tourist jewelry." The piece below is Japanese in origin, and beautifully made.

A Japanese bracelet in what is often called damascene work, but sometimes erroneously labeled damascene enameling. Damascene work is often associated with Spain and with Japan, and also with so-called "tourist jewelry." This piece, however, is beautifully crafted, with stylized irises interspersed with very lovely and detailed landscapes. Marked Amita Japan silver; measures 7" x 1.125". *Courtesy of Robin Allison.*

niello–Niello is, to some extent, the reverse of damascene work: It involves placing a dark metal into hollows in a lighter metal. Niello work, in many ways more difficult to manufacture than enameled pieces, can resemble taille d'épargne enameling, although it is usually a bit bolder.

A Victorian watch in silver and niello, the niello forming a quatrefoil pattern with a dragon in the center. Niello, the art of filling spaces in a lighter metal with insets of a darker metal, can be rather hard to distinguish from metal enameled in black, especially champlevé enamel in black. Undeciphered marks; measures 2.25" x 1.375". *Courtesy of Robin Allison.*

A pendant or large charm in 18K gold and niello. Here, even more than in the example above, it is difficult to decide whether the black pattern is formed by niello or by enamel. In general, however, niello has a less shiny appearance than enamel, and also is often less fine than, for example, taille d'épargne enameling. Measures approximately 1.875" in length; marked Portugal.

pate de verre (pronounced pot di vair')–Of all of the non-enamel techniques, pate de verre (literally meaning *glass paste*) most closely resembles enameling: It uses ground or powdered colored glass, sometimes placed in molds, and heated until it fuses. Some enamelists in fact work with both enamel and pate de verre. The main difference between pate de verre and enameling is that enamel is fused to metal, and pate de verre is not.

A butterfly in pate de verre. While pate de verre in many ways resembles enameling, it seems to produce an effect that is far more translucent than enameling–other than, of course, plique-à-jour enameling–because it is totally formed of fused glass, rather than glass applied to metal. It also appears to create designs that are a bit coarser than those created by enamel, in part because enamel can be painted and otherwise given nuances not found in most pate de verre. Marked GAR (for G. Argy-Rousseau, a noted art glass artist). *Courtesy of Robin Allison.*

Toshikane–Although this is really a brand name rather than a sub-genre of jewelry, it is sometimes applied to other glazed porcelain jewelry from Japan not made by Toshikane. Often found in smaller pieces such as earrings and cufflinks, Toshikane can also be found in larger items such as bracelets. This Japanese company produces porcelain jewelry often set on a silver backing; its pieces can be rather smooth and flat, or contain a good deal of relief and dimensionality. The bracelet below is nicely raised and textured.

A bracelet by Toshikane of Japan. Sometimes referred to as Toshikane enamel, the jewelry produced by Toshikane is really made of enameled *porcelain* applied to silver, rather than glass fused to silver or another metal. While some of Toshikane's pieces are quite beautiful, as is this one, with its floral theme in bas relief, they are not true enamels. Marks for Toshikane, Japan, and silver; measures 7.5" x .75".

Endnotes Chapter Two

[1] Enamel can also be *torch-fired*, that is, fired by holding an open flame near the enameled piece to heat and melt the enamel. The heat is clearly not as evenly distributed as it would be in a kiln, and torch-firing can lead to some interesting results. It also seems highly impractical for mass-production.

[2] According to Andrews, *Ancient Egyptian Jewelry*, and other sources, faience–or frit–made its first appearance during the proto-dynastic period, that is, before 3000 B.C.

[3] For the most part, frit was composed mainly of quartz mixed with small amounts of lime and ash or natron. This frit, which could be tinted to a number of different colors, is sometimes called *faience*. However, this is a misnomer, as true faience is a ceramic material named for the Italian city of Faenza where it was first produced.

[4] This information comes from EnamelsOnline.com; their article, "Enameling Overview: The History of Enameling," states that, "We do not know when or where enameling originated. The earliest surviving enamels, Minoan and Mycenaean date from about 1400-1425 [sic] B.C." and cites as the oldest surviving enameled piece a ring that has "gold repoussé with enamel in embossed depression and cloisonné enameled [sic] decorating the bezel and band."

[5] This information comes from several sources, including an article by Maev Kennedy in the British newspaper *The Guardian*, May 12, 2002; there are many other descriptions of Anglo-Saxon enameling.

[6] A personal communication from Emily Wheat, intern at the Newark Museum, who in researching her thesis on Renaissance jewelry, read Cellini's works on jewelry and goldsmithing, and found no mention in them of plique-à-jour enamel.

[7] Lucien Falize, cited in Snowman (1990, 73), said this of his bracelets with Gothic lettering: "'[These] bracelets are intimate mementos... They will no longer be broken up, but will be handed down as family heirloom, as precious as illuminated parchments.'" Incorporated in this sentiment may be an awareness that jewelry as art, as opposed to jewelry as wealth, would be less likely to be broken up as its value was in its design and workmanship, rather than in costly gemstones. Perhaps Falize was aware that much of the great Renaissance goldsmith Cellini's work was melted down for the intrinsic value of the gold and other precious materials he used. (However, his arguably best-known piece, the Francis I *saltier*–or salt cellar–in gold and enamel, was stolen in May 2003. It was estimated to have a value of 37 million British pounds–obviously much more than the intrinsic value of the gold, enamel, and ebony used to create it.)

Price Guide for Chapter Two

p. 80: AN drgnfl w/ pansy bkl $500-$600; vint Meka grn trns btrfl br $20-$45; **p. 81:** Nk 14K chmpl f-m-n fob $75-$85; Vict chmpl cflks w/ poppy $200; vint Chin clsn bclt $500-$550; vint Chin "basket" e/r $250-$300; vint Chin clsn thmb $15-$25; **p. 82:** Vict p-wtch w/ horse $400-$450; ant turq guil br $100-$125; vint cost guil & clsn br $15-$30; **p. 83: Guilloche roses:** Brit Vict lckt w/ pail $100-$225; Fr ant lckt w/ yell rose $300-$350; 2 Nor br: t. AD br $50-$100, I.H. $50-$125; Edw bclt $350-$400; **p. 84:** AD neck w/ red blk & wh enam $225-$300; vint perf w/ bow $125-$150; vint perf w/ co bl $150-$200; vint cpt with lt bl brd $200-$250; vint S.Cov. cost pend $15-$25; Coro cost e/r $15-$25 **p. 85:** vint guil cat w/ mrr lckt $350-$400; U.S. AN guil w/ b-t iris br $250-$300; Nk AN 14K w/ cit & prls br $500-$700; lg Nk 14K w/ prls br $1000-$1250; Nk AN lt ppl flr br w/ sm dmd $400-$750; **p. 86:** A&C 14K w/ prl mrng flr br $225-$400; Nk Vict 14K w/ prl mrng flr br $750-$900; **p. 87:** M.H. ant fest neck $800-$1000; Fr ant 18K Lim pnd $250-$400; **p. 88:** U.S. guil br w/ bee pail $150-$275; AN 14K w/ sm dmd & prl dngl grn plq neck $500-$1200; AN plq neck w/ cit & prl dngl $400-$500; sm Eg rev scrb br $75-$125; **p. 89:** vint Mo. cost flr br $15-25 Vict 14K w/ sm dmd st-p $170-$300; 18K t-d'J slide $150-$400; **p. 90:** Vict 10K cflnk w/ mnstn & cherub trsfr $350-$400; Vict 14K onyx pend w/ cherub trsfr $1750; U.S. vint 14K p-wtch w/ trsfr enam flrs $750-$1000; Vict p-wtch w/ trsfr $450-$500; **p. 92:** vint Jap dam bclt $150-$200; nie grf lckt $350-$375; 18K nie charm $150-300; Fr AN p-de-v btrfl pend $2000-$2250; vint Tosh. bclt $400-$500.

Chapter Three
Movers and Makers:
Notable Names in Enameled Jewelry

But search the land of living men,
Where wilt thou find their like agen?

—Sir Walter Scott, *Marmion*

The great innovations in enameling of the late nineteenth century were developed by designers and makers of rare talent. These were people who, like Lucien Falize, not only felt that enamel was an important art, but who also had the power to envision, experiment, and perfect new techniques or master older ones.

Their names still resonate today. The Falizes, father and son, who purportedly developed enamel *sur paillons*, and who created some of the most exquisite enameled pieces ever made. The genius jeweler René Lalique, whose use of enamel, most of all plique-à-jour, gave Art Nouveau jewelry an ethereal, otherworldly look. The New York firm of Tiffany & Co., which created the most sought-after of all flower pins (or, as one expert put it, "the holy grail of flower-pin collecting"), the Tiffany orchids, with their exotic design and wonderful combination of materials and color. The renowned Carl Fabergé, whose name has become synonymous with luxurious jewelry and extravagant Easter eggs housed in the collections of the wealthy few, and who created sumptuously enameled and jewel-encrusted confections for European royalty and nobles. The brilliant Charles Ashbee, who mastered the art of painting with Limoges enamels, and inspired other Arts and Crafts jewelers to adopt the technique.

And there were others, whose names may not be quite as well known, but who were master jewelers and designers nonetheless. To this list might be added the names Eugène Fontenay (and his brilliant enamelist Eugène Richet), Louis Aucoc, Frédéric Boucheron, Eugène Feuillatre, and Lucien Gaillard in France; Child & Child, Charles Horner, Mrs. Newman, and Robert Phillips, in Great Britain; and in the United States, Marcus & Co., Riker Brothers, and a number of other makers who, based in Newark, New Jersey, created lovely enameled jewelry for middle-class America.

René Lalique, Genius Jeweler

When Nature has work to be done, she creates a genius to do it.

—Ralph Waldo Emerson, "Method of Nature"

The name of the great designer René Lalique is so closely linked with Art Nouveau that "Lalique style" was sometimes used as a synonym for Art Nouveau. Although Lalique apprenticed with Louis Aucoc and later studied at England's Sydenham College, he developed a unique vision that, combined with his novel use of materials such as glass, horn, and ivory, made him the undisputed master of the new art. His pieces show an interesting dichotomy of seeming simplicity in the spare Japanese style, and amazingly intricate fabrication. Nature, whether trees, flowers, water, peacocks, dragonflies, or Woman, underlies almost all of his work. He used flowers in bracelets, pendants, hair ornaments. Elaborately crafted yet seemingly simple irises and poppies and hydrangeas—often in plique-à-jour enamel– appear in his jewelry.

Among other things, Lalique made plique-à-jour enamel almost a standard feature of great Art Nouveau jewelry. Most of his works contain this translucent enamel, which he used to such great effect. But other types of enamel are also found in his work; he used opaque and iridescent enamels with equally brilliant results.

Many of the pieces he created were done on commission for the wealthy Armenian oil baron Calouste Gulbenkian; these are now housed in the Museu Calouste Gulbenkian, in Lisbon, Portugal. Few pieces of Lalique's work come on the market, as so many are already lodged in museums and private collections.

Art Nouveau was as evanescent as the life-span of a dragonfly, as elusive the mythical beings it often portrayed. Its fevered inspiration and elaborate fabrication made its impetus almost impossible to sustain, and by 1915 the only Art Nouveau pieces being produced were sterile imitations of the once truly innovative style. René Lalique himself had already abandoned the movement with which he was so identified and had turned his talents to glass design.

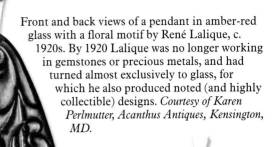

Front and back views of a pendant in amber-red glass with a floral motif by René Lalique, c. 1920s. By 1920 Lalique was no longer working in gemstones or precious metals, and had turned almost exclusively to glass, for which he also produced noted (and highly collectible) designs. *Courtesy of Karen Perlmutter, Acanthus Antiques, Kensington, MD.*

A pendant in gold, silver, diamonds, and plique-à-jour enamel by René Lalique, the genius jeweler whose designs exemplify the best of Art Nouveau design. The pendant consists of four feathers in plique-à-jour enamel, set off by diamond quills. The design is deceptively simple and elegant, while the execution is superlative. *Courtesy of Nelson Rarities, Portland, ME.*

Other European Designers

Although no other name in jewelry is as much associated with an entire movement as that of René Lalique, whose jewelry epitomizes Art Nouveau, Lalique did not suddenly appear as if by magic in a world devoid of fine jewelry. His predecessors were great jewelers such as Frédéric Boucheron, Louis Aucoc, and of course the Falizes.

Louis Aucoc

Louis Aucoc, *fils* (son) was the son of Louis Aucoc *aîné* (the elder), thus inheriting a flourishing jewelry and goldsmithing establishment.[1] He was for the years 1876-1878 René Lalique's master, although he was of course later eclipsed by his famous pupil. Nevertheless, he designed jewelry during the golden age of Art Nouveau, and used some of the same materials and techniques as Lalique, including plique-à-jour enamel.

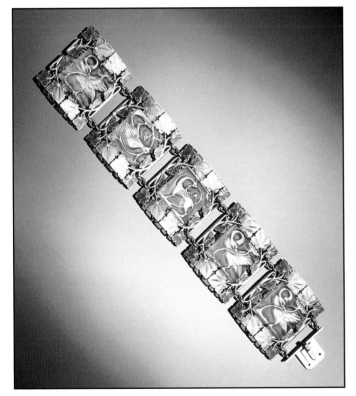

An unusual bracelet by Lalique, in gold, carved glass, and plique-à-jour enamel. The bracelet is formed of five plaques, each rimmed with stylized, rather geometric, plique-à-jour leaves. The carved glass insets in three cases depict the same creature, possibly a mythical bird with an elongated neck, holding a lotus blossom in its beak. The other two contain two different creatures, both also fantastical, and also with lotus blossoms. *Courtesy of Nelson Rarities, Portland, ME.*

Art Nouveau plaque au cou (neck plaque) by Louis Aucoc, in gold, platinum, enamel, and diamonds, approximately 3", c. 1900. The plique-à-jour enamel is superb, with the petals overlapping and the leaves folded over for a very dimensional look. The curving lines, here set with diamonds, are a signature element of Art Nouveau design. *Courtesy of the Newark Museum, Newark, NJ.*

Frédéric Boucheron

Frédéric Boucheron founded the Paris company that bears his name in 1858. Like those in the Aesthetic Movement, Boucheron seems to have found little to admire in the prevailing archaeological revival jewelry. His descendent Alain Boucheron notes that Frédéric Boucheron chose "nature as his theme" in contrast to the "finery" of the age, and notes that, like Art Nouveau designers, Frédéric also found inspiration in Japanese decorative arts. (Snowman, 1990, 78-80)

Boucheron was also interested in enamel, and used translucent as well as other types of enamel, such as *grisaille*. Like his successors in the Art Nouveau movement, Boucheron also used non-precious materials; Alain Boucheron writes that Frédéric "combined simple materials in totally original ways; rock-crystal and wood, for instance, were matched with the rarest precious stones." (Snowman, 1990, 78) Like Tiffany and other jewelers, Boucheron employed the most talented artisans to fashion the jewels that adorned queens and courtesans, tsars and tycoons alike. And, like Tiffany's establishment, Boucheron's continued through several generations, furnishing opulent jewelry for the fashionable.

Boucheron's work does not truly fall into any one category. He was versatile, and designs from his firm show that versatility. Some of his pieces can be considered Renaissance revival pieces, reminiscent of the grand designs of the great Renaissance goldsmith Benvenuto Cellini. While Boucheron created some pieces that can be considered Art Nouveau, when Art Nouveau had run its course he adapted accordingly, producing Art Deco jewelry during the 1920s.

A watch in gold and plique-à-jour enamel by Boucheron, c. 1900, with an intricately carved floral motif. *Courtesy of Nelson Rarities, Portland, ME.*

A late 19th century handbag by the famous French house Boucheron. This fascinating piece has cherubs, or *putti*, in grisaille-like enamel, grisaille being an intricate process that involves multiple layers of black and white, somewhat like silk-screening, until the design is built up. Guilloche enamel forms the center, with a laurel wreath in diamonds; white enamel frames the top and bottom of the guilloche enamel. *Courtesy of Nelson Rarities, Portland, ME.*

Alexis and Lucien Falize

Although their jewelry is much sought-after, the French father and son noted for their work with enameling techniques belong to no particular movement. Like Boucheron, they created work in the Renaissance revival style, but Lucien also favored Asian motifs for many of his cloisonné pieces–which may be the most exquisite examples of cloisonné ever created. Both are considered to have claims to the innovative enamel *sur paillons* (both claimed credit, and it is possible that *sur paillons* was developed by father and son in collaboration). Enamel *sur paillons* was used in their Gothic pieces to create works that resembled illuminated manuscripts; in fact, Alexis Falize was of the opinion that, unlike jewelry of the past, which was often cannibalized for its precious gems and metals, their jewelry would be preserved as family heirlooms much as illuminated manuscripts had been. In other words, he regarded the jewelry they produced as art, rather than wealth–a philosophy later reprised in the Art Nouveau and Arts and Crafts movement. Lucien also used guilloche enamel in cloisonné pieces. Working in collaboration with the brilliant enamelist Antoine Tard, the Falizes made of enameling a high art form.

An elaborate pendant in Renaissance revival style by Falize. The piece has two fantastic creatures, half-woman, half grotesque, flanking a central round with two cameos, a black cameo of a male head wearing a helmet, and a woman's profile in white behind the black cameo. Two faces in profile set below the feet of the beasts also form part of the frame, as does an urn with acanthus leaves set at the top. A simpler piece much like this one– minus the cameos and the enameled heads–can be found in Snowman, *The Master Jewelers.* The similar pendant was apparently exhibited at the Paris Exhibition of 1889. *Courtesy of Nelson Rarities, Portland, ME.*

A pair of cloisonné cufflinks by Lucien Falize, c. 1880. These cufflinks, in light blue enamel against which are set birds and bamboo shoots, show cloisonné at its best. The design also displays the marked Japanese influence that often inspired Falize, especially in his cloisonné pieces. *Courtesy of S. J. Phillips, London.*

Eugène Fontenay

Considered one of the master jewelers of nineteenth-century France, Fontenay thought of himself primarily as a goldsmith (*orfèvre*) rather than a jeweler, or stone-setter (*bijoutier*) (the sharp division between the two was a fact of jewelry-making in nineteenth-century France, although later jewelers such as Falize argued against making such distinctions). However, he did undertake many commissions that involved setting stones, especially from mid-Eastern and Eastern potentates.

His goldwork shows a mastery of some of the prevailing techniques that arose in conjunction with the demand for revival jewelry: He fashioned gold into intricate designs, used granulé work, and overall showed a tasteful restraint sometimes lacking in other pieces of the period. He also employed the talented enamelist Eugène Richet; the two collaborated on pieces, such as the demi-parure below, that made use of scenes from Classical mythology and other revivalist themes.

A demi-parure attributed to famed goldsmith/jeweler Eugène Fontenay, consisting of earrings and a pendant/locket in various karats of gold, enamel, and pearls. Fontenay, who considered himself primarily a goldsmith, was skilled in the new techniques brought about by the archaeological revivals of the period, such as granulation and filigree. With his extremely talented enamelist, Eugène Richet, he created some of the most beautiful jewelry made during the mid 19th century, often using scenes from antiquity or mythology. Here, his subject appears to be Aphrodite, accompanied by a cherub, or Eros, in enameling so finely done that her clothing seems actually to move. The earrings, also decorated with Eros, are interesting because in each one he plays a different instrument: a drum in the leftmost earring, a lute in the other. The pendant/locket measures 3.76" x 1.375", earrings 3" x 1.375". *Courtesy of Robin Allison.*

Carlo Giuliano

Starting, apparently, as a student and then business partner of the Castellanis (who alone largely began the fashion for archaeological revival jewelry), Carlo Giuliano accompanied Alessandro Castellani to London, where he perhaps intended to begin a branch of the Castellani firm. However, in 1863 he registered his own mark with the Worshipful Company of Goldsmiths. (Snowman, 1990, 15) He began producing his own work, which was often marketed by other jewelers, including the prominent Robert Phillips.[2] However, for whatever reason, Giuliano soon began producing jewelry in the Renaissance revival style fashionable at the time. Among other features of his jewelry was the use of enamel, usually opaque and often in vivid colors.

A cross in gold, enamel, and pearls by the famed 19th century designer Carlo Giuliano. Giuliano originally designed archaeological revival pieces, but not long after setting up shop in London switched to making jewelry in the lighter, easier-to-wear Renaissance style. *Courtesy of Nelson Rarities, Portland, ME.*

A pendant in 18K gold, enamel, ruby, and pearl, by Carlo Giuliano, in the Renaissance revival style, complete with swirls, stylized fleur-de-lis elements, and enamel shading from white to pastel pink and green. *Courtesy of Nelson Rarities, Portland, ME.*

Lluís Masriera

Like Louis Aucoc (and the American Louis Comfort Tiffany), Lluís Masriera was born into a dynasty of already established jewelers in Barcelona, Spain. Barcelona was in many ways a center of Art Nouveau, or as the Spanish called it, *modernismo*. It was the home of the visionary Antoni Gaudí, who was to Art Nouveau architecture what René Lalique was to Art Nouveau jewelry. Lluís Masriera, inspired by the revolutionary movement, created pieces that exemplify some of the most typical motifs of Art Nouveau design. His jewelry primarily used the female form in his so-called nymph pieces, draped in realistically rendered–and artfully enameled–gowns, and often outfitted with gossamer plique-à-jour wings. Other pieces representative of his work were insect pendants with plique-à-jour wings, and floral pendants. While his work was often derivative, it was also beautifully executed; perhaps no other jeweler surpassed his ability to depict the draped female form. His company, later known as Masriera y Carrera, produced Art Nouveau jewelry into the 1920s. Recently Masriera began using their nineteenth century molds to produce "original" (although hardly antique) Art Nouveau jewelry.

A "nymph" pendant by the Barcelona maker Masriera y Carrera, in 18K gold, enamel, and a diamond, 1" x 1.5" including bail, c. 1920. The nymph, or young woman, wears an engraved headdress typical of the maker, an opalescent enameled gown, and holds a branch of leaves in translucent green enamel. The leafy branch curves to form part of the pendant's frame. Women and nature are a not uncommon theme of Art Nouveau jewelers, the woman often being depicted with flowers or leaves. The back of the pendant is chased to mirror the front.

Theodor Fahrner

One of the giants in German jewelry production and design, Fahrner was based in Pforzheim, which his and other firms such as Heinrich Levinger's helped make a center of German jewelry manufacturing. He was considered an innovator: He hired outside designers; he worked in materials including iron to make jewelry more accessible to the average German; he was a leader in the Jugendstil movement, both influenced by and influencing other designers in the Arts and Crafts movement and in Art Deco. His firm continued to produce jewelry until the 1980s.

The jewelry pictured below is typical of the spare, clean, timeless lines of his jewelry, which could easily be labeled either Jugendstil or Art Deco.

A pendant by Theodor Fahrner, in silver, enamel, citrine, and onyx. In a style that might be labeled either Art Deco or Jugendstil, Fahrner created geometric designs intended for mass production. Marked TF 935; measures 3" x 1.125".

A brooch by Theodor Farhner, in silver, enamel, marcasites, onyx, and topaz, with the central rectangular stone flanked on either side with stylized elements decorated with enamel onyx. The brooch could probably be labeled Jugenstil or Art Deco–it has a relatively geometric, clean design that falls into both categories. However, it also has flowing elements also somewhat reminiscent of Arts and Crafts or Art Nouveau. Marked TF sterling; 2.375" x .875". *Courtesy of Robin Allison.*

A necklace in silver, enamel, and amethyst by German designer/manufacturer Heinrich Levinger. This necklace, which might be termed Jugendstil in design, also shows the influence of the British Arts and Crafts movement in Europe. The lines, rather like stylized branches ending in circular leaves, which form the cells for the champlevé enamel in darker and lighter shades of blue, along with the amethyst dangle, show definite Arts and Crafts influence. Marked HL, silver; measures 2" x 1.5". *Courtesy of Robin Allison.*

Carl Hermann

Little is known about this German maker, who tended to use floral motifs rather than the geometric forms commonly found in the new Jugendstil movement sweeping Germany at the end of the nineteenth century. Like Fahrner and Levinger, he was based in Pforzheim c. 1900. The lovely plique bracelet in the introduction (p. 16) was also made by Hermann.

Two necklaces by Carl Hermann, in 900 silver, pastes, and plique-à-jour enamel, with the top one also having a baroque pearl dangle. These two necklaces, which are basically the same necklace in different shades of enamel, show Hermann's use of floral motifs, as does the bracelet by him featured in the introduction. Also a good example of how striking a difference color can make to the appearance of a piece of jewelry. *Courtesy of Robin Allison.*

Heinrich Levinger

Heinrich Levinger founded the firm that bears his name in the late 19th century. Like Farhner and Hermann, he was based in Pforzheim. After Levinger's death, the company was renamed Levinger and Bissinger (1903), but after 1909 reverted back to its original name. They produced pieces of the Jugendstil type, and were engaged, like Fahrner, in mass production of jewelry–although Fahrner is better known.

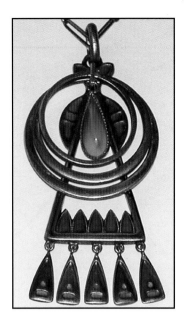

A pendant in silver, enamel, and chrysoprase, by Heinrich Levinger. This interesting piece, with its severe geometrical forms, its nesting silver circles–almost like elements in a mobile–echoed by the plique-à-jour enamel flanking the tear-shaped chrysoprase at their center, the five dangles, could probably be classed as either Art Deco or Jugendstil. Marked HL 900 depose; measures 2" x 1". *Courtesy of Robin Allison.*

A necklace in silver, plique-à-jour enamel, pastes, a mabe pearl, and a baroque pearl, by Heinrich Levinger. While the other two Levinger pieces shown above display marked Arts and Crafts or Jugendstil/Art Deco leanings, this piece has more of an Art Nouveau feel to it, with its plique enamel sweeping up from the central mabe pearl like wings of a scarab that in turn resemble lotus blossoms. Marked HL depose 900; measures 1.75" x 1.5". *Courtesy of Robin Allison.*

A fun, very dimensional piece in silver, enamel, paste, and a pearl, by Meyle & Mayer. The frog brooch, its front legs holding a pearl, its rear legs stretched out behind it, is a cross between the zoologically accurate and the whimsical, enhanced by its vivid green enameling in champlevé partitions that add to its feeling of dimensionality and musculature. Marked for Meyle & Mayer, depose sterling; measures 2.75" x .75". *Courtesy of Robin Allison.*

Meyle & Mayer

Unfortunately, there appears to be very little information on this German firm; they are known primarily through their jewelry, which is versatile and beautiful, and by their makers' marks. Their jewelry cannot be pinned down to one style or period: They produced lovely pieces in the Art Nouveau tradition, such as a beautiful light red bird with plique-à-jour wings (featured in chapter one p. 55), and in a more severe, Jugendstil or Art Deco style. Many of their pieces are in silver; and a number of these also contain plique-à-jour enamel. Other pieces, such as the frog shown above right, do not. Quite possibly the firm was located in Pforzheim, for many years the center of German jewelry production; but this is purely conjecture, rather than fact. A number of their pieces are shown throughout this book.

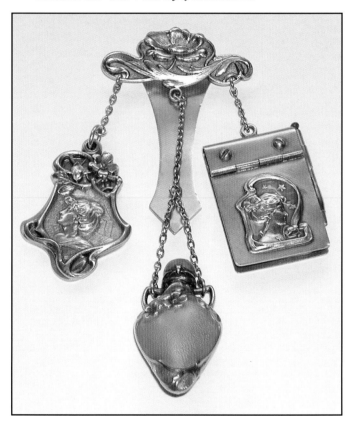

A brooch by Meyle & Mayer in silver and enamel, of a young woman painted in the Limoges style and bordered by deep blue champlevé enamel. Like many Limoges portraits, this one has foil beneath the woman's cap. This piece shows the enormous versatility of Meyle & Mayer, which produced jewelry in the Art Nouveau, Edwardian, and–here–Arts and Crafts style. Marked for Meyle & Mayer, depose sterling; measures 1" x 1". *Courtesy of Robin Allison.*

Perhaps the ultimate in Meyle & Mayer pieces, this chatelaine in sterling silver and enamel is Robin's dream piece. In its own original fitted box, the chatelaine has some very Art Nouveau elements, including the lotus blossoms/water lilies and the women's faces, in profile with upswept hair. Marks for Meyle & Mayer, sterling depose; top piece measures 2" x 1", mirror 2" x 1.325", perfume 2" x 1.125", note pad 2" x 1.25". *Courtesy of Robin Allison.*

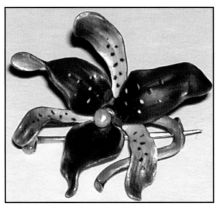

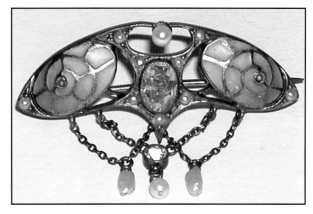

A tiger lily in silver, enamel, and a pearl, by Meyle & Mayer. The free-standing blossom, much in the style of American-made flower pins, is beautifully and realistically enameled in iridescent enamels that, like their American counterparts, include shading and markings. Usual markings for this manufacturer; measures 1.625" x 1.5". *Courtesy of Robin Allison.*

A wonderful brooch in silver, plique-à-jour enamel, aquamarines (or pastes), and pearls, by Meyle & Mayer. Here the color of the central stone is picked up by the blue plique enamel, done in cells that spiral around much like a conch shell. Another blue stone forms the junction between two chains hanging from the spirals, while four other chains end in pearl drops flanking the central pearl that depends from the lower stone. *Courtesy of Robin Allison.*

A different type of flower piece from Meyle & Mayer, in silver and enamel, showing two violet-colored flowers against a trellis formed of green enamel partitioned by silver. One flower leans over the trellis, and leaves curl up the middle and around the edge, forming the bottom part of the frame. *Courtesy of Robin Allison.*

A Jugendstil pendant in 935 silver, amethyst, enamel, and a pearl, by Meyle & Mayer. The pendant shows a very classic design with a central amethyst surrounded by swirls of silver accented with enamel the color of the stone. An amethyst briolette hangs from chains attached to the curving frame around the amethyst. Usual maker's marks; measures 2.24" x almost 1". *Courtesy of Red Robin Antiques.*

Another Meyle & Mayer piece with a very Art Nouveau theme, this one a dragonfly pendant in silver, pastes, and enamel. The wings are in a lovely bright blue plique-à-jour enamel, decorated with pastes along the edges. A blue paste in the dragonfly's thorax echoes the color of the enamel. Usual marks for this company. *Courtesy of Robin Allison.*

A rather unique piece by Meyle & Mayer, this one possibly transitional, but most likely made during the first decade of the 20th century. The bow at the top adds a rather Victorian look, as do the "frills" at the bottom of the pendant. The pendant, in silver, plique-à-jour enamel, and marcasites, measures 2.375" x 1.625"; usual marks for this firm. *Courtesy of Robin Allison.*

British Designers and Enamelists

Life without industry is guilt; and industry without art is brutality.

—John Ruskin, *Lectures on Art*

Like their continental counterparts working in the traditional style and in Art Nouveau, British designers and enamelists of the period also produced some wonderful work in enamel. However, many of them, because of the Arts and Crafts emphasis on anonymity and egalitarianism, did not always sign their work, and are thus less prominent in the annals of enameling than they might otherwise have been.

Still, there were commercial firms, some of which incorporated elements of Arts and Crafts design, that became quite well known. Possibly the most notable of the British firms mass-producing jewelry in the Arts and Crafts style (as well as other styles) was Charles Horner. The Anglo-German firm Murrle Bennet also sold a line of jewelry through Liberty.

Child & Child

This English firm (based in Kensington) produced commercial jewelry in the Arts and Crafts style around 1900. Their jewelry appears to have been true to the Arts and Crafts philosophy insofar as they produced jewelry that is rather simple in form, with beautiful enamel work. Deviating from the true Arts and Crafts aesthetic, however, their jewelry often is in gold rather than the simpler, more affordable silver favored by most Arts and Crafts jewelers.

A heart-shaped locket in gold and enamel by the London firm Child & Child, c. 1900. The locket has vivid green guilloche enamel surrounded by white, and is in its original box. *Courtesy of Nelson Rarities, Portland, ME.*

This pendant in 14K gold, enamel, amethyst, and pearls from Child & Child was perhaps worn by some lucky late Victorian or Edwardian suffragette. Done in the suffragette colors of **g**reen, **w**hite, and **v**iolet (for **G**ive **W**omen **V**otes), this piece also has elements of Arts and Crafts design, such as the brilliant iridescent green leaves surrounding the amethyst (which is also circled by a ring of white enamel), and the baroque pearls forming part of the frame, as well as irregular dangles suspended from chains of varying lengths. *Courtesy of Robin Allison.*

Charles Horner

As previously noted, Charles Horner was one of the better-known designers for the London department store Liberty, which marketed a mass-produced line of Arts and Crafts jewelry under the Cymric label. His silver jewelry, often enameled in pastel colors or the vivid Arts and Crafts blue-green, is highly collectible.

To some extent, Horner–who continued to produce jewelry even during World War II, when he made rings for the Royal Air Force–was the Henry Ford of Arts and Crafts jewelry. He first made his mark with his invention of the patented Dorcas thimble (made of a thin layer of steel sandwiched between silver) and went on to mass produce jewelry, enameled and otherwise. Among his more commonly found pieces are winged scarabs, thistle brooches and hatpins, butterflies, and guilloche roses in pins, pendants, and even rings.

An Arts and Crafts necklace in sterling silver and green and white enamel marked with the initial CH, for the noted British designer Charles Horner. While the necklace is unmistakably fashioned in the Arts and Crafts tradition–its design is simple and geometric, its roundels free of the cluttered look of so much late Victorian jewelry–it retains elements of its Victorian roots in the multiple elements in its dangles. *Necklace courtesy of Classic Facets, Boulder, CO; photograph by Karryl Salit.*

A necklace in silver and enamel, by Charles Horner. This necklace, with its leaves and bright blue-green enamel found in so many Arts and Crafts pieces, is fairly typical of his work. Other Arts and Crafts influences can be found in this mass-produced piece, such as the enameled dangle hanging from the main part of the necklace. Hallmarked with CH, marks for silver and Chester, and the year; measures approximately 4.25" x 1.125".

Murrle Bennett

The Anglo-German firm of Murrle Bennett sold jewelry manufactured in Pforzheim–at that time a major manufacturing center for German jewelry–in the Arts and Crafts style to Liberty.

An Arts and Crafts pendant by the Anglo-German firm of Murrle-Bennett, which marketed many of their pieces through the department store Liberty of London. The simple design of the piece in silver, its symmetrical geometric nature, the small dangle, and the blue-green enamel are typical both of their pieces, and Arts and Crafts pieces in general. Marked 950 MBCo.; measures 2" x .625". *Courtesy of Robin Allison.*

A brooch by Charles Horner, in a rather more unusual design than those commonly produced by him. The brooch, perhaps with Renaissance revival overtones, has a pale blue maple leaf on a shield affixed to an oval in pale blue and white guilloche enamel, with raised stars. Bears the usual marks for Charles Horner; measures 1.75" x 1.5".

Mrs. Phillip (Charlotte) Newman

Mrs. Newman was one of the truly successful women jewelers of the late nineteenth and early twentieth centuries. Early in her career, she worked as an assistant to John Brogden, a well-known jeweler whose designs were mostly in the archaeological revival style. After his death in 1885, Mrs. Newman branched out on her own; she was not only a designer but also a goldsmith and jeweler. Although some of her work at the end of the nineteenth century used a Celtic motif, thus somewhat fitting into the Arts and Crafts movement, she was not primarily identified with this style. (Karlin, 1993, 84) According to one collector, Mrs. Newman designed "art jewelry." Her designs appear to have been rather eclectic, but display a rather classic elegance and simplicity. In some pieces, she also showed a willingness to create daring color combinations: One pendant by her combines a cabochon amethyst, pink sapphires, and red enameling sparked with small diamonds.

A pendant by the noted designer Mrs. Newman, one of a number of successful women jewelers of the late 19th and early 20th centuries in Great Britain. In this elegant piece, five oval and one round amethyst are set off by white enameled acanthus leaves, with the sixth oval amethyst forming a dangle. *Courtesy of Nelson Rarities, Portland, ME.*

The American Cousins

While famous makers of Victorian, Art Nouveau, and Arts and Crafts jewelry are primarily associated with Europe, American jewelers also played a role in jewelry design. Perhaps the most notable American designer of the era was Louis Comfort Tiffany, whose father, Charles L. Tiffany, started the venerable New York jewelry firm in 1837. Other firms, centered in Newark, New Jersey, created affordable yet attractive jewelry for the American middle class. However, it is probably true that both Louis Tiffany and the Newark makers derived much of their inspiration from the Art Nouveau movement centered in Paris.

Tiffany & Co.

The company founded by Charles L. Tiffany and his partner John B. Young in 1837 enjoyed tremendous success. Although originally a purveyor of stationery, fans, umbrellas, and imported curiosities from China and elsewhere, the firm launched its own line of jewelry in 1840 after briefly selling jewelry imported from abroad.

The company opened branches in Paris, London, and Geneva; in the United States it catered to the rich and famous. Notables such as the great French actress Sarah Bernhardt–also a patroness of Lalique and other French Art Nouveau jewelers–bought sumptuous jewelry at Tiffany's, which specialized in expensive diamonds and pearls. Charles L. Tiffany became a much-decorated entrepreneur (among other honors, he was made a Chevalier of France's Légion d'Honneur).

Although much of Tiffany's output fell into the category "Jewelry as Wealth" against which the Art Nouveau and Arts and Crafts jewelers rebelled, Tiffany & Co. also created smaller objects in enamel.

Tiffany's, inspired by the same aesthetic sense that fueled Art Nouveau, produced a number of orchids in gold, enamel, and precious stones which were exhibited at the Paris Exposition Universelle in 1890; today these are considered among the most desirable flower pins in the entire world of flower pin collectibles. Tiffany's created other enameled jewelry, in keeping with the trend of the times, including other flower brooches–for which they may actually have set the trend.

Miniature portrait of a young child handpainted on ivory under crystal and set in an 18K and white enamel frame made by the renowned New York city firm of Tiffany & Co., 1870, still in its original box. *Portrait courtesy of Classic Facets, Boulder, CO; photograph by Karryl Salit.*

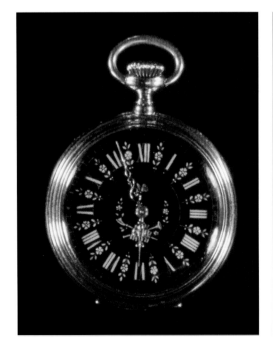

Front and back views of a beautiful late 19th century watch from Tiffany & Co., in gold and enamel using the difficult grisaille technique to depict a long-ago rustic scene. *Courtesy of Nelson Rarities, Portland, ME.*

A pansy in gold, enamel, and a diamond, by Tiffany & Co., c. 1900. The pansy is beautifully enameled in glossy opaque colors showing a wonderful gradation of color, shading from dark markings, pale yellow, cream, light violet, and darker violet. *Courtesy of S. J. Phillips Ltd., London.*

A later enameled piece by Tiffany & Co., in gold and heavy translucent red and opaque white enamel, in the form of a bow. *Courtesy of Bodette Reeves, Odessa, TX.*

Louis Comfort Tiffany

Like the name René Lalique, the name Louis Comfort Tiffany reverberates through time. Just as Lalique's name is forever linked with Art Nouveau jewelry, so is Louis Comfort Tiffany's name linked with Art Nouveau glass. No other name, European or American, is as evocative of Art Nouveau decorative arts as his. His famous stained glass lamps and shades incorporated typical Art Nouveau themes: dragonflies and irises, lilies and poppies.

The son of Charles L. Tiffany, founder of Tiffany & Co., Louis Tiffany early determined on a career in art rather than jewelry. His father, apparently acquiescing with his son's decision not to enter the family firm, provided artistic training for Louis, who proved to be a more than competent painter.

However, in the 1880s, Louis Tiffany became interested in stained glass. He later patented a process for making opalescent, or iridescent glass, known as "favrile glass."[3] Tiffany began creating lampshades with leftover pieces of favrile glass from his stained glass windows, but eventually turned this

from a sideline into a major business. He even worked with Thomas Edison to create shades that would work well with the new electric lighting. In 1900, he began producing freestanding lamps with heavy bronze bases.

However, Tiffany also created jewelry, which for collectors is among some of the most sought-after ever produced. His original intention was to fashion wearable, affordable jewelry incorporating less expensive materials–in effect, the antithesis of the jewelry produced by his father's famous company. In this he somewhat resembled jewelers working in the Arts and Crafts tradition. Like Arts and Crafts and Art Nouveau designers, he frequently used enamel in his pieces.

A striking necklace by the great designer Louis Comfort Tiffany in gold, black opal, demantoid garnet, and plique-à-jour enamel. Although Louis Comfort Tiffany was a leader in Art Nouveau design–his art glass is quintessentially Art Nouveau in its depiction of dragonflies, poppies, and irises–when it came to jewelry his aesthetic was seemingly more in keeping with that of Arts and Crafts. This necklace, while beautifully designed and crafted, essentially presents the balanced design and cleanness of line often found in Arts and Crafts pieces. *Courtesy of Nelson Rarities, Portland, ME.*

Marcus & Co.

Little is actually known about this company, other than the fact that at the end of the nineteenth century, it provided Tiffany & Co. with its only real competition in New York, and perhaps in the greater United States as well. Like Tiffany & Co., Marcus created floral jewelry using plique-à-jour and other enameling techniques. They apparently catered to a wealthy and famous, or perhaps infamous, clientele; the rose brooch below was created for the daughter of Jefferson Davis, former President of the Confederate States of America during the American Civil War.

While probably the most desirable American late Victorian and Art Nouveau jewelry came from the New York firms Tiffany & Co. and Marcus & Co., an entire industry of jewelry manufacturing had grown up in nearby Newark, New Jersey. By the end of the nineteenth century, Newark was already noted as a manufacturing center. It produced, among other things, leather goods and felt hats; it manufactured chemicals and smelted lead; and it was home to Thomas Alva Edison when he invented the ticker tape machine. According to an article in a 1911 encyclopedia, in 1905 Newark was the tenth leading industrial city in the entire United States.

Its jewelry industry was long established by the time the 1911 encyclopedia appeared. While the encyclopedia listed jewelry as a major Newark industry (it claimed the 1905 jewelry output for Newark was valued at $9,258,095.00), it stated that the manufacturing of jewelry began around 1830. It may be that jewelry manufacturing became a major economic factor around that time, but the first record of jewelry being made in Newark is in 1801, when one Epaphras Hinsdale set himself up in business as a jeweler.

So many manufacturers produced enameled floral jewelry around 1900 that dealers and collectors sometimes refer to "Newark enamels" when discussing certain pieces. These pieces are often unsigned but nevertheless have a certain quality that sets them apart from other enameled jewelry. The enameling is careful, detailed, and shades beautifully from light to dark, or through a range of colors. Rather than the bold, bright colors often favored elsewhere, pastels predominate. This jewelry was mass-produced and mass-marketed, intended to reach a wider circle of buyers than the rarified audiences targeted by Art Nouveau designers in Europe; but it was also attractive and wearable.

Although it can be difficult to establish a maker for an unsigned piece, it is not always impossible. Individual makers had their own styles, although many were also quick to pick up on prevailing fashion, or trends. Comparing pieces by various makers can prove instructive. Some makers, such as Krementz, created similar pieces with and without maker's marks. Looking at a marked piece, noting its particular characteristics, and then finding these same characteristics in unmarked pieces can often lead to an "almost positive" identification.

A very unusual brooch by Marcus & Co., c. 1880, with a pearl carved into a rosebud, light green plique-à-jour leaves, and a collet-set dewdrop diamond. This brooch apparently was owned by the daughter of Jefferson Davis, who from 1861-1864 was president of the Confederate States of America. *Courtesy of the Division of Costume and Social History of the Smithsonian Institution, Washington, D.C.*

A beautiful brooch in the form of, possibly, a cherry blossom, in gold, enamel, and a diamond, by Marcus & Co., c. 1890-1900. The enameling, shading from white to pink, the painted veins, the folds and wavy edges to the petals, are all very nicely done. This brooch, save for the added maker's mark, is virtually identical to the flower brooch/pendant pictured in the introduction. *Courtesy of S. J. Phillips Ltd., London.*

Four pairs of cufflinks of different periods, all beautifully enameled, one by the noted New York firm Marcus & Co. Clockwise from left: a) Gold cufflinks with a ground of red enamel bordered by red, with a band of cloisonné enamel in an abstract red-and-black design across the center. b) Cufflinks with black guilloche enamel set with a ruby in the center, with a platinum rim. c) Ornate carved gold cufflinks with monograms on each of the links except for one, which bears an Arabic inscription, with white champlevé enamel. This pair was made by Marcus and Co., c. 1905. d) Art Deco–style cufflinks with three raised bands enameled in dark blue set against horizontal bands of black and green cloisonné enamel. *Courtesy of Nelson Rarities, Portland, Maine.*

What Put the "New" in Newark Enamels?

The thing that hath been, it is that which shall be; and that which is done is that which shall be done: and there is no new thing under the sun.

—*Ecclesiastes*, I:8

Newark enamels, no less than other jewelry, were influenced by prevailing trends. When pansies were popular, a number of makers–not limited to Newark, as Tiffany & Co.'s entry into the pansy sweepstakes shows–made pansies. When Art Nouveau came along, many of the makers created pieces in the Art Nouveau style, translated, it goes without saying, for American tastes and budgets. While it may be difficult to distinguish one Newark maker from another when a piece is unsigned, or unmarked, it is relatively easy to discern that a piece has a Newark (or, less often, New York) origin. Some of the characteristics of unsigned pieces by Newark makers–who failed to leave their mark, so to speak–are:

♦ Careful attention to botanical detail. Veins and markings are painted on, petals have realistic folds and curved edges.
♦ Stamens surrounding a center stone, usually a diamond or pearl. This feature, found on many larger pieces, is also found on some small pieces, such as honeymoon pins, by Krementz and other makers..
♦ Larger pieces with folding bails, allowing them to be worn either as pins or pendants (although this is not unique to Newark enamels).
♦ Matte enamels in pastel colors that often shade from light colors at the center to a deeper shade at a petal's edge. Chips in enamel will usually reveal that these enamels are painted on over a white undercoat.
♦ A diamond or pearl often set in the center of the piece, especially Victorian ones.
♦ Collet-set diamonds on leaves or petals, simulating dewdrops.
♦ Sturdy construction with c-shaped links between petals on the back side of the piece (although one or more makers, including Black, Starr & Frost, used a star-shaped piece of metal as the backing for five-petaled and other flowers).
♦ Usually made of–and stamped on c-clasp–14K gold, although smaller pieces are found in 10K gold; older pieces have curlicue rather than "cuff" c-clasps, which do not allow room for a maker's mark or karat content.
♦ Art Nouveau pieces with shimmering iridescent enamels, sometimes shading from one color to another; green through lavender or pale pink is a not uncommon combination of colors.

Top left:
A small flower pendant and flower brooch in 14K gold, of Newark (or New York) manufacture), in enamel that is both iridescent and opaque. This type of iridescent enameling has been described as enamel that almost appears to have particles of gold suspended in it. The brooch measures 1" x .875"; the pendant also measures .875" in length, including the stem. One characteristic of Newark enamels is that they frequently came in a variety of sizes, tailored to fit a variety of budgets. In most cases the larger and smaller pieces are brooches, but occasionally the smaller piece–as in this example–was in the form of a pendant. The "smaller" piece often included a stem, which made it about as long as the "larger" piece, which was often a larger free-standing flower.

Top right:
Two stick pins with similar flowers–both white, both with five petals–of about the same size (approximately .625" in diameter), both with small diamonds in the center. Can you tell which one is from Newark (or, possibly, New York), and which one is European (probably French)?

Left:
The backs of five pins. Three of them have the usual c- or arch-shaped links reinforcing the petals, but in the other two, the back of the flower pin has a more unusual star-shaped reinforcement at the center. A similar link was used by the maker Starr, Black & Frost, of New York.

Bottom left:
A flower in 14K gold, enamel, and a diamond, c. 1900, of Newark or New York manufacture (possibly attributable to Black, Starr & Frost, which used a star-shaped link for the petals similar to the one on the underside of this piece). Resembling the black violet shown in chapter one, p. 23, this one is in matte pink, with naturalistic folds, shading, and painted veins to the petals. Because matte enamel, given "tooth" by sanding or a light acid, takes paint better than glossy enamel, it was popular for enamelists who wished to give their pieces some detail.
(Note the resemblance between this flower and the flower in matte black enamel for mourning in chapter one.) Folding bail; marked 14K and measures approximately 1.125" x .625".

Left:
A pendant in 14K gold, enamel, and a small pearl, containing a tiny enameled flower in pink. The flower shows, despite its minuscule size, the usual Newark attention to detail: shaded enamel and markings on the matte pink petals. Oddly enough, the leaves are done in an iridescent green, making this piece seem something of a mixture between late Victorian and Art Nouveau. Unidentified maker's mark on bail; measures 1.5" x .5".

Some of the better-known Newark jewelry firms that worked with enameling were Alling Co.; Bippart, Griscom & Osborn; Carter, Gough & Co.; A. J. Hedges; Krementz Co.; Henry Blank, or, with his sometime partner, Whiteside & Blank. A short list of enameled jewelry makers follows, with some information on each, a description of the maker's marks, and photographs showing a little of their design and craftsmanship. Other examples of their work can be found throughout this book. (For more information, Janet Zapata's chapter on Newark jewelers, "The Names Behind the Jewelry," in Ulysses Grant Dietz [ed.] *The Glitter and the Gold*, 1997 is highly recommended; the book itself is an excellent reference volume on Newark-manufactured jewelry of all types.)

Alling Co.

This company is mentioned in Sataloff, *Art Nouveau Jewelry* (1984, 29) as one of the American companies producing Art Nouveau jewelry of a high caliber. Sataloff especially admires their enameling, asserting, "Their enameling was at a level with the French and of very fine quality." Judging by an example of their work, a bracelet in the collection of the Newark Museum, as well as the Alling pieces shown in chapter one, it is hard to dispute Sataloff's assessment.

Records show that Alling Brothers & Company was founded in 1843 (according to Zapata, 1997, 159; other records show 1850, but quite likely Zapata's earlier date is correct). It became Alling Co. in 1881 when Horace Alling retired and William Alling brought two of his sons into the business. The 1915 city directory is the last to mention this firm.

The company's mark was an upside down three-leaf clover with 1 4 stamped in the upper two lobes and A in the lower lobe.

A bracelet from Alling Co. in gold, enamel, and diamonds, c. 1900. The Byzantine woman's face is delicately enameled, with rose-colored cheek, dark red lips, and detail to the eye. The flowing yet carefully arranged hair is typical of Alling's Byzantine women. *Courtesy of the Newark Museum, Newark, NJ.*

Bippart, Griscom & Osborn

According to records, Achille Bippart (born in Germany in 1857) formed his company in 1885. Enameled jewelry crafted in 14K gold was mentioned as a specialty of the firm in its advertisements, the earliest one cited by Zapata (1997, 162) being from 1891. In 1897, when his first partner died, Bippart made Bennet Osborn a partner; and in 1901, Benjamin Griscom became a partner and the name was changed to Bippart, Griscom & Osborn.

The firm produced some of the finest enameled jewelry in Newark. The enameling in their Art Nouveau pieces was in some cases more vivid than usual for Newark makers, using brighter, more saturated colors and forsaking the pastel palette commonly used for floral pieces in that style.

Their maker's mark was a lighted torch, sideways, accompanied by the usual 14K stamp.

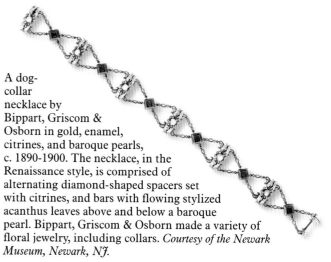

A dog-collar necklace by Bippart, Griscom & Osborn in gold, enamel, citrines, and baroque pearls, c. 1890-1900. The necklace, in the Renaissance style, is comprised of alternating diamond-shaped spacers set with citrines, and bars with flowing stylized acanthus leaves above and below a baroque pearl. Bippart, Griscom & Osborn made a variety of floral jewelry, including collars. *Courtesy of the Newark Museum, Newark, NJ.*

Black, Starr & Frost

Strictly speaking, Black, Starr & Frost does not belong in a list of Newark makers, as it was based in New York City. However, stylistically the one piece of Victorian/Art Nouveau jewelry shown on p. 109 seems similar to that produced by Newark makers. The flower has naturalistic petals in white shading to pink at the edges, with the merest hint of iridescence. The flower is almost undistinguishable from a piece by a Newark maker–except that instead of gold c-shaped links connecting and reinforcing the petals in the flower, a star-shaped gold reinforcement was used. This firm produced a limited number of Art Nouveau pieces, according to Sataloff, "but their work was not very outstanding." (Sataloff, 1984, 29).

This company may lay claim to being the oldest jewelry manufacturing firm in the United States, with one source[4] giving 1810 as the year it was founded. However, like many businesses of the era, it added partners and changed names frequently. It became Ball, Thompson & Black sometime before the middle of the nineteenth century, and around 1855 changed its name to Ball, Black & Co. In 1876, the name was changed again, to Black, Starr & Frost.

The firm has a long and honorable history, and is often mentioned in the same sentence with the names Tiffany & Co., Cartier, Boucheron, and Van Cleef & Arpels. It was one of the few American firms to exhibit at the 1851 Crystal Palace Exposition in London, and along with Tiffany & Co., Whiting, and Gorham was one of the organizers of the Philadelphia Show of Precious Stones. While it still makes fine designer jewelry, it is better known for its silver, both flatware and serving pieces such as bowls and platters, which are highly collectible.

Their output of enameled jewelry, though, seems to have been slight. This is the only enameled piece signed by this maker Dale has seen in many years of collecting.

This company did not have a registered maker's mark. They marked their jewelry simply B. S & F.

A brooch in the form of a rose, in 14K gold, enamel, and diamond, by Black, Starr & Frost, c. 1900. The flower's petals are realistic, and the pin has a nice dimensionality. The petals are enameled in lighter and darker shades of pink, with a hint of iridescence. The diamond dangle presumably imitates a dewdrop. Measures approximately 1.125" in diameter.

Henry Blank – see under Whiteside & Blank

Thomas F. Brogan Co.

Like Black, Starr & Frost, Thomas F. Brogan Co. does not belong in a list of Newark makers, as he was also based in New York City. In terms of quality, however, his work belongs among the best of Newark enamels. The sole piece that represents his work in this book is a late Victorian flower, possibly a primrose, which is enameled with great delicacy and beauty. Very little information seems to be available about Brogan, other than his maker's mark, which was a simple five-pointed star in outline.

A nicely made flower in gold and enamel by Thomas Brogan of New York, c. 1900. The flower, with five heart-shaped petals, has matte enamel in cream shading to pink. Stamens surround the central disk. *Courtesy of S. J. Phillips Ltd., London.*

D. de W. Brokaw

Like Black, Starr & Frost and Thomas F. Brogan, D. de W. Brokaw was a jeweler located in New York City. His output of enameled jewelry was limited, and jewelry by him appears rarely on the market. Nevertheless, the one piece of his displayed here shows great dimensionality in the realistically depicted petals. A gold rim around the edges of the petals (which are enameled on both sides) adds interest to the piece. The design, however, is not original. This type of cabbage rose may have originated with Tiffany & Co., but whatever its original maker, can be found in the repertoire of a number of Newark makers. The size of this piece, however, and the amount of metal used in its creation seems to point to a wealthier than usual clientele.

Brokaw's mark was a circle enclosing the usual 14K with two acorns on a stem below.

A large cabbage rose in 14K gold, purple enamel, and a diamond dangle, by New York maker D. de W. Brokaw. The pin, which measures approximately 1.75" in diameter, displays great dimensionality. As with most pins of this type, its petals are enameled on both sides.

Carter, Gough & Co. (formerly Carter, Howe & Co., etc.)

Aaron Carter, who had apprenticed with the Newark jewelers Taylor & Baldwin, in 1841 went into business for himself. After a number of changes in partners (with attendant name changes to the company; at least a dozen names are listed for the company between 1841 and 1915), the name of the company was changed to Carter, Gough & Co. in 1915. For over sixty years, Carter remained the senior partner.

The firm was a thriving one. By 1878, it was noted that Carter's was among the largest manufacturers of jewelry in the world, with an annual production of jewelry worth over two million dollars. The company's maker's mark as Carter, Howe resembled a sideways arrowhead containing the letter C.

A brooch in 14K gold and enamel, showing a lovely Art Nouveau woman's face in profile surrounded by a wreath of oak leaves in a pale, iridescent enamel typical of American Art Nouveau jewelry, by the Newark firm headed by Aaron Carter, c. 1900. Marked with maker's mark, 14K; measures 1" in diameter. *Courtesy of Robin Allison.*

Another brooch by the Newark firm Carter, Howe & Co. (later Carter, Gough & Co.), in 14K gold and enamel, c. 1900. The brooch, in the very typically Art Nouveau theme of Woman and Nature, shows a woman with a rather piquant face juxtaposed with flowers, leaves, and buds in iridescent enamel. Marked with Carter's maker's mark, and 14K; measures approximately 1.125" x 1". The flower's center possibly at one time contained either a pearl or–less likely–a diamond.

A small oval brooch in 14K gold, enamel, and pearls, by the Newark maker Taylor & Baldwin. This firm employed Aaron Carter before he left to start his own firm, Carter, Gough & Co. (earlier Carter, Howe & Co.).

Crane Theurer

Crane Theurer was effectively established in 1895 when David Crane and E.F.C. Theurer assumed the debts of their employer A.J. Valentine and set up as manufacturers of jewelry under their own names. They continued in existence until around the onset of World War II. They produced jewelry that seems very typical of the place and the time.

Their maker's mark was a T with a C crossing the T's downstroke.

An orchid in 14K gold, enamel, a diamond, and a small pearl, by Crane Theurer, c. 1900. The flower is enameled in the matte black commonly found in Victorian mourning jewelry; it almost undoubtedly possessed a more colorful counterpart enameled in colors appropriate for an orchid. Marked CT 14K; measures approximately 1" x 1".

A.J. Hedges

Andrew J. Hedges, having previously been associated in business with David C. Dodd, formed the company bearing his name in 1877. According to Zapata (1997, 171) Hedges advertised a line of jewelry in 14K, including enameled pieces set with stones, and "'odd jewelry' featuring insects, lizards, butterflies, and turtles ..."

A.J. Hedges produced a considerable number of enameled flowers, including the pansies fashionable in the late Victorian period as well as the wild roses shown here. The enameling on these pieces is among the finest produced by Newark, with delicate shading and realistic markings. Or, to quote Sataloff, "They are known for their small pieces with exceptionally fine enameling." (Sataloff, 1984, 30).

The maker's mark for A.J. Hedges was a capital H, with 14 above the letter's crossbar, and K below it.

A set of matching brooch and earrings by A. J. Hedges in gold, enamel, and pearls, c. 1890-1900, with a nicely formed and enameled wild rose, and smaller earrings with the same enameling and detail to the petals. Marked H, 14K; brooch measures approximately 1.375" in diameter, earrings approximately .875" in diameter.

Krementz & Co.

A good deal is known about this company, in part because of their long history. George Krementz, a native of Germany, learned his trade at Alling, Hall & Dodd. In 1866 he formed Alling & Krementz with Stephen Alling; accounts of Krementz & Co. usually date the founding of the company to this year, although the firm bearing that name was established three years later, in 1869.

Much of Krementz & Co.'s business lay in manufacturing its one-piece collar buttons, for which George Krementz had patented a new design in 1884. The firm's earliest mark–a button sometimes described as an umbrella with two handles–reflects the company's success with its collar buttons.

However, Krementz also created some of the country's finest mass-produced jewelry. In the late Victorian period, it produced jewelry with small blue champlevé forget-me-nots, a design that apparently was copied by other manufacturers. Their flower jewelry, including honeymoon pins, is among the finest of its kind.

One thing that distinguished Krementz & Co. was not only its innovative designs, but its ability to adapt to trends. When Art Nouveau jewelry became fashionable, Krementz & Co. adopted Art Nouveau designs, translating the high-flown European jewels into jewelry suitable for its American audience. Their Art Nouveau jewelry is among the best created for mass consumption in the United States, and enameling on their pieces is extremely fine.

Krementz & Co. later marketed a number of lines. Their Diana line continued to supply 14K gold jewelry, but jewelry marked KREMENTZ is usually gold-plated using Krementz's "Rold Gold" process. Krementz pieces, whether 14K, gold-plated, or the 18K and platinum jewelry featuring colored stones (sold under the name Krementz Gemstones), remained popular. The company sold its lines to various companies, including Colibri and Tiffany & Co., in the late 1990s, although Richard Krementz, grandson of the firm's founder, continues to make designer jewelry with colored stones set in platinum and 18K gold.

In this book, Krementz pieces are more numerous than those of any other Newark (or New York) maker. Possibly this is because pieces by Krementz come on the market more often, and possibly because they simply produced more pieces. They especially produced a variety of honeymoon pins, apparently in some quantity. (Also, of course, there is some preference for Krementz pieces on the part of one of the authors.)

An advertisement by Krementz probably from the 1960s.

The Business of Beauty: Krementz Through Time

A thing of beauty is a joy forever:
Its loveliness increases; it will never
Pass into nothingness…

—John Keats, *Endymion*

Partly because it was in business longer than any other jewelry manufacturer in Newark, Krementz & Co. left us a legacy of pieces that were not only attractive, but also tailored to fit the times. When honeymoon pins were the rage, Krementz made honeymoon pins–and arguably made them better than anyone else: Their miniature flowers had stamens; some had chased gold edges; others were set in crescents dotted with champlevé forget-me-nots. When mourning pieces were in vogue, Krementz made mourning pieces. When Art Nouveau traveled the Atlantic from France, Krementz adapted unaffordable one-of-a-kind pieces to American tastes and pocketbooks, mass producing Art Nouveau jewelry for the middle-class American consumer. Still later, Krementz adapted to the fashion for costume jewelry. Throughout its long history, it rarely, if ever, sacrificed quality to expedience.

A Krementz brooch in the form of a wreath of oak leaves and acorns, in 14K gold and matte black enamel. This pin, with its circular form, motif, and enamel, is typical of late Victorian mourning jewelry. In the language of flowers, the oak leaf represented strength. Measures approximately 1" in diameter, marked with maker's mark and 14K.

A selection of four honeymoon pins by Krementz. Two of the pins have the same small pink flower, each with a pearl in the center surrounded by tiny gold stamens. The crescent of one is plain, however, while the other has the small blue champlevé flowers popular at the time. The pansy shows the chased gold edge sometimes found on small Krementz flowers in honeymoon pins. The iris pin, with its iridescent enamel and crescent with striations suggesting a leaf, is more along the lines of an Art Nouveau piece. All marked with Krementz's mark, and 14K.

Two small pins by Krementz. The top one, enameled in iridescent pink shading through pale green, resembles an iris leaf, with the small pearl perhaps suggesting an iris blossom. The lower pin has a small violet, also in the iridescent enamel found in Art Nouveau pieces rather than the matte or glossy enamel more often found in Victorian flowers; the violet, however, is more suggestive of a Victorian than an Art Nouveau motif. Both marked for Krementz, and 14K.

A cherub brooch, in 14K gold, enamel, diamonds, and a large baroque pearl, by Krementz. The cherub's wings, upstretched above his head, have beautifully carved gold feathers beneath the enamel. The entire piece has a lovely sculptural feel to it, even more so when compared with the similarly sculptural cherub carved in coral.

A flower pin in the form of a violet, in 14K gold, enamel, seed pearls, and a small diamond. While this particular pin is not marked with Krementz's maker's mark, it is a Krementz piece; its exact copy, one marked with Krementz's mark, is in the Newark museum. Furthermore, seed pearls lining the edges or placed at the tips of petals (or, in the case of four-leaf clovers, of leaves) is a hallmark of some Krementz pieces. Marked 14K.

Another pin, this one with a stylized flower in iridescent enamel, possibly a lotus blossom, in a curved navette-like frame. Marked Krementz, 14K; measures approximately 1.25" across.

Three different irises by Krementz, c. 1900. The first, with its glossy pink petals, shows an almost Japanese aesthetic, while the one on the right, in iridescent enamel, is more typically Art Nouveau. The middle flower, with a collet-set diamond probably meant to suggest a dewdrop, is the most realistically rendered of the three, and, with its matte enamel, painted veining, and naturalistic look, seems more Victorian in character. All marked 14K, with maker's mark; the leftmost brooch measures 1.75" x .5", the rightmost one 1.125" x .625".

A pin by Krementz in 14K gold, enamel, pearls, moss agate, and a diamond, c. 1900. The symmetrical pin is designed around a central agate, rather unusual in Newark jewelry of the era, and has stylized leaves in iridescent enamel shading from green to gold to light red or pink at the ends, as seen earlier in the small leaf pin. As in the other pin, the flowers here are also suggested by pearls. Marked 14K, maker's mark; measures approximately 1" x .75".

A pin in 14K gold, enamel, and small diamonds, by Krementz. The pin features two carved gold birds (originally labeled swans, but more likely cranes) forming a frame for a green background against which bloom three white, very dimensional (they in fact stand away from the background) tulips. What is truly interesting about this piece is that it was almost certainly based on a piece by the French Art Nouveau jeweler Antoine Bricteux–a piece with an amazingly similar design by Bricteux resides in Germany's Schmuckmuseum. Bricteux's piece is larger; its green background is of plique-à-jour enamel rather than enamel on gold, and the three flowers are very dimensional enameled calla lilies; but the resemblance is too close to be coincidental. This piece, perhaps more than any other, shows how Krementz adopted and adapted European Art Nouveau design for mass consumption by the American middle classes. Maker's mark, 14K; approximately 1.125" x 1".

An unusual brooch by Krementz, with three stylized lotus blossoms–almost having an Egyptian revival look–twined around a central opal, with two diamond accents. Unfortunately the opal in this piece is crazed, and has a crack through the center. Marked 14K, with Krementz's mark; measures approximately 1.25" high.

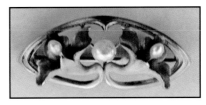

An Art Nouveau brooch in 14K gold, enamel, and pearls, by Krementz, with two symmetrical stylized flowers in iridescent pink shading to green, each with a pearl in the center, and with a third pearl completing the design. Maker's mark, 14K; measures 1.25" x 1".

113

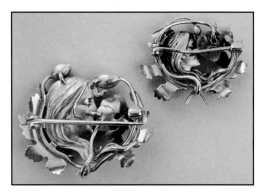

Another "Art Nouveau" woman by Krementz, this one much later, gold-filled, and without enamel. Krementz continued to use themes from their past on into the 20th century, as this brooch shows. Marked KREMENTZ on the pin stem. The gold-filled and glass grape leaf pin is reminiscent of Victorian jewelry.

A very small pin by Krementz, again appropriating an Art Nouveau motif: the grotesque woman. Here the woman is fanged, possibly a vampire woman, with a swirling maelstrom of hair forming the texture of most of the brooch. Despite its small size (it measures about 1" across), the piece shows a good deal of attention to detail. Maker's mark, 14K.

Two brooches by Krementz, each showing a woman with a flower that resembles a poppy. These two brooches are the "large" and "medium" versions of a theme that also came in "small"–about the size of a quarter. The faces of the women in both brooches are beautifully done in iridescent enamel, as opposed to, for example, the women in the Carter, Howe pieces where the face is left in gold. In the larger version, the poppy and leaves that form part of the frame are very dimensional; in the medium version, somewhat less so. Both pieces are very nicely chased on the reverse. This design has been called by an expert the best translation of European Art Nouveau into American mass-produced jewelry; but, begging to differ, the cranes with tulips shows extremely well a very direct appropriation of an Art Nouveau piece. Larger brooch measures approximately 1.375" across; medium about 1.125" across; the small version, not shown, measures approximately 1" in diameter; maker's mark, 14K.

A truly lovely seagull in silver, enamel, and a pearl, by the German firm Meyle & Mayer. The seagull, its wings outstretched in flight, carries a pearl in its beak. While wings and tail are done in plique-à-jour enamel, the cells of which are shaped to form the outlines of feathers, the body itself is done in enamel so iridescent and glowing it very much resembles a pearl or mother-of-pearl. Usual mark for Meyle & Mayer, depose sterling; measures 3.5" x .75". *Courtesy of Robin Allison.*

Krementz's version of the Meyle & Mayer seagull on p. 114, in 14K gold, enamel, and diamonds. Here the seagull's wings are also outstretched in flight, with small diamonds along the upper edges adding interest to the piece. While Krementz did not attempt plique-à-jour enameling, it did suggest the feathers through basse taille markings. Like Krementz's Woman with Poppy pieces, this seagull brooch is nicely chased on the reverse, with markings that show feathers, beak, eye. Maker's mark, 14K; measures approximately 1.375" x .625".

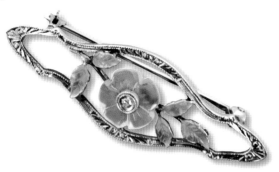

An Edwardian pin by Krementz, in 14K gold, enamel, opalescent quartz, and a small diamond. Given the prevailing preference for white metal, Krementz manufactured this piece in white gold rather than yellow, and also replaced what might have been a colorful flower with shimmery opalescent quartz, centered with a small diamond. Here only the leaves are enameled, in a rather subdued green. Maker's mark, 14K; measures 1.25" in width.

The small enameled blue forget-me-nots with which Krementz once adorned honeymoon pins continued to appear in Krementz's pieces even after the company began to produce primarily costume jewelry in the 1930s. Here the small blue flowers are placed in a frame made of stylized bamboo in the shape of a house–very much in the style of the 1960s.

Riker Bros.

Riker Bros. was originally founded in 1846 as Riker & Tay. When Tay left the business and William Riker's three sons joined the firm, it became Riker & Sons; eventually, with William Riker's retirement from the jewelry manufacturing business, it became Riker Bros. (1892).

Riker was one of the few American companies to use plique-à-jour enameling, and in general produced jewelry of a very high quality. They are listed by Sataloff (1985, 65) as one of the American firms producing fine Art Nouveau jewelry.

Riker Bros. maker's mark was a sideways scimitar with an R above it.

An unusual floral brooch by Riker Bros., with an abstract flower in gold, enamel, and pearl, c. 1900. The red translucent enamel is striking, and somewhat unusual, as red enamels tend to lose their color easily if not properly fired. *Courtesy of S. J. Phillips Ltd., London.*

Whiteside & Blank

More is known about Henry Blank, one of the founders of Whiteside & Blank, than perhaps any other Newark jeweler–largely because he sailed on the *Titanic*, and survived

A wonderful Edwardian necklace in gold, enamel, diamond, and pearls by Whiteside & Blank. This elaborate piece, with a diamond set in iridescent blue guilloche enamel surrounded by white champlevé enamel, decorated with carved gold acanthus leaves, also features a pearl tassel hanging from a bell-shaped cover also with iridescent blue guilloche enamel and white accents. *Courtesy of Nelson Rarities, Portland, ME.*

the disastrous voyage. For this he was at times ostracized, it being felt that, as a man, he should have given up his place in the lifeboat to a woman or a child: "Women and children first" had been the rule on the night the great ship sank.

Henry Blank was a talented jeweler who had mastered gold- and platinum-smithing before he turned twenty-one. In 1899, after having worked for the Prudential Insurance Co., he became the junior partner in the jewelry manufacturing company Whiteside & Blank. When Newton Whiteside retired from the business in 1917, it became Henry Blank & Co.

According to Janet Zapata, in her account of Newark jewelers (Dietz, ed., 1997, 163), Whiteside & Blank was one of the few firms that used plique-à-jour enameling. The company was also the first to market women's wristwatches, as well as a variety of different watches–diamond watches, ring watches, watches with colored gems–unique to Whiteside & Blank.

Their enameling was of very high quality and, as can be seen in the photograph below, Whiteside & Blank created complicated designs with beautiful workmanship.

On the commonly used 14K gold, the company's logo was a crescent moon with an arrow through the center

While Whiteside & Blank created large, impressive pieces such as the Edwardian necklace pictured on p. 115, it also made much smaller pieces, such as the beauty pin (shown in chapter one) as well as this small button pin–measuring approximately .75" in diameter, in gold, enamel, transfers, and a small diamond chip. Marked with maker's mark, and 14K.

An undistinguished little pin in gold, enamel, diamond, and pearl, by Henry Blank. The pin has two clover-like flowers enameled in opaque white, the larger with a diamond in the center, the smaller with a pearl. There is some attempt at depicting veins in green. A missing triangle on one petal may be a manufacturing defect as is sometimes seen near the center of a piece, where the enamelist did not quite cover the entire petal.

Wordley, Allsop & Bliss

This firm originally began as Wordley, Allsop & Bloemke in 1907. Bloemke left, and was replaced by Harry A. Bliss in 1915, and the company name was changed accordingly.

Although they did produce some enameled jewelry, the quality seems to be rather mediocre overall, undistinguished by design, fabrication, or enameling.

Their maker's mark is a capital W with curved sides, with a counter-stroke on the left forming an A, and a figure shaped like a 3 leaning against the right stroke to form a B.

A lovely 14K gold and enamel pendant with a baroque pearl dangle, from the Newark maker Whiteside & Blank, c. 1900. The translucent white enamel lets the underlying metalwork show through, with raised gold dots punctuating the enamel. The flowing gold leaves, the pearl dangle, and the shape of the frame all show Art Nouveau influence. *Pendant courtesy of Classic Facets, Boulder, CO; photograph by Karryl Salit.*

A lovely flower in gold, enamel, and a pearl, by Whiteside & Blank. The flower is in an iridescent peach enamel shading from light to dark, with painted veins. A curving stem holds a pearl "bud." *Courtesy of S. J. Phillips Ltd., London.*

A pin in 14K gold, enamel, and pearls by Wordley, Allsop & Bliss, c. 1895. The pin's three cloverleaves are in a bright iridescent green enamel, with intervening bands of gold to suggest the leaves' shading. The leaves also show heavy engraved striations.

Other American Firms

Charles M. Robbins

Based–as were a number of other firms–in Attleboro, Massachusetts, Charles M. Robbins was founded in 1892. At one time, it allegedly employed more enamelists than any other American company. It produced a number of different kinds of pieces, including the charming Arts and Crafts–like pictorial piece below. The company is still in existence today.

For their maker's mark, please refer to Appendix A.

A marvelous pendant by the Massachusetts-based maker Charles M. Robbins, in silver and enamel. The pendant, unusually for American-made jewelry, is very much in the Arts and Crafts style, with its spare symmetry, geometrical shapes, and hand-painted scene–this one of a seascape featuring a sailboat in the central panel, sky, seagulls, and clouds in the upper panel, and the boat's reflection in the sea in the lower panel. Maker's mark, sterling; measures 2.25" x 1.5". *Courtesy of Robin Allison.*

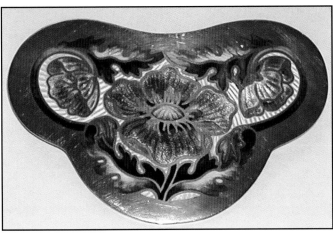

Another piece by Robbins Co., this one a brooch featuring poppies and leaves in silver and enamel. This piece is much more the standard type of brooch produced by some American firms in the Art Nouveau style; typical are the champlevé divisions for the flowers' petals and leaves, the basse taille striations to the petals, and the white guilloche background. While this piece is attractive, it does not truly compare with a similar poppy brooch produced by Watson Co. Maker's mark, sterling; measures 2.75" x 1.625". *Courtesy of Robin Allison.*

Watson Co.

Like Charles M. Robbins, Watson was also based in Massachusetts, and was well known for its fine silver workmanship. Besides serving pieces and silverware, Watson produced a number of enameled brooches, many with flowers in an Art Nouveau style. Their output was such that their pieces remain fairly easy to find.

For their maker's mark, please refer to Appendix A.

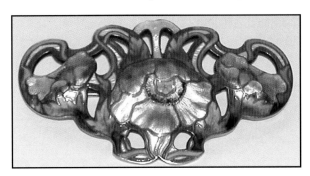

A charming brooch by Watson Co., in silver and enamel, with a design of three poppies and leaves in a flowing frame. Both the flowing design and the deep, lustrous enameling make this a very interesting piece visually, and a wonderful interpretation of Art Nouveau design. Maker's marks, sterling; measures 2.75" x 1.625". *Courtesy of Robin Allison.*

Later Makers

Speak of the moderns without contempt, and of the ancients without idolatry.

—Earl of Chesterfield, in a letter to his son

Although it is difficult not to evince a certain amount of reverence for the great masters of the nineteenth and early twentieth centuries, it should not keep us from recognizing the talent of those who followed them. The Scandinavians produced some wonderful designers working in enamel, while the Germans, led by Theodor Fahrner, created spare, timeless pieces. Margot de Taxco created a wealth of fine enameled pieces, a legacy both for her country and for collectors everywhere.

While it is not possible to mention all of the fine designers and enamelists who worked during the span of the twentieth century, it would seem wrong not to include a few of our favorites. Among these are:

David Andersen

The output of Norwegian David Andersen is truly prodigious, and rivaled by few working in enamel. His pieces range from traditional, incorporating Scandinavian themes; to figural pieces incorporating owls, peacocks, fish, and above all, the leaves and butterflies for which he is perhaps best known; to the unabashedly modern. As one friend noted, part of Andersen's success was that, like Carl Fabergé a century earlier, he produced lines of jewelry in colors that matched. Thus a woman could buy a leaf pin and bracelets and, years later, complete the set by purchasing a necklace and earrings in the same pattern, and the same color. Yet some of Andersen's jewelry is highly distinctive; for example, he produced a highly sought-after monarch butterfly enameled in such naturalistic detail and coloring that it is immediately recognizable.

A brooch and bracelet by David Andersen, both pieces in the deep blue enamel for which he is known, and each using a motif with which he is particularly associated: birch leaves in the bracelet, and a butterfly brooch. *Jewelry courtesy of Classic Facets; photograph by Karryl Salit.*

A pendant by David Andersen in an extremely modern, abstract form which nevertheless bears a couple of his signature marks: the basse taille work–here circles and lines–and the deep blue enamel. Marked 925S David Andersen; measures 4" x 2.375". *Courtesy of Robin Allison.*

Alice Caviness

Alice Caviness was a talented designer who worked with German companies in Pforzheim to create enameled silver jewelry, often containing marcasites, as well as designing costume pieces. Her silver pieces are often figural, including ladybugs, dragonflies, leaves, shells, and butterflies such as the one shown below.

A vintage butterfly, c. 1950, by designer Alice Caviness, in gilt-washed sterling silver and enamel, with articulated wings. Marked Germany, sterling silver, and with Caviness's name; measures approximately 1.625" across.

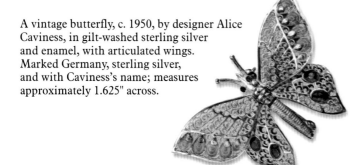

Marius Hammer

Marius Hammer does not fit the "modern" category nearly as well as the others included in this section. His production actually began around 1890, when he fashioned festoon necklaces, cascading brooches, and guilloche enameled pieces. He also made pieces incorporating traditional Scandinavian elements. His enameling was extraordinary, and included a beautiful pale opalescent green that almost looks like melted pearls.

A bracelet in silver and enamel by Marius Hammer. Hammer, who worked in the Scandinavian Arts and Crafts tradition known as Skonwerk, created a number of lovely pieces with enamel. The design of this bracelet is rather spare, yet timeless, with black enameled diamond shapes linked by curving white guilloche links. Hammer created both geometric, non-figural pieces such as this one, as well as figural pieces. Marks for Hammer, 925S; measures 7.5" x .75". *Courtesy of Robin Allison.*

Aksel Holmsen

Another Norwegian, Holmsen also worked within the Scandinavian tradition of fine enameling. His pieces also range from the traditional, such as his brooches with guilloche enamel and roses; to winter scenes; to the figural, such as his orchids and butterflies. Perhaps the motif with which he is most distinctively associated is the Viking ship, fashioned into a brooch in a number of colors.

A brooch by Norwegian Aksel Holmsen, in silver and enamel, with a typical Scandinavian scene of a polar bear on an ice floe, snow-covered mountains in the background. Similar scenes can be found in bracelets and brooches by other Scandinavian makers, such as David Andersen. Marks for Holmsen, 925S; measures 2.875" in diameter. *Courtesy of Robin Allison.*

Other Makers

Although David Andersen is probably the best-known Norwegian maker, Norway and Denmark both produced other fine craftsmen who worked in silver and enamel. Among these are *Ole Petter Raasch Olsen* (whose OPRO company is still active), famous for his butterflies (two of which are pictured in chapter four, Butterflies Through Time). *Hroar Prydz* also produced some lovely butterflies, as well as leaves. *Ivar T. Holt,* working in Norway, also made some fine pieces. In Denmark, by far the best known designer of modern jewelry is *Georg Jensen,* but very little of his work is enameled. However, the Denmark-based companies *Meka* and *Volmar Bahner* did manufacture enameled jewelry, including the almost stereotypically Scandinavian butterflies and leaves.

Margot de Taxco

Margot van Vorhies Carr was so successful a designer and artisan that she became identified with her adopted home, and today is almost universally known as Margot de Taxco. She created imaginative pieces in a variety of styles ranging from Arts and Crafts to Art Deco to exotic pieces incorporating themes derived from ancient Egypt, Asia, and meso-American cultures. She was noted for her use of basse taille and champlevé enameling, and while she did make jewelry without enamel, her enameled pieces seem to be more highly sought after by collectors.

A parure by Margot de Taxco, consisting of a butterfly brooch, a floral pendant/brooch and matching floral earrings, all in shades of purple, green, and blue. All pieces signed Margot de Taxco sterling, and have an ID number: pendant brooch, measuring 2" x 1.625" with a 20" chain is No. 5860; the earrings, 1" x .875", are also 5860; and the butterfly pendant, 2.25" x 1.875, is 5628. *Courtesy of Robin Allison.*

Endnotes Chapter Three

[1] In France of the nineteenth century, a major–although rather contrived–distinction was made between jewelers, called *bijoutiers* or *joiailliers* (*bijoux* were objects of less value and therefore less importance than *joiailles,* which by the prevailing definition made pieces in which valuable gems dominated), and goldsmiths, known as *orfèvriers.* The great jeweler and chronicler Henri Vever wrote:
What is therefore a piece of jewelry, and what distinguishes it from a *bijou,* properly speaking? A piece of jewelry differs from a *bijou* in the sense that diamonds and precious stones must in it have a *preponderant* importance, and essentially dominate it." (Michael Koch, in var., *Belle Époque of French Jewellery,* 1990, 7; translation mine.)

[2] Robert Phillips was apparently a leading proponent of the archaeological revival school, having been influenced to some extent by the Castellanis. He was also among the most successful of the British jewelers of the era, being the only English jeweler to receive a Gold Medal at the Paris Universal Exposition of 1867 (Bury, 1991, 465).

[3] There is some evidence that Tiffany was not the first to devise the glass for which he became so famous. According to stained glass expert Julie Sloan, Tiffany learned about the process of creating opalescent glass to be used in stained glass windows (rather than the usual smaller dishes and vases for which it was then employed in a pressed glass, rather than sheet, form) from an older, and at that point more famous, stained glass designer named John LaFarge. LaFarge received a patent for his opalescent process eight months before Tiffany applied for his patent. Although Tiffany's patent was not for a process, but rather for a method of *construction* using glass produced by LaFarge's process, the end result was that neither one could create stained glass windows using opalescent glass without violating the other's patent. The two, originally on such good terms that LaFarge shared his revolutionary technique with Tiffany, eventually ended up bitter enemies. Youth prevailed, however; LaFarge's career was then waning, while Tiffany's was just beginning. In the end, Tiffany became almost universally famous, while LaFarge's name remains in comparative obscurity, although he is apparently highly regarded by experts on stained glass. (Julie Sloan, "The Rivalry Between Louis Comfort Tiffany and John LaFarge," *Nineteenth Century,* Fall, 1997)

[4] This date came from on online history of Black, Starr & Frost put out by the company itself. However, other information came from a variety of sources.

Price Guide for Chapter Three

Chapter Four
Signs and Wonders:
Symbolism in Victorian, Arts and Crafts,
Art Nouveau, and Other Enameled Jewelry

Signs are taken for wonders. "We would see a sign!"
The word within a word, unable to speak a word
Swaddled with darkness.
In depraved May, dogwood and chestnut, flowering
judas,
To be eaten, to be divided, to be drunk
Among whispers.

—T. S. Eliot, *Gerontion*

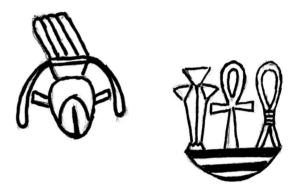

There is probably no period in history when jewelry did
not contain some element of symbolism. It may even be that
one of the primary reasons for the creation of jewelry in antiquity was not merely to display wealth and power, but to
create talismans that would bring the wearer good fortune
and ward off evil. A number of the cloisonné Egyptian pieces
found in jewelry of the Twelfth Dynasty took the form of
amulets. For example, two pendants from the tomb of Princess Khnumet at Dashur wish their owner "joy" and "all life
and protection behind her."

Two amuletic clasps (called "motto clasps" by Andrews) found in
the Twelfth Dynasty tomb of Princess Khnumet, at Dashur,
Egypt. The one at the left wishes its wearer "joy" (literally,
"broadness of heart"); the right hand one says "all life and
protection behind (her)."

An Egyptian revival amulet necklace in silver and enamel, reminiscent of amulet jewelry found in the Twelfth
Dynasty tombs of Princesses Sithathor and Khnumet. In addition to a central ankh, this necklace also contains
two pharaohs wearing stylized crowns, two *sa*-amulets, and two lotus blossoms. *Courtesy of Robin Allison.*

Jewelry found in Tutankhamon's Eighteenth Dynasty tomb was also laden with meaning. Many of the pieces depict Egyptian deities, such as the sky goddess Nut, or contain hieroglyphs for "protection" or "eternity."

Even everyday Egyptians wore amulets made of steatite or faience. Often these amulets took the form of an ankh (the hieroglyph meaning "life" or "live"), an Eye of Horus intended to convey protection and health, or a *sa*-amulet, also for protection. Scarabs were also popular amulets.

An ancient Egyptian scarab (identifiable as such by the hieroglyphs on the back, which contain the name of the falcon god Horus) carved of steatite in a modern silver and plique-à-jour enamel winged setting, possibly c. 1920-1930. The scarab was often used as an amulet in ancient Egypt. Winged scarabs are common motifs found in Egyptian revival jewelry of the 19th and 20th centuries. Winged figures of Isis and Hathor are also frequently found in Egyptian revival jewelry, perhaps because the feathered wings allowed jewelers and manufacturers to create displays of colored enameling.

Elsewhere in the Near East, jewelry was based on myths and symbols. Persian kings wore roundels of gold fashioned into *bas relief* motifs such as lions, suggestive of kingly power. Classical Greek and Roman jewelry depicted gods and goddesses and mythological scenes in cameos or intaglio carvings; Pan and Aphrodite (Venus) were popular subjects. Later, Christian jewelry used recognizable symbols such as the cross, or scenes such as Saint George and the Dragon.

Victorian jewelry also drew on mythological or Biblical themes, especially in the cameos so much in vogue. Many of them depicted Classical scenes, such as nymphs, muses, or Athena. Another popular theme, found in a number of cameos, is the Old Testament-inspired "Rebecca at the Well." Cryptic meanings were hidden in honeymoon pins and DEAREST rings; and they existed as well in the floral jewelry of the late Victorian era. In French jewelry, motifs from mythology were present in the popular pins depicting griffons and dragons and the occasional chimera or basilisk. Some important pieces, such as Frédéric Boucheron's elaborate 1880s chatelaine featuring Apollo's chariot drawn by enameled white horses, also incorporated Classical mythology. Still others, such as Lucien Falize's pendant depicting Moses's messengers Caleb and Joshua returning from the promised land with a bunch of grapes, drew on Biblical themes.

Much of the jewelry of the late nineteenth century seems imbued with symbolism: The endless array of peacocks, the nymph-like women, the flowers, the insects, the mythological or grotesque beings inhabiting the jewelry of the period are portentous with hidden meanings.

And hidden they often were; as Karlin notes, obscurity appeared to be, if it was not in fact, the true intention of the Art Nouveau–if not the Arts and Crafts–adherents and their kindred Symbolist artists: "Symbolist paintings were often intentionally obscure—'the superiority of the artist was matched only by that of the select few who could understand him'" writes Karlin, quoting artist George de Feure (Karlin, 1993, 157). And, according to another source, René Lalique designed some of his jewels, especially those incorporating the sleeping female face with other motifs such as serpents, as "small, symbolic works" (Koch et al., 1990, 138).

While the Symbolists inspired Art Nouveau, Arts and Crafts jewelers appear to have been influenced by the Aesthetic Movement, with its somewhat unfathomable emphasis on peacocks: peacock paintings and drawings, peacock wallpaper and fabric, even peacock bindings abound in Aesthetic art as well as Arts and Crafts.

An allegorical Art Nouveau piece in gold and champlevé enamel. While this piece is stylistically Art Nouveau–the writhing lines make it typical of the genre–it is full of medieval symbolism. St. George slays the dragon, hideous in its death throes–here it ranks as one of the Art Nouveau grotesques–while saving the maiden, chained to a rock. The horse wears the fleur-de-lis of France on its enameled caparison. The peacock stands above the woman, possibly representing resurrection. The champlevé enamel is used to wonderful effect to delineate folds on the dragon's wings. *Courtesy of Nelson Rarities, Portland, ME.*

Two peacock drawings by the Aesthetic Movement artist Aubrey Beardsley. The first is an illustration for the front cover of Aesthetic author Oscar Wilde's play *Salome*. The "peacock skirt" in the second would appear to symbolize vanity.

It was perhaps the Art Nouveau movement, however, that made the most interesting use of symbols, drawing on already existing traditions in mythology and religion, as well as newly discovered Near and Far Eastern motifs. Although the continental Art Nouveau appears to have been influenced to some extent by the British Arts and Crafts movement–both rebelled against the prevailing emphasis on display of wealth rather than good design and craftsmanship too often found in more conventional jewelry of the era–Art Nouveau had other influences that in the end pushed it away from the simpler style embraced by the British.

As previously noted, the Art Nouveau movement was heavily influenced by the Symbolist Movement that took hold in Europe beginning in the 1860s. The Symbolist Movement is said to have begun with the publication of the French poet Charles Baudelaire's book *Les fleurs du mal* (*The Flowers of Evil*) in 1857. As its name implies, the Symbolists used symbols to represent ideas. And while the Symbolist Movement was primarily literary, it did extend to art and jewelry. Art Nouveau attempted to achieve what the Symbolist poet Stephan Mallarmé articulated as a goal: "One of the chief principles of Art Nouveau proposed that the aim of art was to *suggest* reality–in Mallarmé's words, 'to suggest it, that's the dream.'" (Becker, 1985, 9)

Art Nouveau was influenced by the symbolism of mythology, especially Classical mythology, as well as other literary sources. The accomplished designer and enamelist Eugène Feuillâtre, for example, used the theme of the drowned Ophelia, from Shakespeare's play *Hamlet*, to create one of the most beautiful of all Art Nouveau pieces. In Feuillâtre's necklace, Ophelia's face carved out of moonstone shines through a layer of plique-à-jour enamel creating a watery grave out of which grow water lilies, cattails, and other vegetation in opaque enamel.

> Her robe, ungirt from clasp to hem,
> No wrought flowers did adorn,
> But a white rose of Mary's gift,
> For service meekly worn…
> —Dante Gabriel Rossetti, "The Blessed Damozel"

According to Karlin (1993), another motif popular with Arts and Crafts jewelers was the galleon or sailing ship, which appears to harken back to days of yore. In this, the pre-Raphaelite influence can perhaps be detected, as it can in the dress espoused by Arts and Crafts leaders and the flowing hair common to women depicted in both the Arts and Crafts and Art Nouveau movements.

The Symbolists not only had a rich legacy of symbolism and hidden meanings in Classical mythology, but also inherited symbolism from medieval and Renaissance Christian painting. In this tradition, plants and birds were especially meaningful. The dove, for example, is a well-known symbol of peace. The lily, present in many Annunciation scenes, symbolized the Virgin Birth, while the white rose was a symbol of Mary's chastity. The violet stood for modesty, the lily-of-the-valley purity. The strawberry represented rewards for good deeds.

A vintage costume brooch in brass-colored base metal and enamel, c. 1960, representing a galleon. The galleon, perhaps because it harkened back to medieval and Renaissance times, was especially popular as a theme with Arts and Crafts designers, and can be found even in buttons such as those designed by William Hasseler for the London department store Liberty. It remains a popular theme in jewelry from Spain, where this brooch was made. Measures 1.75" x 1.5".

A vintage brooch by David Andersen in silver and enamel, c. 1960. Here the guilloche enamel is decorated not with the usual rose, but with strawberries and their flowers. It is set against the background of a medieval illustrated manuscript leaf with a strawberry in the design along the right margin. Also included are two strawberry charms, one new in silver and the other a vintage charm in 14K gold. Brooch measures approximately 1.125" x .75" and is marked David Andersen, Norway, 925S.

A Victorian pin carved in ivory, the white of which can possibly be taken as a symbol of purity, with a white rose and lilies-of-the-valley, also symbolizing purity or innocence. The lily-of-the-valley beads are also carved from ivory, and probably date to the late 19th or early 20th century. Lilies-of-the-valley were often incorporated into Victorian mourning jewelry, with pearls set in gold forming the flowers against a black background (as in the Victorian mourning demi-parure in chapter one) but obviously ivory was also used. Brooch measures 2.25" x 1.25". Unmarked, but with an old c-clasp.

Classical Mythology and Other Symbolic Sources

The gods, that mortal beauty chase,
Still in a tree did end their race:
Apollo hunted Daphne so
Only that she might laurel grow;
And Pan did after Syrinx speed,
Not as a nymph, but for a reed.

—Andrew Marvell, "The Garden"

The French artist Henri Matisse is said to have believed that there existed, and that he could often find, a flower inside every person.[1] And indeed, in his 1914 painting *Mademsoiselle Yvonne Landsberg*, his subject appears enveloped in petal-like lines, "a natural emanation, unfolding a delicacy of her own, as a flower might unfold." (Gowing, 1979, 126) The ancient Greeks and Romans might be said to have believed the opposite: that inside every flower–and tree, animal, bird, and insect, every river and mountain–there dwelt the spirit of a god, a mortal being, or a demi-god.

In one Greek myth Dryope turned into a tree after picking a lotis blossom–which was really the nymph Lotis, who had changed into a flower while fleeing a pursuer. Just before Dryope became totally paralyzed, and before her mouth was covered by bark, she uttered this warning meant for her infant son: "[B]id him be careful of riverbanks, and beware how he plucks flowers, remembering that every bush he sees may be a goddess in disguise." (Bulfinch, 1981, 90) It appears that the ancients found one way of understanding the world and its non-human fellow dwellers through mythology, which for the Greeks and Romans explained the origin of many creatures.

Greek and Roman mythology is full of transformation myths, many preserved for us in the Roman poet Ovid's work *Metamorphoses*. In this work, Ovid related a number of myths in which figures, often nymphs, become animals or plants or even natural forces. In one transformation myth, for example, the nymph Echo, whose love for Narcissus goes unnoticed, fades away and becomes merely, well, an echo. In another myth, while attempting to escape unwanted attentions, the nymph Arethusa is transformed into a fountain by the goddess Artemis.

Flowers and trees form the basis of a number of transformation myths. The nymph Clytie, for example, fades away and dies for love of the sun god Apollo. After her death, she is transformed into the heliotrope, or sunflower, which daily follows the sun on its path through the sky. In another myth the nymph Daphne, pursued by Apollo and attempting to escape him, is turned into a laurel tree by the goddess Artemis, who among her other duties protected virgins. The laurel then became sacred to Apollo, presumably because of his love for Daphne. The god Pan chased after the nymph Syrinx, only to have her transformed into the reeds from which he made the Pan pipes for which he was noted. The youth Narcissus, in love with his own face reflected in a pool of water, pines away and dies; after his death, he is transformed into the flower that bears his name.

124

A brooch in silver gilt and enamel, c. 1900, by Norwegian designer Marius Hammer. The brooch, in the form of a laurel wreath with leaves in filigree against vertical silver wires, is embellished with dots of pearlescent light green enamel and–in true Arts and Crafts tradition–has a small dangle also dotted with green enamel. Mark for Hammer; measures approximately 1" across.

In other transformations, people or gods became birds or animals. Zeus himself chose to become a swan, and in this guise seduced the nymph Leda. The watchful Argus's thousand eyes were placed on the peacock's tails after Argus was slain while guarding Zeus's lover Io (herself transformed into a cow). Yet another nymph, Callisto, was transformed into a bear by Artemis after becoming pregnant by Zeus; in a further transformation, she became the constellation Ursa Major.

Perhaps more than other creatures, birds in classical mythology were associated with deities. The peacock was associated with Hera, the owl with the goddess of wisdom Athena (Minerva), the cockerel with the messenger god Hermes (Mercury), the dove with Aphrodite (Venus), the swan with Apollo, and the eagle with Jupiter (Zeus).

An Art Nouveau brooch in silver and enamel, featuring a rooster in champlevé enamel with basse taille markings against a guilloche trellis pattern set with stars. The strutting rooster is nicely stylized, yet bears touches of realism in the colors and feathers. A fine representation of Chanticleer. Marked sterling, RD 1910 for an unknown North American (probably Canadian) maker; measures 1.75" in diameter. *Courtesy of Robin Allison.*

Insects also were not exempt from transformation myths. In one Greek myth Arachne, noted for her weaving, challenged the goddess Athena to a contest to see who could produce the best tapestry. As Athena was the goddess of weaving as well as wisdom, this challenge was an insult, and for her hybris Arachne was changed into the ever-weaving spider from which arachnids derive their name. The Greek goddess of the dawn, Eos, so loved a mortal named Tithonus that she begged Zeus to have Tithonus made immortal. However, she forgot to ask that he remain forever young, with the result that he grew older and older until he withered into a cricket–or, in other versions, a locust.

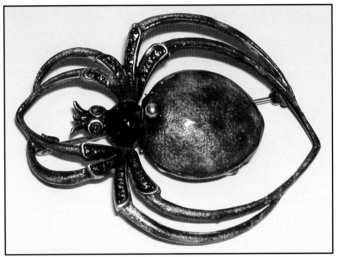

A vintage brooch that opens to reveal a watch, in sterling silver, enamel, and marcasites, in the form of a spider. While the spider is somewhat stylized, it is recognizably an arachnid. In myths and legends, spiders often take on unpleasant attributes; in one Sioux legend, Unktomi the spider tricks two widows and makes soup out of their two babies, which he has been left to guard while the women search for plums. However, while arachnophobes perhaps outnumber arachnophiles, spiders can be found in jewelry from many periods. Made by the Swiss company Eska; measures 2.25" x 1.75". *Courtesy of Robin Allison.*

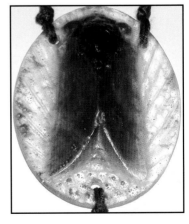

A pendant in *pate de verre* (please see chapter two for more information on this technique) in the form of a locust. The locust's folded wings are in an amber glass, while the head–all that is visible of the rest of its body–is in much darker glass. In Greek mythology, Tithonus was immortal, but grew ever older, at last becoming a locust. Signed GAR (for G. Argy-Rousseau, a noted glass artist) and measures 2.25" x 1.75". *Courtesy of Robin Allison.*

Modern Literary Influences

Though not as rich a source for allegorical or symbolic jewelry as ancient mythology or older literary sources such as the Bible, Greek and Roman writers, or William Shakespeare, modern literature has provided some themes for more recent jewelry. One fun piece alludes to Frank R. Stockton's often anthologized short story, "The Lady–or the Tiger?" Another draws on a fairy tale by Danish writer Hans Christian Andersen.

A watch in 14K gold and enamel, by the American watchmaking firm Elgin. Unusually, this Art Deco watch has a lady–stylized and very Deco, down to the sleek cap of hair–to one side of the watch face, and a tiger–also sleek, stylized, snarling, and lurking in tall grasses–on the other. It seems likely that this combination of the lady and the tiger was meant to evoke the much-anthologized short story classic, "The Lady–or the Tiger?" A most unusual piece of jewelry, measuring 1.125" x .625. *Courtesy of Robin Allison.*

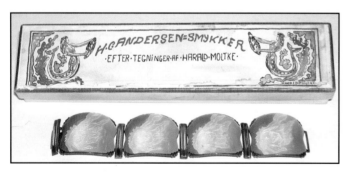

A bracelet in silver and enamel, by the Danish designer Harald Moltke, showing the Snow Queen from the fairy tale of the same name by Danish author Hans Christian Andersen. Moltke, as is known from promotional material in the bracelet's original box, also created other pieces based on Andersen fairy tales, including perhaps the most famous Andersen story of all, "The Little Mermaid." Marks for Moltke, sterling, Denmark; measures 6.5" x 1.25". *Courtesy of Robin Allison.*

Other Influences: Egyptian and Eastern Myths and Religions

Scattering fire, Uraeus serpents guard the Tombs' tremendous gate;
While Thoth holds the trembling balance, weighs the heart and seals its fate.

Mathilde Blind, "Tombs of the Kings"

There is no question that Art Nouveau jewelry took much of its inspiration, whether indirectly or directly, from Classical mythology; the myriad nymphs, graces, satyrs, and other mythical beings portrayed in jewelry of the movement attest to this. However, Art Nouveau was probably also in part inspired by aspects of the nineteenth century revival movements, which provided a wealth of iconic designs and motifs from the ancient world, not merely those of Greece and Rome but also those of ancient Egypt. Japan too, newly accessible, was a font of not just form and style but also meaningful iconography; and thus Chinese culture, which so greatly influenced the Japanese, probably featured as well. Interestingly, many symbols from China can be explained by homophony, or two words that sound alike creating associations. The bat, though feared in many cultures, was to the Chinese a symbol of good fortune because the Chinese words for "bat" and "luck" are so alike (both are *fu*). (Biedermann, 1994, 30)

No less than for the ancient Greeks and Romans, and later for Christians drawing on both Old and New Testament traditions, nature provided symbolic motifs for the Egyptian, Chinese, Japanese, and other cultures. The lotus, for example, was imbued with meaning for ancient Egyptians, for the Chinese, Buddhists, and Hindus. The peacock as well can be found as a symbol in many cultures, as can the eagle, the dove, the raven, and the crane.

Perhaps because of its great antiquity and its relative isolation from other cultures until the first millennium B.C., Egypt provided a number of unique motifs. And, due to the several Egyptian revival phases, Egyptian signs and symbols are fairly prominent in nineteenth century jewelry. The falcon, for example, was peculiarly prominent in Egyptian religion, first as a solar deity and later in a triad with Isis and Osiris, who figured as his mother and father. The myth of Isis and Osiris and their son Horus provided several signs used in amulets, including the *djed*-pillar (see the list of symbols below). Another symbol unique to Egypt was the scarab, the beetle thought by Egyptians to push the sun in its daily transit across the sky.

Grotesque or Mythical Creatures

Come not between the dragon and his wrath.

—William Shakespeare, *King Lear*

Although Victorian, Arts and Crafts, and Art Nouveau drew heavily on themes or motifs from nature, mythical creatures were also popular. Among the most common beasts were dragons and griffons, with the occasional chimera and basilisk thrown in. Some of these creatures come from Classical mythology. Others, such as the unicorn, have largely Christian associations, while still others, such as Egypt's sphinx, are from non-European traditions that passed into Classical myths. Art Nouveau designers were not loath to create their own mythical beings when necessity arose: The Art Nouveau repertoire is full of woman-butterflies, woman-dragonflies, and other "grotesques." In this as well, however, they may have drawn upon earlier tradition: Artists had created drawings of women as plants and flowers long before Art Nouveau.

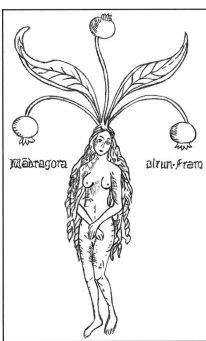

The idea of women melded with plants (or insects) was not a new one. Here, a drawing based on a medieval herbal drawing of a man-drake-woman.

Because it is sometimes difficult to distinguish a stylized dragon from a griffon, or a sphinx from a chimera, jewelry representing these creatures has been placed together at the end of this section. The types of grotesque and mythological creatures seemingly found most often in jewelry are:

basilisk–A mythical being, the lizard-like basilisk was said to have a gaze that turned humans to stone. It was a symbol for Christians as well as ancient Greeks and Romans, and figures in the writings of, among others, Saint Augustine and the mystic writer Saint Hildegard of Bingen. It symbolized lust, one of the seven deadly sins. (Biedemann, 1994, 29)

chimera–A mythical creature from Classical mythology, the chimera or chimaera was part lion, part goat, and part snake. In one myth, the chimera was slain by the hero Bellerophon, who rode the winged horse Pegasus. Like the basilisk, the chimera in Christian iconography sometimes represented demonic forces. The chimera appears in nineteenth century French jewelry, tra-

ditional as well as Art Nouveau. The jeweler Eugène Fontenay created an archaeological revival chimera brooch with an enameled scene of a chimera being tamed by an unidentified Greek figure (who resembles in some ways the god Hermes). The brooch bears the Greek words "H XIMAIPA" in granulation under the enameled picture.

dragon–The dragon seems to be an almost universally occurring image; one might even believe in a collective unconscious memory of dinosaurs, so prevalent is this ferocious mythical creature. It is found in China, in Classical mythology, in Christian stories. Often it has evil overtones: In Egyptian mythology, the snake or dragon Apophis swallowed the sun, Re, each night. Apophis also had to be overcome by the dead on their way to the afterlife just as Re overcame it each morning. In medieval literature, dragons ravished maidens and battled Saint George, becoming in essence a symbol of evil. In other tales, the dragon hoarded its treasure, which it guarded fiercely. However, in China the turquoise dragon was a symbol of imperial power, the East and the rising sun, and spring rain; the white dragon was the symbol of the West and death (white being the color of mourning in China as well as ancient Egypt).

griffon–A mythical being encountered in Greek mythology, the griffon (also spelled *gryphon* or *griffin*) had the body of a lion and the head of an eagle. It was also a winged creature. Biedermann (1994, 159) sees the griffon as having roots in the Assyrian cherub, a winged lion with the head of a man. Whatever the validity of this claim, the griffon, composed as it was of an eagle–king of the birds–and a lion–king of the beasts–was a symbol of strength. It was a very popular motif in nineteenth century jewelry, especially French, where it can be found in innumerable stickpins and brooches.

A wonderful brooch in unmarked silver, showing a mythical beast, most likely a dragon, in Limoges (or Limoges-like) enamel, with an Arts and Crafts silver setting studded with turquoise, pearls, and with pearl dangles. The fire-breathing beast has a coiled snake-like tail, wings, and a head possibly representing a stylized lion. Measures 1.5" x 1.375". *Courtesy of Robin Allison.*

A striking French Gothic revival pendant with Art Nouveau overtones–the flowing lines of both monster and the frame, the vivid expression both seem in the Art Nouveau style–depicting a chimera, in gold, diamond, and guilloche enamel. The guilloche enameling is wonderfully textured, as it leads to the chimera's target–the diamond at the center of an enameled bull's-eye. The chimera was frequently depicted in late 19th century French jewelry, along with dragons and the occasional basilisk. *Courtesy of Nelson Rarities, Portland, ME.*

A very unusual pair of Chinese earrings in unmarked gold-washed silver and enamel in the form of dragons, possibly late 19th century (definitely pre-1920). Like other Chinese pieces, these are embellished with wire cloisons, here filled with blue and green enamel suitable for dragons; these colors are reprised in the many dangles hanging from the dragons' bodies. In Eastern mythology, dragons were often symbols of power, as well as harbingers of fortunate events such as spring rains. Measure 1.75" x 1.375". *Courtesy of Robin Allison.*

A marvelous Japanese buckle in unmarked silver and enamel, showing a dragon, with its head surrounded by the coils of its body. Unlike the dragons in the Chinese earrings shown above, this dragon is very detailed, down to the scales on its body, its gaping mouth enameled in red, its yellow and black eyes, the claws in which it holds a blue enameled disk, and the whiskers curving upward from its face. Measures 2.125" x 1.625". *Courtesy of Robin Allison.*

A fantastic necklace in sterling silver, enamel, mabe pearl, and garnets (perhaps paste), showing two fabulous creatures–possibly griffons, as they have the heads of eagles, and are winged–facing one another across a red (paste) gem. With its medieval revival theme and its combination of silver, mabe pearl, and (possibly) paste, this piece has something of an Austro-Hungarian look to it. Marked Geschutzt (German meaning "protected by law"); measures 1.875" x 1.25". *Courtesy of Robin Allison.*

Another wonderful dragon piece, this one a brooch in silver and enamel by noted Mexican designer Margot de Taxco. Here the dragon has a Mayan look, seen for example in its eye and stylized fire. While dragons played no great part in meso-American mythology and lore, the serpent was especially important. And in fact what seems to be a dragon may represent the feathered serpent Qetzalqoatl. However, it should be noted that Margot de Taxco drew not only on themes from her adopted Mexico, but Asian, Egyptian, and other cultures as well. The piece shows Margot's usual fine champlevé and basse taille work. Signed Margot de Taxco, sterling, with the ID no. 8783; measures 2.625" in diameter. *Courtesy of Robin Allison.*

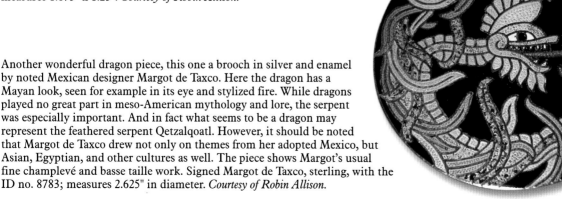

A Brief List of Some of the More Common Symbols

The following is a short alphabetical list of some of the symbols more commonly used in nineteenth and twentieth century jewelry, whether Victorian, Arts and Crafts, Art Nouveau, Egyptian revival, or later, with meanings taken from a variety of sources and cultures.

Amon (also spelled *Amun*)–From the Late Kingdom on, Amon was the most powerful of Egyptian gods. His name meant "secret" or "hidden one" in Egyptian. Originally a local god of Thebes, home of Eighteenth Dynasty rulers, Amon was sometimes portrayed with a ram's head. His name was also combined with that of the solar god Re; as Amon-Re, the powerful god was often depicted with a falcon's head, the falcon being associated with solar deities in ancient Egypt. As such, he is depicted in one Egyptian revival brooch (see under *falcon*).

ankh– the Egyptian word and hieroglyph for "life," it is thought to be also the sign for a sandal strap, which was a homophone for "life." The hieroglyph was prominent in amulets, including royal pectorals.

A wonderful Egyptian revival pendant in 800 silver, plique-à-jour enamel, opals, garnets, and baroque pearls. The central element of the pendant is an ankh in pink and turquoise enamel, flanked by stylized lotus blossoms. The use of chains and baroque pearls in this piece give it an interesting Arts and Crafts look, a departure from the usual Art Deco Egyptian revival pieces. Measures 3.875" x 1.625". *Courtesy of Robin Allison.*

Two similar Egyptian revival bracelets in silver and enamel, both with winged scarabs and *ba*-birds, as well as winged serpents. True to Egyptian representations of the *ba*, these are human-headed birds; the heads have the ceremonial beard associated with kingship. Unusually, the bracelet on the bottom, with the plique-à-jour enamel rather than the champlevé, has the winged scarab set with a faceted aquamarine, rather than the scaraboid cabochons usually found (and seen in the second bracelet). The bracelet without plique is marked sterling Germany, and measures 6.625" x 1"; the plique bracelet measures 7.25" by 1" and is marked sterling. *Courtesy of Robin Allison.*

Aphrodite or *Venus*–The Greek and Roman goddess of love, she was associated with the dove. In mythology, she was awarded the Golden Apple of Discord, and in reward gave Helen of Troy to Paris, thus starting the Trojan War. She was noted for her beauty, and is sometimes portrayed in cameos and other jewelry from the nineteenth century.

Apollo–In Classical mythology Apollo was featured in several of the transformation myths: He pursued the nymph Daphne (transformed into a laurel tree), and spurned Clytie (turned into a sunflower). He was also endowed with the gift of prophecy, and the ancient Greeks are said to have consulted his oracle at Delphi, where he spoke through the priestess Pythia.

A Victorian sterling silver heart charm with a bas relief enameled sunflower. Oddly enough, the sunflower seldom occurs in other types of Victorian (or later) jewelry, such as flower pins. A charm similar to this one can be found in chapter one, under Hearts Through Time. Measures 1.25" x 1.25". *Courtesy of Robin Allison.*

Apophis–see under *snake*

Athena or *Minerva*–The warlike goddess of wisdom was often portrayed wearing a helmet (as in the Limoges enamel below, on p. 136, flanking the picture of Dionysus). Unlike Artemis, Athena was no protectress of women. In the trial of Orestes, who killed his mother Clytemnestra and was in turn haunted by the Furies, Athena voted with male deities who exonerated Orestes. Their argument: Because the father alone contributes matter–the seed that grows into the child; the woman merely serves as incubator–in a child's creation, a mother does not count in the same way a father does. Athena is associated with the owl as well as with the olive tree, her gift to the people of Athens for naming their city after her. (For a depiction of Athena in a Limoges enamel, please see below under *Dionysus*.)

ba–The ancient Egyptians believed that the body was survived primarily by two different souls. One, the *ka*, is generally assumed to have represented a person's double; the *ka* lingered in the tomb, inhabiting statues of the dead, carrying out functions such as eating and drinking offerings left for the deceased. The other, the *ba*, is often represented as a bird with a human head–complete with ceremonial beard. The *ba* flitted around the tomb, but also traveled on the solar barque at night. The *ba*–bird is occasionally found in Egyptian revival pieces.

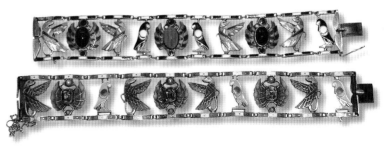

Bacchus–see under *Dionysus*

basilisk–see above, under *Grotesque or Mythical Creatures*

bat–InClassical mythology, the souls of the dead were sometimes said to flit about in the afterlife like bats; however, the bat was considered intelligent but timid. Later European legends were less kind to the bat, and associated it with vampires (perhaps because of the discovery of the Central American vampire bat, which does drink blood; most other bats eat either fruit or insects). However, in China, the bat was considered a symbol of good fortune, perhaps because the Chinese words for "bat" and "luck" are both pronounced *fu*. The bat is frequently carved in jade or ivory as a symbol of luck.

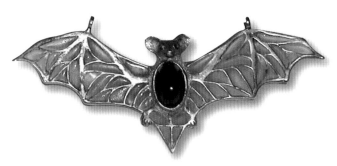

An Art Nouveau pendant in silver, plique-à-jour enamel, and paste, in the form of a bat with outspread wings. The cells are made in such a way that they seem to mimic the veining in a bat's wings, as well as its arms and legs. The unenameled head is nicely dimensional, with a protruding nose, concave ears, and red eyes. While bats are often considered scary in Western tradition–associated with vampires as well as with such real-life threats as rabies–in China they are symbols of good fortune. The back of this piece is very detailed. Marked 900 silver; measures 2.25" x .875". *Courtesy of Robin Allison.*

bee–Of all insects, the bee may be the most symbolic as well as the most useful, providing both honey and bee's wax. As the source of honey, it is associated with sweetness. Because of its relentless pursuit of flowers' nectar, it is also associated with hard work or industriousness. To the ancient Egyptians, it was the royal symbol of Lower Egypt; the Egyptian kingly titles included the phrase "He of the sedge (symbol of Upper Egypt) and the bee." The Chinese, because the word for "bee" is similar to that for the title "count," considered the bee a symbol of professional or social advancement. Christian philosophers saw the bee as a symbol of the faithful, who gathered around the church as bees swarm about their hive.

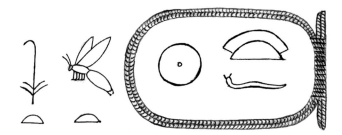

A drawing of the *n-sw bity* ("he of the sedge and the bee") name, which preceded the king's prenomen–in this case that of Khephren, owner of one of the three great pyramids.

Two vintage pins in silver, enamel, and marcasites, in the form of bees, both from Germany. Although the wings on the two bees are of different shapes, folded back in one, spread in the other, and there are other small variations as well, the coloring of the wings–turquoise blue in the one on the right, turquoise shading to purple in the leftmost pin–and the bodies are similar, and point to the same manufacturer for both. Bees in jewelry, both with and without enamel, are fairly popular, and formed one subtype of Brazilian jewelry (as in the earrings below). Both marked sterling Germany; the leftmost one measures 1.125" x .875", the one on the right 1.375" x .75". *Courtesy of Robin Allison.*

A pair of earrings, c. 1960, from Brazil, in gold, pearls, and rubies, in the shape of bees. Such apian jewelry was very common in Brazil mid-20th century, in pins and earrings, worn by both tourists and native Brazilians alike. Despite their sting, bees have long been associated with industry and, of course, the honey they produce.

beetle–The scarabaeus, or dung beetle, pushes its eggs before it in a round ball; the ancient Egyptians saw this as an embodiment of the force that daily pushes the sun through the sky. The scarab thus became a powerful symbol in Egyptian mythology, and is frequently found in amulets; a heart-scarab was placed on a mummified body where the heart had been in life. The scarab also figures prominently in Egyptian revival jewelry, often as a winged scarab.

An Egyptian revival bracelet in 800 silver and enamel, featuring cobalt blue and turquoise enameled scarabs set between ovals containing stylized lotus blossoms. Interestingly, the scarabs have a guilloche or basse taille background that adds shimmer, possibly seeking to emulate the iridescence found in some beetles in nature. The usual colors of dark blue, turquoise, and red, commonly found in Egyptian revival jewelry, represent the stones most often used in ancient Egyptian cloisonné jewelry as well as more modern replications. In ancient Egypt, both the lotus and the scarab represented coming into being, or creation. Measures 6.5" x .875". *Courtesy of Robin Allison.*

bluebird–A symbol of happiness, as in Maurice Maeterlink's play *The Bluebird*, in which two rather impoverished children wait for the bluebird to bring them relief from their unfortunate situation, the bluebird was a popular motif in Victorian jewelry, and also used by makers such as Charles Horner (please refer to chapter one for examples of such brooches). In these pieces, it is often found with a forked tail, such as a swallow might have. Nevertheless, it is fairly clear that such pieces were meant to represent bluebirds–the bright coloring leaves little doubt.

A locket in silver and enamel, with a bluebird and a robin perched in a cherry tree painted against a white guilloche background, by Norwegian designer Aksel Holmsen. While bluebirds are fairly frequently found in Victorian and later pieces, robins are encountered much less often–and Robin was delighted to have found this one! Maker's mark, 925S; measures 1.25" in diameter. *Courtesy of Robin Allison.*

butterfly–Symbolic in many cultures, the butterfly often represents metamorphosis. It also symbolizes beauty, or the transitory nature of life and beauty. In some pre-Aryan Indian religions, butterflies were thought to be the souls of the reincarnated dead.

A Bevy of Butterflies: Butterflies Through Time

> When thou dost ask me blessing, I'll kneel down
> And ask of thee forgiveness: and we'll live,
> And pray, and sing, and tell old tales, and laugh
> At gilded butterflies.
>
> —William Shakespeare, *King Lear*

> The leaves fall early this autumn, in wind.
> The paired butterflies are already yellow with
> August
> Over the grass in the west garden;
> They hurt me. I grow older.
>
> —Ezra Pound, *The River Merchant's Wife: A Letter,* by Rhiaku

Perhaps because their brilliant colors and exotic markings, their iridescent wingspans and their evanescent life span fascinate us, butterflies are more often found in figural enameled jewelry than any motif other than flowers. Scandinavian enamelists, particularly Norwegians such as David Andersen, Hroar Prydz, and OPRO, have made enameled butterflies almost a cottage industry. But the Victorians also loved butterflies, as did British firms that followed that era, such as John Atkins & Sons, noted for their large, brightly hued butterfly brooches.

A Victorian veil clip in 14K gold and enamel, in the form of a butterfly with articulated wings. The enameling is extremely fine, with cloisonné-like separations (probably in reality achieved through champlevé depressions set off by textured gold lines rather than by the use of wire to create cells) delineating various parts of the wings and their markings. The enamel shades beautifully, from pale blue through pink, darker through lighter pink, with cobalt blue outlining the wings, and deep red circles marking the top and bottom wings. The body of the butterfly, in gold, is constructed so that the wings move, but overall this piece seems less concerned with a realistic depiction of a butterfly than with the creation of a lovely piece of jewelry. Undeciphered maker's mark; measures 1" x .625". *Courtesy of Robin Allison.*

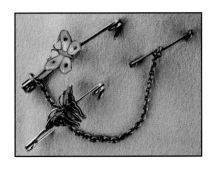

A pair of Victorian cufflinks in silver and enamel, in the shape of very stylized butterflies showing what appears to be a marked Asian influence in both design and color, as well as in the cloisonné-like cells created by champlevé depressions. Interestingly, the two butterflies show different coloring in some of their markings, as well as in the main color: The dominant yellow in the wings of the butterfly on the right appears as brown in the wings in the left cufflink. Unmarked silver, measuring almost 1" in diameter. *Courtesy of Red Robin Antiques.*

Two small pins in silver and enamel, each with a small butterfly resting on the wire pin. The lower pin, with the butterfly done in dark green "bubble" enamel found in some Arts and Crafts pieces, is by designer Charles Horner. The upper pin, probably British c. 1900, has a butterfly enameled in lighter blue of an almost aquamarine hue, with red markings, similar to a design found in some larger butterfly brooches by the Birmingham maker John Atkins & Sons (although this particular piece is unmarked). Each pin measures approximately 1.25" in length, with the butterflies measuring approximately .5" wide. The Charles Horner pin is marked CH, and sterling, but without the usual marks for Chester and the year of manufacture.

An Arts and Crafts butterfly brooch in unmarked silver, enamel, and mabe pearl, showing many elements of Arts and Crafts design: a handcrafted look; stylized geometrical squareness to the wings, along with cutout circles for "markings"; the inclusion of the central mabe pearl; and the signature blue-and-green enamel, here with a "bubble" look created by basse taille circles. Measures 2.5" x .875". *Courtesy of Robin Allison.*

An interesting necklace in sterling silver and enamel, with three circular links in black enamel decorated by a butterfly with folded wings; and linked by elements containing seven graduated circles in black, yellow, and green which are similar to, but do not exactly replicate, the colors used for the butterflies, and which give something of an Art Deco look to the piece. Enameled section measures 6.5" x .625". *Courtesy of Robin Allison.*

An Art Nouveau take on the butterfly, here in a brooch by the German firm Meyle & Mayer, in silver, plique-à-jour enamel, seed pearls, and paste gems. Like other pieces from this maker, this one is beautifully designed and executed, with the lines forming the cells indicating both the veining of the wings, and their markings. The enamel is done in lovely pastel shades of pinks and greens, with paste gems set in the corners of each wing. Seed pearls set in silver form a scalloped design near the edge of each wing, while the body of the insect–with basse taille striations–is also set with paste and small pearls. Marks for Meyle & Mayer, depose, sterling; measures 2.75" x 1.75". *Courtesy of Robin Allison.*

A butterfly brooch in silver and enamel, by the Birmingham maker John Atkins & Sons, c. 1918. While this firm created other types of jewelry, including bar pins as well as other figural jewelry such as dragonflies, it seems to have specialized in butterflies. These appear fairly frequently at auction, often designated as Art Deco pieces, probably more due to date of manufacture rather than for any reason to do with style or design. The firm's pieces were well made, with fine enameling and with underlying basse taille designs to indicate the wings' veins (in this piece those markings are not easily seen due to the dark color of the enamel). Measures approximately 2.625" across, with anchor mark, lion passe, S for the year 1918/1919, and maker's mark (J A & S in a diamond divided into four quadrants).

A smaller butterfly brooch, measuring approximately 1.125" across, by the Birmingham maker JA&S, this one in a pale green shading to darker at the wings' edges. The color and the red markings on the wings are very similar to the hues in the very small butterfly pictured with the Charles Horner butterfly; although it is unmarked, it seems a reasonable guess that it too was manufactured by JA&S. Marked sterling, maker.

Four butterfly brooches by Norwegian makers. Top: A butterfly by Ole Peter Raasch Olsen (OPRO), in basse taille ochre, brown, and black enamel. Center, left: A small brooch by Aksel Holmsen, in dark blue and white basse taille enamel; right: Another butterfly, in purple basse taille enamel, by OPRO, which still produces enameled jewelry in some quantity. Bottom: A butterfly by Hroar Prydz, who is noted for his butterflies. All marked for sterling silver, with maker's marks; all mid-20th century except for the purple OPRO, which is c. 1980.

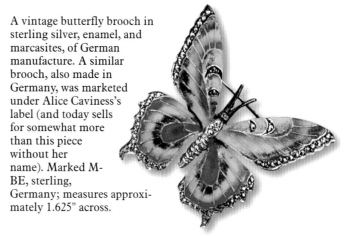

A vintage butterfly brooch in sterling silver, enamel, and marcasites, of German manufacture. A similar brooch, also made in Germany, was marketed under Alice Caviness's label (and today sells for somewhat more than this piece without her name). Marked M-BE, sterling, Germany; measures approximately 1.625" across.

A large enameled butterfly brooch by Norwegian maker David Andersen, in sterling silver and enamel, c. 1950. In this piece, Andersen has used basse taille engraving to create patterns in the yellow- and orange-enameled wings, and in the orange body of the butterfly. The basse taille pattern uses both small straight lines and tiny dots inside larger designs. Measures approximately 2.5" x 1.5" and is marked David Andersen, sterling, Norway.

A small Art Deco butterfly in sterling silver and green basse taille enamel, possibly by the British maker John Atkins and Sons. This piece is marked only for silver content and not for maker. Especially distinctive are the antennae on butterflies by J.A.& S., which are almost horizontal.

Another, larger butterfly by the German maker M-BE, in sterling silver, enamel, and marcasites. Marked as above; measures 2.125" x 1.75". *Courtesy of Robin Allison.*

A vintage butterfly brooch in silver gilt filigree and enamel, perhaps c. 1940. Similar brooches are sometimes described as having plique-à-jour enamel, because the filigree work underlying the enamel allows light to pass through; however, the enamel is not formed in backless cells, and thus is not truly plique-à-jour. Marked sterling; measures approximately 1.375" across.

A more modern Taxco butterfly brooch in silver and enamel, by Maya de Taxco, measuring approximately 1.125" across.

A demi-parure by noted Mexican designer Margot de Taxco, in silver and enamel. The necklace is formed of oblong silver links enameled in black, with a central butterfly in champlevé enamel of various colors, including a vivid red, turquoise, and mottled greens and grays. Interestingly the matching earrings, rather than consisting of complete butterflies, take elements from the butterfly to create an abstract design. Signed sterling, with the number 5628; the brooch/pendant, on a 15" chain, measures 2.125" x 1.875", the earrings 1" x .625". *Courtesy of Robin Allison.*

A pair of earrings by famed costume designer Miriam Haskell, in brass and opaque matte turquoise enamel. These earrings are perhaps most notable for their simplicity of design and enameling; stamped out of a single sheet of metal, very little effort was made to create realistic features such as dimensionality, markings, or wing structures. Measure 1" x .75"; marked Haskell on earring screw backs.

Another butterfly from Taxco in silver and enamel, this one c. 1960 and marked ATI, Mexico, sterling. Measures approximately 1.375" across.

A brooch in copper and enamel by the maker Matisse (also known as Matisse Renoir). A hallmark of pieces by this maker is the use of copper designs, often geometric, over the enamel. Like all of their pieces, this one is done in hard enamel.

cat–Throughout history, cats have seemingly been either revered or reviled. In ancient Egypt, the cat was worshiped as the goddess Bastet. On the other hand, to superstitious medieval Europeans, the cat was sometimes seen as a witch's familiar. Even today, black cats are considered unlucky.

A cute Victorian brooch in silver, enamel, and paste, with a black cat in champlevé enamel sitting on an area textured possibly to represent a floor. The cat's blue paste eyes add a nice touch of color to this charming piece. Marked WS Ltd. sterling; measures 1" in diameter. *Courtesy of Robin Allison.*

cherub–Perhaps no other mythological creature has undergone so drastic a transformation as has the cherub. Originally, in ancient Assyria, the cherub was a winged lion with the head of a bearded man. Monumental stone statues of cherubs in this guise have been found in Mesopotamia. The cherub then became one of the orders of angels in the Old Testament, second in importance only to the seraphim. The cherub was next transformed into one aspect of the god Cupid or Eros, shooting arrows at mortals to make them fall in love. Finally, the cherub became an angelic child; in this last guise, it is sometimes given the Italian name *putto* (plural *putti*).

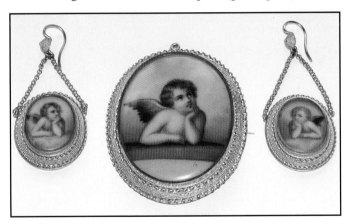

A demi-parure in 18K gold and porcelain consisting of a brooch/locket and earrings painted with cherubs in a thoughtful pose. The gold work, with its granulation and texture, is reminiscent of that in archaeological revival pieces. Cherubs were among the more popular themes used in Victorian jewelry, and can be found in enamel, on porcelain, in transfers, as well as in other decorative arts. Brooch measures 2.125" x 1.875", earrings 2.25" x .875". *Courtesy of Robin Allison.*

Another Victorian cherub, this one on a Wedgwood china plaque. The cherub itself, mostly in the bas relief common to Wedgwood items, here has added dimensionality in the protruding leg and the arm holding a muff (while with the other hand the cherub releases snow).

chimera–see above under *Grotesque and Mythical Creatures*

chrysanthemum–Depending on its color, the chrysanthemum had various meanings in the language of flowers: Red was a declaration of love, white stood for truth, and yellow for cheerfulness or, somewhat contradictorily, slighted love. However, the chrysanthemum is also a symbol of Japan, and as such appears often in its floral jewelry and other decorative arts. (For an example of a Japanese chrysanthemum piece, please refer to chapter one, p. 62, under Asian jewelry.)

A brooch in sterling silver and enamel, with a white chrysanthemum (in the language of flowers, signifying "truth") in basse taille against a guilloche background, of New England manufacture. Marked for Chas. M. Robbins, sterling; measures 2.875" x 1.75". *Courtesy of Robin Allison.*

cockerel or *rooster*–The rooster is associated with the Greek messenger god Hermes (Mercury), but also appears in medieval tales as Chanticleer, the boastful barnyard ruler–he appears, for example, in Geoffrey Chaucer's *Canterbury Tales*, where he is described in the following manner:

> His comb was redder than the fine coral, Embattell'd as it were a castle wall. His bill was black, and as the jet it shone; Like azure were his legges and his toes; His nailes whiter than the lily flow'r, And like the burnish'd gold was his colour.

The rooster's crowing was supposed to have almost magical powers: It could ward off lions and basilisks, and raise the sun. Chinese mythology also portrays the rooster in positive light; not only is it one of the signs of the Chinese zodiac, but the white rooster was also thought to drive away demons, while the red variety protected one from fire. Using the homonymic sounds of the words for "cock" (*kung-chi*) and "crow" (*ming*), the Chinese heard the word *kung-ming* ("merit and fame") in the rooster's crow.

A vintage brooch in silver, enamel, and marcasites, in the form of a strutting rooster. While the rooster is stylized–colorful enamel in curlicues represents its tail, with marcasites set in the topmost swirl–some attempt at realism is made in the depiction of neck and wing feathers. Marked Germany sterling; measures 2.375" x 2.25". *Courtesy of Robin Allison.*

Dionysus or *Bacchus*–In Classical mythology, Dionysus was a son of Zeus who introduced the grapevine and wine to humankind, thus dispelling care. As his Roman counterpart Bacchus, he was the god of intoxication and revelry, and gave his name to the word "bacchanalian"–wild to the point of ecstasy. He is associated with grapes, wine, satyrs, and frenzied women.

A 19th century pendant watch depicting the god Dionysus (Roman Bacchus). Dionysus/ Bacchus, the god of wine and the vine, was often depicted with a beard and a garland of grapes and grape leaves. The watch is flanked by two Limoges brooches; the helmeted woman might very well be a depiction of the goddess Athena, who is often shown wearing a helmet. *Courtesy of Nelson Rarities, Portland, ME.*

djed-pillar–In the Egyptian myth "Isis and Osiris," Osiris, king of the gods, was slain by his jealous brother Set. To ensure that Osiris was truly powerless, Set hacked Osiris's body into pieces, and scattered these pieces up and down Egypt. Isis searched the length of the land, found Osiris's body parts, and reassembled them. His backbone, or *djed*-pillar, found at Busiris became a symbol of strength and a popular Egyptian amulet.

dove–The dove in Classical mythology was associated with the goddess of love, Aphrodite (Venus). In the Old Testament, the dove is one of two birds sent out by Moses to ascertain whether or not the great deluge had ended. The dove returned with an olive branch, and has since become a symbol of peace. This symbolism continued into Christian iconography, where the dove also represents the Holy Spirit or Holy Ghost, and as such is present in most renditions of the Annunciation. Because of its association with Aphrodite, the dove is often portrayed with her son Eros (depicted as a cherub).

A charming Victorian brooch in 14K gold, enameled porcelain, and pearls, depicting a cherub in a chariot pulled by four white doves. Measures 1.625" x 1.5". *Courtesy of Robin Allison.*

A Victorian brooch in silver, gutta percha (a plastic, fairly hard substance made of rubber and other materials, and sometimes used in Victorian jewelry), and transfer enameling, showing a coy cherub with two white doves. Measures 2" x 1.625". *Courtesy of Robin Allison.*

dragon–see above, under *Grotesque and Mythical Creatures*

*Lonesomely clings the dragonfly to the underside of the leaf
Ah! The autumn rain.*

—Japanese poem

dragonfly–Although the dragonfly seems to have little symbolism in Classical mythology, it nevertheless was a favorite theme of Art Nouveau jewelers and decorative artists. In fact, like the plique-à-jour from which its wings were often formed in Art Nouveau pieces, it almost epitomizes the movement. It is found in pieces by almost every major Art Nouveau jeweler, and in the stained glass lampshades of Louis Comfort Tiffany. The dragonfly, significantly enough, is called a *nymph* while in its aquatic larval stage, which may last for up to two or three years. Also significant, given the *Japonisme* that to some extent influenced Art Nouveau, the dragonfly is important in Japanese mythology, poetry, and art. *Shoryo Tombo* ("dragonfly of the dead") is the name given to the dragonfly that carries the souls of dead ancestors to their descendants during the Bon festival. In other traditions, such as some Native American myths, dragonflies also represent the souls of the dead. However, like the butterfly they also seem to symbolize metamorphosis: The watery nymph becomes the beautiful iridescent dragonfly.

A beautiful Art Nouveau dragonfly brooch in gold, enamel, demantoid garnets, diamonds, and rubies. The iridescent enamel with accents of red and green seems to capture the wonderful delicate coloring of dragonfly wings. *Courtesy of Nelson Rarities, Portland, ME.*

A small perfume jar in the Art Nouveau style, with an iridescent enameled dragonfly against bright red with iridescent swirls.

eye–The eye, so important to human perception, is not surprisingly a recurrent motif in mythology, literature, and superstition. In some myths, the eye has the obvious meaning of watchfulness, wakefulness, alertness. Argos, the watchman in Greek mythology set by jealous Hera to guard Zeus's lover Io, had a thousand eyes, of which only two could close at any one time. When he nevertheless failed at his task, being overtaken and slain by Hermes, Hera placed his eyes upon the tail feathers of the peacock, her favorite bird. In some cultures, an amulet in the shape of an eye can be a protective amulet; in others, it brings bad luck. Brazilians, influenced by their *macumba* (Brazilian form of voodoo) tradition, wear an amulet called a *figa* (a clenched hand with the thumb protruding between the index and middle fingers), to ward off the evil eye.

A pendant in 18K gold, enamel, and glass, representing an eye and intended to serve as a good luck charm. This one was made in Egypt; however, bracelets and necklaces with round enameled "eyes" have recently been in vogue.

Eye of Horus–The Eye of Horus was one of the most common and most powerful of Egyptian amulets. The falcon god Horus, originally a solar god but early incorporated into the myth of Isis and Osiris, lost his eye to the evil god Set. (Some scholars feel that this myth may reflect an awe of the darkness of solar eclipses.) Later he regained it, and it became a symbol of wholeness. In ancient accounting, the Eye of Horus, divided into parts such as the iris and the eyebrow, was used to write fractions.

The Eye of Horus, which was a powerful amulet in ancient Egypt, symbolized "wholeness" or "soundness." It was also used to measure grain, with each part of the eye representing a fraction. Together, these fractions add up to 63/64; the missing 1/64, it has been suggested, was supposedly supplied by magic.

$\frac{1}{2}$ $\frac{1}{4}$ $\frac{1}{16}$ $\frac{1}{8}$ $\frac{1}{32}$ $\frac{1}{64}$

falcon–The falcon in ancient Egypt was associated with solar gods, perhaps because of the falcon's ability to soar seemingly close to the sun. First a symbol of the god Horus, the falcon later became associated with the god Re-Harakhty (Re of the Two Horizons); both gods were portrayed as a falcon or a human body with a falcon's head. The falcon appears as a motif both in ancient Egyptian jewelry and Egyptian revival jewelry. The falcon hieroglyph, standing for the god Horus's name, was a powerful talisman, and occurred often in amulets.

feather–The feather, not surprisingly, is a symbol of lightness (in the sense of not weighty rather than not dark) and gracefulness. In ancient Egyptian mythology, Osiris–king of the underworld–weighed the hearts of the dead against a feather; only those whose hearts were lighter than the feather were allowed to pass through to the hereafter. The same feather was a symbol of the goddess of truth and justice, Ma'at. Peacock feathers, so prominent in Arts and Crafts and Art Nouveau jewelry, represented the eyes of Argus in Classical mythology; but were probably more prized for their striking iridescent beauty than for their symbolism by nineteenth century artists.

fish–The fish is symbolic in many traditions, including Christian; as an acronym for the Greek words **I**esus **Ch**ristos **Th**eou **H**uious **S**oter ("Jesus Christ of God the son, savior," *ichthus* being the Greek word for "fish"), it became an early sign by which Christians identified themselves. The apostles were called "fishers of men," giving Christians a further identification with fish. In Mediterranean tradition, the fish was a symbol of good luck, and in the New Testament, the parable of loaves and fishes makes fish a metaphor for abundance. In China, the fish symbolized happiness and, as elsewhere, plenty. However, in ancient Egypt fish were considered somewhat unclean, perhaps because of their association with the myth of Isis and Osiris, in which a fish swallowed Osiris's phallus, thus rendering him unable to procreate and as a result, unable to rule upon earth.

An unusual Victorian brooch/watch pin in onyx, gold, enamel, diamond chips, and a pearl, c. 1890. The pin shows a fish head in champlevé enamel, holding a pearl in its mouth. In many cultures the fish symbolizes abundance; a fish holding a pearl might represent even more abundance or good luck. This unmarked piece appears to be hand-made, but possibly represents a "married" piece with a newer (possibly Asian) fish melded to an older onyx pin. Unmarked; measures 1.5" x 1.125".

137

A charming fish bracelet in silver and enamel, by noted–and very collectible–Mexican designer Margot de Taxco. The bracelet is comprised of four articulated fish, enameled in Margot's combination of champlevé and basse taille enameling, with the added interest of a mottling in the colors of the enamel. An unusual detail is the dangling fish charm hanging from the clasp and adjacent fish, reprising the four fish in the body of the bracelet. Signed, with ID no. 5701; measures 7.75" x 1.375". *Courtesy of Robin Allison.*

frog–In Native American myths, the frog is sometimes associated with abundance, the meaning given it in Zuni carved fetishes. In ancient Egypt, the symbol for a tadpole was used to represent the number 100,000. Possibly the frog, like the dragonfly (though not so beautiful or suitable for Art Nouveau jewelry), also represented metamorphosis.

A darling vintage frog brooch in silver, enamel, and marcasites, with eyes of either paste or small garnets. The translucent green enamel, framed by rows of marcasites, shows the basse taille markings representing the texture of the frog's skin. Marked Germany sterling; measures 1.125" x 1.125". *Courtesy of Robin Allison.*

What wond'rous life is this I lead!
Ripe apples drop about my head;
The luscious clusters of the vine
Upon my mouth do crush their wine
—Andrew Marvell, "The Garden"

grape–The grape is often identified with the Roman god Bacchus (or the Greek Dionysus), and as such symbolizes the intoxicating power of the grape made into wine. However, it also symbolizes, like other fruits, abundance; and it often appears in pictures of the cornucopia, or horn of plenty. It was a fairly popular motif in late nineteenth century jewelry, and seems to be among the leaves most often depicted in jewelry, along with oak leaves and ivy.

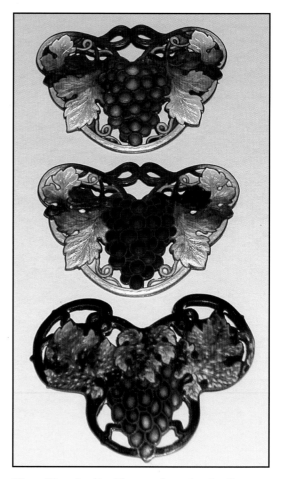

Three Victorian/Art Nouveau brooches in silver and enamel, in the form of bunches of grapes, vines, and leaves. The top two brooches are identical save for the color of the grapes; the bottom one is similar, though clearly not from the same mold or press as the other two. Basse taille enameling gives texture to the leaves in all three brooches, while the grapes are formed by champlevé depressions. Top two brooches marked sterling and measure 2.5" x 1.75"; bottom brooch marked for Watson Co., sterling, and measures 2.625" x 2.125". *Courtesy of Robin Allison.*

griffon–see above, under *Grotesque and Mythical Creatures*

horns–Horns have a number of different associations. There is the horn that holds fruit, "the horn of plenty" (or cornucopia). There is the *shofar*, used to usher in the New Year in Jewish tradition. In Egyptian mythology, horns are often found on goddesses, especially Isis and Hathor. In some depictions, Hathor has the head of a cow; but in others, the horns indicate her partly bovine nature. In Christian lore, however, horns–along with cloven feet–are associated with the devil. This association may come from the goat's association with the lecherous half-man, half-goat satyrs often linked with the god Dionysus (Bacchus) in Classical mythology.

A Victorian watch in 935 silver and niello, with an interesting and unusual combination of a horned demon–in the center–with a winged cherub below it. Horns are often associated with demons and devils, perhaps because of the association of the goat with unruly satyrs. Of Swiss manufacture; measures 1.875" in diameter. *Courtesy of Robin Allison.*

A brooch in unmarked silver and plique-à-jour enamel, 1.25" by 1.25", with the face of a demon–or possibly a satyr–set against the green enamel and framed by flowers, buds, and flowing Art Nouveau leaves. Here the horns are more vestigial; the face's unpleasant, almost sneering, expression and deep-set eyes seem to convey evil or unpleasantness enough on their own. *Courtesy of Robin Allison.*

ibis–The ibis in Egyptian mythology represents the god of wisdom and writing Thoth, who was depicted usually with a human body and an ibis head. Thoth stood by as Osiris weighed souls in the hereafter, and jotted down the results.

Isis–In the best-known Egyptian myth, Isis was the wife of the god-king Osiris, slain by his jealous brother Set. To ensure that Osiris was well and truly dead, Set hacked his brother's body into pieces and strewed them up and down the length of Egypt. Isis, the faithful wife, searched far and wide to find the pieces and, when she had gathered them all, she reunited her husband's body and used her magic arts to bring him back to life. The girdle of Isis was one of the more popular amulets in ancient Egypt, believed to confer special protection.

An Egyptian revival pin in silver and champlevé enamel depicting a winged goddess, probably Isis, in the usual Egyptian revival colors of turquoise, dark blue, and red. Isis and Ma'at–the goddess of justice and order–were often depicted with wings, possibly as a sign that they protected humankind, or possibly as an indication of their association with the sun or the air. If this were meant to represent Ma'at, the goddess should be wearing the feather of justice on her head. Marked silver; aproximately 2" across.

ivy–See under *Ivy* in chapter five.

laurel–In Classical mythology, the laurel tree was sacred to Apollo, the god of the sun and healing arts. He was attached to the laurel tree because Daphne, the nymph he had loved and pursued, was transformed into this tree. Because of Daphne's metamorphosis, the laurel stood for immortality. The laurel leaf also signified triumph, accomplishment, and victory, and as such was made into crowns for ancient Greek Olympic champions, and later crowned Roman emperors. The laurel wreath also occurs in nineteenth century jewelry–as, for example, in the handbag by Boucheron is shown in chapter three, p. 96.

A bar pin in 14K gold, enamel, and a small pearl, by the Newark maker Whiteside & Blank, c. 1900. The pin is done in a combination of medium blue guilloche enamel with plain white enamel that swirls around at the ends in champlevé depressions. Unusually, the center of the pin contains a series of unenameled laurel leaves that branch out on either side of a small pearl. Marked 14K on c-clasp, with maker's mark; measures approximately 1.25" across.

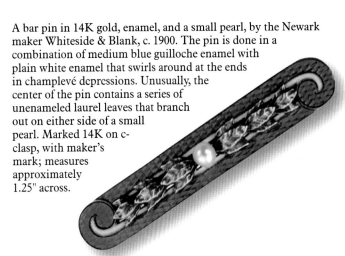

lily–The lily has in some traditions been considered a symbol of purity. In Arthurian legend, Elaine, the Lily Maid of Astolat, sweet and pure, died for love of Sir Lancelot. In Christian tradition, the white Madonna lily is associated with Mary.

An Art Nouveau brooch in sterling silver and enamel, with three white Madonna lilies, their petals and leaves having basse taille markings to indicate the texture and structure of the flowers' components. As its name implies, the Madonna lily has long been associated with the Virgin Mary in Christian iconography; according to the seventh century English cleric and scholar Venerable Bede, the flowers' snowy white petals symbolize the purity of her body, while the golden anthers represent her soul glowing with heavenly light. Measures 2.5" x 1.5". *Courtesy of Robin Allison.*

lion–Worshiped as the goddess Sekhmet in ancient Egypt, the lion still commands respect as the king of the beasts. A not uncommon theme for Victorian jewelers, lions are found on lockets, brooches, and stickpins.

An unusual late Georgian or early Victorian locket, in 18K gold, enamel, diamond chips, and pearls. Most unusually, the lion–done in transfer enameling–is purple; perhaps, Robin feels, indicating a membership in a secret society, or even possibly some aspect of heraldry. Also unusual is the half-ring set with pearls held in the lion's mouth. This rather gives the lion the appearance of a Victorian doorknocker, with the lion intended both to announce and to guard. Measures 1.25" x 1" including bail. *Courtesy of Robin Allison.*

lizard–In ancient Egypt, the hieroglyph for the word "many" was a lizard. In medieval heraldry, the lizard is found on coats-of-arms, signifying courage, and in some cases foresight.

A colorful Art Deco watch by the Roxy watch company, in 935 silver and enamel, with a lizard in bold green enamel against a blue background; measures 1.375" x 1". *Courtesy of Robin Allison.*

An interesting Art Nouveau watch in silver and guilloche enamel, with three lizards almost encircling and forming a border for the watch. The tails of the upper two lizards curve around to form the loops to which the chain is attached. The tail of the lizard on the bottom also forms a loop, possibly originally intended to hold a pearl or other dangle. *Courtesy of Robin Allison.*

lotus–The lotus, a popular Art Nouveau motif, is among the most symbolic of flowers. In fact, in her book *The Illustrated Language of Flowers*, Frances Kelly goes so far as to say that the lotus was the most important of symbolic flowers in ancient times, and is the flower most frequently found in Near and Far Eastern art. (Kelly, 1992, 38) And in fact the lotus flower is found in artwork and texts from a number of ancient cultures. In ancient Egypt, for example, the lotus came to be identified with the country itself. The Egyptians had a number of creation myths; in one of them, the lotus blossomed from the primordial mound, and was a symbol of emerging life. Tutankhamon's Eighteenth Dynasty tomb contained a sculpture of the boy king's head springing from a lotus blossom. The lotus is also found in scenes in Egyptian temples and tombs. The lotus, as well as the papyrus, was used in the design of columns in monumental buildings.

In Eastern mythology, the lotus is also a symbolic flower. The Buddhist chant or mantra *Om mane padme oum* literally means "hail to the jewel in the lotus." Some interpretations of this mantra give it a sexual meaning; others appear to refer to Buddha himself. In some iconic images, Buddha is shown sitting serenely on a lotus blossom, his legs folded in what is known as the lotus position.

In Buddist tradition, Buddha is often shown seated on a lotus throne, as in this drawing.

A marvelous pair of Egyptian revival earrings, in silver, enamel, and pink quartz, consisting of a series of three stylized lotus blossoms–graduated in size–which end in scarabs carved from pink quartz. The earring screw backs are attached to yet another lotus blossom flanked by buds. After the scarab (winged or otherwise), the stylized lotus appears to be the element most often found in Egyptian revival jewelry. Marked sterling, Germany; measure 2.75" x .625". *Courtesy of Robin Allison.*

A drawing of a statue from the tomb of Tutankhamon, showing the head and neck of the king as a small boy emerging from a lotus blossom. In one Egyptian creation myth, the lotus blossom emerged from the primordial mound, and with it, life.

oak–See under *Oak* in chapter five.

orchid–Orchids, so lush and rich and yet existing as parasites living on air, were extremely popular floral motifs in both late Victorian and Art Nouveau jewelry. Given their relatively recent introduction to the Old World from the Americas, they had little place in European tradition, Classical or medieval. However, their beauty made them appropriate subjects for the jeweler; Tiffany & Co. produced a number of elaborately enameled and jeweled orchid brooches. Sataloff (1985, unnumbered), describing an amazing orchid created by Georges Fouquet out of a walnut-shaped baroque pearl, 18K gold, translucent enamel, and diamonds, notes that: "The pearl is veined and flesh-colored to resemble an anatomic specimen that may well have reminded Fouquet that the orchid flower was named by the ancients because of its resemblance to the male gonad."

Two vintage flower pins in silver, enamel, and marcasites. While the flower on the left, with its folded petals and stamens, seems to represent lilies, less likely several calla lilies (the blue-to-purple enamel seems inconsistent with this identification, as do the multiple stamens), the brooch on the right is quite clearly a stylized orchid, complete with brown spots on the petals. The similarities between the two flowers makes the speculation that they came from the same maker hard to resist, although the different silver content might be inconsistent with this. The lily measures 2.375" x 2.125" and is marked 935 silver; the orchid is 2.25" x 1.875" and in 830 silver. *Courtesy of Robin Allison.*

Ma'at–The goddess of justice and order in ancient Egypt, Ma'at was usually portrayed wearing a feather on her head. This feather was weighed against the hearts of the dead in the scales of justice. Ma'at, along with Osiris (as presiding judge) and Thoth (recorder of the verdict), was often present in scenes in which the heart was judged in the afterlife.

Minerva–see under *Athena*

nymph–Nymphs, or nubile young women, were a common theme in Art Nouveau jewelry. In Greek mythology, nymphs were the spirits of nature, daughters of Zeus who were not quite divine, but certainly not human. Nymphs were sometimes divided according to the sphere they inhabited: Naiads were water nymphs, Oreads dwelled in mountains, Dryads were nymphs who lived in forests, Nereids belonged to the ocean. As beautiful young women, they also symbolized dark forces; their beauty could lead to madness, and glimpsed in the middle of the day, they could inspire sudden terror. (Compte, 1991, 142)

Art Nouveau pendant in 18K gold, plique-à-jour enamel, and diamonds, possibly c. 1900, approximately 1" x 1.125". The pendant depicts a nymph set against what appears to be a pond with water lilies; the enamel work behind the woman's face seems to be in the form of a lotus or water lily blossom, while another water lily blooms on the left side of the frame, in gold set with a diamond. The nymph-woman also wears a flower on her shoulder. The pendant has the Swiss hallmark for 18K gold, but the pendant may have been made in France for export to Switzerland.

owl–Associated with the goddess Athena, the owl has long been a symbol of wisdom. In jewelry, it is very often found in charms intended for recent graduates, sometimes wearing an enameled mortarboard. Native American lore, though, often viewed the owl as a harbinger of misfortune, and even death.

An Occurrence of Owls: Owls Through Time

> *There was an old owl liv'd in an oak*
> *The more he heard, the less he spoke;*
> *The less he spoke, the more he heard*
> *O, if men were all like that wise bird!*
>
> —Quote from the British humor magazine *Punch,* 1875

Perhaps because people find them endearing, even cute, owls occur frequently in figural jewelry. They were made by the Victorians, and they were made by more modern jewelers producing both fine and costume jewelry. Sometimes they are realistically rendered, but more often they are stylized–yet still quite recognizable as that wise bird.

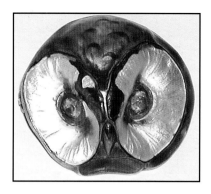

A Victorian brooch in silver, enamel, and green paste gems, in the shape of an owl's head, by the German firm Meyle & Mayer. Some attempt has been made to create naturalistic effects, such as the feathers on the head in a darker brown enamel, and basse taille markings around the eyes. The owl head remained popular as a motif with some twentieth century costume jewelry makers, such as the well-known Joseph Mazur (Jomaz), who produced such brooches in some quantity. Usual maker's marks; measures 1.125" in diameter. *Courtesy of Robin Allison.*

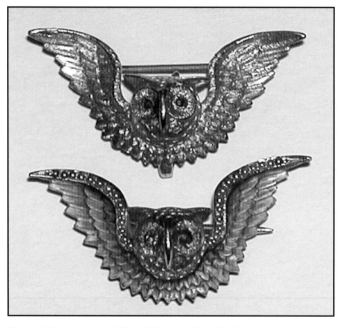

Two owl brooches in 14K gold and rubies, the bottom one also with enamel and pearls, by the notable Newark maker Riker Bros. As with the three bracelets from the same mold by David Andersen (for which please see the introduction), these two brooches show what a difference enameling can make in the appearance of a piece of jewelry. Just as today some antique enameled jewelry commands higher prices than similar pieces without enamel, the enameled owl was also probably a more expensive piece when manufactured; the pearls edging its outspread wings would indicate a higher price than that asked for the relatively unadorned gold owl. In true Art Nouveau style, the owls convey more the *essence* of an owl rather than a naturalistic representation–although the feathering along the wings is nicely realized in carved gold. Both marked with maker's mark, 14K, and measure 1.625" x .5". *Courtesy of Robin Allison.*

A small gold-filled and enamel owl pin by the American costume jewelry firm Wells, probably from the 1930s. Despite its tiny size, the owl is more-or-less realistically depicted, with basse taille feathering under the translucent light turquoise enamel. The owl is perched on a curving spray of leaves. Measures approximately 1" in diameter; marked Wells and GF on the reverse.

A vintage brooch in silver and enamel, possibly of Norwegian or other Scandinavian origins, in the form of an owl. Unlike other vintage owls, this one is not particularly stylized, and the mottled grays and browns in the enamel are apparently meant to represent an owl's true coloring. Marked sterling on the reverse, with no other identifying marks; measures approximately .875" x 1.125".

A wonderful cigarette case in 935 silver and enamel, with a hand-painted scene of an owl perched in a branch by moonlight. The design is done against a guilloche diamond background, which unlike some guilloche backgrounds does not seem intended to convey or create any effect of lighting. Nevertheless, this is one of Dale's favorite pieces from Robin's collection, partly because the owl is so beautifully rendered, and partly because the crescent moon hanging among ethereal branches and the mountain background create a wonderfully atmospheric mood. German hallmarks; measures 3.5" x 3.25". *Courtesy of Robin Allison.*

A charming owl brooch by Norwegian David Andersen in silver and enamel, probably c. 1950. Although the owl is quite stylized and very symmetrical, the piece nicely conveys a sense of "owl" through the wide black eyes surrounded by yellow enamel over basse taille striations, and the grid of "feathers" on the owl's chest. A number of similar pieces were made by Andersen, some in hues including the bright blue for which he is known, others in more subdued garb, such as the wintry hues seen here. Measures 1.5" x 1.125" and marked David Andersen 925S. *Courtesy of Robin Allison.*

A set of vintage earrings and brooch in sterling silver, enamel, and marcasites by Alice Caviness, with small stylized owls perched on branches in yellow, green, and blue enamel, with brown spots dotting the chest, and red paste eyes. The earrings match the owl on the right in the brooch, both in size and shape, and in coloring. Signed and marked sterling; brooch measures 1.125" x .75", earrings .75" x .5". *Courtesy of Robin Allison.*

A group of three costume owl brooches, by well-known costume designers Eisenberg (better known for his heavily rhinestone-encrusted "Eisenberg ice" pieces) on the right, and Boucher on the left. The owl on the lower left, in gold-tone metal, hard enamel, rhinestones, and paste, is a reproduction of an antique "fine" French piece.

peacock–The peacock has been symbolic in a number of cultures and periods, though often with different meanings. For example, in China it was a symbol of beauty and dignity. In Christianity, because of a legend in which the flesh of the peacock will not burn but remains pure white when exposed to fire, it is a symbol of resurrection. In more modern times, it is a symbol of pride and vanity. The English artist Aubrey Beardsley, associated with the Aesthetic Movement, drew pictures of women wearing peacock capes, possibly as a sign of vanity.

An Arts and Crafts bar pin in silver and enamel, with a hand-painted design depicting a peacock with its tail trailing behind it. While Arts and Crafts peacocks are most often shown with their tails fanned, the better to depict the feathers' exotic coloring and markings, this one was designed to accommodate the very narrow bar pin. *Pin courtesy of Classic Facets, Boulder, CO; photo courtesy of Karryl Salit.*

A fairly recent peacock brooch in silver, enamel, and garnets, probably made in India or elsewhere in Asia. While peacocks usually serve as a canvas for the enamelist's skill, here cabochon garnets rather than enamel add color and interest to the tail, which is cupped slightly forward to give a sense of dimensionality.

poppy–see under *Poppy* in chapter five.

Re or *Ra*–One of the most powerful gods in ancient Egyptian mythology, Re was the god of the sun. As a solar deity, he later became identified with the falcon god Horus, and was sometimes referred to as Re-Harakhty or Re, Falcon of the Two Horizons. He is frequently depicted with the body of a man and the head of a falcon surmounted by a solar globe. (For a depiction of Re, please see above under *falcon*.)

rooster–see under *cockerel*

rose–While largely absent from Near Eastern and Far Eastern symbolism (the biblical "rose of Sharon" is usually said to refer to the *Hybiscus syriacus* of the mallow family rather than a true rose), the rose is one of the most widely represented symbolic flowers in European art and literature. The white rose is in medieval art a symbol of purity, and is sometimes associated with the Virgin Mary. It is also a symbol of secrecy and silence: A white rose suspended from the ceiling of a medieval meeting hall meant that everything said or done at the gathering was to remain secret; hence the Latin phrase *sub rosa*, literally "under the rose," used to refer to covert or confidential matters. During the English civil wars known as the Wars of the Roses, the red rose symbolized the House of Lancaster, while the white rose symbolized its rival, the House of York.

A wonderful Tudor rose brooch by British maker Robert Phillips. The brooch has beautiful dark green leaves and five red-and-white Tudor roses with nicely dimensional roses springing from a simple three-pronged fork. The Wars of the Roses, which split England apart, were fought by the houses of York, symbolized by the white rose, and Lancaster, symbolized by the red rose. The country was reunited by the Tudor monarch Henry VII, and the Tudor rose symbolizes the union of both red and white roses, and of both belligerent factions. *Courtesy of Nelson Rarities, Portland, ME.*

sa amulet–This sign, the hieroglyph meaning "protection," was found in the jewelry of the Twelfth Dynasty princess Khnumet, whose tomb was discovered at Dashur in 1895. Her jewelry, among the finest ever made in ancient Egypt, included a number of cloisonné pieces made of gold inlaid with semi-precious stones cut to fit the cloisons. Some of these pieces included amulets wishing her happiness, life, prosperity, strength, and other good attributes. Modern jewelers adapted some of the designs found in her jewelry, creating amulet necklaces that emulate the ones she wore.

scarab–see under *beetle*

snake–Ever since Eve, the snake or serpent has been considered a sign of evil. In ancient Egypt, however, the serpent appeared on the kings' crowns as the *uraeus* representing Udjat, the tutelary goddess of Lower Egypt. Even so, Egyptian mythology for the most part portrays serpents as evil: The demonic Apophis, lurking in the underworld, is a snake that daily devours the sun as the earth sinks into darkness. Yet despite its unwholesome reputation, the snake has been a popular motif in jewelry throughout history. One ring from Roman-ruled Egypt has the form of a coiled gold snake that winds its way around the finger a number of times. In Victorian times, snake bracelets were common, in large part because such a bracelet was Prince Albert's engagement present to Victoria. Some snake bracelets have lucky charms dangling from their mouths, perhaps an indication that such snakes could bring good fortune.

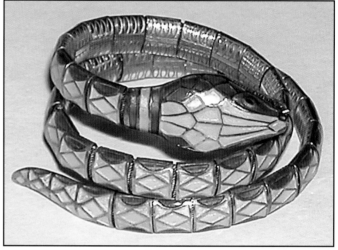

An Art Deco bracelet in 925 silver and enamel in the form of a coiled snake, c. 1930s. Its Art Deco style is seen in the geometric, stylized scales–diamonds and triangles–in bold glossy green enamel against pale green and yellow. Measures 11" x .5". *Courtesy of Robin Allison.*

An amulet necklace similar to that shown at the beginning of this chapter, with the same elements: a central ankh, *sa* amulets, pharaohs' heads (these facing front rather than in profile, and wearing a headdress rather than the Two Crowns), and lotus blossoms, all in champlevé enamel in the usual red, turquoise, and dark blue. Charms measure from .25" to .75" on a 16" chain. *Courtesy of Robin Allison.*

A matching articulated snake necklace and bracelet in silver and enamel, from the Mexican silver center, Taxco. The snakes are enameled in champlevé divisions used to indicate the snakes' scales. Each snake holds its tail in its mouth. Snakes, both in this design and one using only snakes' heads–in rings, earrings, bolo ties, bracelets–are among the more frequently found pieces from Taxco. Marked AF sterling Mexico; necklace measures 19" x .75", bracelet 8" x .75". *Courtesy of Robin Allison.*

swallow–The swallow is an important symbol in both Europe and Asia. In Cassical legend, it was a harbinger of spring; Greek songs refer to it as a sign of spring, and the phrase "one swallow does not make a summer" is known from the texts of the philosopher Aristotle and the comedic playwright Aristophanes. In China as well, the swallow was a portent of spring's arrival. It was also a sign of luck: A swallow nesting at one's house was an omen that promised marital happiness, children, and success. The swallow also symbolized the relationship between older and younger brothers.

A brooch in 14K gold and enamel, by the Newark maker Bippart, Griscom & Osborn, c. 1900. The brooch, depicting two swallows joined at beak and wing in bright iridescent enamel, is somewhat reminiscent of a drawing of two swallows done by an ancient Greek artist on the island of Thera. Measures approximately 1.5" across.

A set in silver and enamel by famed Mexican designer Margot de Taxco in silver and enamel, consisting of a bolo, ring, and earrings with snakes' heads. Signed with ID no. 5554; bolo measures 1.625" in diameter, ring 1.25" x .75", earrings 2.125" x .75".*Courtesy of Robin Allison.*

A drawing, after 16th century B.C. Minoan frescoes on the island of Thera (Santorini), of two swallows in a "kissing" position, apparently showing that swallows connoted connubial bliss even before Greeks settled along the Mediterranean.

swan–The swan represents a complex mixture of purity and prurience. Perhaps because of the myth of Zeus appearing to Leta as a swan and in this guise seducing her, the swan sometimes symbolizes lust or fleshly love. In one medieval account (by the Austrian Franz Unterkircher), the swan has black flesh beneath its white feathers; it thus symbolizes the hypocrite. Most interpretations, however, are more positive. The singing (or northern) swan was associated in Greek mythology with the sun god Apollo; swans were also associated with the goddesses Artemis and Aphrodite, symbolizing feminine grace. Because of their white plumage and grace, swans were also considered a sign of noble purity both in ancient and medieval times. Swans seem prevalent in German and Russian fairy tales and legends; in one tale, a young woman must knit seven tunics out of nettles and place them on her brothers in order to turn them from swans back into humans. In the medieval German *Niebelungenlied* (a collection of sacred texts, myths, and legends), virgins could be turned into swans.

A German Renaissance woodcut of a swan, imputing to it great purity.

thistle–In the language of flowers, the thistle often has unpleasant connotations, signifying revenge and retribution. However, just as the leek is the symbol of Wales (though not nearly so often found in jewelry!), the thistle is the symbol of Scotland, and such appears in a number of unenameled pieces by Charles Horner, as well as later enameled pieces.

A lovely Art Nouveau necklace in 14K gold, plique-à-jour enamel, and pearls, in the form of a stylized swan which itself is in the shape of a heart. Interestingly, the outer plumage, in cells meant to resemble feathers, is in dark enamel, contrasting nicely with the white pearls lining the inner body, head, and neck of the swan. Measures 1.875" x 1.5". *Courtesy of Robin Allison.*

An Austro-Hungarian pendant in silver, enamel, mabe pearl, and a baroque pearl, in the form of a swan depending on two chains from a central enameled element in dark blue with a red flower. The swan is enameled in light blue over basse taille depressions along the neck and body, and champlevé compartments for the longer wing feathers (which also show dark blue lines down the center), with its folded leg in orange. Unfortunately, the swan has experienced some enamel loss, the better allowing us to see the underlying markings and compartments. Undeciphered mark; measures 2.25" x 1.25". *Courtesy of Red Robin Antiques.*

A vintage thistle brooch from Great Britain, in silver, soft enamel, and marcasites. This large brooch is one of a number of thistle brooches produced in the island kingdom, in large part because the thistle is the national symbol of Scotland. Charles Horner produced many stylized thistle pieces, mostly hatpins and brooches, often with faux amethyst crystals representing the actual thistle; however, very few of these were enameled. Unmarked, measures approximately 2.125" across.

146

Tyger! Tyger! Burning bright
In the forests of the night,
What immortal hand or eye
Could frame thy fearful symmetry?
—William Blake, "The Tyger"

tiger–Tigers were especially popular subjects for some Newark jewelers, who made entire parures of tiger jewelry: One such parure contained earrings, cufflinks, bracelets, brooches, and stickpins. All held a diamond in the mouth. There is something about a tiger that draws the eye–possibly its fearful symmetry?

A wonderful beaux art locket in unmarked gold, enamel, and diamonds, most likely of Newark manufacture, c. 1900, with the face of a tiger sculpted and enameled with a fair eye to naturalistic detail, its nose very dimensional, its open mouth holding a diamond between nicely sculpted fangs against a bright red tongue. Measures 1" in diameter. *Courtesy of Robin Allison.*

A watch fob in 14K gold, enamel, and a diamond, with a tiger similar to the one on the locket above holding a diamond in its vividly enameled red mouth. Measures 1" x .75". *Courtesy of Robin Allison.*

A wonderful and unusual necklace in silver, enamel, and lapis, in the form of a scarab flanked not by the usual wings alone, but by vultures with outspread wings. The scarab is enameled in the same shade as the lapis drops that dangle below the vulture's tail, while the wings are in plique-à-jour enamel shading from light green through lavender–colors more often associated with Art Nouveau jewelry rather than Egyptian revival pieces. Interestingly, while the heads flanking the scarab are obviously those of vultures, the bodies seem rather serpentine, almost as if the designer intended to combine the two tutelary goddesses of Upper and Lower Egypt. Measures 3" x 2.125". *Courtesy of Robin Allison.*

turtle–In Aesop's fable, the turtle (or sometimes tortoise), slow but steady, wins the race. Some Native American myths have the turtle holding up the earth.

Two too cute turtle pins in silver, enamel, and marcasites, probably c. 1950. Aside from their coloring–brown for one, brown and green for the other, both with blue eyes–these turtles could be identical twins. Both marked Germany sterling, and measure 1.25" x .75". *Courtesy of Robin Allison.*

Another vintage turtle pin in sterling silver, enamel, and marcasites, this one a bit more stylized than those shown above, and also in profile. This turtle has marcasites decorating the center of each segment of its shell (rather than set around the shell) as well as marcasites inset into its feet and tail. Its scalloped edge, light green eye, and cute little smile give it a somewhat whimsical air. Undeciphered maker's mark; measures 1.625" x .625". *Courtesy of Robin Allison.*

vulture–In many cultures, the vulture is regarded unkindly as a symbol of death, a scavenger who awaits death so it can feed. In ancient Egypt, however, the vulture was the royal tutelary god of Upper Egypt, just as the uraeus serpent represented Lower Egypt. As such, heads of both the serpent and the vulture appear on royal headwear. The vulture– its entire body, not just the head–also formed the queen's headdress. Cleopatra was occasionally depicted wearing the vulture crown, although it dates back to well before her time.

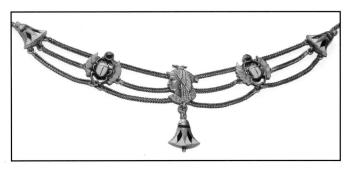

An Egyptian revival necklace in silver gilt and enamel, containing some familiar elements–the winged scarab and stylized lotuses–along with a much less common element in the form of an Egyptian queen wearing the vulture headdress, which is topped by the horns that most often represent Hathor, but which also are associated with Isis. In this piece, the enameling (in typical Egyptian revival colors) is confined to the lotus blossoms and the winged scarabs; the queen has been left in bare silver. Festoon section measures 5.25" x 1.25". *Courtesy of Robin Allison.*

Egyptian revival earrings in brass and enamel, c. 1920s. The earrings, in champlevé enamel, are in the form of the bust of an Egyptian queen wearing a broad collar and the vulture headdress that was an insignia of her status. Interestingly, the enameled portion of the earrings was made in Italy, while the screw backs were made in Germany. *Courtesy of Karen Perlmutter, Acanthus Antiques, Kensington, MD.*

wasp–The wasp is, for the most part, not viewed with favor, as one might expect from its painful sting. The ancient Greek comedic playwright Aristophanes titled his play about litigious Athenians, who spent their time suing one another to amass legal fees, *The Wasps*. In later usage, a hornet sometimes referred to an unpleasant woman; today a hornet's nest implies an unpleasant situation.

A vintage brooch in unmarked silver, enamel, and marcasites, 2.625" x 1.5", in the form of a stylized wasp. The stylized wings are enameled in a translucent light blue, while the body is done in bands of opaque yellow and brown. Not surprisingly, unlike its cousin the bee, the wasp is not an especially popular motif in jewelry. *Courtesy of Robin Allison.*

wheat–Wheat, for all its prosaic nature and plain appearance, has long been a symbol of plenty. In Greek and Roman mythology, Demeter (Ceres) was the goddess of grain. When her only child, Persephone (Proserpina) was kidnapped by Hades (Pluto) and taken to the underworld, Demeter went into mourning and gave up her duties. As a result, the earth grew barren. Zeus demanded that Hades return Persephone to her mother, but Persephone had already eaten six pomegranate seeds (breaking one of the conditions of her return). A compromise was reached in which Persephone spent six months of the year with her mother, and six months with Hades–during which time the earth lay dormant. In Egyptian mythology, wheat (and barley) were symbols of resurrection associated with the Osiris myth. Boards carved in the shape of Osiris' body were drilled with holes. The holes were filled with soil and grain was planted. The wheat (or barley) when it grew represented Osiris' and the earth's renewal. In medieval and Renaissance iconography, wheat was often embroidered on Mary's robes, perhaps as a relic of earlier myths, perhaps as a prayer for a plentiful harvest.

A pendant in 18K gold and plique-à-jour enamel, c. 1920, of French manufacture. The pendant, in the brighter colors found in later plique-à-jour, depicts stalks of wheat, a symbol of abundance important both in Christian symbolism and ancient Egyptian mythology. Measures approximately 1.25" x 1".

wings–Possibly no one single motif occurs quite so frequently in the jewelry pictured in this book. Wings abound: on scarabs, on angels and cherubs, on swans and swallows, on dragons and dragonflies, on bees and butterflies, on vultures, on goddesses. Ever since the mythological Greek architect Daedalus dared gravity and fashioned wings for himself and his son Icarus, wings have spelled for humans a kind of freedom that, air transport aside, is still really available only to birds and insects.

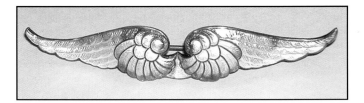

An Art Nouveau brooch in silver and iridescent enamel, in the shape of a pair of wings. The enamel shades ethereally from silver to a very pale lavender; basse taille markings indicate the feathers' barbs, with champlevé depressions used to distinguish the covert feathers. Undeciphered maker's mark; measures 3.5" x .625". *Courtesy of Robin Allison.*

The Language of Flowers

There's rosemary, that's for remembrance; pray, love, remember; and there is pansies, that's for thoughts... There's fennel for you, and columbines; there's rue for you, and here's some for me; we may call it herb of grace o' Sundays. O, you must wear your rue with a difference. There's a daisy. I would give you some violets, but they wither'd all when my father died.

—William Shakespeare, *Hamlet*

A set in silver and enamel, comprising a necklace, bracelet, and earrings. The necklace and bracelet are composed of alternating plaques in silver filigree, and rather circular pansies enameled in glossy purple and yellow, with a fair amount of realism. The earrings, although they are enameled in the same colors, probably did not originally belong with this set, as they display much more naturalistic markings in black on the lower petals, and also are less disk-like than the pansies in the necklace and bracelet. However, the fact that earrings in the same colors and the same basic design could be found to match two pieces meant to be worn together attests to the pansy's popularity in jewelry. Sterling; bracelet measures 6.75" x 1", necklace 16.5" with enameled section 5" x 1", earrings .75" in diameter. *Courtesy of Robin Allison.*

Anyone who has ever read or heard Ophelia's "mad scene" from Shakespeare's *Hamlet* has had an introduction to the language of flowers. Ophelia, in her speech, mentions several flowers (and herbs). Some of their meanings are known today: Columbines symbolize folly, daisies represent innocence, and violets stand for hope. And pansies, of course, are for thoughts–they derive their name from the French word *pensée*, which means "thought."

From ancient times on, people have given meanings to flowers, based on myths and legends or on some property of the flower itself. For the pansy, this property is its name, just as the forget-me-not's name holds its meaning. Other meanings are slightly more contrived: The bachelor's button, in one list, is said to mean "single blessedness," and in another list represents "celibacy." For other flowers, such as the sunflower, the meaning comes from a Greek myth. However, until the beginning of the nineteenth century, no one had thought to create a dictionary of floral meanings; that is, there was no "codified" language of flowers.[2]

There is no color, no flower, no weed, no fruit, herb, pebble, or feather that has not a verse belonging to it; and you may quarrel, reproach, or send letters of passion, friendship, or even news, without ever inking your fingers.

Thus wrote Lady Mary Wortley Montagu to a friend in 1716. Lady Mary was at the time residing in Constantinople, where her husband was the British ambassador to the Sublime Porte (as the Turkish government was then known).

Although the idea of certain flowers as symbols dates back to ancient times, a complete formal language of flowers, in which specific meanings were ascribed to many common flowers and leaves, apparently entered modern Western culture through the Middle East–through Lady Mary Wortley Montagu.

Lady Mary Wortley Montagu was one of the most interesting women of her time. The daughter of a duke, she eloped with Edward Wortley Montagu when her father forbade their marriage. When her husband was assigned to Constantinople, she made an adventure of it, veiling herself like her Turkish counterparts, entering their public baths, frequenting their bazaars. She was also a poet of some repute, acquainted with many of the literary figures of her day. And, among other things, she brought back from Turkey the concept of vaccination against smallpox, which she had witnessed first-hand during her sojourn there, and which she described in great detail in one of her letters. (Her letters, at her request, were first published in 1763, a year after her death.)

In her witty letters to friends and family from Turkey, she also mentioned the custom of *selam* (from the Turkish for "peace," used as a greeting). Selam involved the use of objects as diverse as pearls and peacock feathers, coal and cloves, as a means of covert communication. And thus, almost as an afterthought to her amazing life, she began what later became known as the language of flowers.[3]

The English poet Elizabeth Barrett Browning alludes to the Eastern antecedents of the language of flowers in her poem "A Flower in a Letter":

Love's language may be talked with these;
To work out choicest sentences
No language can be meeter;
And, such being used in Eastern bowers,
Young maids may wonder if the flowers
Or meanings be the sweeter.

It may be that Lady Mary Wortley Montagu's words fell on ground already fertilized by the eighteenth century fascination with botany, which can be seen in the hand-colored illustrated books of the period.

Indeed, it might be said that the eighteenth and the nineteenth centuries constituted something of a Golden Age of Botany. In 1753, the Swedish naturalist Carl Linnaeus published his monumental taxonomic classification of plants, demonstrating the ways in which plants can be said to be related. During the same period, the great British explorer Captain James Cook was making his historic voyages to the South Seas, taking with him scientists such as the Swedish botanist Daniel Solander. New plants, South American orchids, Chinese tiger lilies and bleeding hearts, were being introduced to Europe for the first time. Moreover, new hybrids were being created in European gardens; the larger modern version of the iris was introduced, and in the 1840s a new form of the pansy was created in London's Kew Gardens. With the introduction of so many new and exotic plants, gardening was now not only a genteel pursuit, but a fascinating one as well. Members of the French court circulated lists of flowers and their meanings, while France's Empress Eugénie worked ambitiously on her gardens, which she was said to love almost as much as she loved jewelry.

An eighteenth century botanical print showing various types of poppies, c. 1759, hand-colored and most likely taken from an entire book of such prints. Books on botany became very popular during the eighteenth century, accompanying a surge in botanical knowledge engendered by the collection of heretofore unknown plant species on sea voyages, and the colonization of the newly settled (by Europeans) continents of North and South America, Africa, and Australia, as well as the opening of trade with China and Japan.

Traipsing Through Time: Botany on the *Bounty*

How many people know that the *HMS Bounty* was, before the famous mutiny, engaged on a botanical mission? Funded in part by the great English botanist Joseph Banks and in part by the British government, the *Bounty* was on its way to the South Seas, where it was to collect a large quantity of breadfruit saplings. These were in turn to be transported to the Caribbean, where they would be planted to provide cheap, abundant food for slaves and other plantation workers. (This mission does make one wonder if Captain Bligh didn't deserve his fate.)

The *Bounty's* voyage was not atypical. From the mid-eighteenth century, when Linnaeus first classified plants into phylae and genera and species, through a large part of the Victorian era, botany was something of a fad. In fact, the nineteenth century was the culmination of what might be called a Golden Age of Botany, which was marked by the following events:

♦ 1753–Linnaeus publishes his *Species Plantarum*, the first modern classification of plant life, and establishes himself as the father of taxonomy.
♦ 1759–The Royal Botanic Gardens at Kew, London, England are established.
♦ 1768–Partly at the urging of (and with funding by) Banks, Captain James Cook sets sail on the *Endeavour* with botanists Banks and Solander on board, in what is in large part a plant-hunting expedition.
♦ 1771–The *Endeavour* returns to England with specimens of many new plants, including Australian honeysuckle, acacia, and eucalyptus.
♦ 1787–William Curtis founds the *Botanical Magazine*, which goes on to be the longest-published botanical magazine.
♦ 1810–Robert Brown's publication of *Prodromus Florae Noviae Hollandiae* marks the beginning of publications on the flora of Australia.
♦ 1842–The Treaty of Nanking cedes Hong Kong to Britain and opens Chinese ports to European and American trade; as a result, the tiger lily and bleeding heart, among others, are introduced to Europe.
♦ 1848–The first of the new breed of pansies–larger, showier–is bred at Kew Gardens.
♦ 1854–James Veitch, a renowned British nursery owner, achieves the first hybrid orchid.
♦ 1856–Owen Jones publishes his noted work, *The Grammar of Ornament*, suggesting ways in which plants might be used for inspiration rather than minute replication, and how they might be adapted for use in decorative design.
♦ 1859–Charles Darwin publishes his important work, *The Evolution of Species*.
♦ 1866–Austrian monk Gregor Mendel publishes his work on the genetics of plants.
♦ 1874-1886–Ruskin's influential *Proserpina* describes in detail the way plants grow.
♦ 1883–William Robinson publishes one of the first major books for flower gardeners, *The English Flower Garden*.

The Lovers' Lexicon

It may be that this preoccupation with botany, as well as the need of those living in a repressed society, made Victorian England ripe for the language of flowers.

It was the French rather than the British, however, who first took up the idea of forging a symbolic language based on the Turkish system of covert communication. The French often referred to this language as *Selam,* using its Turkish name. Although lists of flowers and their meanings circulated in the French court, the first systematic language of flowers was published in 1819 by Charlotte de la Tour (a pseudonym for Madame Louise Cortambert) as *Le langage des fleurs.* From the title alone, it can be seen that the European version of the secret language borrowed, at least as an idea, from the Turks differed from the original: As in an untended garden, the plants have taken over; there no longer room for objects such as pearls, coal, cloth, or hair in this new westernized system of communication.

It was the same in other European countries, possibly because Charlotte de la Tour's book was widely circulated, translated, and copied. The covert language was purely botanical. *Selam oder die Sprache der Blumen (Selam or the Language of the Flowers),* by Johann Symansk was published in 1823, the same year that saw the first English book on the language of flowers, *Flora Domestica or the Portable Flower Garden,* by Elizabeth Kent. More—many more—books followed. In her comprehensive book, *Tussie-Mussies: The Victorian Art of Expressing Yourself in the Language of Flowers,* Geraldine Adamich Laufer writes: "It has been reckoned that fifty-seven writers produced ninety-eight books on the Language of Flowers, in two hundred twenty-seven editions between 1800 and 1937." (Laufer, 1993, 12)

Many of the meanings in the guides to the language of flowers were undoubtedly invented. Others, however, were based on older myths and legends, some of them cited above. A number of the books mentioned by Laufer or illustrated in her book not only listed the meanings in the contemporary floral idiom, but referred back to Classical allusions; a book published in London and New York by Frederick Warne and Co. was entitled *The Language and Sentiment of Flowers and the Classical Floral Legends.* (Laufer, 1993, 11) The English writer Dr. Henry Phillips gave historical antecedents for meanings in the language of flowers in his two books, *Flora Historica* and *Floral Emblems* (published in 1824 and 1825 respectively).

A brief history of the language of flowers was given by Thomas E. Hill in his *Manual of Social and Business Forms,* published in Chicago in 1905:

> The language of flowers has a long history. Plants and flowers have been given meanings through myths, legends, and folklore all over the world. The Myrtle was sacred to Aphrodite and the Lotus flower has represented divine female fertility in the Orient for over 5,000 years. The language of flowers as the western world knows it today, was started in Constantinople in the 1600's and was brought to England in 1716 [sic] by Lady Mary Wortley Montagu who had spent time in Turkey with her husband. It developed and flourished through out Europe for many decades.

It was in Victorian times that the language of flowers reached the height of its popularity and became part of the wider culture. Victorian mores had much to do with the flourishing idiom of flowers. Gardening was considered a respectable pastime for women in a culture much taken with botany. Flowers were also considered an appropriate, even optimal, gift. The nineteenth century American poet and essayist Ralph Waldo Emerson wrote, in his essay entitled "Gifts" (1844):

> Flowers and fruit are always fit presents; flowers because they are a proud assertion that a ray of beauty outvalues all the utilities of the world... [T]hese delicates look like the frolic and interference of love and beauty. Men used to tell us that we love flattery, even though we are not deceived by it, because it shows that we are of importance enough to be courted. Something like that pleasure, the flowers give us: what am I to whom these sweet hints are addressed?

Given the prevailing social climate, it is easy to see why the Victorians were so taken with the language of flowers. Just as the so-called "language of stones" (discussed in chapter one) allowed lovers to exchange tokens of affection, the language of flowers permitted the disclosure of emotions otherwise repressed by a culture in which propriety reigned. Etiquette demanded that unmarried men and women keep a respectable distance from the opposite sex. Young women were chaperoned or went about in groups. Holding hands was considered loose behavior, while kissing was forbidden except between husband and wife or a young woman and her fiancé.

The Rules—Nineteenth Century Version

Michelle J. Hoppe, in her article "Courting the Victorian Woman," lists a number of strictures young woman were expected to follow:

◆ A single women never addressed a gentleman without an introduction.
◆ A single woman never walked out alone. Her chaperone had to be older and preferably married.
◆ If she had progressed to the stage of courtship in which she walked out with a gentleman, they always walked apart. A gentleman could offer his hand over rough spots, the only contact he was allowed with a woman who was not his fiancée.
◆ Proper women never rode alone in a closed carriage with a man who wasn't a relative.
◆ The proper woman would never call upon an unmarried gentleman at his place of residence.
◆ She couldn't receive a man at home if she was alone. Another family member had to be present in the room.

Given the severe restrictions under which young men and women conducted their social lives, it might be considered amazing that they ever reached the stage where they entered into engagements.

Fan Facts

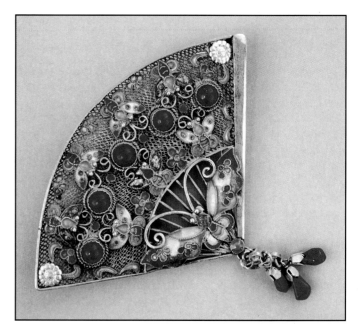

A Chinese export brooch in silver gilt, cloisonné enamel, and lapis lazuli, c. 1920, approximately 2.5" across, in the shape of an open fan decorated with lapis cabochons and enamel butterflies. Typical of Chinese export pieces, this one is done in a mesh overlain by the enamel cloisons. Small lapis dangles in place of tassels finish off the piece. Fans, popular accessories in Victorian times, also became fashionable as pieces of jewelry. As with butterflies, their lovely and colorful designs as well as their pleasing shape made them very suitable for jewelry, enameled or otherwise.

A copy of sheet music to a nineteenth century song entitled "Flirting with a Fan." Flirting with fans became another way for young men and women to communicate in a society in which young people were not expected to mingle with those of the opposite sex. Pamphlets on the proper art of flirting with a fan were written and sold, much like the even more popular tracts on the language of flowers. And flirting with fans was apparently popular enough to inspire the song "Flirting Behind a Fan" listed on the cover of "Popular Songs Composed and Sung by Mlle. Rosa Marliani."

However, youth is inventive. Young women, with aids such as the guide entitled *How to Flirt with a Fan*, used their fans to let young men know that they were single, or that they were engaged, or that they wanted to make a (presumably forbidden) assignation. Flirting with a fan was well within the bounds of acceptable behavior, and there seems to have been a fairly well-known repertoire of signals:

- Fan fast: I am independent
- Fan slow: I am engaged
- Fan with right hand in front of face: Come hither
- Fan with left hand in front of face: Please leave me
- Fan wide open: Love
- Fan half open: Friendship
- Fan shut: Hate
- Fan swinging: Will you see me home?

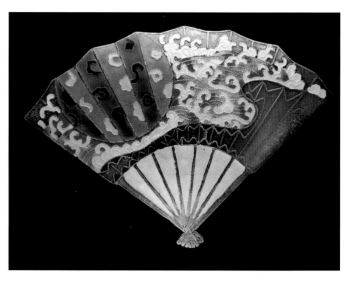

A large brooch in the shape of a fan in gilded silver and enamel, c. 1930, approximately 4.0" x 2.75". This pin, of Chinese origins, is a veritable potpourri of enameling techniques: The white enamel between the fan's "sticks" is champlevé enamel; the yellow and orange sun is done in a combination of champlevé and cloisonné enamel, with the cloisonné in turn used to create a basse taille effect; and the blue and white stylized swirling clouds and sky are done in cloisonné. Unmarked, but tested silver.

Two more modern fan brooches, one from Thailand, the other from Spain. The Thai fan is in silver, with blue enamel; numerous examples of this type of jewelry–probably made for tourists and for export–exist, but more often are decorated with stylized Thai dancers in silver against the enamel. The Spanish fan, decorated in black enamel against a gold-tone metal, is also very typical of export or tourist jewelry from that country.

A modern costume brooch in the shape of a fan, with three dimensional flower and butterfly added to the pleated metal of the fan. Although done in base metal, it is enameled in true vitreous enamel, which either failed to cover, or was lost, at the top where the flower was attached.

And young people of both sexes communicated with flowers. As can be adduced by the statistics cited above from Laufer's *Tussie-Mussies*, the language of flowers was everywhere. In Victorian England and the United States, the language of flowers sometimes appeared in ephemera: A small book entitled *How to Flirt with a Fan* contained at the back a short glossary of flower meanings,[4] while a late Victorian game called "Flirt" consisted of cards printed with flowers; the player was supposed to pick a card and discern meanings.[5] At the opposite extreme, however, many books on the subject became best-sellers with a great deal of staying power. For example, *Flora's Interpreter* by Sarah Josepha Hale, first published in 1832, had by 1857 sold over 40,000 copies (Laufer, 1993, 12). Even Kate Greenaway, the hugely popular illustrator of children's books, wrote and illustrated her own version of the language of flowers. With renewed interest in the language of flowers, Greenaway's book has gone through a number of reprintings.

And the language of flowers could also be found in the most common, respectable, and perhaps even mundane, of publications. Collier's 1882 *Cyclopedia of Commercial and Social Information and Treasury of Useful and Entertaining Knowledge* contained a lengthy article on the language of flowers compiled by Nugent Robinson. In the following flowery observation that opens Robinson's section on the language of flowers, Robinson somewhat indirectly refers to the Eastern origins of this language:

> How the universal heart of man blesses flowers! They are wreathed round the cradle, the marriage-altar, and the tomb. The Persian in the far East delights in their perfume, and writes his love in nosegays... The Cupid of the ancient Hindoos tipped his arrows with flowers, and orange-flowers are a bridal crown with us, a nation of yesterday. Flowers garlanded the Grecian altar, and hung in votive wreath before the Christian shrine...
>
> Flowers have a language of their own, and it is this bright particular language that we would teach our readers. How charmingly a young gentleman can speak to a young lady, and with what eloquent silence in this delightful language. How delicately she can respond, the beautiful little flowers telling her tale in perfumed words; what a delicate story the myrtle or the rose tells! How unhappy that which basil, or yellow rose reveals, while ivy is the most faithful of all.

Robinson begins his list with a short poem:

ALMOND–HOPE
In our dreams of a happier hour
That alights upon misery's brow
 Springs out of the silvery almond flower
That blooms on a leafless bough.

A long list of flowers and their meanings then follows.

A single flower could be rich with meaning; and a bouquet could contain an entire paragraph. Small bunches of flowers, called tussy-mussies, were often exchanged.

The language of flowers was also popular in Germany. The *Dictionary of Symbolism* (Biedermann, 1994, 137-139) contains a partial list of German flower symbolism. The great mystery writer Agatha Christie included the language of flowers in a short story featuring her rather old-fashioned detective Miss Jane Marple. In this story, "The Four Suspects," Miss Marple uses her botanical knowledge to illuminate obscure facts in a murder case. She tells her listeners that as a young woman she had a German governess who instructed her in the language of flowers. Given that Agatha Christie herself had endured a sheltered Victorian upbringing complete with governesses, it is probably safe to assume that she too had been instructed in, or at least exposed to, the language of flowers.

While the language of flowers might have seemed old-fashioned in the 1940s when Agatha Christie wrote her story, today it is undergoing a revival. Numerous books, ranging from simple lists with attractive illustrations to books containing a great deal of research and explanation, can be found in bookstores and libraries everywhere. Kate Greenaway's book has been reprinted by several publishers. A glance at the bibliography at the end of this book will shows how prevalent books on this subject have become. Florists and wedding floral designers offer partial lists of meaning in their advertising and on their web sites.

Flowers call to us. They speak a language we almost hear.
Each flower's color seems an announcement.
　　　　　　　　　　—Gretchen Scoble, *The Meaning of Flowers*

Although flowers appeal to our emotions, as Frances Kelly (1992, 2) notes, quoting a Zen Buddhist maxim, "Flowers do not speak." For most flowers, the meaning assigned is arbitrary. And, as might be expected, given the rather artificial nature of the language of flowers, the various lists of flowers and their significance do not always agree. At times, it seems that some authors of lists have given somewhat random meanings to the more obscure flowers. For example, one list claims that the cherry blossom, so prevalent in Chinese and Japanese art and culture, signifies a good education. But why should it? Did the compiler of that particular list associate the blossom with young women graduating from school in the spring, perhaps wearing flowing white gowns and hair bedecked with delicate pink cherry blossoms? Or did the compiler decide that as cherry trees need to be pruned and carefully tended–or "educated"–when they are young, that the cherry tree or blossom signifies training, or education?

As previously noted, some flower meanings come from myths and legends, or formed part of popular lore. In other cases, the meaning of a flower might be found in poetry or prose that antedates the Victorian language of flowers. When Robert Burns wrote "My love is like a red, red rose" he made an association that has lasted well over a century. Most lists agree that a red rose signifies passionate love, and red roses abound on Valentine's Day.

With such floral fervor present in the air, it is hardly surprising that flower pins became popular at around the same time that the language of flowers had its heyday. When Dale first started collecting, before she had heard of the language of flowers, she wondered at the relatively narrow range of flowers depicted in jewelry. Why so many pansies? Why no red roses? Why no marigolds, or narcissus, or–living as she was in Colorado, where it was the state flower–columbine? The reason is now a bit clearer. The red rose (or any red flower

Flower fever was everywhere. It expressed itself in jewelry, paintings, books on the language of flowers–and in china, which well-bred women painted as a hobby. These floral plates, painted by Dale's great-grandmother, are typical of the era. Not surprisingly, pansies and wild roses were among the flowers represented.

declaring passion) was probably too ardent for the restrained Victorian suitor. The marigold, narcissus, and columbine, on the other hand, have disagreeable meanings. The marigold represents "despair," "jealousy," or a "vulgar mind." The narcissus means "egotism," and the columbine, "folly."

Pansies, though, were the ideal flower, conveying the most acceptable of meanings. For who could take offense at a flower which said, "Thoughts" or "My thoughts are with you?" And, as we have already seen, in Victorian times pansies predominated when it came to flower pins and other floral jewelry.

Endnotes Chapter Four

[1]This view was mentioned by a critic discussing Picasso and Matisse exhibit in New York, *Charlie Rose Show*, April 12, 2003.
[2]However, there does seem to have been an older European tradition, perhaps from a Dutch guide published in the sixteenth century; this has been alluded to in some sources. And it may have been this tradition that gave Shakespeare the meanings of flowers for his Ophelia "mad scene." At least some of the meanings in Ophelia's speech were not a creation of Shakespeare's inventive mind, but rather refer to established associations still in use today. Also, he quite likely used symbols with which his audience was familiar, in the expectation that they would understand the allusions.

[3]Shakespeare's words, written long before Lady Mary Wortley Montagu set pen to paper, make it clear that there was already in place a symbolism attached to flowers based on Western tradition; Classical myths, medieval symbolism, and medicinal properties of herbs all contributed to this tradition. Still, Lady Mary's description of *selam* did inspire a new type of lexicon.
[4]Such an ephemeral guide was offered for sale on eBay in May, 2003; although some of the pages at the back were missing, enough was left to show that it also included a flower glossary.
[5]Personal communication from Robin Lamoreux, who owns such a game, bought by her mother at an antique shop. Laufer (1993, 19) also has a picture of this type of card game. The cards are printed with floral pictures, with the flowers' meanings given.

Price Guide for Chapter Four

p. 121 : Eg rev amlt neck $300-$400; **p. 122:** Eg rev pl wg-scar $750-$1000; **p. 123:** Sp galleon br $25-$35; **p. 124:** D.A. strawberry br $50-$100; **p. 125:** M.H. laurel br $125-$200; AN rooster br $350-$400; vint brn spider wtch $500-$550; vint spider lckt $300-$400; AN p-d'v locust $1200-$2000; **p. 126:** AD 14K lady/tiger w/w $2000-$2500; vint Dan snow queen bclt $500-$750; **p. 127:** A&C/Gth rev Lim dragon br w/ turq & prls $450-$500; **p. 128:** A&C dragon neck w/ prls & pst $400-$450; vint Chin clsn dragon e/r $400-$500; ant Jap dragon bkl $$400-$500; vint M.de T. chmp dragon br $350-$500; **p. 129:** Eg rev plq ankh neck $1500-$200; lg Vict sunflower hrt $200-$250; *ba* bclt w/ plq $2500-$3000, w/o $750-$800; **p. 130:** AN plq bat $1200-$1500; 2 vint bee br w/ marc $75-$100 ea; **p. 131:** scrb bclt $300-$350; vint robin & bluebird lckt $200-$250; **Butterflies:** Vict 14K veil clip w/ art wgs $250-$300; **p. 132:** Vict cflnk $350-$400; A&C br w/ mab prl $250-$300; M.M. plq br w/ prls & pst $3000-$3500; 2 v sm Vict pins: C.H. $100-$150; lt bl $65-$100; vint/AD neck $200-$250; lg AD J.A.& S. co bl br $175-$300; **p. 133:** sm J.A.&S. lt grn br $80-$150; lg D.A. vint br $300-$500; med H.P. vint br $100-$175; 4 sm-med br: sm vint co bl & wh A.Hn. $35-$50, sm vint ppl OPRPO $50-$100, med vint yell OPRO $100-$150, sm AD lt grn $150-$200; vint Germ brn & grn br w/ marc $125-$150; vint Germ bl & grn br w/marc $125-$150; **p. 134:** vint fil br $75-$100; vint A.C. fil br w/ art wgs $150-$200; vint M.de T. demi $750-$900; vint Mex br $75-$100; mod Mex lav br $40-$65; vint Mm. Hsk.lt bl cost e/r $35-$75; vint Mat cost br $30-$45; **p. 135:** Vict blk cat br $150-$200; Vict chrb br w/ red bdr $125-$150; Vict 18K porc chrb demi $1500-$2000; AN chrysanthemum br $250-$300; vint rooster br w/ marc $125-$150; **p. 136:** Vict 14K porc chrb w/ doves br $500-$600; **p. 137:** vint AN drgl perf $175-$200; mod 18K eye pend $100-$125; Vict 14K onyx clsn fish wtch-p w/ prl $450-$550; **p. 138:** vint. M.de.T. fish bclt $500; vint frog br w/ marc $125-$150; 3 AN grape br $200-$250 ea; **p. 139:** nie demon p-wtch $500-$600; AN plq demon br $400-$500; Eg rev cost wg Isis br $75-$125; Edw W.& B. 14K bl guil br w/ sm prl & gld laurel lvs $300-$450; **p. 140:** AN chmp lilies br $250-$300; Vict 14K ppl lion lckt w/ prls $1000-$1200; AN lizard p-wtch $500-$600; **p. 141:** Eg rev styl-lot e/r w/ pnk qtz $350-$400; AN plq 18K w/ dmds nymph pend $1250-$2000; 2 vint bl & gr flrs w/ marc $125-$150 ea; **p. 142: Owls:** 2 R.Bro. 14K owl pins: w/ enam & s-prls $750-$1000, w/o $500-$750; M.M. owl head br $200-$250; sm AD/vint Wls. gf owl br $25-$50; vint gr & wh owl br $100-$150; **p. 143:** vint owl cig-c $500-$600; vint D.A. wh & gr styl owl br $125-$175; vint A.C. owl set w/ marc $200-$250; 3 vint cost owl br: Eis. bl, turq & bl $45-$75, Trf. gf bl & grn $25-$45, mod rep w/ rh-st $20-$40; A&C rect peacock br $250-$500; vint peacock w/ garn $60-$85; **p. 144:** Eg rev amlt neck $350-$400; AD snake bclt $350-$450; **p. 145:** vint M.de.T. snake neck & bclt $1500-$2500 set; M.de.T. bclt $750-$1000; B.G.&O. AN swallow br $450-$900; **p. 146:** AN plq swan neck $750-$1000; A-H swan pend $400-$500; vint thistle br w/ marc $125-$150; **p. 147:** BA/AN 14K tiger lckt w/ dmds $400-$650; BA/AN 14K tiger fob w/ dmds $500-$750; 2 vint turtle br w/ marc $75-$100 ea; vint turtle br in prof $75-$125; Eg rev plq vulture neck w/ l/l $2500-$3500; **p. 148:** Eg rev queen neck $350-$400; vint wasp br w/ marc $150; AD plq 18K wheat pend $350-$400; AN wings br $200-$225; **p. 149:** vint fil pansy set $200-$300; **p. 152:** vint Chin exp clsn fan br w/ l/l $350-$450; lg vint Chin exp fan br $125-$300; **p. 153:** 2 vint fan br: Sp cost w/ bl enam $25-$30, Thai w/ bl enam $35-$50; lg cost fan br $15-$25.

Chapter Five
The Jeweled Garden: Flower Pins and the Language of Flowers

The language of love was spoken in flowers; so, too, was it spoken in poetry. Because so many meanings in the language of flowers seem to be associated with poetry–either the poetry using the floral lexicon, or the floral lexicon deriving meaning from the poet's words–it seemed appropriate to include a selection of verses here. These verses are associated with the flowers themselves, or their meanings, and in some cases may perhaps indicate from what source a flower derived at least part of its significance.

A Profusion of Pansies: Pansies through Time

Haply I think on thee,–and then my state
Like to the lark at break of day arising
From sullen earth, sings hymns at heaven's gate;
For thy sweet love remember'd such wealth brings
That then I scorn to change my state with kings.
 —William Shakespeare, Sonnet XXIX

... here's pansies, that's for thoughts
 —William Shakespeare, *Hamlet*

Pansies
thoughts ~ my thoughts are with you

In the language of flowers, pansies–their name derived from the French *pensée*, or "thought"–not surprisingly meant "thoughts" or "thinking of you."

Also not surprisingly, it was the favorite flower pin in late Victorian times. The pansy itself is lovely, and its sentiment beyond reproach.

An unusual Victorian locket in the form of a stand-alone pansy in 14K gold, enamel, with a small diamond in the center, approximately .625" x .875". Lockets of all types, used to hold a lock of a loved one's hair (or, later, a photograph) were popular with the sentimental Victorians. The realistic painting of the pansy's petals and the glossy enamel point to an earlier Victorian date, perhaps c. 1880-1885. The small chip to the enamel on the locket's left edge is unfortunately all too common in enameled pieces this old. When opened, the locket reveals a tiny hinged magnifying glass, which can be raised or lowered.

A spectacular red pansy, in 14K gold, enamel, and a diamond, c. 1895. Pansies are conventionally enameled in shades of yellow and violet, or blue. A red one is extremely rare. Aside from its color, this pansy looks rather similar to the blue pansies shown below. *Courtesy of Karen Perlmutter, Acanthus Antiques, Kensington, MD.*

Two Victorian brooches in unmarked 14K gold, enamel, and diamonds, each having three pansies tied together with twine or ribbon, both probably of Newark or New York manufacture c. 1890. The pin on the right, 1.375" across, is in glossy enamel with enamel shading from deep purple markings on yellow to light violet, nicely detailed markings, and the typical Newark construction with arched supports linking the flowers. The pin on the right, approximately 1.25" in diameter, is in matte enamel in shades of white, yellow, and lavender with more finely drawn markings (as is often the case with matte enamel); it has star-shaped links holding the petals of each flower together, possibly indicating that it was manufactured by Black, Starr & Frost, which is known to have used this type of link.

A rather large pansy in 14K gold, semi glossy enamel, and a diamond, 1.5" in diameter, c. 1890. The diamond, fittingly, is also larger than usual in such brooches. Like many of the larger pieces of the era, this one has a bail that allows it to be worn as a pendant as well as a brooch, although it is not a folding bail. The blue color is somewhat unusual, as most pansies are in shades of violet, often with yellow or white, or both. Marked 14K, with no maker's mark; measures approximately 1.5" in diameter.

A pansy brooch in 14K gold, enamel, and a pearl, remarkably similar to the one shown above, except that instead of a diamond in the center it has a pearl. Otherwise, the folds in the petals, the shade of blue, and the markings on the two pansies are similar enough to make one wonder whether they are from the same maker. One feature of Newark (and probably other) jewelry is that Newark makers often allowed for the substitution of a diamond for a pearl (or a pearl for no stone at all) in basically what was otherwise the same piece. Undecipherable marks; measures .75" in diameter. *Courtesy of Robin Allison.*

A pansy in 14K gold, enamel, pearls, and diamond, c. 1900, from Krementz & Co. The seed pearls around the edge of each petal add an extra touch of elegance to this beautifully enameled piece. Seed pearls at the edges of petals and leaves are featured in a number of pieces produced not only by Krementz, but by other makers such as Crane Theurer. (For other examples of enameled pieces with seed pearl edges, please see chapter one, Cloverleaves Through Time; chapter three, Krementz Through Time; and this chapter, under Violets.) *Courtesy of S. J. Phillips Ltd., London.*

A pansy brooch/pendant in 20K gold, enamel, and diamonds, c. 1900, approximately 1" x 1.125", of unknown manufacture. Although this pansy has a folding bail almost identical to those in Newark pieces, the enameling—in a glossy champlevé that has created gold striations in the petals—has none of the nuances characteristic of Newark flowers. While it was not unusual for Newark makers such as Krementz and Crane Theurer to add seed pearls to the edges of petals and leaves, diamonds are much more unusual. In fact, Dale has seen only one other instance, a pair of French pansy earrings belonging to a collector.

A pair of earrings in 14K gold, enamel, and small diamonds in the shape of pansies, probably of Newark or New York manufacture c. 1900. Like other Newark and New York flower pieces,

these were made with separate petals joined in the center, and reinforced with c-shaped links attaching each petal to its neighbors. The use of matte enamel with very slight iridescence in shades of white, green, and lavender points to Art Nouveau pretensions. These colors are also found in suffragette pieces; however, it seems more reasonable to assume that the colors were chosen for the purpose of design rather than a declaration of political sentiments. Marked 14K, with no maker's mark; measure approximately .875" in diameter.

An unusual watch in the form of a free-standing pansy. Like many pansies from this and later eras, this one has very detailed and naturalistic markings on the petals, as well as enameling that shades from a near-white to a pale lavender at the edges; the top petals are done in a deeper purple. Folds in the metal give this piece a nicely dimensional look, as do the striations in the upper petals. Marked depose; measures 1.75" x 1.5". *Courtesy of Robin Allison.*

A slide locket in 900 silver and enamel, in the form of a free-standing pansy, similar in many ways to the watch shown above. Like the watch, this pansy has very detailed and naturalistic markings on the petals, as well as nicely shaded enameling, with the top petals done in a darker violet, and given a dimensional look. Measures 2.25" x 1.75". *Courtesy of Robin Allison.*

An Art Nouveau buckle in silver and enamel, featuring three pansies in bright, glossy enamel. While each pansy has quite a bit of detail, the overall effect is more that of somewhat stylized rather than naturalistic flowers: The markings on the petals are more sketchy than lifelike, and the colors are done in bands rather than blending together. The exception is the inclusion of small stamens in the center of each blossom. Turtle hallmark; measures 2.25" x 1.75". *Courtesy of Robin Allison.*

A very attractive vintage brooch in 14K gold, enamel, and pearls, c. 1930s-1940s. The enameling on this piece is extremely fine, resembling the best of enameling in Newark and New York pieces created c. 1900. *Courtesy of Karen Perlmutter, Acanthus Antiques, Kensington, MD.*

A vintage brooch in silver gilt, enamel, and a pearl, by the U.S. maker Creed, probably c. 1940. This pansy is, rather unusually, enameled in shades of cream and a peachy pink. Like earlier flower pieces, this one has petals fashioned individually and then joined. Marked Creed, sterling silver; measures 1.5" x 1.25".

Another Creed pansy, probably c. 1960, this one smaller, more stylized, and with a stem and leaves forming part of the design, rather than a single lone flower. Marked Creed, sterling silver; measures 1.25" in diameter including frame.

A lovely pansy brooch in 935 silver, plique-à-jour enamel, and pastes, 1.25" x 1". The blue plique enamel shades very slightly from a tinge of pink near the center. The nature of plique-à-jour enamel, with its obligatory open cells forming the basic underlying structure of a piece, makes it much more suited to stylized rather than truly natural-looking flowers. Similar to the seed pearls edging the Krementz pansy pictured above, the paste gems around the edges of this pansy add an extra bit of flair. *Courtesy of Robin Allison.*

A brooch in silver, guilloche, basse taille, and cloisonné enameling from the New England maker Watson, c. 1900. True cloisonné enameling, rather than champlevé enameling, is not usually encountered in American-made pieces of this period; in fact, so rare was this technique among American makers that this piece is stamped on the back with the words "Genuine cloisonné" in addition to the maker's marks and sterling. Measures approximately 2" x .75".

A pair of pansy earrings in sterling silver and enamel, probably c. 1940 to 1950. Although these are formed in one single piece, the folds to the petals and the deep translucent cobalt enamel give them something of a dimensional look. Realism is added to what are essentially stylized flowers by the yellow and gold centers. Marked sterling, and measure approximately 1" in diameter.

Another pair of pansy earrings in sterling silver and enamel, these by Norwegian designer David Andersen, c. 1950. These pansies, formed of separate petals, are extremely stylized, with only four petals rather than the actual five found in nature (although, possibly to add dimension, the top petals are double, with the petals in back enameled in dark violet instead of the lighter lavender of the front petals).

Andersen created a number of pansy pieces, both earrings and the more commonly found brooches, all with the same stylized look, but in different colors, especially blues. Some wear to a lower petal on one of the earrings reduces the value of the earrings considerably; in better condition, they would probably sell for twice what was actually paid for this pair. Marked David Andersen, Norway, 925S; measure approximately 1.25".

A vintage gold-filled and enamel pansy, with a cultured pearl, by the well-known costume jewelry manufacturer Weiss. Although jewelry by Weiss is often considered among the better costume, this pansy–though well made–is enameled in soft rather than true vitreous enamel.

A pair of small pins by the costume manufacturer Trifari in the form of stylized pansies, probably c. 1960. Like most costume pieces, these are in soft rather than vitreous enamel. Marked Trifari; measure approximately 1.25" in diameter.

An Eloquence of Irises

In Belmont is a lady richly left
And she is fair, and fairer than the word,
Of wondrous virtues; sometimes from her eyes
I did receive fair speechless messages.
—William Shakespeare, *The Merchant of Venice*

Fenc'd up the verdant wall, each beauteous flow'r
Iris all hues, roses and jessamin
Rear'd high their flourished heads…
—John Milton, *Paradise Lost*

Iris
a message ~ eloquence ~ my compliments

In ancient Greek mythology, Iris was the goddess of the rainbow. How fitting that the shimmery iris, "all hues," bears her name. And the iridescent iris was the perfect flower for Art Nouveau enamelists working with their delicate iridescent palette.

Iris also served as the messenger of the gods. In the language of flowers, an iris signified a message–unspoken, like the fair speechless messages from Shakespeare's lady's eyes.

An iridescent Art Nouveau iris in 14K gold, enamel, and pearls that can be worn as a brooch or a pendant, by Whiteside & Blank, c. 1900. The detailed petals, with folds and basse taille markings, are enameled in a luminous iridescent peach that when held a certain way approaches violet. A hook on the back once held a long baroque pearl dangle that, unfortunately, was lost. Marked 14K, maker's mark, and measures approximately 1.5" x 1.375".

A brooch in sterling silver and enamel, c. 1900, featuring a white iris with three cattails. The leaves and petals of the flower are given a look of dimensionality through their curving basse taille markings, while the cattails' texture is conveyed by basse taille dots. Robbins Co. marks, sterling; measures 2.25" by .75". *Courtesy of Robin Allison.*

An iris in 18K gold, enamel, rubies, and turquoise, of Italian manufacture in the Art Nouveau style. The iris and its leaves are very dimensional, but the enamel is less subtle than enamel in Newark pieces, and also seems more fragile, having suffered some wear. Marked 18K, Italy, with no discernable maker's mark; measures approximately 2.25" x 1.5".

A marvelous hatpin in silver and enamel, of Japanese manufacture, in the form of an iris. Although this is very recognizably an iris blossom, the perspective–seeming to view the iris from the top rather than the side–gives this piece a unique look. Marked with a star-shaped maker's mark and Japanese hallmarks; measures 1.5" x .875". *Courtesy of Robin Allison.*

A slide mirror in unmarked silver and enamel, 1.375" in diameter, featuring a very detailed iris (quite possibly created through transfer enameling). The petals add the only color to this piece as the leaves, in typical Art Nouveau style, are of plain metal, heavily carved to add dimension and texture. *Courtesy of Robin Allison.*

An iris stickpin in 14K gold and enamel that is also a fichu pin, meant for pinning lacy collars or shawls around a woman's shoulders–hence the small chain and bar, probably c. 1880. The iris, enameled in matte white, has little detail, but it is completely three-dimensional. Inside, it appears to have been enameled or painted in gold. Iris measures approximately .625".

A pendant in sterling silver and enamel, painted with iris blossoms. This pendant, marked for Birmingham silver, probably falls somewhere between Victorian and Arts and Crafts in style; the obvious hand-painted (and signed) enameling would seem to fall more under the Arts and Crafts rubric, while the detailed naturalistic rendition would appear to be more Victorian.

An Opulence of Orchids

Beauty is the lover's gift.

—William Congreve

Orchid
a belle ~ beauty ~ luxury ~ nobility ~ I await your favors

Orchids, so beautiful and yet appearing to live on air, in the language of flowers must inevitably mean "beauty" or "a belle"–at least in some lexicons. However, the orchid can also signify "luxury," "love," "nobility," or "I await your favors."

Whatever meaning they conveyed to Victorians, they provided ample scope for the talents of the most noted Art Nouveau jewelers.

An orchid in 14K gold, enamel, and a diamond, c. 1890. The orchid, in matte enamel, is realistically painted down to the last spot. Like many larger pieces, this has a folding bail, and can be worn either as a pendant or a brooch. Unmarked but tested 14K gold; measures approximately 1.25" x 1.375".

An orchid in unmarked 14K gold, iridescent enamel, and a diamond, most likely of Newark manufacture, c. 1900. Like most American flower pins in gold from that period, this one is beautifully dimensional, and a very recognizable rendition of an orchid. The iridescent enamel, in pastel hues of green and pink, with a splash of darker pink under the diamond, marks this piece as Art Nouveau in style. It may be an unmarked piece by Krementz. Measures 1.25" x 1.25". *Courtesy of Robin Allison.*

A more modern orchid brooch by Norwegian maker Aksel Holmsen. Although somewhat more stylized than its Victorian counterpart, this is nonetheless very clearly an orchid, as evinced in its form and color. Interest and texture are provided by the basse taille work that characterizes so much of Scandinavian enameled jewelry, while raised champlevé work creates lines along the larger white petals. Marked for sterling, Norway, and maker. *Courtesy of Robin Allison.*

A 19th century botanical print depicting the orchid Cattleya callumata. The spots on this orchid are reminiscent of the spots on the pin in matte enamel, shown above.

A small orchid in 14K gold, enamel, and a pearl, by Whiteside & Blank, c. 1900. The orchid, very dimensional, is enameled in an iridescent peach that is almost opalescent in its softness. Whiteside & Blank also made this same orchid in a larger size, without the stem. Maker's mark, 14K; measures 2" with stem; enameled flower is approximately 1" x .75".

A striking vintage brooch in 800 sterling silver, enamel, and marcasites, in the form of an orchid. The silver has been cast to give an almost ruffled edge to the petals, which are vividly enameled in orange, yellow, and lavender, and accented with marcasites. Measures 3" x 3". *Courtesy of Robin Allison.*

A Vision of Violets

A violet by a mossy stone
Half hidden from the eye!
Fair as a star, when only one
Is shining in the sky.
—William Wordsworth, "She Dwelt Among
the Untrodden Ways"

I know a bank whereon the wild thyme blows,
Where oxlips and the nodding violet grows
Quite over-canopied with luscious woodbine
With sweet musk-roses, and with eglantine.
—William Shakespeare, *A Midsummer Night's Dream*

Violet
modesty
blue
modesty ~ faithfulness ~ loyalty ~ love
purple
you occupy my thoughts

In Greek mythology, the violet sprang up on the spot where weary Orpheus set down his lyre. The violet is sweet, but grows low to the ground: In the language of flowers, the violet most often stands for modesty.

A violet in 14K gold, enamel, and a diamond, probably made in Newark or New York c. 1900. This violet, enameled in a soft matte purple that almost looks sueded, has a folding bail that allows it to be worn as a pendant as well as a brooch. Marked 14K, with no maker's mark; measures approximately 1.125" in diameter.

An adorable slide in unmarked silver gilt and plique-à-jour enamel, .75" in diameter, in the shape of a violet. Although the nature of plique-à-jour enameling sometimes makes a piece look rather stylized, this one is recognizable as a violet due to the number and shape of its petals, as well as its purple hue, which shades from lighter at the center to darker at the edges. An attempt at realism is also conveyed by the small silver stamens in the center. *Courtesy of Robin Allison.*

Another Newark or New York violet, c. 1900, in 14K gold, enamel, and a diamond. Like the other examples of flower pins from that time and place, this one is nicely dimensional, formed of separate petals joined at the center, and has opaque enameling shading from lighter to darker purple, with fine green lines painted to represent veins. The diamond is set in a buttercup setting rather than the more common prong or collet setting. Measures 1" X .875". *Courtesy of Robin Allison.*

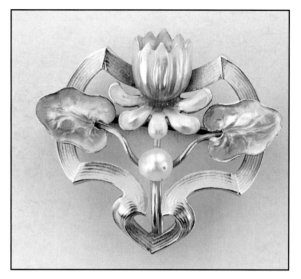

An unusual watch pin in 14K gold, enamel, and a small diamond, in the form of a violet, probably of Newark origins (and possibly by Krementz), c. 1890. Unlike most Newark violets, this one is not enameled in purple, but rather has the light blue champlevé forget-me-nots fashionable for certain types of jewelry in the late 19th century. However, this is a rather different piece in that most champlevé forget-me-nots are found in lover's knots and the crescents of honeymoon pins, rather than in figural jewelry. Marked 14K; measures approximately 1.125" x 1".

A Luxurance of Lotuses

> *'Courage!' he said, and pointed toward the land,*
> *'This mounting wave will roll us shoreward soon.'*
> *In the afternoon they came unto a land*
> *In which it seemed always afternoon. ...*
>
> *Surely, surely, slumber is more sweet than toil, the shore*
> *Than labor in the deep mid-ocean,*
> *wind and wave and oar;*
> *Oh rest ye, brother mariners, we will not wander more.*
> —Alfred, Lord Tennyson, *The Lotos-Eaters*

Lotus
divine love ~ eloquence

The lotus, so beautiful and so symbolic, was one of the favored flowers of Art Nouveau jewelers. It was less important to the Victorians, who rarely depicted it in jewelry other than Egyptian revival pieces. In the language of flowers, it meant "divine love" or "eloquence."

In Greek mythology, Odysseus and his crew came upon a land where the strangely hypnotic lotus made them slumber; hence the inspiration for Tennyson's poem *The Lotos-Eaters.*

A lotus brooch in 14K gold, enamel, and a pearl, by Whiteside & Blank, c. 1900. The stylized lotus and leaves are enameled in iridescent peach and green, and in spite of the somewhat angular frame, this piece is very Art Nouveau in style–and lotus blossoms were among the flowers most favored by Art Nouveau designers. Marked 14K, with maker's mark on c-clasp; measures 1.25" x 1".

A lotus brooch in 14K gold and enamel by Bippart, Griscom & Osborn, c. 1900. The bud is tipped in a deep opaque coral, the only vivid touch in the otherwise pale iridescent green of the leaves and bud. Stamped 14K and with maker's mark on c-clasp; approximately 1" x .875".

A Benevolence of Bleeding Hearts

Where your treasure is, there will your heart be also.

—St. Matthew, 6: 21

Bleeding Heart
elegance ~ fidelity

Because the bleeding heart was such a late addition to European and American gardens, most older books on the language of flowers do not include it in their glossaries. However, because it is a lovely and unusual flower, and sometimes used in wedding arrangements, more modern interpretations of its meaning are occasionally given.

A brooch and matching screw-back earrings in 14K gold, enamel, and seed pearls, by Krementz, c. 1900. This is a realistic rendering of bleeding hearts, which are in matte enamel shading beautifully from pale to dark pink, with each blossom ending in a seed pearl. The leaves, on the other hand, are in iridescent enamel. Marked 14K, with maker's mark; brooch measures approximately 2" x 1.25".

Makers often made pins in small, medium, and large versions, but this is the smallest possible version of the above pin. Tiny bleeding hearts, showing the same attention to detail as the larger ones in the above picture, end in seed pearls in a pendant that is only 1.25" long. Also by Krementz, c. 1900.

A bleeding heart (or, equally possibly, a fuschia blossom) in 14K gold, enamel, and a pearl, also by Krementz, c. 1900. The bleeding heart (or fuschia) in this pin is much less realistic than the ones shown above. Its iridescent enamel and the overall impressionistic style clearly mark it as Art Nouveau. Fully marked; measures approximately 1.125" x 1".

A Contentment of Carnations

*The fairest flowers o' the season
Are our carnations and streak'd gillyvors...*

—William Shakespeare, *A Winter's Tale*

Carnation, Pink
maternal love ~ lively and pure affection ~ beauty ~ pride

The carnation's spicy scent has led to its being given the same name as the clove in some Romance languages. In its red version, carnations had a much spicier meaning, too: they indicated passion, as well as deep pure love, and betrothal.

A flower pin in 14K gold, enamel, and an opal, c. 1900, in the form of a stylized pink carnation. This flower pin has no maker's mark, but is very likely from a Newark or New York maker. The stylization and rather geometric nature of this piece mark it as quite possibly Edwardian, although the carved gold stem seems more Victorian in character. As is usual in Newark enamels, the petals shade from a lighter to a slightly darker pink at the edges, and are also painted with thin lines to indicate veins. Marked 14K, with curlicue c-clasp; blossom measures approximately 1" in diameter, with stem brooch is 1.625".

A Delight of Daisies

There grew pied wind-flowers and violets,
Daisies, those pearled Arcturi [stars] of the earth,
The constellated flower that never sets.
            —Percy Bysshe Shelley, "The Question"

Daisy
innocence ~ simplicity

The daisy's name comes from the old English "day's eye," or sun. And with its yellow disk surrounded by a pale array of petals, it truly does resemble the sun. In the language of flowers, it almost invariably means "innocence." In popular lore, pulling its petals until all are gone and repeating "She/he loves me, she/he loves me not" can tell a person whether or not her or his affection is returned.

A Victorian brooch in 14K gold and enamel, probably of Newark or New York manufacture, c. 1890, in the form of a bunch of daisies gathered into a bouquet tied with a thin gold rope. As is the case with many Newark enamels, this one has small gold c-links holding the flowers together. No maker's mark; measures approximately 1.375" x 1.125".

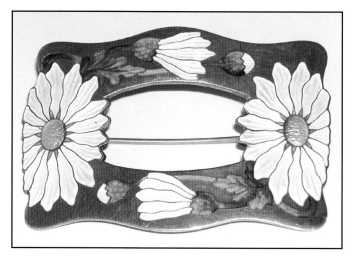

A brooch in sterling silver and enamel, 2.75" x 2", with two daisies, leaves, and buds around a wavy rectangle, very likely of New England manufacture. As in other pieces of this type, the iridescent enameling over basse taille markings creates a fairly naturalistic texture, especially to the gold disks of the flowers. *Courtesy of Robin Allison.*

A much more unusual floral brooch in sterling silver and enamel, by the Massachusetts firm Watson Co. with a daisy in champlevé enamel against guilloche enameling on an almost cruciform background. This piece shows Watson's usual fine basse taille work in the petals and disk of the daisy. Maker's marks, sterling; measures 2" x 1.5". *Courtesy of Robin Allison.*

An Art Nouveau brooch by a North American (probably Canadian) maker, c. 1900, an oval decorated with a wreath of daisies in champlevé enamel. Measures 2.5" by 1.625"; marked sterling RH. *Courtesy of Robin Allison.*

Faithfulness of Forget-Me-Nots

—William Shakespeare, Sonnet CXVI

Forget-Me-Not
true love ~ hope ~ remembrance ~ do not forget me

Given the forget-me-not's name, and the legend of how this name was bestowed, it is not surprising that in most flower lexicons it means "true love."

According to legend, a young knight stood on a sloping riverbank, picking the small blue flowers for the young woman he loved. Somehow he slipped and fell into the river, and the current carried him away. As he was swept out of sight, his voice was heard saying, "Forget me not!"

Three forget-me-nots in unmarked 14K gold, enamel, and diamonds, c. 1885-1890. The construction of the pin, as well as its curlicue c-clasp, mark it as relatively early, as does perhaps the glossy enamel. Some attempt at giving the blossoms an appearance of naturalness has been made by adding stamens, but this attempt is thwarted by the unnatural disk-like petals. Measures approximately 1.5" x 1.25"

Jauntiness of Jonquils

—Sir John Betjeman "May-Day Song for North Oxford"

Jonquil
I desire a return of affection ~ have pity on my passion

The jonquil, that jaunty colorful harbinger of spring, in the language of flowers has a rather plaintive message–"I desire of return of affection" or "have pity on my passion"–which may help explain why this wonderful flower is found less frequently than forget-me-nots, pansies, and violets in late Victorian floral jewelry.

A darling Victorian daffodil or jonquil in unmarked silver, enamel, and seed pearls. The flower and its buds are enameled, but the stem and leaves are set with the seed pearls often found in late Victorian jewelry. The flower is realistically enameled in white, with a creamy yellow edged in orange on the

An unusual flower brooch in gold, enamel, diamond, and pearl, c. 1890. This pin, with its symmetrical mirror-image flowers composed of six petals around a central cup, is framed by leaves with dark green basse taille enamel and buds crossing at the top. Carved gold stems cross at the bottom, above a pearl dangle. *Courtesy of Nelson Rarities, Portland, ME.*

A Victorian locket in unmarked silver and enamel (possibly a transfer), with a floral design including two jonquils in the same colors as the Victorian one shown above. Most likely American; measures 1.75" x 1.375" (not including bail). *Courtesy of Robin Allison.*

A less stylized rendition of the lily-of-the-valley in silver, enamel, ivory, and marcasites, c. 1920. In this version, the flowers are represented by ivory drops carved to resemble the blossoms, while the leaf, edged with marcasites, has basse taille striations indicating its structure.

An Art Nouveau brooch in silver and enamel, with a jonquil in champlevé enamel against a guilloche background by the Massachusetts-based Shepard Co., c. 1900. Basse taille markings indicate the folds and texture of the petals and the structures of the leaves. Like the other jonquils shown above, this one has white leaves and a yellow trumpet, although this latter lacks the red/orange edging. Marked; measures 2.125" x 1.5". *Courtesy of Robin Allison.*

Loveliness of the Lily-of-the-Valley

Not in Utopia–subterranean fields,–
Or some secreted island, Heaven knows where!
But in the very world, which is the world
Of all of us,–the place where, in the end
We find our happiness, or not at all!
—William Wordsworth, *A Poet's Epitaph*

Lily-of-the-Valley
return of happiness ~ purity ~ delicacy

The lily-of-the-valley, long associated with purity as well as the arrival of spring, in the lexicons of the language of flowers most often means "return of happiness." In medieval symbolism, it stood for purity and, like the white rose and white lily, was sometimes associated with the Virgin Mary: According to one legend, her tears turned into this flower as she wept at the cross, and thus the flower is sometimes called "Mary's tears." It has also been called "ladder to heaven" and "Jacob's tears," and has been considered a symbol of the second coming of Christ.

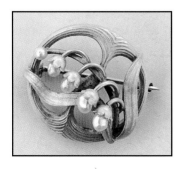

An Art Nouveau pin with stylized lilies-of-the-valley, in 14K gold, enamel, and pearls, by Krementz. A motif in some mourning jewelry, sprigs of lily-of-the-valley are occasionally found on jet or onyx bar pins, formed of pearls set in gold. Fully marked; measures approximately .875" in diameter.

Peace of Poppies

Not poppy, nor mandragora,
Nor all the drowsy syrups of the world,
Shall ever medicine thee to that sweet sleep
Which thou ow'dst yesterday.
—William Shakespeare, *Othello*

But pleasures are like poppies spread—
You seize the flow'r, its bloom is shed;
Or like the snow falls in the river—
A moment white—then melts for ever.
—Robert Burns, *Tam o' Shanter*

In Flanders fields the poppies blow
Between the crosses, row on row,
That mark our place...
If ye break faith with us who die
We shall not sleep, though poppies grow
In Flanders fields.
—Dr. John McCrae, "In Flanders Fields"

Poppy
forgetfulness ~ sleep ~ fleeting pleasure
orange
vanity
red
forgetfulness ~ extravagant pleasure

The poppy, with its obvious medicinal opiate properties, early received its association with sleep. In Greek mythology, it was the flower of Morpheus, the god of sleep and dreams. Because its petals are so delicate, so fragile, the poppy also signifies "fleeting pleasure" in the floral lexicon. More recently, with Dr. McCrae's World War I poem and its association with fallen soldiers, the poppy has come to be associated with remembrance–almost the complete opposite of its original meaning! Along with the iris, the lotus, and the orchid, it is one of the flowers most frequently found in Art Nouveau jewelry.

167

A poppy brooch in sterling silver and enamel, with a naturalistically rendered poppy in champlevé with basse taille markings. The stem and leaves in this piece are beautifully shaded from a dark green at the bottom, through light green, yellow, to a white that almost blends in with the guilloche background. The flower itself is in a deep red enamel, one of the harder shades to achieve in enameling (reds tend to burn out more quickly than other colors when fired). Measures 2.5" x 1.875". *Courtesy of Robin Allison.*

A marvelous brooch in gold and enamel, c. 1900, showing a poppy so realistically formed that its petals almost seem alive, with their folds and frilled edges. The enameling on the flower is equally fine, a gorgeous orangey-pink at the edge shading from a creamy center. Two buds have a deeper green enamel, while carved gold leaves are set against a lighter green plique-à-jour enamel. *Courtesy of Nelson Rarities, Portland, ME.*

A Promise of Primroses

Primrose first born child of Ver [spring],
Merry Springtime's Harbinger.
—John Fletcher (with William Shakespeare),
Two Noble Kinsmen

O fairest flower, no sooner blown but blasted,
Soft silken primrose fading timelessly.
—John Milton, "On the Death of a Fair Infant"

Primrose
childhood ~ early youth ~ innocence ~ gaiety ~ sorrow

The early-flowering primrose is often associated with childhood and early youth; as Milton's poem indicates, it can also imply sorrow.

A late Victorian primrose, or primula (the name often given to pink primroses to distinguish them from the more usual yellow ones) in 14K gold, enamel, and a pearl, c. 1890-1895. The glossy pink enamel shows some faint attempt to create differentiation in color, but lacks the detail of most Newark flowers, especially those in matte enamel. The stamens have been added to create a touch of verisimilitude, and the frame surrounding the primrose blossom has been given knots in an attempt to make it look like wood. The triangular piece missing enamel near the center of one petal appears to be a manufacturing flaw rather than later loss of enamel. (This flaw is occasionally found in an area where loss through wear would not be expected, and may be the result of stone-setting.) Approximately 1" in diameter.

Romance of Roses

Rose
cabbage
ambassador of love
pink
grace ~ beauty ~ femininity
red
love ~ passion ~ beauty
white
silence ~ secrecy ~ I am worthy of you ~ love ~ respect
yellow
friendship ~ jealousy ~ distinction ~ unfaithful ~ decrease of
love on better acquaintance

Probably no flower has been more glorified in poem and song than the rose. Also, there may be no other flower with quite so many different varieties and colors as the rose. In nineteenth century flower pins, the red rose is almost never found (too passionate? too bold a statement?). Nor, for good reason, is the yellow rose—jealousy and infidelity are usually not reasons for presenting a loved one with a gift of jewelry. Cabbage roses, however, occur fairly frequently, as do roses in delicate shades of pink so pale they border on white. Most of the major Newark and New York manufacturers of enameled jewelry seem to have come up with a version of the rose. (For further examples, please see chapter three.)

However, it does seem that with so many colors and so many meanings to choose from, the nineteenth century suitor might have been satisfied with roses alone.

A late Victorian or early Edwardian pin in 10K gold, enamel, and a tiny diamond, in the form of a wild rose, most likely of Newark or New York origins. As in other pieces in lower karat gold–as well as in later Edwardian pieces where color was shunned–here only the leaves are enameled, in a pale shimmery green. Although this would have been considered a relatively inexpensive piece of jewelry at the time of manufacture, it nevertheless has a very small diamond set in the center. Marked 10K, with no maker's mark; measures approximately 1.125" across. *Courtesy of Bodette Reeves, Odessa, TX.*

Sweet Suffering and Sweet Peas

Sweet Pea
departure ~ delicate pleasures ~ meet me ~ farewell

In most versions of the language of flowers, sweet peas stand for departure, or farewell. "Parting is such sweet sorrow," wrote the Bard. But he also wrote, in *Twelfth Night*, "O mistress mine! where are you roaming?/ O! stay and hear; your true love's coming,/ That can sing both high and low,/ Trip no further, pretty sweeting;/ Journeys end in lovers meeting."

A purple rose in 14K gold, matte enamel, and a diamond dangle, c. 1900. Pins such as this one, with a stem rather than a blossom alone, are sometimes the "small" version of a larger piece by the same maker. A diamond dangle, perhaps meant to represent a dew drop, is a common feature of rose pins of the era. Marked 14K, with no maker's mark; enameled flower measures approximately .625" in diameter, with stem 1.875".

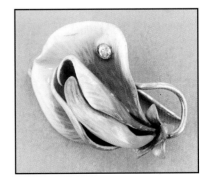

A sweet little sweet pea by Krementz, in 14K gold, enamel, and a diamond, c. 1900. The glossy enamel is nicely shaded, and delicate lines indicate the petals' veining. While the green tip of the sweet pea is in the same glossy enamel as the rest of the blossom, the rudimentary leaves, or sepals, are in iridescent green. This mixture of matte or glossy enamel in flowers with iridescent enamel for the leaves is occasionally found in Newark enamels. The collet-set diamond, not infrequently found on petals and leaves in Newark enamels, undoubtedly represents a dewdrop. Marked 14K and maker's mark on c-clasp; measures approximately 1.125" across.

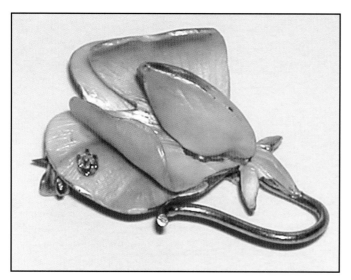

Another sweet pea brooch of Newark or New York manufacture, in 14K gold, enamel, and a diamond, c. 1900. This one is enameled in the iridescent enamel often found in Art Nouveau pieces, in the pale pink shading to green also favored by designers of jewelry in this genre. Here the diamond dewdrop is set in prongs, rather than in a collet. Measures approximately 1.25" x .75". *Courtesy of Robin Allison.*

A third sweet pea brooch, in 14K gold and enamel, by Bippart, Griscom & Osborn, c. 1900. This sweet pea blossom is enameled in iridescent enamel shading from pale green-gold at the edges to a delicate violet at the center. The enameling in this brooch has a more metallic look than the enamel in the second sweet pea brooch. The brooch features a chatelaine or watch hook at the back. *Courtesy of the Newark Museum, Newark, NJ.*

A Tumult of Tulips

Here tulips bloom as they are told;
Unkempt about those hedges blows
An English unofficial rose.
—Rupert Brooke, "The Old Vicarage, Grantchester"

Tulip
fame ~ consuming love ~ happy years ~ memory
red
ardent love
pink
dreaminess ~ imagination ~ love
white
lost love
yellow
hopeless love

Like the rose, the tulip comes in a variety of colors, many of which were assigned meanings in the language of flowers. However, many of the meanings seem to convey a message about love–whether ardent, hopeless, or lost. But while red roses–also signifying ardent passion–are uncommon in late nineteenth and early twentieth century floral pieces, red tulips seem to have been used more freely.

Because the tulip was introduced to Europe relatively late (albeit earlier than the bleeding heart) from Asia, it had no real place in ancient mythology or medieval lore. Thus the meanings given it seem rather artificial, based neither on tradition nor any particular attribute of the flower itself, nor on its name (which comes from the Turkish *tulbend*, meaning "turban," due to the flower's resemblance to a turban). Historically, the tulip is perhaps most famous for the huge investments made in its bulbs by speculators in seventeenth century Holland; this frenzy is at the center of Alexander Dumas' novel *The Black Tulip*.

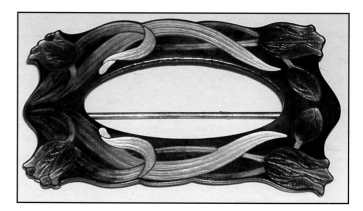

An Art Nouveau brooch in sterling silver and enamel, very likely made in New England, with a design of red tulips (signifying ardent love in the language of flowers), buds and leaves around a wavy-edged rectangular brooch similar in shape to one of the daisy brooches shown above. The four tulips and their two buds are in glossy enamel over basse taille work, and shade from red at the bottom to a deep pink at the edges. The leaves are similarly shaded from dark green through lighter green, yellow, and white. Measures 3" x 1.875". *Courtesy of Robin Allison.*

A Windfall of Leaves

How vainly men themselves amaze
To win the palm, the oak, or bays [laurel];
And their unceasing labours see
Crown'd from some single herb or tree,
Whose short and narrow vergèd shade
Does prudently their toils upbraid;
While all flowers and all trees do close
To weave the garlands of repose.

—Andrew Marvell, "The Garden"

In spite of Marvell's views on the vanity of striving to win laurels, so to speak, leaves had their place in the language of flowers. In the various flower dictionaries, they are almost as frequently represented as their fairer cousins, the flowers. However, with a few exceptions–including the almost ubiquitous cloverleaves–they do occur less frequently in floral jewelry.

Unlike most leaves, ivy is fairly well represented, especially in small circle pins. Sycamore leaves, too, seem to have been manufactured more than other leaves. Sataloff notes this in his book ("Sycamore leaves are very common, especially in American jewelry." *Art Nouveau Jewelry*, 1985), but places no special interpretation on this fact. In later jewelry, maple leaves abound, possibly in part because of their connection with Canada (and in fact, many maple leaf pins were made as tourist items).

The following is a sample of some leaves with their meanings in the language of flowers. Most, though not all, were produced by American firms. While the laurel leaf, for example, seems to have been a favored motif of French jewelers, usually these leaves serve as decoration on larger pieces (such as the handbag by Boucheron described in chapter three) rather than in pieces standing on their own.

Grape
charity ~ intemperance ~ intoxication ~ domestic happiness

Two brooches in 14K gold, enamel, and pearls, both in the shape of grape leaves, with small pearls representing the grapes themselves. Both are probably of American manufacture, c. 1900. The smaller one, which measures about .875" across, is marked 14K; the larger single leaf, measuring approximately 1.25" x 1", is unmarked but tested 14K . That fact, along with the glossy enamel, points to an earlier date for this particular piece. Both show detail in the dimensional folds of the leaves, and basse taille markings.

Holly
foresight ~ domestic happiness

A small honeymoon pin with an unusual holly motif, in 14K gold, enamel, and a small coral berry, c. 1890. The iridescent green of the leaves shades to gold at the edges, which show a bit of wear. While the giver might have been thinking of the yuletide season when presenting this pin, he might also have been thinking of the domestic happiness and foresight that holly signifies in the language of flowers. Measures approximately 1" in length.

Ivy
domestic happiness ~ friendship ~ constancy ~ ambition

A lovely brooch in the form of an ivy leaf in gold, plique-à-jour enamel, and a diamond. The plique-à-jour enamel is a deep green, set in cloisons that form its network of veins, with the gold at the edges curving slightly up. The collet-set diamond on leaves and petals, presumably representing a dew drop, is not uncommon. *Courtesy of Nelson Rarities, Portland, ME.*

Two circle pins in 14K gold, enamel, and diamonds (and, in the smaller one, pearls) c. 1900, and probably of Newark or New York manufacture. Circle pins with ivy leaves are not uncommon, as ivy seems to have been a motif used in mourning jewelry, as well perhaps for expressing hopes of friendship and fidelity. The leaves in both pieces are white, although similar pins with translucent green enamel were also manufactured. Larger pin measures approximately 1.125" in diameter, the smaller approximately .875".

Maple
beauty ~ elegance ~ reserve

The last red leaf is whirl'd away;
The rooks are blown about the skies.
  —Alfred Lord Tennyson, *In Memorium A. H. H.*

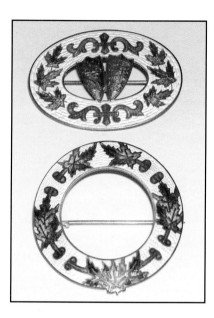

Two similar vintage brooches in silver and guilloche enamel, with maple leaves. Additionally, the oval maple leaf has two silver shields set in the center, somewhat like the Charles Horner pin that also contains a shield adorned with a maple leaf. All of the leaves, in champlevé enamel, are in the bright greens, reds, yellow, and orange often found in maple leaves. *Courtesy of Robin Allison.*

Two vintage maple leaves in silver, marcasites, and enamel, both marked sterling silver Germany. The brooches are very dimensional, with notable folds and veining, and are enameled in almost identical colors, leading to the suspicion that they were manufactured by the same company. The larger, broader one, however, is marked Alice Caviness; many of her sterling pieces were manufactured in Germany.

Left:
A large maple leaf (approximately 2.25" across) in sterling silver and enamel, by Norwegian designer Hroar Prydz. Unlike most maple leaves, this one is enameled in a glossy translucent light yellow, with a darker yellow or gold towards the center, with brown near the end of the leaf where the stem would attach. Fully marked for that maker.

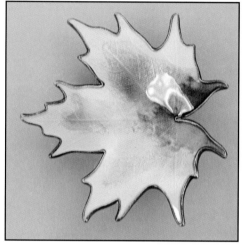

Two vintage maple leaf brooches in silver and enamel, most likely of American manufacture and quite possibly by the same company, as both are very similar. The smaller one, however, is marked with the letters EN in a circle, while the larger is marked BMCo. Both leaves are very two-dimensional, showing none of the folds found in their German counterparts. The bright green, red, orange, and yellow appear to be colors often used to enamel such maple leaves, perhaps meant to indicate that they were changing into their fall colors.

An interesting vintage brooch, with a maple leaf–in the usual bright colors–set against an oval enameled with a deep blue border, and with dots of white that almost mimic pearls. *Courtesy of Robin Allison.*

A brooch in 14K gold, enamel, and pearls by the Newark maker Krementz, c. 1900. The brooch, in the form of three oak leaves set with pearl "acorns," is nicely dimensional, and beautifully enameled in light green shading through gold and brown. *Courtesy of S J Phillips Ltd., London.*

A Victorian brooch in 14K gold with an enamel accent, in the form of two oak leaves in carved gold, with an acorn dangle. The cap of the acorn is enameled in a variegated green, adding the only touch of color to the piece. Measures 1.75" in width.

Sycamore
curiosity

A maple leaf in copper and enamel, by the costume jewelry manufacturer Matisse (also known as Matisse Renoir). Typical of their designs, this one has a copper curlicue–possibly representing the leaf's stem–curled on top of the enamel, which is in a deep vitreous red edged at the top in black. The enamel also seems to contain metallic flecks.

Two leaf brooches in 14K gold, enamel, and–in the larger–a small diamond, and–in the smaller–small pearls. The similar brooches, each with a grouping of colorfully enameled leaves, appear at first to be larger and smaller versions by the same maker; but in fact, the larger brooch (measuring 1.375" in width) is by Bippart, Griscom & Osborn, and appears to represent sycamore leaves, while the smaller (.875" across) is by Whiteside & Blank and may represent more serrated oak leaves (though the bright colors would seem to contradict this identification). Sataloff, in his book on Art Nouveau jewelry, mentions that sycamore leaves are frequently found in jewelry of the period, without attaching any particular significance to that fact. In the language of flowers, the sycamore leaf meant curiosity; and the larger brooch, transfixed by a pin tipped in a diamond as if real leaves worn on a lapel, is indeed something of a curiosity.

Price Guide for Chapter Five

p. 156: Pansies: Vict 14K lckt $600-$1000; 2 Vict 3-pansy br: l. $600-$1450; r. $550-$1250; Vict 14K br w/ dmd $1000-$1250; **p. 157:** Vict 14K br w/ prl $500-$600; AN 14K e/r $750-$1200; AN sl-lckt $500-$600; AN p-wtch $600-$750; AN bkl $400-$450; **p. 158:** plq br $250-$300; W. clsn br $250-$350; pnk Crd. br $35-$65; sm Crd. br $25-$50; co bl e/r $35-$60; **p. 159:** D.A. e/r $35-$100; Wss. gf br $35-$60; Trf. cost br $20-$35/pr; **Irises:** W.& B. br/pend $1000-$1750; **p. 160:** AN br w/ cattail $200-$250; AN ht-p 300-$350; lg Ital br $1000-$1250; Vict 14K fch-p $450-$650; AN sl-mrr $500-$600; **p. 161: Orchids:** Nk Vict 14K wh & lav br/pend $1200-$1700; Nk AN 14K irid br/pend $1000-$1200; A. Hn. lav & wh br $125-$175; **p. 162:** sm W.& B. br $500-$1240; lg vint br w/ marc $350-$400; **Violets:** Nk Vict 14K w/ dmd br/pend $1000-$1500; plq br $200-$250; **p. 163:** Nk 14K br w/ dmd $500-$600; Nk 14K irid br w/ dmd, s-prls $750-$900; Nk 14K wtch/p w/ dmd & chmp f-m-n $350-$600; W.&B. AN 14K w/ prl irid lotus wtch/p $600-$900; B.G.&O. AN 14K lotus br $550-$700; **p. 164:** Kr. 14K w/ s-prls bleed hrt demi $2400-$3500; Kr. Vict 14K w/ s-prl bleed hrt pend $450-$600; Kr. AN 14K irid bleed hrt br $750-$1000; Nk Vict 14K pnk car-

nation w/ opl $1250-$1500; **p. 165: Daisies:** Nk Vct 14K br $400-$600; AN rect br $350-$400; AN Xifrm br $250-$300; AN R.H. br $300-$400; **p. 166:** Nk Vict 14K w/ dmds f-m-n br $750-$900; Vict 14K w/ s-prls jonquil br $250-$300; **p. 167:** Vict jonquil lckt $400-$500; AN jonquil br $250-$300; Kr. AN 14K irid lily/valley br $600-$1000; vint lily/valley br w/ marc $400-$500; **p. 168:** chmp poppy br $350-$375; AN rect red poppy br $250-$300; Nk Vict 14K w/ prl pnk primrose br $500-$750; **p. 169:** sm Nk 14K w/ dmd rose br $600-$750; sm 10K w/ dmd rose br $150-$250; Kr. 14K w/ dmd sweetpea br $1000-$1250; **p. 170:** Nk AN irid 14K w/ dmd sweetpea br $1000-$1250; AN tulip br $250-$300; **p. 171:** Lg 14K w/ prls grape br $700-$800; sm 14K w/ s-prls br $250-$300; Nk 14K w/ crl hon/pin $300-$400; 2 Nk 14K w/ dmds cir br $600-$750 ea; **p. 172: Maple leaves:** sm Nk Vict/AN 14K w/ dmd & s-prls br $350-$450; C.H. A&C oval br $400-$600; sm vint Ger br w/ marc $50-$75, Ger A.C. br w/ marc $75-$100; vint EN. br $50-$60, vint BMCo. br $75-$100; vint oval br w/ bl brd $200-$225; vint guil br $125-$175 ea; lg H.P.br $125-$150; **p. 173:** Mat. cost br $30-$85;14K oak leaf br $450-$600; B.G.&O. lg 14K w/ dmd sycamore br $750-$1000; W.&B. sm 14K w/ prls br $300-$350.

Chapter Six

Collecting Enameled Jewelry

What to Look For, and Where to Find It

Creating a pricing guide for vintage and antique enameled jewelry is difficult, because price depends so much on a number of factors, including age, condition, size, gold karat content, and the maker of the piece (think of this as the brand name). Also important are what, if any, gemstones are included in the piece, and their value. For some stones, such as amethysts and citrines, the value might be minimal; while others, such as diamonds or demantoid garnets of any size, can add considerably to the value, or the cost, of a piece of jewelry.

Another factor, often overlooked, is *where* you shop for jewelry. Prices in New York and London, for example, are considerably higher than prices in, say, the midwestern United States, the Pacific northwest, and some parts of New England, the mid-Atlantic states, and the south. The prices in Texas and California seem to lie somewhere in between the most expensive and the least pricy. Dale once called a dealer in New York about an Art Nouveau pendant by the Newark maker Bippart, Griscom & Osborn. It was a lovely piece, but her jaw almost dropped when she was quoted a price of nearly $30,000. Yes, it was beautiful and yes, it did have a rather large demantoid garnet, but... Dealers on the internet sometimes, but not always, give great value for the money. It pays to comparison shop; and, with the internet and the number of online catalogs–ranging from those put out by Bond Street jewelers in London to those listed by independent dealers working from their homes–available, comparing price, quality, and value has become relatively easy. (See Appendix B for the names of some of the dealers and vendors who sell the types of enameled jewelry featured in this book.)

Name brands cost more. The mark of a world-renowned designer such as Louis Comfort Tiffany or René Lalique can send the price of a piece of jewelry into the stratosphere. Richard Fautaux, antique jewelry expert at the Canadian auction firm Dupuis (cited in the online Canadian business publication, *Perks*), notes, "A name can take a piece of jewelry far beyond any intrinsic value. A marked piece is like a signed Picasso." This is true for enameled jewelry just as it is for more conventional jewelry. A piece made by one of the Falizes and their wonderful enamelist Tard will cost considerably more than one made by an anonymous jeweler (a Falize bracelet might run upwards of $60,000); of course, it will also show its higher quality in design and execution. The jewelry created by René Lalique before he began to work almost exclusively in glass is considered by many the acme of Art Nouveau jewelry, and anything with his signature can be expected to fetch premium prices. Such jewelry is on offer at relatively few places, and auctions at major houses such as Sotheby's and Christie's may be the easiest way to find these rare pieces. G. Fouquet is another French jeweler whose pieces are rare, and costly. Other makers whose names command high prices are Plisson & Hartz, P. Wolfers, Vever, Gaillard, Cartier, and Gautrait. In the United States, Tiffany & Co. and Marcus & Co. were among the foremost makers of enameled Art Nouveau as well as traditional jewelry. As with paintings, a piece actually *marked* by one of the better-known makers will usually bring more than a piece merely *attributed* to a maker.

Assuming that jewelry by makers such as those named above *is* on the market, the prices asked for their pieces are usually beyond the budgets of most collectors. Prices for pieces by such makers vary, as already noted, depending on a number of factors, including size. A bracelet by Lucien Falize was recently offered for sale for about $70,000; smaller pieces such as pins or pendants by the Falizes might be priced in the $10,000 to $30,000 range. Thus it is reasonable for a beginning collector or one simply seeking to add to an existing collection to look elsewhere for new acquisitions.

There are still many pieces of antique enameled jewelry for sale, although jewelry from the Victorian, early Arts and Crafts, and Art Nouveau periods is becoming harder to find, as well as costlier. Gold jewelry with a higher gold content, especially 18K and higher, will be more expensive than 10K or 12K pieces. Many pieces of good American jewelry were made in 14K gold, and they also tend to be more expensive than those in 10K and 12K gold. If you are interested in a certain period rather than a certain maker, then buying an unmarked piece in lower karat gold, or silver, may make more sense than buying a marked higher karat piece from the same period. As can be seen from the pricing guides at the end of each chapter, silver pieces almost always sell for less than gold ones, and also are often quite a bit larger. However, as always, there are exceptions: Silver pieces by makers such as Meyle & Mayer can be every bit as expensive as a smaller Newark enamel in gold, especially if the Meyle & Mayer piece contains plique-à-jour enamel.

Some of the better-known American makers of enameled jewelry during the late nineteenth and early twentieth centuries were located in Newark, New Jersey; their pieces are sometimes referred to as Newark enamels. Among these makers were Krementz; Riker Brothers; A.J. Hedges; Bippart,

Griscom & Osborn; H. Blank, or Whiteside & Blank; Wordley, Alsop & Bliss; and Alling. Starting about 1895, most of the makers marked their pieces (see Appendix A: A List of Some Commonly Found Makers' Marks), but before that time marking seems to have been fairly random. To an experienced collector, some pieces may look like they were manufactured by, say, Krementz, but without a maker's mark, nothing is entirely certain. As already noted, prices for pieces marked by these makers may be higher than prices for unmarked jewelry, but this is less certain than for jewelry from the truly famous names such as Lalique, Tiffany, Fouquet, and Falize. (It should also be noted that Krementz, which primarily produced gold-filled jewelry after the heyday of Newark enamels, is collectible primarily as *costume jewelry* rather than fine jewelry except for pieces produced during the Victorian and Edwardian periods.)

One fairly simple way of telling whether a piece of jewelry is truly an antique rather than a reproduction is the clasp. Unless it has been replaced with a later safety clasp, Victorian pieces usually have a c-clasp–that is, a piece of gold formed into a c-shape in which the pin rests. Earlier c-clasps tend to have a rather curlicue shape, while later ones are more like half a cuff, giving room for the maker to stamp gold content and, often, a maker's mark.

If you don't particularly care *when* a piece of jewelry was made, but are more interested in the quality of the workmanship and enameling, then perhaps you might consider *vintage* enameled jewelry from the 1930s, 1940s, or 1950s. A good value in this area is Scandinavian pieces in the Arts and Crafts tradition. Perhaps the best-known of these makers is the Norwegian David Andersen. His pieces are usually in sterling silver rather than gold, are marked either D - A (for earlier pieces) or David Andersen, along with 925S Sterling Norway. The workmanship and enameling of his pieces, which tend to run heavily to butterfly brooches and bracelets with roundels or leaves, is extremely fine; and his pieces remain affordable, in the $50 to $500 range. His work makes striking use of basse taille and guilloche enameling, with translucent enamel in a range of colors (although blue does seem to be a recurring color). His work is also relatively easy to find in vintage jewelry stores or online catalogues. Other Scandinavian designers to consider are Hans Hansen of Denmark (although his pieces tend to be much more modernistic than Andersen's), Meka (also Danish), Aksel Holmsen, and Hroar Prydz (the latter two Norwegian).

Also highly collectible–yet still relatively available–are pieces from Mexico, especially those from Taxco. Margot de Taxco is by far the best known, and most expensive, of the Taxco makers, but pieces by other Taxco artists also come on the market, often at very affordable prices.

Another area the beginning collector of enameled jewelry might explore is Japanese enamels from the 1920s on. Toshikane is one of the better-known makers of so-called enameled jewelry, and still relatively affordable. However, it is important to note that Toshikane is enameled on *porcelain* over silver. And while some of its pieces, such as bracelets with painted flowers, are extremely attractive, some Toshikane, depicting sculpted faces of old men or gods as in the set shown below, is not always to Western taste. Some of the Japanese jewelry from the 1920s and 1930s, however, is quite beautiful.

A set of matching earrings, bracelet, and a ring, by the Japanese maker Toshikane. While many Toshikane pieces contain flowers and birds, others are done in motifs perhaps not quite so appealing to Western tastes, such as this set showing various Japanese deities. *Courtesy of Robin Allison.*

Yet another possibility is collecting modern jewelry either made with original molds, or made to look like antique jewelry. For the first category, the Barcelona (Spain) jewelry firm of Masriera has begun to manufacture jewelry using molds that originally created Art Nouveau jewelry from about 1895 up to the 1920s. Whereas an original Masriera piece might cost upward of $6000, the modern reproductions are more reasonable; a small piece might cost about $2000, while a larger piece or one with plique-à-jour enamel might cost from $3000 on up. The price primarily depends on size, intricacy, and materials used; many of their modern pieces include diamonds and pearls.

While modern Art Nouveau pieces have been on the market for a number of decades, a more recent trend is the production of modern Arts and Crafts jewelry. There are now a number of new Arts and Crafts pieces–either reproductions of Arts and Crafts pieces or pieces in the Arts and Crafts style– on the market, but these are usually sold as new pieces *based on* designs by makers such as William Hasseler, Charles Horner, Archibald Knox, and Murrle Bennett, rather than as pieces *by* those makers.

Art Nouveau–or Art New-Faux?

As an aside, it must be noted that it is easy to be led astray, especially by makers who misrepresent modern pieces as authentic. One account (Sataloff, 1984, 13) mentions a collector who was offered "'eight beautiful pieces in the Art Nouveau style. Some of these were enameled, some were *plique à jour*, and all were stamped "Cashiera," a maker of particularly fine antique jewelry in Portugal in the 1900s.'" However, as Sataloff's source noted, "'They were not authentic; to be more exact, they were "revival pieces."'" (1984, 13) (The name "Cashiera" may be a typo for Masriera, a firm that later merged with Carrera to become Masriera y Carrera. It is Masriera that represents their modern pieces as period pieces.) Also, some makers of more modern new-faux pieces may incorporate diamonds and other stones of an older cut, making a newer piece look far older than it really is. When purchasing a supposed "period piece," be sure to ask the question: Is it Art Nouveau, or Art new-faux?

The piece shown here, from Robin's collection, is a modern enameled piece in silver with carnelian accents. The Byzantine woman is comparable, in both style and execution, to similar pieces produced c. 1900. But rather than having, say, a guilloche background providing texture and light, the light green background is broken up with jagged lines. The silver work, too, seems flat when compared with the carved gold and silver of true period pieces. On the other hand, it is probably a bit more available, and a lot more affordable, than its antique forerunners.

A modern Art Nouveau necklace in silver, enamel, and coral, showing a Byzantine woman in profile, with the long flowing hair and elaborate headdress typical in such pieces. In many ways, she very closely resembles the Byzantine women created c. 1900 by makers such as Alling. However, the enameling is not quite as fine, and the light green background punctuated by occasional jagged lines is not as appealing as, for example, the guilloche backgrounds found in some lady pieces. Also, compared to the more flowing and textured frames found in genuine Art Nouveau jewelry, this silver frame seems graceless and clumsy. *Courtesy of Robin Allison.*

A well-known television personality designs and markets a line of jewelry based on pieces in her own collection. The brooch below is based on a poppy flower made c. 1900 by the Newark company Bippart, Griscom & Osborn. While the original was made in true Newark fashion, with petals cast separately and then joined to form the flower, this one was cast (in base metal) in one piece. The enamel too is quite different; it has a metallic cast not found in the Bippart, Griscom & Osborn piece. However, it is a nice costume piece, and sells for about one-hundreth of what the Newark poppy would cost.

A modern "reproduction" of a Bippart, Griscom & Osborn poppy brooch, created and sold by a television personality. This one is made out of base metal crudely molded in one piece rather than having individually cast petals, and the enamel on the flower is glaringly metallic rather than soft and nuanced, as in the original. *Courtesy of Bodette Reeves, Odessa, TX.*

There are also a number of enameled flower pins, rings, earrings, and pendants being manufactured in France and Brazil. Many of these are available on the internet from various companies in the United States and Europe. One drawback to these modern enameled pieces is that, unfortunately, the intricacies of the techniques employed by the master enamelists of the past seem to have been lost. Modern plique-à-jour enamel, for example, is thicker, brighter, and less nuanced than true Art Nouveau plique-à-jour. The gossamer quality seems to have evaporated with time. An acquaintance recently sold a consignment of plique-à-jour butterflies that had been made within the past few years, possibly in this country (although they were unmarked, they were in 14K gold). While the enamel was beautifully done, it was thicker and less transparent than plique-à-jour created by Art Nouveau enamelists working in the years 1885 to 1915. Enamel other than plique-à-jour is also a bit coarser; it is glossier, thicker, and more monochromatic than older enamels. And very seldom do we find the iridescence that makes American Art Nouveau enameled pieces so alluring.

That said, aside from age, the maker's name, and materials used, with all other things being equal, size and condition seem to be the factors that most affect the price of antique American and European enameled jewelry. Because enamel is glass, it is relatively fragile, and many older pieces have suffered chipping, dings, scratching, and other types of enamel loss. A small amount of chipping or flaking around the edges of, say, a petal on a flower pin might be barely noticeable to the naked eye, and might be expected to have fairly minimal effect on the pin's price. On the other hand, a large chip that bares a substantial portion of a petal's underlying enamel or metal can drastically lower the value–and, hopefully, the price–of a piece.

For example, last year a dealer offered Dale a large pin consisting of a central flower surrounded by daisies. One of the petals in the central flower had a chip that had taken away about one-fourth of the upper enamel. (Two of the surrounding daisies were missing petals, as well, but this seemed a minor defect compared to the rather large area of missing enamel.) Dale bought the pin because it was very similar to another pin in her collection and she wanted to compare the two; also, aside from the chip, she *liked* the pin. If the pin had been in perfect, or near perfect, condition, the dealer would have asked several thousand dollars for it; as it was, he sold it to her for considerably less. The pin is shown below; the damaged (and repaired) petal is on the bottom left-hand side of the central flower.

When buying an enameled piece, it's wise to examine the prospective purchase with a jeweler's loupe, which will often reveal or magnify flaws unseen by the naked eye. If you are purchasing a piece sight unseen, ask the dealer about any damage to the enamel. If there is significant loss, you should receive a substantial discount. And if the piece is not as described, a reputable dealer will allow you to return the jewelry if you aren't satisfied with its condition. Do make sure to ask about return policies before buying anything, especially if you haven't had a chance to inspect it first-hand.

Smaller pieces are not only easier to find than larger pieces, but are more affordable. Most of the enameled stick pins, often with a pansy or other flower but sometimes with

A brooch in 14K gold, enamel, and a small diamond, undoubtedly of Newark or New York manufacture c. 1900. Although this brooch is not marked, certain elements make it clear that it was created by the company that made the unusual sickle, primrose, daisy, and forget-me-not brooch shown in chapter one. For one thing, the diamonds in both are in an unusual buttercup setting; additionally, the daisies in the two pieces are virtually identical, while the central flowers also show certain similarities. Like many of the larger brooches manufactured in Newark, this one has a folding bail that allows it to be worn as a pendant. However, because there was a large chip missing on a lower petal (since cosmetically repaired with craft enamels), and because two of the daisies are missing petals, this piece was sold at a fraction of the price one in better condition would command.

other motifs, are quite affordable compared to other forms of antique jewelry, even though they may be intricately detailed. Circle pins with small flowers also can be more affordable.

The so-called honeymoon pins made from about 1880 to 1900 are usually small; this means that less gold, less enameling, and sometimes–though not always–less detail was used in their manufacture. However, recently some of these miniature pieces have had asking prices of more than $300. Some Newark makers created larger and smaller versions of the same piece, probably to fit long ago budgets. The good news is that the smaller versions also fit more easily into modern budgets: The asking price for the medium-sized version of Krementz's "Woman with Poppy" pin was $1000 less than the asking price for the larger version.

And What You Should Expect to Pay

As mentioned previously, prices for enameled jewelry will vary widely. The factors affecting cost are primarily:

♦ Location–as they say in real estate, location is everything. And where you shop can mean the difference between paying $700 for an orchid pin by a Newark maker in, say, Oregon, or twice that much–or more–for roughly the same pin on New York City's Fifth Avenue.

♦ Maker's name–if the maker is someone famous like Lalique or Tiffany, expect to pay much more; but, on the upside, also expect wonderful craftsmanship. A maker's mark from a noted maker may also add to the cost as well as the value of a piece.

♦ Age–a true period piece in good condition will usually sell for more than a more modern piece, or a reproduction. However, if there is any question at all about the age of a particular piece, be sure to ask; a reputable dealer should stand behind his or her appraisal, and be willing to give a refund if he or she happens to be wrong.

♦ Materials–most pieces in 18K gold will cost more than those made of lower karat gold, or of silver; diamonds, natural pearls, or other gemstones may also add to the price.

♦ Condition–a pin with the enamel in perfect shape–not chipped, flaked, or cracked—will inevitably cost more than a pin with flaws; the larger the flaw, the more it should detract from both the price and the value.

♦ Type of enamel–as can be seen from the pricing guides, plique-à-jour enamel can add considerably to the cost of a piece. Robin's two similar Egyptian revival bracelets (which can be found under *ba* in chapter four on p. 129 demonstrate this very well: The bracelet *with* plique-à-jour enamel is priced at $2500-$3000, whereas the bracelet with *plain* enameling has a price of about $750. In general, plique-à-jour pieces are becoming harder to find. Those from the true Art Nouveau period, with their more delicate plique-à-jour enamel, are especially rare, and costly. In Arts and Crafts pieces, Limoges enameling–another difficult technique–may add to the cost of a piece.

♦ Size–in general, larger pieces are pricier than smaller pieces, although other factors–such as those mentioned above–may outweigh this; overall, however, collecting stickpins or honeymoon pins may cost less than collecting larger flower pins or other pieces. This also applies to pieces in silver, although perhaps not quite as dramatically as to pieces in gold.

When Dale started collecting flower pins, a nice one from a good Newark maker cost about $800 from a relatively expensive dealer. Her first collection of nine flower pins cost slightly under $10,000, or slightly more than $1000 a pin. But as she wrote in the preface, the pins varied considerably in size and quality. It would be almost impossible to put a price on each one individually. The largest brooch, the cherry blossom shown in the introduction, although not marked is identical to one made by Marcus & Co. (shown in chapter three), and today might sell for as much as $4000 from a high-end dealer or shop.

More recent purchases have run the range from $9 (for the small David Andersen water lily pendant with missing enamel shown below); $60 for a small gold stickpin with a seed pearl cross topped by a willow leaf; $175 for a c. 1900 silver and cloisonné enamel pin by the Massachusetts maker Watson Co. (in chapter five p. 158); $800 for a Krementz violet; $2400 for a matching wild roses brooch/pendant and earrings by A. J. Hedges; to considerably more for the two Krementz "woman with poppy" pins (these all c. 1900 and found in chapter three under their respective makers).

A small water lily pendant signed D-A for Norwegian David Andersen; it has a fairly good sized chip to the green enamel above the petals, but it was sold for $9 primarily because the person who had it basically was not interested in enameled jewelry.

A small circle pin in 14k gold, enamel, and baroque pearls, c. 1900, with the small blue forget-me-nots that were so popular in late Victorian jewelry. Because the flowers on this brooch are smaller— and, more important, contain less gold—this piece and ones like it should cost considerably less than brooches that consist of a single large blossom, or several larger blossoms. Unmarked, but tested 14K; measures about 1.125" in diameter.

Robin, however, feels that such prices are unrealistically inflated, and that armed with a little knowledge, and a lot of determination, no one needs to pay such upscale prices. And in the past year, having discovered the joys of online auctions, Dale was able to purchase a pair of Krementz cloverleaf earrings (complete with seed pearl edges) for under $200, and a nearly matching brooch/pendant for under $400 (a similar one in a shop owned by an acquaintance had an asking price of over $1000).

However, even good deals may not fit one's budget, and in that case, short of taking on massive debt, there is usually no other option than to grit one's teeth, and walk away. Robin tells a rather wistful story of a genuine period Art Nouveau necklace from France, which she was offered for about $25,000. No way was she going to pay that much even though a) it was a good price for a piece that realistically might have fetched up to $100,000; and b) it was a to-die-for piece, with moving enameled bats–and she collects birds and bats! She now drools fondly from time-to-time over a picture the dealer was kind enough to give her.

Re-enameling

The innocent and the beautiful
Have no enemy but time.

—William Butler Yeats,
"In Memory of Eva Gore-Booth…"

As noted above, because enamel, like other forms of glass, is fragile, finding enameled pieces in perfect condition can be difficult. However, a flaw such as scratching, chipping, wear along the edges, or–in the case of flower pins–the loss of an entire petal, can not only mar the beauty of an enameled piece, but it can also significantly lower its value. In some cases, the difference in cost between a perfect piece and a piece with, say, a noticeable chip can be as much as a couple of thousand dollars.

Does that mean that one should avoid buying that flawed flower pin, or that blemished bracelet? It depends. If the damage is not too great, cosmetic repair is possible. And one might find a great bargain on a pin that, in perfect condition would cost as much as a thousand dollars, but with a chip or two along the edges could be had for as little as two or three hundred dollars.

One dealer told a story about a European buyer who snapped up damaged enamels. What, he wondered, was the purpose? Who wants to wear a pin that has numerous chips along the edges, or a bracelet with multiple scratches?

The answer: Probably no one. But…

An accident–a spring-loaded box that was a bit *too* springy, so that some pins bounced onto a hard tile floor when the box was opened–left several pins in Dale's collection with noticeable chips. And in the one case related above, she also bought a damaged pin in spite of the large chip on one petal (the missing petals from the surrounding daisies were, alas, beyond repair). She called a noted enamelist, and asked if he could repair the enamel loss. Not without seeing the pins, he replied; so she sent them off. Within a couple of weeks, he returned them. The enameling, he explained, was too complicated. The enamel had been applied in layers, the colors were too delicately shaded, and the individual details such as painted veins could not be duplicated. He was sorry, but there was nothing he could do.

Dale decided she liked the pins too much to leave them in their pathetic state, and began to investigate other methods of repair. Kiln-fired enamel, it appeared, was not an option. What about enamels that didn't need heat?

In the end, she decided to experiment with craft enamels–acrylics or polymers that need little or no heat to bond with metal. The outcome was not perfect, but with practice she got better.

The enamels that seemed to work best were Delta's Permenamel line. This type of enamel is not baked, which means that if the color doesn't match perfectly, or the enamel isn't applied properly, it can be wiped or scraped off (using a small, delicate tool, of course; toothpicks work well). For the Newark enamels colors in the more pastel range, such as Tropical Pink seemed to work. Delta's Opalescent White is also quite useful. It serves to lighten colors, as well as creating the proper pearlescent hue for some enamels.

Delta also makes iridescent craft enamel. When re-enameling Art Nouveau pins with iridescent enamel, one can mix a little of this iridescent enamel with opalescent white and then add it to the premixed color until the right hue is obtained.

Delta's Permenamel is air-dried. After a piece is dry, Delta does make a clear glaze that protects the very soft enamel. Whether or not to use this glaze is a matter of preference. While it does protect the enamel, it also adds a sheen that may not be entirely compatible with nineteenth century enamel, especially matte enamel. There is also a liquid meant to prepare metal for the enamel. For the most part, however, the pieces re-enameled still retained some or all of the white under-enamel, and thus did not need to be prepped.

Because this enamel is wet and rather sticky, it is almost impossible to re-create the fine lines found in nineteenth century enamels, such as veins or markings on petals. Even with the finest brush–one with two or three hairs–this sort of painting with the enamel proved impossible. However, as most chips occur around the edges of petals, re-enameling with cold enamel is still a useful technique for repairing minor damage.

And, it should also be noted that, in most cases, the repair can be detected by a knowledgeable collector or dealer. This type of cosmetic repair should be used only on pieces that are meant to be kept and enjoyed, rather than damaged pieces bought to be resold. On no account should someone, whether collector, dealer, or casual buyer, ever purchase a damaged piece with the intention of re-enameling it and selling it as an original piece. This cannot be emphasized strongly enough. Most dealers, as well as collectors with a good eye and a jeweler's loupe, will be able to detect re-enameling unless it is a) done in true vitreous enamel, and b) applied by a master enamelist who specializes in working on period pieces–a rare individual indeed. For example, the stickpin shown here, bought online, sports a fairly awful re-enameling job, with gold enamel added to the center of the petals, replacing the finely drawn veins one might expect to see in an antique floral piece.

So, the caveat: Being able to repair damage *cosmetically* does not mean that buying a damaged piece will ever be a good investment. If you should happen to fall in love with a less-than-

perfect piece, however, and find its lower price an inducement, then a cosmetic repair to make it more wearable makes sense.

A flower stickpin, bought over the internet, which upon inspection "in person" proved to have a very bad job of re-enameling, illustrating not only the perils of re-enameling, but also of buying from less-than-reputable dealers.

Appendix A
A List of Some Important Makers' Marks

Newark and New York Maker's Marks for Manufacturers of Enameled Jewelry

Alling Co.

Bippart, Griscom & Osborn

B.S.F.

Black, Starr & Frost: used the initials B.S.F. as their mark

Bride & Tinkler

Thomas F. Brogan Co.

D. de W. Brokaw

Carter, Howe (var. Carter, Grough etc.)

Crane Theurer

A.J. Hedges

Krementz & Co.

Link & Angell

Riker Bros.

Whiteside & Blank

Wordley, Allsop & Bliss

American Manufacturers Based in Massachusetts

CMR

Charles M. Robbins

Shepherd Co.

Thomae Co.

Watson Co.

British Manufacturers

John Atkins & Sons (later also J.A.&S.)

Child & Child

C.H.

Charles Horner

German Manufacturers

Theodor Fahrner

Carl Hermann

Heinrich Levinger

Meyle & Mayer

Norwegian Manufacturers

Andersen & Scheinpflug

David Andersen (Later D.A.; D. Andersen; David Andersen)

Marius Hammer

Norwegian Manufacturers (Cont'd)

Aksel Holmsen

Ivar T. Holt

Ole Peter Raasch-Olsen

Hroar Prydz

Tone Viegeland

181

Appendix B
A Short List of Dealers Who Carry Enameled Jewelry

Please note: This list is by no means comprehensive, and there are many other fine dealers who carry antique and twentieth century enameled jewelry besides those few mentioned here. However, this list contains, for the most part, the addresses (virtual or real) of dealers with whom we have done business, whom we have found to be honest and fair, and whose items are as described in catalogs or on web sites. Those few dealers whom we know only by reputation carry a wide or unusual selection of enameled items, and have web sites well worth visiting.

About Mimi's Gems
P.O. Box 458, Methuen, MA 01844
www.mimideeartwear.com

Acanthus Antiques
4132 Howard Ave., Kensington, MD 20895

Adin
Vestingstraat 16, 2018, Antwerpen, Belgium
www.adin.be

Bijoux Extraordinaire Ltd.
P.O. Box 1424, Manchester, NH 03105-1424
www.jewelryexpert.com

Carol Lane Antiques
P.O. Box 434, Riverdale, NY 10471

Caroline's Jewelry with a Past
www.carolinesjewelry.com

Granite Pail Collectibles
granitepail.com

Joden World Resources
144 S. Broad Street, Grove City, PA 16127

Kensington House Antiques
www.kensingtonhouse.com

Megan McGee's
www.meganmcgees.com

Nelson Rarities
Two Monument Square, 7th Floor
Box 453, Portland, ME 04112

Red Robin Antiques
www.redrobinantiques.com

S. J. Phillips
139 New Bond St., London W1A 3DL, England

Tadema Gallery
10 Charlton Place, Camden Passage
Islington, London N1 8AJ

Tildenwood Antiques
North Bethesda, MD

Uncommon Treasures
3526 SE Hawthorne Boulevard, Portland, OR 97214

Van den Bosch
1. Georgian Village, Camden Passage
Islington, London N1

Glossary

acrotistic jewelry–a term sometimes used to refer to jewelry such as DEAREST and REGARD lockets and rings, where the first letter of a series of stones set in order spells out the desired word; see also *Language of Stones*.

Aesthetic Movement–a movement that is believed to have begun in Germany in the 1850s with the publication of Baumgarten's *Aestetica*. From there it spread to France and, in the 1870s, England. While the philosophy underlying the Aesthetic Movement does not appear to be extremely well articulated, one of its tenets appears to be Art for Art's sake; the French writer Theophile Gautier wrote that "Nothing is really beautiful unless it is useless." (Lambourne, 10). Aestheticism found expression in both the arts and architecture, and in literature. Art, especially that of James McNeill Whistler, was influenced by the Japanese, whose decorative arts became available with the opening of Japan by Commodore Perry's visit. A limited number of Japanese imported pieces were on display at the 1851 Great Exposition in the Crystal Palace in London. Especially admired seem to have been Japanese blue-and-white pottery, painting, and textiles. Aside from Japanese themes, a favorite motif of the movement was the peacock, which appeared in fabric design, wallpaper, and Whistler's famous Peacock Room (built for shipping baron Leyland). Other names associated with the Aesthetic Movement are Swinburne, Wilde, Beardsley, Burne-Jones, and Alma-Tadema. The *pre-Raphelites* are also associated with Aestheticism by some. Although the Aesthetic Movement had little influence on jewelry, it did influence and perhaps spark the Arts and Crafts movement; John Ruskin and William Morris were associated with both movements.

Aesthetic period–a term sometimes applied to the *late Victorian* period.

agate–a finely-grained form of *chalcedony* in which *opal* is often mixed, and which is layered in bands or stripes; not usually considered a precious material, banded agate was commonly used in Victorian Scottish jewelry as well as in some Arts and Crafts jewelry.

alloy–a term that refers to any combination of metals, precious or base; the first alloy was that combining tin and copper to form bronze, giving rise to the Bronze Age named after the alloy. Gold often is used in alloys, as only 24 karat gold is pure, or fine, gold. Gold can be given different shades, such as white, green, or pink, depending upon which metals are alloyed with it, and in what proportions.

almandine–a garnet composed of iron aluminum silicate and having a deep, rich red color.

amber–fossilized sap of ancient trees, its characteristic color being a rich translucent, at times almost transparent deep gold. Amber sometimes incorporates insects or flora, giving it added interest. Besides the color named for it, amber is also found in deeper brown, reddish-brown, orangy-red, light olive green, and an opaque yellow mottled with white known as "butterscotch amber." Amber was one of the non-traditional materials used in Art Nouveau and Arts and Crafts jewelry.

amethyst–a clear purple or bluish violet variety of quartz occurring in crystals and much used in jewelry in many periods. Amethysts can be found in most areas of the world; they were prized by the ancient Greeks as protection against drunkenness (hence their name, which comes from the Greek for "not drunk") and were used as early as the XIIth Dynasty (about 2000 B. C.) in Egyptian jewelry

amulet–any object worn either as magical protection against evil or as invocation of a deity's aid. Amulets were especially common in ancient Egypt, and featured jewelry in the form of scarabs, the Eye of Horus, and the *djed*-pillar representing the backbone of the god Osiris (see Chapter Four).

angelskin coral–coral of a near-white color with only tinges of pink, today considered of value along with the more traditional red and pink coral.

aquamarine–a stone ranging from very light blue (this variety notably found in Russia) to a deeper blue (such as those found in Brazil), often with a hint of green, hence its name, which means "sea water" in Latin. Aquamarines are a form of beryl and, as such, are related to emeralds.

archaeological revival–a general term subsuming the various jewelry (and other decorative arts) revivals based on 19th century discoveries of Etruscan, Greek, and other ancient arts and crafts. Discoveries at Pompey, Troy, Ninevah, Egypt, Greece, and Etruscan Italy all helped fuel revivals of ancient jewelry.

Art Deco–a style of decorative arts and architecture that appeared in the 1920s, although it was presaged by the more geometric jewelry of the *Edwardian* period. Highly geometric, the finest Art Deco jewelry was made of platinum and included diamonds, often with other precious stones such as sapphires and rubies, and featured elaborate filigree work. Enamel, when used at all, was primarily present as an accent rather than a major feature of the jewelry. Opaque stones such as jade and onyx were also popular in Art Deco jewelry, as was the depiction of lithe, sleek animals such as greyhounds, borzois, and leopards. Art Deco is also sometimes referred to as *Art Moderne*.

Art Nouveau–a movement that lasted only from about 1890 to 1910, it nonetheless produced some of the greatest jewelry of that or any period. Begun in Belgium, its major proponents were French, including the famous jeweler René Lalique. Art Nouveau took its themes from nature; favorite motifs were the dragonfly, the lotus, the peacock, and the female form. The movement also broke with the past in using non-precious materials such as horn and glass, and made great use of enamel, one of its most characteristic materials. In addition to Lalique, other notable names associated with Art Nouveau are Louis Comfort Tiffany, Georges Fouquet and the Spanish architect-designer Antoni Gaudí.

Arts and Crafts–a movement that began in mid- to late 19th century England. Heavily based on the artistic and critical theories of William Morris and John Ruskin, it was formed largely as a reaction to the industrial age and mass production, with the accompanying decline in design and reduction of workers from craftsmen and artisans to soulless factory workers. One of its aims was to restore dignity and satisfaction in their labor to those practicing crafts such as wood- and metalworking. In addition to creating superior design and workmanship, the Arts and Crafts movement also intended to make goods that the average person could afford. It thus focused on using materials such as copper and silver instead of gold and platinum, and opals, mother-of-pearl, and enamel instead of precious stones in its jewelry. An interesting offshoot of this movement was the large number of women who took part in it, producing jewelry, embroidery, textiles, pottery and other decorative arts emphasized by the Arts and Crafts philosophy. Names associated with the Arts and Crafts movement, besides those of Morris and Ruskin, are Ashbee, Fisher, Dawson, Horner, and Mrs. Newman. Also associated with Arts and Crafts was the London department store Liberty, which carried Arts and Crafts designs in jewelry and textiles. This store was so much associated with Arts and Crafts that in Italy Art Nouveau was sometimes called *stilo Liberty*.

bail or bale–the ring or loop on a pendant through which passes the chain holding the pendant; in more elaborate jewelry, the bail is sometimes enameled or set with diamonds or other stones.

baroque pearl–a pearl, either freshwater or ocean, in a shape other than round; elongated baroque pearls were especially popular with Art Nouveau and Arts and Crafts jewelers, who used them as dangles from pins, necklaces and pendants.

base metal–any combination of alloys of non-precious metals; also sometimes called *pot metal* or *white metal*.

bas relief–in French, literally "low relief," the carving of an object such as a decorated wall or a vase or piece of jewelry such as a cameo with a motif or scene in raised form that is nonetheless not especially sculptural or three-dimensional.

basse taille–literally "low form," in enameling the use of engraved, stamped, pressed designs visible under translucent enamel.

beauty pin–a small pin, usually of elongated oval shape in silver or gold and enamel popular during the first years of the 20th century.

beaux arts–literally, "beautiful arts," this is a relatively recent term when applied to jewelry. In general, it appears to be in some sense a catch-all category for pieces that do not quite fit into Arts and Crafts, Art Nouveau, Victorian, or Edwardian. Pieces such as the tiger jewelry produced in some quantity in Newark c. 1900 fit into this category.

belle époque–literally meaning "beautiful era," the phrase is commonly used to refer to the period from c. 1890 to the beginning of World War I in August, 1914, but sometimes is also used as a synonym for the Edwardian period. The *belle époque* is characterized by luxury and enjoyment of life, with pleasure a goal of the upper classes. However, the term can be used to apply to any supposed "golden age" of beauty and pleasure, and has been used to refer to the grand era of the French jeweler's art during the 19th century.

beryl–a stone formed in crystals as a silicate of beryllium and aluminum, beryl can be white or golden, but in its blue form it is called *aquamarine*, and when green is an *emerald*.

Bohemian garnet–a common form of garnet having a deep purplish-red color, commonly used in Victorian jewelry, and also called *pyrope*.

brass–an alloy of copper and zinc, tin or other metals that is usually yellowish in hue. Harder and more ductile than copper, it was used for belt buckles, costume jewelry, and in Art Nouveau and Arts and Crafts jewelry and metalwork.

briolette–a stone cut in the shape of a three-dimensional teardrop, and having its entire surface covered with triangular facets.

bronze–an alloy of copper and tin, one of the first if not the first alloys fashioned, giving its name to the Bronze Age and prized for being harder and more durable than copper. Bronze was used for a number of purposes, especially sculptural, by Art Nouveau artists, designers and jewelers, as in the elaborate lamp bases designed by Louis Comfort Tiffany, and is still much used in modern sculpture.

bulla–a rounded ornament having a rather convex curve used in *Classical revival* jewelry primarily for brooches, pendants and earrings in the Roman or Etruscan style, often decoration with granulation, twisted wire and cabochon stones.

buttercup setting–a setting in which prongs are set above a circle fluted or molded into petal-like shapes, this type of setting was popular in late Victorian jewelry and used in some Newark flower enamels.

c-clasp–a simple curved clasp in the shape of a "c" used on most 19th century (and earlier) brooches and pins to hold the pin in place. In later jewelry it was replaced by the *safety clasp*.

cabochon–a stone that is smooth and rounded on top, as opposed to faceted. Opaque gems such as *coral, jade, lapis lazuli, onyx,* and *turquoise* are often used in cabochon form, and occasionally other stones such as *amethysts, carnelian, garnets,* and moonstones are found as cabochons.

cameo–a shell or stone carved in relief with, usually, a human face or one or more human or mythological figures, the cameo has been known since ancient Greek and Roman times. In the Victorian era, cameos were very much in vogue, and often depicted historical or mythological scenes, such as Rebecca at the well, or nymphs, muses, and other Classical themes. Cameos were also used to create miniature portraits of relatives and other loved ones. Their use fits in with the Classical revival movements so frequently found in 19th century jewelry.

carat–is used to measure the weight of a precious or semi-precious stone, especially important when describing diamonds; it is sometimes abbreviated c. or ct. Originally it referred to the seed of the carob plant, which was used as a counterweight for precious goods by Arab and other traders. A carat weighs one-fifth of a gram, or 200 milligrams. A hundredth of a carat is called a *point*. Note that the word of the same origin used for gold content is spelled *karat*.

carnelian–an orange-red, deep red, fleshy red or reddish-white form of chalcedony, which being hard polishes well and is much used in jewelry as a cabochon gemstone. Carnelian was one of the favorite stones in ancient Egyptian jewelry and as such can often be found in Egyptian revival jewelry.

Celtic revival–yet another of the revivals so popular in jewelry of the 19th century, this revival was in part associated with Irish nationalism. Also, as Karlin notes, a number of ancient Celtic jewels were found in Ireland during the 19th century. Owen Jones published a page of Celtic designs in his Aesthetically-based *Grammar of Ornament*, and the Celtic revival also took root in the Arts and Crafts movement. Common themes were variously-arranged groups of three often triangular shapes, possibly based on the Irish shamrock; harps, Celtic knots, and elaborately entwined serpents were also prominent. In their Scottish jewelry, Victorian and Arts and Crafts artist-designers produced jewelry in which banded *agate* was widely featured, as were thistles, a national symbol of Scotland.

chalcedony–a translucent variety of quartz with crystals too small for the human eye to easily discern, usually occurring in a uniform blue or bluish-gray color.

champlevé–literally, "raised field" (or ground), a type of enameling in which enamel is *wet-packed* into a sunken area in the surrounding metal created by hammering, casting, or pressing.

chase–to decorate a metal, especially silver, surface with a pattern of lines created by using a hammer and tools without a cutting edge.

chatelaine–in French literally "mistress of the castle or manor," a chatelaine is a device meant to be hooked to a belt or brooch to hold any number of useful items such as thimbles, needle cases, magnifying glasses, keys, pens, pencils, small tablets of paper, scissors, and watches, quite popular in Victorian times. Occasionally hooks on the backs of pins or brooches from which watches or other object could be suspended are referred to as chatelaine hooks.

chinoiserie–the use of Chinese-style decoration and motifs in art, architecture, and the decorative arts; chinoiserie was most popular in late 18th century Europe, and influenced design such as that of the furniture of Thomas Chippendale. Although adherents of the *Aesthetic Movement* and jewelers such as Lucien Falize were more influenced by Japanese decorative arts than by Chinese, cloisonné enamel is more common to Chinese objects and Chinese art undoubtedly had some effect on 19th century jewelry.

choker–a close fitting necklace, especially popular in Art Nouveau, Arts and Crafts, *fin-de-siècle*, and Edwardian jewelry.

chrysoprase–an apple-green variety of *chalcedony*, it was used in Arts and Crafts, Art Nouveau, and Art Deco jewelry, although it had not formerly been considered a precious gemstone. Lalique made use of chrysoprase in, among other jewels, his dragonfly-woman plaquet now housed in the Museu Calouste Gulbenkian in Lisbon, Portugal, and one of the iconic pieces of the Art Nouveau movement.

citrine–a form of quartz that ranges in hue from a pale yellow to a deep gold sometimes confused with imperial topaz, used in jewelry especially Art Nouveau and Arts and Crafts, as both favored less expensive materials either to make jewelry more affordable or to emphasize design rather than costly materials.

Classical revival–the name used to refer to various revival movements in jewelry (and other decorative arts) during the 19th century, including Greek, Roman and *Etruscan* revivals inspired in part by archeological discoveries made in the 1800s and also in part by Caetano's donation of his extensive collection of Classical artifacts to the Louvre Museum in Paris.

cloisonné–a form of enameling in which cells, or cloisons, are created by wire to form a design, and then filled with *wet-packed* enamel. Cloisonné is often said to have begun in ancient Egypt, where the cells were in the earliest jewelry filled with stones cut to fit them, and only later was *faience* (a form of enameled earthenware) substituted for the rarer *turquoise* or *lapis lazuli*. This type of enameling was popular with some 19th century jewelers, especially the father and son designer-artists Alexis and Lucien Falize, who used it to create jewelry based on Asian, most especially Japanese, decorative arts.

cold enamel–a term not much in use, it can be used to refer to enameling that is done without the high temperatures used in kilns to fuse *hard enamel*. Some craft enamels, such as Delta Permenamel©, might be considered cold enamels; these can be used to effect minor repairs on enameled jewelry that has small chips or other flaws.

collet–a metal band that surrounds and supports a stone, collets were not infrequently used in Newark floral enamels to set diamonds against enameled leaves or petals, giving the impression of a dew drop.

copper–a metallic element with a warm hue deeper than gold and redder than bronze, it was used in less expensive costume jewelry and also in much of the Arts and Crafts jewelry and metalwork, where it was prized for a number of reasons, including its affordability, its warmth, its ability to take enamel well, and its retention of the hammer marks that showed a piece to be handmade.

coral–a natural material formed by colonies of small marine animals, it was very popular in Victorian jewelry, especially carved into cameos, cherubs, flowers, leaves, branches and clusters of grapes. The most valuable coral is a deep red, with pink and orange-red coral also popular. Near-white coral with only tinges of pink, called *angelskin*, is also deemed valuable. Less frequently, coral can also be found in black and a less warm shade of white than angelskin.

corundum–a mineral formed as aluminum oxide occurring in brightly-colored rhombohedral crystals which, as gemstones, are usually referred to either as *ruby* if true red, or *sapphire* if any other color, such as pink, yellow, or blue, blue being the color usually associated with sapphires. It is thought by some that the sapphire of the Old Testament is really *lapis lazuli*. Corundum is very hard, ranking as a 9 on the *Mohs' scale*, coming directly after diamonds, which are 10 on the scale.

cultured pearl–is not one that's been to the Louvre, as the old joke goes, but a pearl created artificially by introducing an irritant under the mantle of an oyster (or other bivalve); the oyster then begins to form a pearl around the irritant, as it would do naturally in response to an irritant. In modern jewelry, natural pearls are seldom found, having been replaced by the much more accessible, available, and controllable cultured pearl. Like the mabe pearl, cultured pearls were first produced in some quantity by Mikimoto. Although it is difficult to tell some natural pearls from cultured ones without x-raying them, in general natural pearls are more lustrous, having built up more of the nacre that creates the pearl's outer coat.

Cymric–a line of silver jewelry in the Arts and Crafts style produced for Liberty & Co., the London department store noted, among other things, for its textile designs. Most of the Cymric jewelry was produced in Birmingham by the W. H. Haseler firm. The noted Arts and Crafts leader Charles Ashbee felt that the Cymric line contributed to the downfall of the Guild of Handicraft because it created and mass-produced a less expensive version of the Guild's work, thus undercutting the Guild and decreasing the demand for its products.

damascene work–a type of metal-working sometimes confused with enameling; in some respects the reverse of *niello*, damascene work creates a pattern by inserting lighter-hued metals into a darker metal background.

demantoid garnet–first used in the mid-1800s, it is a rare, bright green form of garnet usually found in relatively small stones. Said to have the highest dispersion of all colored stones on the market, it is very sparkly and highly prized.

demi-parure–literally, "half a set." This term is sometimes used to refer to a set of jewelry that is not a complete suite, but which contains (usually) earrings and a matching brooch, pendant, or necklace. See *parure*.

depose–in jewelry, a French term for "protected by law," a version of the English trademarked or copyrighted. It is found on some French jewelry, and was also used by makers in other European countries, such as Germany's Meyle and Mayer.

dispersion–the selective separation of light into its spectrum of colors by refraction or diffraction.

dog collar–a wide choker popularized in Edwardian England by Queen Alexandra, who was noted for her long, graceful neck.

Edwardian–historical period named after Victoria's son, who succeeded to the throne upon her death in 1901 and died himself in 1910. Like the era named after his mother, the tag Edwardian is often applied to the manners, mores, and style of the period encompassed by his reign. Edwardian jewelry used white metals–primarily *platinum* but also *white gold*–in preference to gold, diamonds and *precious gems* were preferred over the *semi-precious* or non-precious materials favored in *Art Nouveau* and *Arts and Crafts* jewelry.

Egyptian revival–a trend in decorative arts that has had several incarnations, especially in late Victorian times and the 1920s, influenced by 19th century archaeological finds and the discovery of King Tutankhamon's unlooted tomb in 1922. Scarabs–sometimes authentically ancient but more often not–in faience, semi-precious stones, and enamel appear often in Egyptian revival jewelry, and enamel to simulate ancient Egyptian stone cloisonné work is very common.

emerald–a pure grass-green gem variety of *beryl* traditionally considered one of the true *precious gems* (along with *rubies, sapphires, pearls,* and diamonds). Because emeralds are softer than many gemstones, they tend to have more flaws and fractures than harder stones, and thus what might be considered a defect in a sapphire can be acceptable in an emerald. The best emeralds are said to come from South America, particularly Colombia; but emeralds were also used in jewelry from India and Russia well before the discovery of the Colombian emerald fields.

enamel–powdered glass often in bright colors, it was first widely used during the *Renaissance* by goldsmiths such as Benvenuto Cellini. Older forms of enamel glass were generally leaded, but today most enamelists work with lead-free materials. Enameling, especially cobalt blue, black, *taille d'épargne, cloisonné,* and *Limoges,* was popular in the Victorian age, but enameling really came into its own with the *Arts and Crafts* and *Art Nouveau* movements, in the jewelry of which it was almost an obligatory element. Arts and Crafts jewelers are said to have developed an *iridescent* blue-green enamel, and also made use of Limoges enamel. Art Nouveau jewelers and enamelists perfected *plique-à-jour* enamel, and it is one of the hallmarks of Art Nouveau pieces. Enamel can be glossy, *matte, iridescent, opaque, translucent* and, in more modern enameling, *opalescent*.

engraving–the art of incising a pattern, using a sharp tool intended for that purpose, on metal; names or dates, for example, are often engraved on the inside of a ring or bracelet, or the back of a watch or charm.

Etruscan revival–one of the more prominent revival movements during the last half of the 19th century, it attempted to reproduce for modern wear jewelry based on that fashioned by the Etruscans. A people of mysterious origins (speaking what is probably a non—Indo-European language) who predated the Romans in Italy, the Etruscans were considered among the best goldsmiths in the ancient world, producing some of the finest of all ancient jewelry. Their art relied on delicate *granulation* and wire twisted into ropes or elaborate designs, including *filigree*. The revival of their jewelry began in Italy with the discovery of Etruscan jewelry in what is today Tuscany. The major jewelers most associated with the Etruscan revival are Castellani and Giuliano. Castellani is said to have mastered the technique of granulation used in Etruscan jewelry.

faience–a form of pottery used in ancient Egypt and in modern reproductions, usually fired with a dark blue glaze to simulate lapis lazuli or a lighter blue or blue-green glaze to simulate turquoise.

festoon–an often chain decoration draped and hanging between two points; chain festoons on necklaces were popular with Arts and Crafts and some Art Nouveau jewelers.

fibula–an ancient form of pin used by Greeks and Romans to fasten clothing, it was occasionally produced in the 19th century by archaeological revival jewelers.

fichu–a woman's triangular shawl often of lace or sheer white cloth, worn over the shoulders or to fill in a low neckline, fastened with pins, some of which were in Victorian times specially manufactured for that purpose.

figural jewelry–a piece of jewelry in the form of an object, which can be a face, a flower, a ship, an angel, an insect, etc.

filigree–the art of creating elaborate designs using thin wire, especially popular in *Etruscan* and *Classical* revival jewelry, and in late *Victorian*, *Edwardian*, and *Art Deco* jewelry. The use of *platinum*, which is noted for its strength and ductility, beginning in the late Victorian period made possible finer, thinner, and more elaborate filigree settings for diamonds and other stones, although filigree work could and did exist on its own.

fin-de-siècle–literally, "end of the century," referring to the end of the 19th century and considered by some to apply to decorative arts and jewelry in a style apart from those falling under the rubrics *Victorian*, *Edwardian*, *Arts* and *Crafts*, and *Art Nouveau*.

fine gold or silver–pure gold (24 karat) or silver unalloyed with any other metal; the great Arts and Crafts enamelist Alexander Fisher asserted that only pure metals–copper or fine silver or fine gold– were suitable for enameling, and many modern enamelists still adhere to this dictum. However, as demonstrated by British, European, and American enamelists and manufacturers who created enameled pieces in 18 karat, or even 10 karat, 12 karat, and 14 karat gold, this is manifestly not true.

foil–an extremely thin sheet of pure silver or gold, often used with certain enameling techniques, such as *Limoges*, to create a shimmery metallic accent. Also sometimes referred to as *paillons*.

fossilized–having been made into a fossil, that is, having had organic material replaced by inorganic material in the form of a mineral.

freshwater pearl–a pearl formed in a mollusk, often a clam, that lives in rivers rather than in salty oceans or seas. Freshwater pearls are usually irregularly shaped or *baroque*, have less nacre than ocean pearls, and are thus much less costly than natural or even cultured ocean pearls. For this reason, they were sometimes used by Art Nouveau and Arts and Crafts jewelers, who concentrated less on precious substances than on design and subtlety.

garnet–a transparent silicate mineral that comes in several varieties including the most common *Bohemian*–or *pyrope*–form much used in Victorian jewelry and having an deep purplish-red hue, *demantoid* (green) and *rhodolite* (having a pinker or more purplish hue than the *almandine* or pyrope) forms.

Georgian–the period immediately preceding the *Victorian* era in English history in which the Hanoverian kings George I through George IV reigned, beginning in 1714 and ending with the crowning of Queen Victorian in 1837. The Georgian period is noted among other things for its architecture, often in the Classical style, its well-crafted furniture, and its fine silversmithing. Certain motifs, such as the scallop shell, were especially popular with Georgian craftsmen and designers. Also, a Chinese influence was pronounced at the end of the 18th century, manifesting itself, for example, in the furniture designs of Thomas Chippendale. Georgian jewelry often features pieces in which 18K gold and silver are mixed, as it was considered most appropriate to set diamonds in white metal.

gold–a metallic element prized since great antiquity for its beauty and malleability, its purity is measured in *karats* (abbreviated K), with pure gold being 24 karats. Gold of less than 24K is more commonly used in jewelry than pure, or fine, gold, with 10K, 12K and 14K being common in the United States, 18K in France and other European countries, and 15K almost unique to Great Britain. Depending on the metals used in gold *alloys*, gold can be pink or

white; gold with a greenish tint was also popular in English Georgian and some 19th century European jewelry.

gold-filled–a term used for a thin sheet of gold mechanically applied to the surface of base or other metal; in the United States, to be labeled "gold-filled," a piece must contain .05, or one-twentieth, of gold by weight.

Gothic revival–one of the many revivals found in 19th century decorative arts and architecture, its jewelry used *medieval* motifs such as quatrefoils and circles in twisted wire and gold beads; gargoyles, among other mythical beings, were not uncommon in 19th century French jewelry. However, it appears seemingly less in jewelry than in other decorative arts such as furniture. In France it was sometimes known as *style cathédrale*

Grand Period–a term sometimes applied to the mid-Victorian period (1861–1885).

granulation–the use of very small balls of gold to create designs, it was used in Egyptian jewelry of the XIIth dynasty (around 2000 B. C.) and perfected by Etruscan goldsmiths. It is a signature of Etruscan revival jewelry, this "lost art" supposedly having been rediscovered and perfected by the Italian jeweler Castellani. Also called *granulé work*.

Greek revival–a revival movement that formed part of the *archaeological revivals* during the 19th century, influencing architecture and decorative arts alike. Greek revival jewelry is characterized by earrings in the shape of amphorae (earthenware vessels used to store wine and oil), *fibulae*, and gold-work with intricately twisted wire.

grisaille–literally, "grayed" in French, grisaille is a form of enameling not often employed, as it is exceedingly time-consuming and difficult. It uses enamels only in black and white to create detailed paintings that somewhat resemble old sepia photographs, except that they are in shades of gray rather than brown.

guilloche–literally French for "machine-turned," it is in enameling the use of a metal with regular, often wavy or geometric, patterns over which *translucent* enamel is fired, allowing the machine-created design to show through. While guilloche enamel was used by 19th century jewelers and designers such as the great Alexis and Lucien Falize and Carl Fabergé, it became truly popular for use in *Art Deco* objects such as powder compacts and cigarette cases.

hallmark–a mark that identifies the gold (or less often, the silver) content of precious metals used in manufacturing jewelry and other objects; hallmarks, such as the French eagle or the Swiss wolf, can also indicate the country or city of origin of a piece. Originally hallmarks were stamped by governments to attest to the purity of a gold or silver piece. See also *maker's mark*.

hard enamel–enamel that is fired at a high temperature, and thus is harder and more durable than soft enamel. Modern enamel is usually fired somewhere between 1400 and 1600 degrees Fahrenheit.

honeymoon pin–a Victorian pin, perhaps originally meant to be given to a wife on her honeymoon by her husband, with an often enameled flower or flowers held in a crescent; as often the case with Victoriana, the pin conveys its meaning indirectly, with the flower providing the "honey," and the crescent being the "moon."

iridescent–a term indicating a material, such as enamel, that exhibits the colors of the rainbows especially in shifting patterns of different hues depending on the movement of light; iridescent enamel was especially popular with American firms that manufactured enameled jewelry in the Art Nouveau style. It was also used effectively in jeweled insects, especially dragonflies whose bodies and wings are naturally iridescent, birds, and the wings of mythical beings such as fairies.

ivory–a now banned material as it is too often obtained by slaughtering mature elephants for their tusks, ivory can also come from walrus tusks and, in fossilized form, mammoth tusks. Ivory carved into flowers was in vogue in middle and late Victorian jewelry, and was also used in men's cufflinks, sometimes imported from India, China, or Japan. As its warm hue somewhat resembles light human skin, ivory was used in Art Nouveau jewelry to create women's faces and figures. It was also used to create birds, insects, and other naturalistic motifs.

jade–a name given to two separate stones, *jadeite* and *nephrite*. Although jadeite is the more valuable form of jade, its use is relatively recent, and most ancient Asian jade pieces are made of nephrite.

jadeite–a mineral composed of sodium aluminum silicate, found primarily in Burma. While apple green and rich clear green jade are prized, other colors of jade are considered equally or even more valuable. Among the most valuable colors are red and lavender. It is usually either carved or cut into cabochons to be set in jewelry. Jadeite also occurs in white, brown, yellow, dark green (called spinach jade), and black, as well as in combinations sometimes given prosaic names, such as muttonfat (a mottled tan) or more poetic names such as moss on snow (green and white jade).

Japonisme–the use of Japanese decorative arts, newly discovered in the 19th century with the reopening of Japan's ports, especially after Commodore Perry's visit with four warships to Tokyo on March 31, 1853. Japanese influence can be seen in the work of artists of the Aesthetic Movement, such as Whistler, and found perhaps its finest expression in the cloisonné enamels designed by Lucien Falize and executed by the great enamelist Tard.

jet–a fossilized form of coal popular during Victorian times in mourning jewelry; it can be faceted or carved into various shapes.

Jubilee enamel–a type of brightly colored iridescent enamel developed for Queen Victoria's 60th jubilee celebration in 1897.

Jugendstil– literally, "youth style," the term used for Art Nouveau in Germany. Today the name most associated with *Jugendstil* is that of Theodor Fahrner, who produced affordable handcrafted jewelry set with semi-precious stones.

language of stones–a term sometimes applied to *acrostic* jewelry in which the first letters of the names of stones spell out a message such as REGARD (ruby, emerald, garnet, amethyst, diamond) or DEAREST (diamond, emerald, amethyst, ruby, emerald, sapphire, topaz)

lapis lazuli–a semi-precious stone used since ancient times; it is primarily composed of lazurite, a mineral with a complex chemical structure, and occurs as a deep opaque blue, often with inclusions of iron or other metals. It was one of the three primary stones used in ancient Egyptian jewelry (the others being *turquoise* and *carnelian*), and probably is the "sapphire" referred to in the Bible. In medieval times it was ground and used as a pigment in, for example, illuminated manuscripts.

Limoges–a type of painting with enamel named for the French city in which it was developed; the enamels are mixed with essential oils, lavender for fine details and clove for backgrounds, often applied over silver or gold foil. Limoges was also the home of some of the finest china manufactured during the 19th and 20th centuries, and is still known for its painted china souvenir boxes, often in odd shapes such as shoes, cakes, flower carts, and musical instruments.

locket–literally a piece of jewelry intended to hold a lock of a loved one's hair (a concept very much in vogue especially before the invention of photography made other types of souvenirs accessible and affordable), lockets were very popular in the 19th century, and remained popular with Art Nouveau jewelers who often created on them the *bas relief* design of a woman's head in profile; often lockets were decorated with stones, enamel, or engraving.

mabe pearl–a hemispherical cultured pearl first created by the Japanese pearl magnate Mikimoto; mabe pearls were among the materials favored by some artists for *Arts and Crafts* jewelry.

maker's mark–a mark, usually very small, specific to a jeweler or jewelry manufacturing firm to indicate the manufacturer of a piece of jewelry. Maker's marks were often used by 19th century European jewelers; in the United States, they seem to have come into vogue c. 1880. On pins and brooches, the maker's mark is often found on the *c-clasp*. However, many pieces of jewelry, even those made by famous jewelers such as Alexis and Lucien Falize, are not marked. (See also Appendix A: Marks of makers of enameled jewelry in Europe and the United States.)

marcasite–a small dark crystal, usually crystalized iron pyrite, used in more affordable pieces of *Victorian, Edwardian,* and *Art Deco* jewelry, often set in silver.

matte–having a flat, rather than a shiny or glossy surface. In enameling, this is achieved by etching the fired and hardened enamel with weak acid, or by buffing it with a light-grained emery or sand-paper. Enamel prepared in this fashion holds a painted design, transfer, or lettering much better than does glossy enamel.

medieval–refers to the historical period following the collapse of the Roman empire and immediately preceding the European Renaissance, lasting from about 500 to 1500 A.D., very often also called the Middle Ages. Like many such terms referring primarily to a historical period, the term medieval also covers the art, architecture, decorative arts, customs, and literature of the people living during that time. The period is noted for its Gothic cathedrals with their flying buttresses, gargoyles, and stained glass rose windows; religious paintings that were primarily flat, lacking perspective or elaborate backgrounds; beautifully illustrated, hand-drawn and colored illuminated manuscripts predating the invention of movable type by Gutenberg; and beautifully woven textiles; otherwise, decorative arts appear to have been more functional than ornamental. The later part of the period saw the rise of trade guilds, which were to some extent copied by guilds of handicrafts at the beginning of the *Arts and Crafts* movement. The Gothic revival based some of its principles and designs on those of the Middle Ages.

micro-mosaic–a technique used especially in Italian jewelry, and popular in Victorian times, that uses tiny chips of stone to create a pattern, often floral; this technique in effect makes very very tiny mosaics for use in jewelry.

modernismo–the Spanish term for *Art Nouveau*; probably the most notable practitioner of Art Nouveau in Spain was the famous architect and designer Antoni Gaudí, who created marvelously organic buildings–one has a roof-line tiled to resemble a dragon–in Barcelona. Jewelry, however, was not ignored by Barcelona adherents of *modernismo*, and the firms of Masriera and Carrera, among others, created some beautiful Art Nouveau pieces featuring *plique-à-jour* and other enameling.

Mohs' scale–named after the German minerologist Friedrich Mohs (who died in 1839), a scale used to measure the hardness of stones and minerals, with 1, exemplified by talc, being the softest and 10, exemplified by the diamond, being the hardest.

mother-of-pearl–the soft, usually iridescent material produced by certain mollusks, especially oysters and abalone, to line their shells, this inexpensive material was favored especially by jewelers working in the *Arts and Crafts* tradition, in pieces where it was often combined with enamel.

nacre–sometimes synonymous with mother-of-pearl, it can refer to calcium carbonate deposited as a lining to their shells by some mollusks; but it can also refer to the depth and luster of the iridescent layers deposited by mollusks on the pearls they form.

natural pearl–a pearl formed by a mollusk, usually an oyster, without it having had grains of sand or other irritating substances introduced by man. Such pearls are today quite rare, and usually cultured pearls–those created through the intervention of human agents–are found in modern jewelry.

navette–literally meaning "small ship," it refers primarily to an elongated stone pointed at both ends, synonymous with a marquis cut; but is also sometimes used to refer to elongated frames in Victorian and Art Nouveau brooches and pendants that have more-or-less the same shape. Art Nouveau frames, however, usually contain flowing lines not found in earlier Victorian ones.

nephrite–one of the two–and the less valuable of the two–minerals known as *jade*. The original jade, especially prized by the Chinese, was nephrite, which commonly occurs in a rather darker green than the best *jadeite*, the other form of jade. Nephrite is named after the Greek word for "kidney," as it was in ancient times considered a remedy for kidney disorders and worn above the kidneys. White versions of this form of jade are also not uncommon.

niello–from the Latin for "blackish," this term refers to an alloy of sulphur with silver, copper or lead to create a deep black metal; in niello work, metals are engraved or incised, with the incisions then being filled with niello metal; the end result can sometimes resemble enameling.

onyx–a somewhat opaque form of chalcedony that in its natural state is most often found with thin lines of alternating black, white, and brown; some onyx, however, is artificially dyed black. It is found in some *Art Deco* jewelry, when the contrast between black and white materials was desired

opal–a very soft semi-precious stone formed of hydrated (containing water) amorphous silica; it is noted for the shifting play of iridescent colors, also called the opal's fire. Opals come in various types and colors, with the black opals of Australia usually considered the most valuable. Other types include boulder opals, which often are infused with iridescent blues and greens; fire opals, which usually contain red or pink glints. Milky opals, which are white with less fire than other opals and Mexican opals, which are often almost a monochrome orangish color leaning either toward red or toward brown, are less desirable types of opal. Opals, especially the blue-green boulder opals, were very frequently used in Arts and Crafts jewelry, often to indicate the coloring of peacock feathers or of water.

opalescent–named after the shifting colors of opals, this term can refer to enamel that also exhibits a soft iridescence that is less marked than that of true iridescent enamels and perhaps closer to the nacre of mother-of-pearl or pearls.

opaque–a term applied to materials, such as certain enamels, that are impervious to rays of light, and thus do not allow it to pass through; compare with *transparent* and *translucent*.

paillon(s)–a term that in jewelry has two similar but distinct meanings: a) it refers to the thin sheets of metal foil–gold, silver, or copper–placed under enamel to create a glittery effect; and b) it refers to a shape made out of thin gold or silver, and placed under enamel as an element in the design. Paillons of the latter type can be found as stars, fleurs-de-lis, ribbons, and even insects.

parure–another term for a set, or suite, of matching jewelry. In Victorian times, a complete parure often consisted of one or more bracelets, a brooch, earrings, and necklace, all matching.

paste–a brilliant glass with a high lead content used to manufacture artificial colored stones.

pate de verre–literally "glass paste," a type of material akin to enameling in that it uses ground or powdered glass of different hues which are then molded or otherwise formed into the desired shape and fired at high temperatures. The main difference between true enamel and pate de verre is that enamel is fused to glass, while pate de verre is not.

pearl–a gem formed in a mollusk by layers of calcium carbonate (with some organic matter included) around an object introduced into the mollusk's shell and causing it some irritation (against which the nacre acts as a sort of bandage). Pearls are formed most often in oysters and clams, but beautiful pink, almost coral-colored, pearls can be produced by the conch. Irregular pearls are called *baroque* pearls, and were much favored in *Art Nouveau* and *Arts and Crafts* jewelry both because of their lower cost and because of their interesting shapes. *Seed pearls* are tiny, usually natural, pearls; these were often used in the settings of Victorian jewelry, and also alone, woven into flowers and other designs.

plaque au cou–a plaque to be worn on the neck, usually either fixed to a ribbon, or held by several chains or strands of pearls; such neck pieces were fashionable in the late 19th century, and a number were designed by Art Nouveau jewelers such as Lalique.

plique-à-jour–a type of enameling in which cells created by wire or cut-out forms in metal are filled with *wet-packed* enamel and then fired on mica or some other substance to which the enamel will not adhere. Similar to *cloisonné* enamel, it differs in not having a metal backing; thus the fired enamel lets light shine through and creates a stained-glass effect. Plique-à-jour enamel can also be shaded within the same cloison or cell, so that delicate effects of color can be achieved. Although the origins of plique-à-jour enameling are obscure, and even its name usually lacks an etymology, it was perfected and used to wonderful effect by Art Nouveau designers and jewelers such as René Lalique, and is now considered a hallmark of jewelry from that movement.

precious gems–while today the distinction between precious and *semiprecious* stones has largely been dropped, historically only diamonds, emeralds, pearls, rubies, and sapphires were considered precious gemstones.

precious metals–few in number, including only platinum, gold, silver.

platinum–a very heavy metallic element that is grayish-white in color, it is the most valuable of all the precious metals, both because it occurs less frequently than gold or silver, and because it possesses useful properties: Platinum expands and contracts little, is very malleable and ductile, and above all is very strong. Not used in jewelry until the mid- to later part of the 19th century, it became popular during the *Edwardian* period as it was strong enough to be used in thin, ornate *filigree* work. Georgians and 18th and 19th century European jewelers believed that only a white metal, silver or white gold, was suitable for setting diamonds, as white metal showed them off to better effect than gold; however, neither silver nor white gold was strong or ductile enough to allow very fine filigree work. Also, unlike silver, platinum does not tarnish. Platinum was also the metal of choice in most *Art Deco* jewelry, for the same reasons that made it popular in the *Edwardian* era.

pre-Raphaelite–a movement named for the belief of its adherents that all art produced after the great Italian Renaissance artist Raphael was degenerate. Two of the main proponents of this movement were the English brother and sister Dante and Cristina Rossetti. Women portrayed in pre-Raphaelite paintings wore loose, drapey clothing and long flowing hair, presaging the depiction of women, especially in jewelry, of the Art Nouveau movement. This movement cannot be entirely separated from either the *Arts and Crafts* or the *Aesthetic Movement*, as some of its motifs and tenets were adopted by both of the above-mentioned movements.

quartz–a mineral, silicon dioxide, that occurs in usually clear crystals, but can also be found in crystals colored yellow, purple, brown, or green. The yellow form of quartz is known as *citrine*, while the purple is *amethyst*; both were widely used in Victorian jewelry, and a deep yellow citrine can be mistaken for imperial *topaz*.

quatrefoil–a shape that has four, usually rounded, lobes around a central circle, somewhat resembling a four-leaf clover.

Renaissance–the historical period immediately following the medieval, considered by many to have begun with the Italian scholar Erasmus's discovery of the Classical texts of Aristotle and other Greek philosophers. While the Renaissance reached some European countries later than others, it is generally considered to have begun c. 1500 A.D. It produced a flowering of scholarship and literature aided by Gutenberg's invention of the printing press (the idea having come from China), and also was marked by artist-geniuses such as Michelangelo and Leonardo da Vinci. In England it is sometimes thought to have begun during the reigns of the Tudor monarchs, especially Elizabeth I.

Renaissance revival–yet another 19th century revival, this one taking its themes and motifs from the Renaissance, apparently aiming for both beauty of design and quality of workmanship. A number of designs for Renaissance revival jewelry with flowing lines and floral motifs in which enameling played a large part were created by the great jewelers Alexis and Lucien Falize. Falize father and son also fashioned jewelry with lettering and decoration that resembled illuminated manuscripts. Other motifs of the Renaissance revival were grotesque creatures such as dragons and female figures with the heads of beasts.

Romantic Period–a term sometimes given to the early Victorian period.

repoussé–literally "pressed back" in French, the decoration of a metal object with a design in relief; true *repoussé* work is created by pushing the design out from the back of the piece, usually by hammering.

rose cut–a manner of cutting stones, especially diamonds, in use before more modern ways of cutting stones to best bring out their sparkle emerged; basically the stone was cut to resemble a rose, having twenty-four facets rising up to the table

ruby–one of the *precious gems*, a red variety of *corundum*. Ruby is the most valuable form of corundum, all other forms being referred to as *sapphires*. The best rubies are said to come from Burma.

safety clasp–an innovation introduced in the later part of the 19th century, in the 20th century almost completely replacing the older *c-clasp* in fine jewelry; the safety clasp has a mechanical hinged hook operated by a lever that allows the clasp to be opened and then, unlike the c-clasp, completely closed around a brooch's pin to hold it firmly in place.

sapphire–a catch-all term used to refer to all *corundum* gemstones that are not red, or rubies; while traditionally sapphires are thought of as being blue–the best being a medium blue rather than the more common dark inky blue–sapphires also come in pink, yellow, and purple.

seed pearl–a very tiny pearl, usually natural, widely used in Victorian jewelry set in gold or, less often, silver; used in frames surrounding enameled pieces or other gems; or used alone, being woven or otherwise formed into various designs such as flowers. Seed pearls, perhaps because of their small size and hence modesty, are often found in smaller pieces such as might have been worn by children or very young women.

semi-precious stones–while as noted above under *precious gems* the distinction between precious and semi-precious stones has today more-or-less largely been done away with, traditionally semi-precious stones included colored varieties of quartz such as citrines and amethysts, opals, topaz, jade, tourmalines, aquamarines, jade, coral, and varieties of chalcedony used in jewelry.

silver–a metallic element that is the least valuable of the precious metals. In ancient times it was used for coinage and some jewelry, although the ancients for the most part preferred gold to silver. *Fine*, or pure, silver was believed to be better than silver alloys for holding enamel. Silver marked *sterling* is 925 parts silver, although some jewelry is made in 935 silver. Less valuable than gold, it was used primarily for jewelry of lesser importance, belt buckles, buttons, and similar objects. However, because Georgian and some European jewelers believed that only a white metal could show off a diamond to its best advantage, it is sometimes used together with 18 karat gold, especially in 18th century jewelry but also in some 19th century pieces, most notably before the introduction of *white gold*.

silver gilt–seems to be a term sometimes used interchangeably with *vermeil*, but which can also refer to a thin wash, rather than a layer, of gold placed over silver.

soapstone–see under *steatite*.

spinel–a semi-precious stone formed as an oxide of magnesium and aluminum occurring in octahedral crystals; of great hardness, it is in its pink or red forms used as a gemstone.

steatite–a form of talc usually occurring in large masses, and having a green-gray or brownish color; also often called *soapstone*. Steatite was used in Egyptian carving, both for utilitarian objects and for scarabs.

sterling–a hallmark used for silver that is 925 parts sterling, used in both England and the United States, as well as in Scandinavian and some other European countries.

stile liberty or stile floreal–names given to Art Nouveau in Italy; the first name because of the notable association of the great London store Liberty with Arts and Craft designs in textiles, jewelry and other decorative arts.

style cathédrale–a phrase used in 19th century France that was for the most part synonymous with *Gothic revival*.

suffragette jewelry–jewelry made in the *Edwardian* era and continuing until about 1916, it contained the suffragette colors of Green, White and Violet, the initials of these colors standing for "Give Women the Vote." Suffragette jewelry is often in pearls (white), peridot (green), and amethyst (violet), but enameled suffragette pieces are found in Arts and Crafts-style jewelry as well as Art Nouveau and Edwardian.

sur paillons–literally "over little pieces of straw," a form of enameling developed either by Lucien or Alexis Falize (both father and son having claimed credit for the innovation) or by both working together, it involved setting small pieces or shavings of gold under translucent brightly colored enamel to create a wonderful shimmering effect.

symbolism—often a literary term, in art and jewelry it refers to the use of one object, such as a bird, flower, tree, mythological figure, insect–to represent something else; for example, the peacock, a common theme in Art Nouveau and Arts and Crafts jewelry, can stand for beauty, pride, or resurrection, depending on one's interpretation. Symbolism was heavily used especially in Art Nouveau jewelry.

Symbolist Movement–a movement said to have begun with the publication of French poet Charles Baudelaire's *Les fleurs du mal (The Flowers of Evil)* in 1857; this movement and some of its tenets affected Art Nouveau jewelers, much of whose work is heavily symbolic in nature. (See chapter four.)

taille d'épargne (also sometimes spelled taille d'épergne)–a type of enameling popular in Victorian times, in which black enamel was used to fill patterns incised against a background of gold onto which a repeated pattern had been engraved; the black enamel made pieces fashioned with taille d'épargne enameling suitable to be worn as mourning jewelry.

topaz–a semi-precious stone composed of a silicate of aluminum and occurring either in crystalline form or in masses, it is usually transparent or translucent white, but in its gem variety can occur in yellow, reddish brown, and a deep golden color (sometimes referred to as "imperial" topaz).

tourmaline–a very complex mineral composed of borosilicate, fluoride and hydroxide of aluminum, iron, calcium, magnesium, lithium and sodium, which usually occurs in three-, six- or nine-sided prisms with a hardness of 7 to 7.5 on the *Mohs' scale*. In color it can range from white through pink, red, green, blue-green, and blue, and is most valuable in its deep pink or blue varieties. It was not much used as a gemstone before 1900, but can be found in some Arts and Crafts and Art Nouveau jewelry.

translucent–though sometimes used synonymously with *transparent*, a more specialized meaning for this term is admitting and diffusing light so that objects beyond cannot be readily seen; that is, a material somewhere between transparent and *opaque* in terms of allowing objects to be viewed through it. Some semi-precious stones, such as carnelian and opal, are translucent, admitting some light to create a somewhat glowing effect, but not transparent enough to allow one to see through them.

transparent–a material through which light can pass without appreciable scattering, so that bodies below the transparent substance can be easily seen; in enameling, a usually colored but otherwise clear enamel through which foil, engraved patterns (such as those created for *guilloche* or *basse taille* enameling), or other materials can be seen.

turquoise–a mineral with an incredibly complicated structure that occurs in the colors blue, blue-green, or greenish gray, being most prized in a pure, almost sky, blue variety found in Persian and Arizona turquoise. Persian turquoise, frequently used in Victorian jewelry, is thought to be the only type of turquoise that does not contain matrix. Turquoise was known and valued in antiquity; being one of the stones most used in Egyptian jewelry; it therefore is sometimes found in Egyptian revival jewelry, although seemingly not used as often as *lapis lazuli* or *carnelian*.

vermeil–silver with gold overlaid.

Victorian–a term that refers not only to the tenure of the longest-reigning monarch in British history, from 1837 to 1901, but also to the customs, manners, literature, art, architecture, furniture, decorative arts, and jewelry in fashion during her reign. Because Victoria's reign was so long, the era is often divided into periods each encompassing about twenty years: early Victorian (1840-1860), mid-Victorian (1861-1885) and late Victorian (1886-1901). Jewelry from the Victorian age in England and the United States is characterized by sentimentality, numerous revival movements, heaviness of design and execution, and jewelry intended to be worn by those in mourning; Victoria's beloved husband Prince Albert died in 1861, and Victoria remained more-or-less in mourning for the rest of her life. Mourning thus became a very fashionable pastime in the later years of Victoria's reign.

white gold–a pale alloy of gold that somewhat resembles silver or platinum, in which gold is combined with nickel and sometimes with other elements such as tin and zinc. Developed in the mid-1800s to replace silver especially for the setting of diamonds, it had the advantage of not tarnishing. White gold can come in 18 karat as well as in combinations containing a lesser percentage of gold, such as 14 karat. However, in most fine jewelry platinum is preferred to gold because it is stronger and more ductile.

Bibliography

[Anon.] *Flower Fairies - The Meaning of Flowers*. Poems and pictures by Cicely Mary Barker. London, England: Frederick Warne, 1996.

Adams, Steven. *The Art of the Pre-Raphaelites*. Seacaucus, New Jersey: Chartwell Books, 1988.

Andrews, Carol. *Ancient Egyptian Jewelry*. New York, New York: Henry N. Abrams, 1997.

Barker, Cicely Mary. *The Complete Book of the Flower Fairies*. London: Frederick Warne, 1996.

Becker, Vivienne. *Art Nouveau Jewelry*. New York, New York: E.P. Dutton, New York.

Biedermann, Hans, *Dictionary of Symbolism: Cultural Icons and the Meanings Behind Them* [James Hulbert, trans.]. New York, New York: Meridican, 1994

Bourne, Eleanor. *Heritage of Flowers*. New York, New York: George Putnam's Sons, n.d.

Bulfinch, Thomas. *Myths of Greece and Rome*. Introduction by Joseph Campbell. Compiled by Bryan Holme. New York, New York: Penguin Books, 1981.

Bury, Shirley. *Jewellery 1789-1910: The International Era*. Volume II: 1862-1910. Woodbridge, Suffolk, England: Antique Collectors' Club, 1991.

Catalog, Tate Museum, *The Pre-Raphaelites*. Tate Gallery Publications Department, Millbank, London, 1984.

Coats, Peter, *Flowers in History*. New York, New York: Viking Press, 1970.

Compte, Fernand. *The Wordsworth Dictionary of Mythology*. Ware, Hertferdshire: Cumberland House, 1998.

Dietz, Ulysses G., [ed.] *The Glitter & the Gold*. Newark, New Jersey: Newark Museum, 1997.

Gardiner, Alan. *Ancient Egyptian Grammar*. Oxford, England: Oxford University Press, 1963.

Gere, Charlotte. *Victorian Jewelry Design*. Chicago, Illinois: Henry Regnery Company, 1972.

Gordon, Lesley. *The Mystery and Magic of Trees and Flowers*. Exeter, England: Webb & Bower, 1985.

Greenaway, Kate. *Language of Flowers*. New York, New York: Dover, 1992 (reprint; originally published by Routledge, London, 1884).

Hase-Schmundt, Ulrike von, Christianne Weber, and Ingeborg Becker. *Jewelry . . . between Avantgarde and Tradition: Art Nouveau, Art Deco, the 1950s*. Atglen, Pennsylvania: Schiffer Publishing Ltd., 1991.

Hay, Roy and Patrick M. Sybnge. *The Color Dictionary of Flowers & Plants for Home & Garden*. New York, New York: Crown Publishers, Inc. n.d.

James, T. G. H. *Tutankhamun*. Friedman/Fairfax, 2000.

Karlin, Elyse Zorn. *Jewelry and Metalwork in the Arts and Crafts Tradition*. Atglen, Pennsylvania: Schiffer Publishing Ltd., 1993.

Kelly, Frances. *The Illustrated Language of Flowers: Magic, Meaning and Lore*. South Yarra, Victoria, Australia: Viking O'Neil, 1992.

Koch, Michael et al. *The Belle Epoque of French Jewellery 1850-1910: Jewellery making in Paris 1850-1910*. London, England: Thomas Heneage and Company, 1990-1991.

Lambourne, Lionel. *The Aesthetic Movement*. London, England: Phaidon Press, 1996.

Laufer, Geraldine Adamich, *Tussie-Mussies: The Language of Flowers*. New York, New York: Workman Publishing, 1993.

Luhti, Ann Louise. *Sentimental Jewellery*. Princes Risborough, Buckinghamshire, England: Shire Publications, 1998.

Mourey, Gabriel, Aymer Vallance, et al. *Art Nouveau Jewellery & Fans*. New York, New York: Dover Publications, 1973.

Museu Calouste Gulbenkian. *Sala Lalique*. Introduction by Maria Teresa Gomes Ferreira. Lisbon, Portugal: Fundação Calouste Gulbenkian, n.d.

O'Rush, Claire. *The Enchanted Garden*. New York, New York: Gramercy Books, 1996.

Purcell, Katherine. *Falize: A dynasty of jewelers*. New York, New York: Thames & Hudson, 1999.

Raulet, Sylvie. *Art Deco Jewelry* [trans. Lucinda Gane]. New York, New York: Rizzoli International Publications, 1985.

Robinson, Fanny. *The Country Flowers of a Victorian Lady*. New York, New York: Harper Collins, 1999.

Rodway, Averil. *A Literary Herbal*. New York, New York: G.P. Putnam's Sons. n.d.

Sataloff, Joseph. *Art Nouveau Jewelry*. Bryn Mawr, Pennsylvania: Dorrance and Co., 1984.

Scoble, Gretchen and Ann Field. *The Meaning of Flowers*. San Francisco, California: Chronicle Books, 1998.

Snowman, A. Kenneth, [ed.] *The Master Jewelers*. New York, New York (what a wonderful town!): Harry N. Abrams, 1990.

Spence, Lewis, *Egypt, Myths and Legends*. London, England: Studio Editions, 1994.

Stuart, David, *The Garden Triumphant: A Victorian Legacy*. New York, New York: Harper & Row, 1988.

Velez, Pilar, *Masriera Jewellery: 200 Years of History*. Barcelona, Spain: Àmbit Serveis Editorials, 1999.

Volpe, Tod M. And Beth Cathers. *Treasures of the American Arts and Crafts Movement, 1890-1920*. New York, New York: Harry N. Abrams, 1988.

Weisberg, Gabriel P. *Art Nouveau Bing: Paris Style 1900*. Harry N. Abrams, New York, in association with The Smithsonian Traveling Exhibition Service, 1986.

Zapata, Janet. *The Jewelry and Enamels of Louis Comfort Tiffany*. New York, New York: Harry N. Abrams, 1983.

Index

Index to Photographs of Pieces by Notable Makers